WILLIAM H. PIVAR

Guide to Passing the Pearson VUE Real Estate Exam

NINTH EDITION

Dearborn™
Real Estate Education

This publication is designed to provide accurate and authoritative information in regard to the subject matter covered. It is sold with the understanding that the publisher is not engaged in rendering legal, accounting, or other professional advice. If legal advice or other expert assistance is required, the services of a competent professional should be sought.

President: Dr. Andrew Temte
Chief Learning Officer: Dr. Tim Smaby
Executive Director, Real Estate Education: Melissa Kleeman-Moy
Development Editor: Christopher Kugler

GUIDE TO PASSING THE PEARSON VUE REAL ESTATE EXAM NINTH EDITION
©2015 Kaplan, Inc.
Published by DF Institute, Inc., d/b/a Dearborn Real Estate Education
332 Front St. S., Suite 501
La Crosse, WI 54601

Printed in the United States of America
First revision, March 2017
ISBN: 978-1-4754-2613-7
PPN: 1970-0609

CONTENTS

INTRODUCTION

In compiling this study guide for the salesperson and broker examinations administered by Pearson VUE, we have tried to provide the necessary information to candidates before they take the examination. Note, however, that Pearson VUE is not responsible for the content of this book. The structure of this book follows the content outline that was put together by Pearson VUE and has been accepted by various jurisdictions for use in their licensure process. Pearson VUE is a testing service and as such is responsible for the structure of testing programs.

This guide was written for salesperson and broker examinations in all of the Pearson VUE exam states. If your class instructor does not cover all the material in this guide, it may be because some material or terminology is not covered in your state examination. Keep in mind, however, that you can never know too much, especially when preparing for a career in which you will aid buyers and sellers in making some of their most important life decisions.

Because the intent of this study guide is to provide helpful information to candidates preparing for the examination, we hope you find this ninth edition to be of value. We wish you success on the examination and in your career.

ACKNOWLEDGMENTS

This new edition owes much to its reviewers. The time and effort that go into a review are considerable. My very special thanks go to Anita Hill for her assistance with the ninth edition of the *Guide to Passing the Pearson VUE Real Estate Exam.*

I would also like to recognize those real estate educators who provided valuable assistance with past editions of the *Guide to Passing the Pearson VUE Real Estate Exam*:

- Ron Baker, Alamo Real Estate Institute, San Antonio, Texas

- Thomas Battle, Real Estate Certification Program, Bloomington, Indiana

- Dr. Kenneth Beer, Beer School of Real Estate, Milford, Indiana

- Stephanie Blackburn, Jones College, Denver, Colorado

- Darryl Bradshaw, President, Mykut Real Estate School, Lynwood, Washington

- Richard Clemmer, D&D School of Real Estate, Johnson City, Tennessee

- Kay Knox Crawford, Continual Learning Institute, Nashville, Tennessee

- Jeff Dudley, Century 21 North Shore Real Estate School, North Andover, Massachusetts

- Rick Foster, Foster Real Estate Education, Maine

- Michael C. Glazer, Ivy Tech State College, Indianapolis, Indiana

- Katharine Hale, Arizona School of Real Estate and Business, Scottsdale, Arizona

- C. Van Hilty, Van Education Center, Colorado

- Cheryl Jimerson, Jones Real Estate College, Colorado

- Kent Keahey, Broadway School of Real Estate, Hot Springs, Arkansas

- Ron L. Kelton, Director, Kelton Schools, Arkansas

- Peggy McConnochie, Alaska Coastal Homes, Inc., Juneau, Alaska

- Walt McLaughlin, McColly School of Real Estate, Indiana

- John Morgan, Morgan Testing Services, Waterford, Connecticut

- Jerry W. Passon, Dean of Student Services, North Central Institute, Clarksville, Tennessee

- Janice Price, Partners Real Estate School, Highland, Indiana

- Larry D. Rickard, Realty School of Kansas, Wichita, Kansas

- Phyllis Rudnick, Annex Real Estate School, Quincy, Massachusetts

- Joan Sheppard, Sheppard & Associates, Anchorage, Alaska

■ Marie Spodek, Professional Real Estate Services, David City, Nebraska

■ Arnold Stringham, Stringham Real Estate School, Salt Lake City, Utah

■ Ruth Vella, Omega Real Estate School, Wilmington, Delaware

■ Jerry Wooten, Tucker School of Real Estate, Indianapolis, Indiana

—William H. Pivar

THE PEARSON VUE EXAMINATION

ABOUT THE EXAMINATION

Pearson VUE (www.pearsonvue.com) is the global leader in electronic testing services for academic admissions, certification, and licensure programs. Pearson VUE offers exams through the world's largest network of more than 4,000 test centers in 145 countries, providing testing services for information technology, regulatory and certification boards, and academic, government, and corporate clients. Its innovative technology offers the security and control required by admissions, licensure, and certification programs, while its commitment to service provides customers with an unmatched testing experience. Pearson VUE is a business of Pearson (NYSE: PSO; LSE: PSON), the international media company, whose other businesses include the Financial Times Group, Pearson Education, and the Penguin Group.

The exam is administered under contract with state licensing authorities and is not designed to be a test of language ability, reading, or test-taking skill. Its purpose is to identify candidates who have sufficient skills and knowledge to serve the interests of the public, and to lead those who are lacking in these skills to further study. The material you will be tested on was selected after analyzing numerous responses from real estate salespeople and brokers as to the scope of tasks required by their profession and the knowledge and skills needed to perform these tasks.

Bear in mind that the purpose of a licensing exam is not to disqualify applicants but to protect the public. This is done by requiring real estate salespeople and brokers to have the knowledge necessary to meet their professional obligations.

The Pearson VUE real estate examination is divided into two parts: Part One covers general topics and Part Two covers state laws. All questions are of the four-answer multiple-choice variety. The general portion of the real estate exam is made up of 80 scored items, which are distributed as noted in the following content outlines. Approximately 10% of the scored items on the general examination will involve mathematical computations.

The general examination also contains five pretest items that are not counted toward the score. These items are used to gather statistics on performance and to help assess appropriateness for use on future examinations. Because pretest items look exactly like items that are scored, candidates should answer all the items on the examination.

Your state portion of the examination will consist of 30 to 110 questions (determined by state licensing authority). The state portion will also include pretest questions that will not count for your score. Pretest questions will not appear to be different from other questions and will not be identified as pretest questions.

You will have four hours to take your examination. Most states allow 150 minutes for the general portion and 90 minutes for the state portion, but this can vary by state. The passing score for each state is established by the state real estate agency based on standards of competence that are deemed appropriate for licensure. Questions are based on topics that real estate salespeople or brokers actually deal with in the course of their work. Questions appear at the end of each chapter, to test your understanding of the material presented.

Key words such as *generally*, *approximately*, *best*, and *most likely* will appear in all caps. While Pearson VUE avoids using negative questions in the general portion of the examination, negative questions might be used in the state-specific portion of your examination, so you should be prepared to see them. The possibility of inclusion of a negative question reinforces the need for careful reading.

The examination may contain case-study questions in which a block of information is given, followed by two or three related questions. However, questions stand alone and are not based on preceding answers. Thus, one wrong answer does not affect the score on another question.

Questions are carefully reviewed to make certain there are no clues to the answer that could aid a candidate who doesn't know the material. Each question is either a clear and straightforward statement that calls for one of four answers, or it is an incomplete statement (stem) to be completed with the correct answer.

Each question has one right answer that will be clear to those candidates prepared for the examination. Wrong answers are often distracters that either tend to confuse or seem plausible to someone who does not fully understand what is sought. These wrong answers are likely to come from any of the following:

- Common misconceptions
- Common errors (a math answer resulting from a common computation error is likely to agree with one of the distracters)
- A carefully worded but incorrect statement that will appear plausible to an uninformed candidate
- Statements that, although true, are not really relevant to the question

The exam takes a positive approach to achieve fair measurement of a candidate's knowledge and skills. Therefore, do not fear your examination but treat it as an opportunity to demonstrate the knowledge and skills you have acquired to serve others as a real estate salesperson or broker.

Your state licensing agency will provide you with a copy of the *Real Estate Candidate Handbook*, which sets forth the content outline for both the general and state portions of the examination. You can access and print out your state real estate candidate handbook on the internet. Google the name of your state and real estate candidate handbook. It is recommended that you use state manuals to study for the state section of your examination. These manuals contain specific state laws and may be available from your state licensing agency. Any required prelicensing educational requirements can be obtained from your state department of real estate.

The following sections present the general content outline for the general portion of your Pearson VUE salesperson and brokers examinations. This book is arranged to follow these outlines as closely as possible.

GENERAL EXAM CONTENT OUTLINE FOR SALESPERSONS (EFFECTIVE APRIL 1, 2014)

I. **Real Property Characteristics, Definitions, Ownership, Restrictions, and Transfer (12)**
    A. Definitions, descriptions, and ways to hold title
        1. Elements of real and personal property
        2. Property description and area calculations
        3. Estates in real property
        4. Forms of ownership, rights, interests, and obligations
    B. Land-use controls and restrictions
        1. Government controls
        2. Private controls—nonmonetary
        3. Private controls—mortgage (deed of trust) and liens
    C. Transfer/alienation of title to real property
        1. Voluntary
        2. Involuntary
        3. Protections
        4. Partition/severance (voluntary or involuntary)
        5. Deeds and warranties: validity, types, and covenants
        6. Title and title insurance

II. **Property Valuation (7)**
    A. Principles, types, and estimates of property value
        1. Valuation definition, purpose, and process
        2. Characteristics
        3. Valuation principles
        4. Approaches to value
        5. Depreciation/obsolescence
        6. Appraisals and fair market value
        7. Math calculations
        8. Influences on property value
        9. Comparative market analysis (CMA)
    B. Investment analysis
        1. Application of principles
        2. Math calculations

III. **Contracts and Relationships With Buyers and Sellers (14)**
    A. Contract elements
        1. Validity
        2. Void/voidable
        3. Enforceable/unenforceable (statute of frauds)
        4. Executory/executed
    B. Listing contracts
        1. General purpose/definition of listing
        2. Types
        3. Required elements
        4. Establishing listing price
        5. Responsibilities
        6. Compensation arrangement

C. Buyer representation agreements
1. General purpose
2. Types
3. Required elements
4. Responsibilities
5. Compensation arrangement
D. Sales contracts
1. Terminology
2. Procedures
3. Standard parts
4. Contingencies and misc. provisions
5. Contractual rights and obligations
6. Disputes and dispute resolution terms
7. Delivery and acceptance
E. Option contracts
F. Agency relationships and responsibilities
1. Types of relationships—definitions
2. Relationship powers and obligations

IV. **Property Conditions and Disclosures (9)**
A. Federal environmental regulations
1. Lead-based paint
2. CERCLA
3. Asbestos
4. Wetlands and floodplains
B. Environmental issues
1. Mold
2. Radon
3. Protected species
4. Other
C. Material and other property disclosure

V. **Risk Management (6)**
A. Types of insurance
1. General liability
2. Errors and omissions
3. Hazard and flood
4. Other insurance
B. Recordkeeping
1. Contracts
2. Accounting
3. Other important documents
C. Privacy, security, and confidentiality
1. Security measures and controls
2. Systems and programs
3. Electronic communication and social media
4. Personal safety
D. Scope of expertise

VI. Federal Laws Governing Real Estate Activities (9)
    A. Antidiscrimination/fair housing acts
        1. Protected classes
        2. Advertising
        3. Enforcement/penalties
    B. Americans with Disabilities Act (ADA)
    C. Restraint of Trade (Sherman Act, etc.)
    D. Lending (Regulation Z, etc.)
    E. Privacy (Privacy Act, etc.)
    F. Marketing
        1. Real Estate Settlement Procedures Act (RESPA)
        2. Do not call
    G. Other regulations that apply

VII. Financing the Transaction and Settlement (8)
    A. Financing components
        1. Financing instruments
        2. Financing sources (primary and secondary mortgage markets, seller financing)
        3. Types of loans
        4. Financing clauses, terminology, and cost of money (calculation)
        5. Lending issues
    B. Lender requirements and obligations
        1. Private mortgage insurance (PMI)
        2. FHA requirements
        3. VA requirements
        4. Escrow/impound account
        5. Credit report
        6. Assumption requirements
        7. Appraisal requirements
        8. Hazard and flood insurance
        9. Federal financing and credit regulation
    C. Settlement/closing
        1. Procedures and forms
        2. Closing costs and calculations
        3. Documents, title, and recording

VIII. Leases, Rents, and Property Management (5)
    A. Types and elements of leases
        1. Leasehold estates
        2. Types of leases
        3. Lease clauses and provisions
    B. Lessor and lessee rights, responsibilities, liabilities, and recourse
        1. Owned and leased inclusions
        2. Reversionary rights of owners
        3. Unit-related disclosures
        4. Effect of sale/transfer/foreclosure
        5. Evictions
        6. Tenant improvements
        7. Termination of a lease
        8. Breach
        9. Security deposit guidelines and procedures

    C. Property management contracts and obligations of parties
        1.   Contracts and contractual relationships
        2.   Manager's obligations, duties, and liabilities
        3.   Owner's obligations, duties, and liabilities
        4.   Management/owner math calculations

IX.   Brokerage Operations (6)
    A. Trust accounts
        1.   Earnest money
        2.   Commingling
        3.   Conversion of funds
    B. Advertising
    C. Forms of business ownership
        1.   Corporation
        2.   Partnership (general and limited)
        3.   Limited liability company
        4.   Sole proprietorship
    D. Independent contractors vs. employee

X.   Ethical and Legal Business Practices (4)
    A. Misrepresentation issues
    B. Implied duty of good faith
    C. Due diligence
    D. Unauthorized practice of law

GENERAL EXAM CONTENT OUTLINE FOR BROKERS (EFFECTIVE APRIL 1, 2014)

I.   Real Property Characteristics, Definitions, Ownership, Restrictions, and Transfer (9)
    A. Definitions, descriptions, and ways to hold title
        1.   Elements of real and personal property
        2.   Property description and area calculations
        3.   Estates in real property
        4.   Forms of ownership, rights, interests, and obligations
    B. Land-use controls and restrictions
        1.   Government controls
        2.   Private controls—covenants and restrictions
        3.   Private controls—mortgage (deed of trust) and liens
    C. Transfer/alienation of title to real property
        1.   Voluntary
        2.   Involuntary
        3.   Protections
        4.   Partition/severance (voluntary or involuntary)
        5.   Deeds and warranties: validity, types, and covenants
        6.   Title and title insurance

II.   Property Valuation and Appraisal (9)
    A. Market analysis/broker price opinion
        1.   Definition and purpose
        2.   Process
        3.   Requirements

B. Appraisal
   1. Definition and purpose
   2. Process
   3. Requirements
   4. Three approaches to value
C. Investment analysis
   1. Application of principles
   2. Math calculations
   3. Commercial-investment property types

III. Contracts and Relationships With Buyers and Sellers (17)
A. Contract elements
   1. Authority
   2. Validity
   3. Void/voidable
   4. Enforceable/unenforceable (statute of frauds)
   5. Unilateral/bilateral
   6. Executory/executed
B. Contracts with buyers and sellers
   1. General purpose/definition of listing
   2. Types
   3. Required elements
   4. Establishing listing price
   5. Responsibilities
C. Commission agreements
   1. Negotiation of commission
   2. Who may collect?
   3. Other compensation arrangements
   4. Math: licensee compensation/commission
D. Sales contracts
   1. Terminology
   2. Procedures
   3. Standard parts
   4. Contingencies and miscellaneous provisions
   5. Contractual rights and obligations
   6. Disputes and dispute resolution terms
E. Distressed property sales
F. Licensee relationships and responsibilities
   1. Types of relationships—definitions
   2. Relationship powers and obligations

IV. Property Valuation and Appraisal (9)
A. Market analysis/broker price opinion
   1. Definition and purpose
   2. Process
   3. Requirements
B. Appraisal
   1. Definition and purpose
   2. Process
   3. Requirements
   4. Three approaches to value

C. Investment analysis
    1. Application of principles
    2. Math calculations
    3. Commercial-investment property types

V.   Contracts and Relationships With Buyers and Sellers (17)
A. Contract elements
    1. Authority
    2. Validity
    3. Void/voidable
    4. Enforceable/unenforceable (statute of frauds)
    5. Unilateral/bilateral
    6. Executory/executed
B. Contracts with buyers and sellers
    1. General purpose/definition of listing
    2. Types
    3. Required elements
    4. Establishing listing price
    5. Responsibilities
C. Commission agreements
    1. Negotiation of commission
    2. Who may collect
    3. Other compensation arrangements
    4. Math: licensee compensation/commission
D. Sales contracts
    1. Terminology
    2. Procedures
    3. Standard parts
    4. Contingencies and misc. provisions
    5. Contractual rights and obligations
    6. Disputes and dispute resolution terms
E. Distressed property sales
F. Licensee relationships and responsibilities
    1. Types of relationships—definitions
    2. Relationship powers and obligations

VI.   Property Conditions and Disclosures (8)
A. Federal environmental regulations
    1. Lead-based paint
    2. CERCLA
    3. Asbestos
    4. Wetlands and floodplains
B. Environmental issues
    1. Mold
    2. Radon
    3. Protected species
    4. Other
C. Material and other property disclosures
D. Liability considerations

VII. Federal Laws Governing Real Estate Activities (7)

    A. Antidiscrimination/fair housing acts
        1. Protected classes
        2. Advertising
        3. Enforcement/penalties
    B. Americans with Disabilities Act (ADA)
    C. Restraint of Trade (Sherman Act, etc.)
    D. Lending (Regulation Z, etc.)
    E. Privacy (Privacy Act, etc.)
    F. Marketing
        1. Real Estate Settlement Procedures Act (RESPA)
        2. Do not call
    G. Other regulations that apply

VIII. Financing the Transaction and Settlement (9)

    A. Financing components
        1. Financing instruments
        2. Financing sources (primary and secondary mortgage markets, seller financing)
        3. Types of loans
        4. Financing clauses, terminology, and cost of money (calculation)
        5. Lending issues
    B. Lender requirements and obligations
        1. Private mortgage insurance (PMI)
        2. FHA requirements
        3. VA requirements
        4. Escrow/impound account
        5. Credit report
        6. Assumption requirements
        7. Appraisal requirements
        8. Hazard and flood insurance
        9. Federal financing and credit regulation
    C. Settlement/closing
        1. Procedures and forms
        2. Closing costs and calculations
        3. Documents, title, and recording

IX. Leases, Rents, and Property Management (7)

    A. Types and elements of leases
        1. Leasehold estates
        2. Types of leases
        3. Lease clauses and provisions
    B. Lessor and lessee rights, responsibilities, liabilities, and recourse
        1. Owned and leased inclusions
        2. Reversionary rights of owners
        3. Rental-related discriminatory laws
        4. Unit-related disclosures
        5. Effect of sale/transfer/foreclosure
        6. Evictions
        7. Tenant improvements
        8. Termination of a lease
        9. Breach

    C. Property management contracts and obligations of parties
       1. Contracts and contractual relationships
       2. Manager's obligations, duties, and liabilities
       3. Owner's obligations, duties, and liabilities
       4. Management/owner math calculations

X.   **Brokerage Operations (14)**
    A. Broker management of funds
       1. Earnest money
       2. Commingling
       3. Conversion of funds
    B. Supervision and management
       1. Broker-salesperson relationship
       2. Office operations
       3. Training
       4. Recordkeeping
       5. Activities requiring a license
    C. Advertising
    D. Ethical and legal business practices
       1. Misrepresentation
       2. Implied duty of good faith
       3. Due diligence
       4. Unauthorized practice of law
       5. Marketing practices
    E. Forms of business ownership
    F. Independent contractors vs. employee
    G. Regulatory compliance

HOW TO STUDY

Any career decision requires preparation, and preparing for a career in real estate takes time and dedication. Although your motivation to spend the time necessary must come from within, a few simple suggestions can make the hours you spend more productive.

1. Study daily, if possible.   You will retain much more information if you study over many days than if you try to cram everything into a few marathon sessions. Set aside particular blocks of time for study; early mornings are preferable because you are more likely to be at your mental peak for the day. Try to avoid study periods after heavy meals or in too warm a study area because a nap might take precedence over concentration.

2. Find a quiet place.   While some people have no problem studying in the midst of chaos, most students do best with as few distractions as possible. Such students should use the quietest room in their home for study purposes. Studying near televisions, next to the phone, or even outdoors can be extremely difficult.

3. Break up your study time.   With pressures of work and family, most people don't have large blocks of time to study. Therefore, be opportunistic by taking advantage of short available time periods, even as short as ten minutes. Actually, it is easier to concentrate over a short period than over a long period. If you do have large blocks of time available for studying, break up your study time into blocks no longer than 45 minutes and take a break by doing some other activity for 10 to 15 minutes. A short walk is an excellent way to refresh yourself and aid concentration.

4. Use good study techniques.

Scan.   Before you study each section, spend no more than five minutes scanning the material. A general understanding of what you will study helps your retention. Look for unfamiliar terms in your scanning process. Check the definitions in the text material or glossary.

Read and paraphrase.   After reading each paragraph, stop, close your eyes, and ask yourself what you've read. By putting the material into your own words mentally (or verbally if your study area permits it), your likelihood of retaining the information increases dramatically. By forcing yourself to paraphrase the material, you avoid the likelihood of giving too light a treatment to any one area.

Reread and paraphrase.   A second reading should involve paraphrasing more than one paragraph (for example, whole topic areas).

5. Take the test.   After the second reading, take the quiz at the end of the chapter as if it were an actual examination. If possible, schedule a single block of time for this purpose.

When taking the examinations in this book, use the examination techniques described later in this chapter. Mastering proper exam techniques can mean the extra points that make the difference between passing and failing.

Don't write on the examinations in this book. Use a separate answer sheet. If you mark the examination answers in the book, you will not gain the maximum benefit from a review. You will see the answer and not analyze each question and the answer choices.

On your answer sheet, you should place a "c" next to those answers you are certain of and a "?" next to those you are not certain of. By doing so, checking the answers is more likely to be a learning experience than just a simple evaluation.

6. Check your results.   After taking each test, check your answers. Don't limit your evaluation to those questions you answered incorrectly. Understanding *why* an answer is correct is more important than the fact that it is correct. Pay particular attention to wrong answers that you were certain of. For all wrong answers, ask yourself why you were drawn to that answer and how you will relate to the same material in the future. You don't want that same wrong answer to seem correct in the future.

7. Study before class.   If you are using this book in a license preparation class, complete your study of a subject before it is covered in class. Immediately before class, spend another few minutes quickly scanning the material so it is fresh in your mind.

By coming to class already understanding the topic, you get the greatest possible benefit from your instructor. That is, instead of trying to learn basic facts in class, you can use classroom time as it is meant to be used—asking questions, clarifying difficult points, and learning about changes, as well as material specific to your state.

8. Mark your book.   Highlighting key areas in the text will help you recall and review particularly important points. Too much special emphasis, though, defeats the purpose of making a few points stand out.

Notes on your instructor's comments are best written in the margins. This way, you have one integrated text to study.

9. Know the vocabulary.   Create flashcards for each word you have trouble with. Whenever you have a few minutes free during the day, review your cards. When you feel you have mastered a term, discard that card.

10. Review all material.   While preparing for the Pearson VUE examination, it is a good practice to review on a weekly basis the material you have covered up to that point. This will result in greater review time for material you learned first. This way, you will compensate for the effect of time loss on your memory process. In preparing for your examination, don't limit your review to the material you feel you are weak in or topics you think the exam will emphasize. For a comprehensive review, a good starting point is the review examination section at the end of this book, followed by the text material. Your review should include several readings of the glossary at the end of this book, which will be of great help in tying all the material together. You will find some terms in the glossary that have not been covered in text material. While these terms are less likely to be covered on the general portion of your examination, a familiarity with them is strongly recommended.

Retake the examination in each section as well as the review examinations. These practice examinations are especially beneficial. Of course, the same level of study must be applied to information unique to your state. The five review tests in the back of the book have been weighted to reflect the emphasis given to the areas covered by the general portion of the Pearson VUE examination. The five examinations are weighted in an ascending order of difficulty starting with the Level I examination. After you take each examination, make certain that you understand why your correct answers were correct, as well as why incorrect answers were incorrect, before going on to the next level.

11. Don't become discouraged.   Because of the sheer volume of new material, some students use their confusion as an excuse to drop out. Realize that confusion is normal for the first few weeks (sometimes months) of study; as you progress, things will come together slowly. Students often are well into the review process before they realize they are no longer confused. Whenever you feel you will never get it, think of everyone you know in real estate. The reason they succeeded is not because they are smarter than you but because they refused to quit.

ONLINE PRACTICE TEST

Pearson Vue offers an 80-question online practice test on general real estate subjects. The test costs $19.95 and is available at www.pearsonvue.com/practicetests/realestate.

MENTAL PREPARATION

Know the location of the examination center where you will take your examination and where you will park. Allow time for unexpected traffic delays. If you rush to the examination site with worries about being on time for your appointment, you will likely be in an agitated frame of mind. This can have a negative effect on your examination performance.

It is natural to be nervous before an examination. Even though you understand the material, nervousness can detract from your test-taking ability; remaining calm isn't easy. Even the candidate who appears relaxed has a few butterflies. You can help yourself by avoiding pre-exam socializing with other candidates. Nervousness breeds nervousness, and talking with a group of tense people is not the way to relax.

Some students encounter a difficult question early in the exam and become frustrated, which can have a negative effect on the remainder of their performance. You must keep in mind that one question, no matter how difficult, will not by itself be the difference between success and failure. Everyone taking the examination will have similar problems with a number of questions. If this were not the case, it wouldn't be much of a test.

PERTINENT STATE INFORMATION

At the end of each chapter, we have presented a number of questions under the heading "Your Pertinent State Information." These questions allow you to consider state-specific information that may be covered on the state portion of your licensing examination.

You may want to mark the margins of this book with notes on material for your specific state, because not every question is applicable in every state. If you are using this book in a classroom setting, your instructor will likely point out state-specific material of importance, as well as point out which material you may disregard.

LICENSING REQUIREMENTS

Your state statutes set forth the requirements for licensing as a real estate salesperson or broker. They might include minimum education and age requirements (18), fingerprinting, and taking and passing a real estate examination.

In addition to state requirements, the federal Personal Responsibility and Work Opportunity Act requires that license applicants provide proof of their legal right to be in the United States. The act denies public benefits, which includes professional licensing, to illegal immigrants. The act applies to both original licensing and license renewals.

SITTING FOR THE EXAMINATION

Make a reservation to take your examination by following the instructions in your state candidate handbook.

For individuals with documented disabilities, Pearson VUE provides accommodations, such as a separate testing room, extra testing time and/or a reader or recorder for individuals with mobility or visual impairments who cannot read or write on their own. Special accommodations should be solicited at the time of examination request.

Candidates must check into the test center 30 minutes before their examination, sign a Candidate Rules Agreement, and be photographed. The rules agreement deals with strict confidentiality.

It is important to check your state candidate handbook as to required material to bring to your examination. Candidates who do not present the required items will be denied admission to the examination, be considered absent, and forfeit the entire examination fee. The required items may include

- the confirmation number given when you made your examination request;

- certificates showing completion of state-mandated education and experience requirements (for brokers);

- two forms of identification (including a government-issued identification showing your photograph and signature);

- a surety bond, if required (for broker candidates; see your state candidate guide); and

- a license fee (candidates passing their examination will be required to pay their license fee; credit cards, personal checks or money orders payable to Pearson VUE may be used).

While not required, candidates may bring a battery-powered, handheld calculator. The calculator must be silent, nonprinting, and without a stored memory. Make certain your calculator has fresh batteries. Don't use a solar calculator because the light may be insufficient for sustained use. On the day before your examination, test your calculator with simple addition, subtraction, multiplication, and division problems. A malfunctioning calculator is not grounds for challenging exam results or getting an extension of the time limit. Even a perfect calculator is useless if you can't operate it correctly. If you borrow one or buy a new one for the exam, be certain you understand fully how that model functions.

No dictionaries, books, papers (including scratch paper), or other personal items will be permitted at your examination station. The test administrator will provide material to take notes.

Candidates will be given the opportunity to take a tutorial on the computer on which the examination will be administered. Tutorial time does not reduce examination time. While the examination administrators are not familiar with the examination content, they will answer questions on procedure and use of the computer. Candidates may begin their examination when they are familiar with the computer.

The computer shows each question and records your answers. These are user-friendly programs, even for those who do not have computer or typing experience. This system allows for a paperless examination, eliminates any possibility of grading error, increases exam security, and lets each applicant take a different but equivalent examination. You can move forward or backward through the exam, mark questions for review, and change answers. However, once you start the state-specific portion of your examination, you cannot go back to the general portion of your examination.

The computer system you will be using allows your examination to be scored immediately after completion. You will leave the examination center with a pass or fail score.

Pay attention to any instructions. Cheating will result in your immediate dismissal from the examination room and notification to the state licensing agency. Attempting to copy questions or remove exam material (including your notes) constitutes cheating.

Your examination begins when you put the first question on your monitor and ends automatically after four hours.

Read

Read each question carefully to be sure you understand what is asked. Don't mentally change the wording or assume the question means something other than what it says. If a question makes an assumption, accept it as true; students often read more into a question than is asked. Each question stem should be read carefully and the answer should apply to that specific question. A correct statement that answers the wrong question is still a wrong answer.

While not intended to be tricky, questions on the state-specific portion of your examination could be at a higher level of reading difficulty.

Answer

Read the entire question and every answer before giving your computer answer. If you are not certain of the answer, eliminate what you believe to be the wrong answers and take a guess from the others. An informed candidate should be able to eliminate at least one answer, possibly two; an uninformed candidate will find all four answers plausible. When you have two answers that appear to be right, you should look at the answers in a reverse light. Look for something wrong with one of the answers. The thing that makes it wrong could be in the stem or in the answer.

Words should be interpreted using their common meaning, unless a word has a special meaning in regard to real estate, in which case the real estate meaning should be used. You may find questions that go beyond what you have studied. These questions are intended to test your judgment using what you have learned. They are not intended to be tricky.

Just as in real-life situations, questions may present facts or figures that are not necessary to answer the questions. If careful reading of a question indicates that information given is not relevant to the answer, ignore it.

Because your computer will show whether you have left any question unanswered, it is suggested that you commit yourself to at least two passes through the test. On the first pass do the easy questions—that is, material you are familiar with where the correct answer is obvious to you. When you are finished with the first pass, you will feel good about yourself and be ready for the second pass.

There are two types of questions for which you should leave the question for the second pass. They are

1. questions you absolutely don't know the answers to, and
2. math questions that are likely to be time-consuming—even if you are great at math.

Ideally, when you have completed your first pass, you will feel that you have answered the majority of the questions correctly and you need to answer only a few more right to be on your way to a real estate license. Best of all, you have a lot of time to finish.

Go to the summary page on your computer. Press "Review Unanswered" and the questions left unanswered will come up one after the other. Now finish the examination.

Math Questions

Approximately 10% of your examination questions will require some degree of mathematical calculation.

Before you work out a mathematics question, make a mental estimate of the answer. If your computed answer differs significantly, there's a good chance you made an error in computation. Just because your computed answer agrees exactly with an answer choice does not mean it is correct. Wrong answers are the result of common mistakes, such as reversing dividend and divisor; failing to carry the mathematics to the final step; failing to convert inches to feet, square feet to square yards, cubic feet to cubic yards, and the like; and misplacing a decimal point.

Your computer will show the time remaining, but time shouldn't be a problem unless you really get hung up on a math question. If this is the case, leave it until you have answered the rest of the questions.

After you have completed and reviewed the general portion, go on to the state portion of your examination.

Use Your Time

Remember, you have two and one-half hours to complete the 85 questions on the general portion of the examination. Your examination computer will indicate the time remaining. Don't rush to take a break when you are finished with your state portion. Take time to review the questions and answers. Staying longer can mean more points for you. You will have the time; use it to your advantage.

Reread the questions, asking yourself what is really being asked and then check your answers. You may discover you answered several questions based on the way you thought the question should read and not on what was actually asked. Misreading questions does not excuse a wrong answer.

Changing Answers

Never change an answer for change's sake. Your first decision is usually the best. However, if you discover that you misread a question, or a later question jogs your memory so that you now understand what is sought, change the answer.

Clues

If a question or an answer includes a word that is not familiar to you, it might help you to keep in mind that words ending in "or" are givers, such as *grantor* (one who makes a grant) and *donor* (one who makes a gift). Words ending in "-ee" describe receivers, such as *grantee* and *donee*. Should a word end in "-trix," it designates a woman.

Calculations

For calculations on the examination, unless otherwise indicated, you should

- round off math answers to the nearest whole number;

- assume there are 5,280 feet in a mile and 43,560 square feet in an acre; and

- base prorations on the time scale indicated in the question, which will state if there are assumed to be 360 or 365 days in a year, as well as who is responsible for the date of closing (use the actual days in a month for prorating unless the question indicates otherwise).

Real Property and Ownership

PROPERTY

All property is divided into two categories: real property and personal property.

Elements of Real Property

Real property includes land and the improvements and benefits that transfer or go with the land, such as buildings, fences, trees, water rights, the ground below, mineral rights, air rights, and easements. Historically, ownership included the airspace to the highest heavens, the surface, and the ground below. Today we limit ownership to reasonable airspace. The rights, benefits, and improvements that go with the land are also called **appurtenances**. In most states, mobile homes on permanent foundations are regarded as real property.

Bundle of Rights

The beneficial rights to use, exclude others, lease, encumber, transfer, and inherit are ownership rights called the **bundle of rights**.

Elements of Personal Property

Also called **chattels**, personal property is any property that is not real property. Personal property is generally considered movable, whereas real property is regarded as immovable. Mobile homes on wheels are usually regarded as personal property. Naturally growing plants, perennial crops, and trees (**fructus naturales**) are classified as real property, but cultivated annual crops (**fructus industriales**) are considered personal property.

Real property can become personal property and personal property can become real property. For example, a growing tree is real property, but when cut down, it is personal property. Similarly, lumber from the tree (personal property) becomes real property if it is used to build a dwelling. Personal property becoming real property by becoming attached to real property is the process called **annexation**. **Severance** is the act of removing something from the land. For example, tearing down a building (real property) would leave a pile of bricks and lumber, which is personal property.

Chattels real.   Real estate interests less than fee ownership, such as tenant leasehold interests and mortgages, are called the seemingly contradictory term *chattels real* but are personal property.

FIXTURES

Fixtures are items that were once personal property but have become so affixed to the real property that they have become part of it. Fixtures are transferred with, and are taxed as, real estate.

Tests of Fixture

Courts require that at least one of the following four tests be met to determine that an item is a fixture.

1.   *Agreement.*   A written agreement of the parties as to whether an item is a fixture and will remain with the real estate or will be regarded as personal property will govern the character of the property between the parties.

2.   *Intent.*   Courts determine the intention of the parties if there is no agreement. Intent is considered the most important test of a fixture when there isn't an agreement. Did the parties intend that property would become part of the real estate? It can be difficult to prove intent.

3.   *Attachment or method of annexation.*   Can the item be removed without causing major damage to the real property? Is the method of attachment of a permanent nature?

4.   *Adaptability.*   Adaptability is a legal rather than a physical attachment. If an item is reasonably necessary for the normal use of the property, it probably is a fixture, even though it is not attached.

Relationship of parties.   If the other tests are inconclusive, the law generally favors the buyer in a buyer-seller relationship or the tenant in a landlord-tenant relationship.

Trade fixtures.   Fixtures installed by a tenant for the purpose of conducting a business or trade ordinarily remain personal property and can be removed by the tenant anytime before expiration of the lease. The tenant is liable for any damage caused by the removal.

Emblements.   Cultivated annual crops are personal property. Unless otherwise agreed, tenants have the right to enter the property after expiration of the lease to harvest those crops that were the fruits of their labor.

METHODS OF PROPERTY DESCRIPTIONS

Concentrate on the method(s) of land description used in your state.

There are three methods of legally describing real property: lot, block, and tract; metes and bounds; and government survey. Street addresses and tax-assessor descriptions, while sufficient for some purposes, are considered informal descriptions and are not legal descriptions.

1. Lot, Block, and Tract

State and/or local subdivision law requires recording of a subdivision map. This legal description uses the parcel's designation on the recorded map, as well as recording information. For example:

> Lot 17, Block 4 of Atlantic Heights Third Addition recorded on pages 814–815 in Volume 36 of the official records of the County of Oceanside.

2. Metes and Bounds

Also called **measurements and directions**, this is the oldest method of describing property; it was used extensively in the original 13 states. The metes-and-bounds method shows the boundaries of a parcel by measuring from point to point. The measuring points in a metes-and-bounds description are called **monuments**. Trees, rocks, and rivers are examples of **natural monuments**, whereas iron stakes, fences, and roads are examples of **artificial monuments**. In the case of a difference between stated distances and actual monuments, the actual monuments would prevail. Metes-and-bounds descriptions are given in a clockwise manner, starting at the **point of beginning (POB)** and ending at the POB. If a description fails to end at the POB, it is defective because the property is not encircled. Angles in a metes-and-bounds description are measured in degrees (°), minutes ('), and seconds (") from a north-south line (see Figure 1.1). The size of a metes-and-bounds parcel may be described as "acres MOL." The term **more or less (MOL)** indicates the acreage is not guaranteed to be exact.

FIGURE 1.1

Circle Demonstrating Angles in a Metes-and-Bounds Description

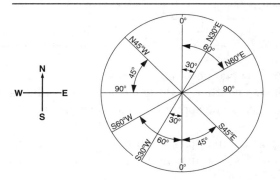

Circle Demonstrating Angles in a Metes-and-Bounds Description

There are 360° in a circle.
There are 180° in a half-circle.
There are 90° in a quarter-circle (right angle).
Each degree is divided into 60 minutes.
Each minute is divided into 60 seconds ($\forall$).
The point of beginning is at the intersection of the two lines (or the center of the circle).
The "bearing" of a course is described by measuring easterly or westerly from the north and south lines.

In cases where the boundary is in dispute, the parties can agree to a boundary line (**doctrine of agreed boundaries**). The agreed boundary is binding on future owners.

Boundaries may be described by natural features.

As a rule, the following apply:

- If a boundary is a private road, the boundary line is the center of the road.
- If a boundary is a navigable river, the boundary line is the average low water line.

- ■ If a boundary is a nonnavigable river, the boundary line is the center of the river.

- ■ If land borders tidelands, the boundary line is the average high-tide line.

3. Government (Rectangular) Survey

Most U.S. land is laid out in a rectangular pattern by government survey. If your state uses the government survey method, pay close attention to the following material. If not, read it, but concentrate more on your own state's method[s] of land description. The government survey method measures land from the intersections of principal surveying lines. Lines going east and west are called **base lines**; those going north and south are called **meridians**. From the intersection of base lines and meridians, land is measured in **townships**. Townships are 6 miles square and contain 36 square miles.

The township marked A in Figure 1.2 is three tiers north of the base line and two ranges east of the meridian line. Therefore, it is designated Tier 3 North, Range 2 East, or T3N, R2E. To have a complete legal description, reference also must be made to the specific base line and meridian.

FIGURE 1.2

Meridians and Base Lines

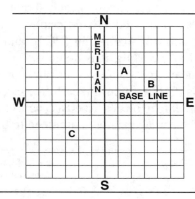

Horizontal rows of townships are called *tiers*. Tiers are either north or south of the base line.

Vertical rows of townships are called *ranges*. Ranges are either east or west of the meridian.

The north and south boundary lines of each township are called *township lines*. The east and west boundary lines of townships are called *range lines*.

Township B is two tiers above or north of the base line and four ranges east of the meridian and, thus, is designated Tier 2 North, Range 4 East, or T2N, R4E, with reference to the appropriate base line and meridian.

Township C is three tiers south of the base line and three ranges west of the meridian and is described as T3S, R3W, with reference to the appropriate base line and meridian.

Correction lines.   If uncorrected, township lines would converge as they go north because of the curvature of the earth. To compensate for the curvature of the earth so as to maintain the square shape of townships, every fourth north/south township line is designated a **correction line** or **guide meridian**. East/west lines every 24 miles are called **standard parallels**. The 24-mile-square (24-mile-by-24 mile) parcels bordered by the guide meridians and standard parallels are called **government checks** or **quadrangles**.

Because of the curvature of the earth, adjustments are made in sections on the north and west boundaries of a township. Eleven sections of a township could be so affected.

Because of lakes and rivers, some quarter sections will have less than 160 acres. Such quarter sections are designated as **government lots** and are identified by a lot number.

Locating Land by Government Survey

Know these measurements:

- One township = 6 miles square (36 square miles)
- One section = 640 acres
- One mile = 5,280 feet
- One acre = 43,560 square feet

To help you understand the size of an acre, a square acre is approximately 208.7 feet square.

Each township is six miles square and contains 36 sections. Each **section** is one mile square and contains 640 acres. Sections in a township are always numbered as shown in Figure 1.3.

FIGURE 1.3

Sections in a Township

N					
6	5	4	3	2	1
7	8	9	10	11	12
18	17	16	15	14	13
19	20	21	22	23	24
30	29	28	27	26	25
31	32	33	34	35	36

W ← → E, S

Adjoining this township are other townships, so east of Section 24 would be Section 19 of the adjoining township. In the same way, south of Section 33 would be Section 4 of another township.

Note that the numbering starts in the upper right-hand corner (NE) and continues in a zigzag pattern (see Figure 1.4).

FIGURE 1.4

Section Numbering Order

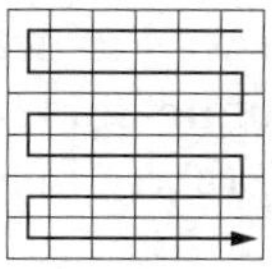

Land is normally described by its location within a specific section. For an example, see Figure 1.5.

FIGURE 1.5

Legal Descriptions of Land Within a Section

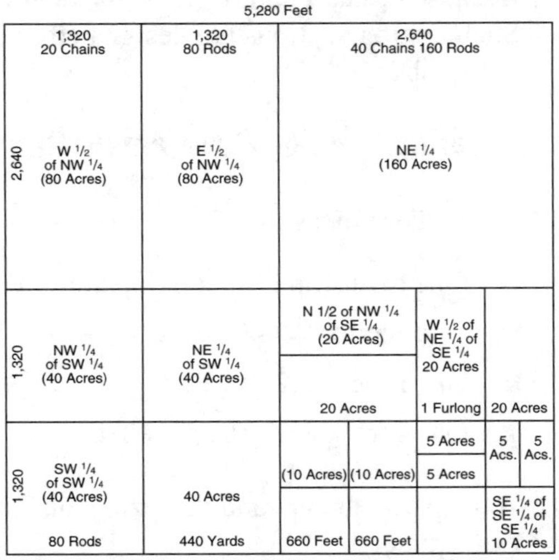

	5,280 Feet		
	1,320 20 Chains	1,320 80 Rods	2,640 40 Chains 160 Rods
2,640	W ½ of NW ¼ (80 Acres)	E ½ of NW ¼ (80 Acres)	NE ¼ (160 Acres)
1,320	NW ¼ of SW ¼ (40 Acres)	NE ¼ of SW ¼ (40 Acres)	N 1/2 of NW ¼ of SE ¼ (20 Acres) / 20 Acres / W ½ of NE ¼ of SE ¼ 20 Acres / 1 Furlong / 20 Acres
1,320	SW ¼ of SW ¼ (40 Acres)	40 Acres	(10 Acres) (10 Acres) / 5 Acres / 5 Acres / 5 Acres 5 Acs. Acs. / SE ¼ of SE ¼ of SE ¼ 10 Acres
	80 Rods	440 Yards	660 Feet	660 Feet

Legal descriptions are not always as simple as finding a ¼ section. Suppose the description is the S½ of the NW¼ of the SE¼ of section 27, T8N, R17W, SBBL&M (San Bernardino base line and meridian). We first find the township by counting 8 north from the base line and 17 west from the meridian. We find the section by the numbering, as previously explained.

We can find the size of a parcel by simply going backward, using its description alone (see Figure 1.6).

FIGURE 1.6

Property Descriptions

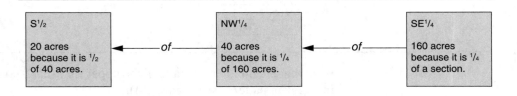

S½
20 acres because it is ½ of 40 acres.   —of—   NW¼
40 acres because it is ¼ of 160 acres.   —of—   SE¼
160 acres because it is ¼ of a section.

Another way to determine size of a parcel by its legal description is to multiply the denominators (bottom number of each fraction) and then divide that number into 640 (acres in a section).

The example given in Figure 1.6 is:

$$½ \times ¼ \times ¼$$

$$2 \times 4 \times 4 = 32$$

$$640 \div 32 = 20 \text{ acres}$$

Because a section is 1 mile square, it has 5,280 feet on each of its four sides. A ¼ section would have 2,640 feet on each side because it is ½ mile. A quarter of a quarter section would have 1,320 feet on each side because it is ¼ mile square.

Benchmarks are permanent markers that have been set by the U.S. National Geodetic Survey. They indicate elevation above sea level. The **datum** or **datum plane** is a horizontal plane from which elevation is measured. Surveyors use it.

Topographical lines are lines on a map that indicate contour of the land. Lines set close together mean the surface has a slope; lines set far apart indicate relatively level land.

ESTATES IN REAL PROPERTY

An estate is the degree or nature of the ownership interest a person has in real property.

Freehold Estates

Freehold estates are estates for an indefinite period of time. Fee simple and life estates are the two basic types of freehold estates. Freehold estates are considered real property.

Fee Simple or Fee Simple Absolute Estates

Fee simple is the highest ownership possible in real property. It is also the most common degree of ownership. All other estates have a lesser interest than fee simple.

Three features characterize fee simple:

1. It has no time limitation.
2. It is freely transferable.
3. It may be inherited.

Fee Simple on Condition Subsequent

An estate on a condition subsequent conveys title, provided a specific condition is met. It does not provide a duration for which title is granted. An example is a grant of property on the condition that it is never used for the sale of alcoholic beverages. If the condition is breached, the grantor must declare the breach and retake the property within a reasonable period of time.

Note that grantor action is not required under a fee simple determinable estate.

Fee Simple Determinable

Like fee simple on a condition subsequent, fee simple determinable is a defeasible estate that can be lost upon the happening of a specified condition.

If a deed specifies that a grant shall be only "for as long as" or while a property is in a particular use, the length of the estate is really determined by the deed. Use for another purpose would automatically end the estate, and no action of the grantor is necessary. An example is a deed to a city for the length of time the property is used as a road; if the road use were to cease, title would revert to the grantor.

Life Estates

In life estates, grantees customarily hold the estate only for their lifetime. Therefore, the property cannot be inherited or encumbered by the life tenant beyond their lifetime. For example, if the life tenant leased the life estate for 20 years but died sooner, the lease would end with the life tenant's death.

It is possible to have a life estate based on the life of a person other than the life tenant, called a **pur autre vie estate**. In such a case, the life tenant or the heirs will have the estate only as long as this other person lives (see Figure 1.7).

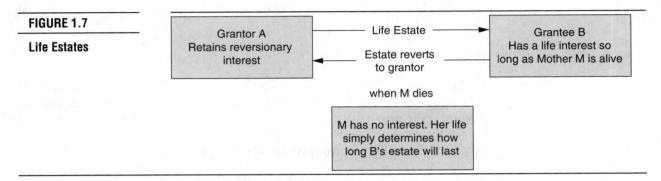

FIGURE 1.7

Life Estates

In the case shown in Figure 1.7, when M dies, B's interest reverts back to A, who would now have a fee simple interest. If B died before M, then B's heirs would inherit B's interest and would be able to enjoy the benefits of the life estate so long as M was alive.

The life tenant must make repairs, pay taxes, and avoid committing **waste**, which is characterized by damage or failure to make repairs. Because the life tenant is under no obligation to insure the premises, future interest holders should secure their own insurance if they wish to be protected.

Lenders sometimes lend on a life estate but require that the life tenant take out a life insurance policy that will pay off the loan in the event of the life tenant's death. As an alternative, a lender might require that any future interest holders join in signing the mortgage.

Reversionary and remainder estates.   On the death of a life tenant, the property reverts to the grantor or to the grantor's heirs (if either retained a reversionary interest) or to a named third party who has a remainder interest (see Figure 1.8).

If the conveyance shown in the diagram were from A to B for life and then to C, C or C's heirs would be certain of receiving the estate, so they would have a **vested remainder** interest.

If, however, the conveyance were from A to B for life and then to C if C is still alive, C must outlive B in order to obtain the property. In this case, C would have a **contingent remainder** interest.

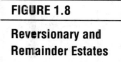

FIGURE 1.8

Reversionary and Remainder Estates

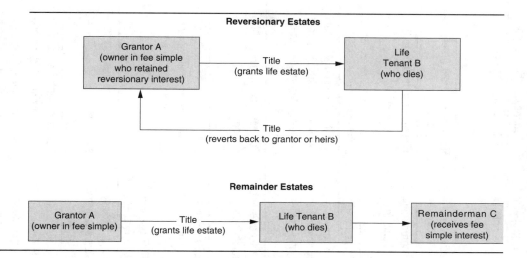

Creation.   A life estate may be created by will, by grant where the grantor conveys a life estate, or by reservation where the grantor conveys the real property but reserves a life estate. In addition, a number of states recognize dower and curtesy as legal life estates created by law.

Dower.   A wife's right to a life estate or an ownership interest in her husband's home upon his death is called **dower**. Some states don't provide dower interests, and dower varies among the states where it is provided.

Curtesy.   A husband's right to a life estate in the wife's property upon her death is called **curtesy**. Usually, a one-third interest applies to curtesy. Not all states provide the right of curtesy.

In some states, homestead rights also create a legal life estate, giving a widow and minor children the right to occupy the homestead for life after the husband's death.

Termination.   A life estate can be lost by **merger**. If the same party acquired the life tenant's interest, as well as the interests of the reversionary or remainder interest holder, the life estate would be lost through a merger. The single owner would now have a fee simple estate. Through the merger, the lesser interest is merged into the greater fee simple interest. A person cannot own a property in fee simple and also have a lesser interest as a life tenant.

Nonfreehold or Less-Than-Freehold Estates (Leasehold)

Leasehold interests of tenants are nonfreehold estates. Unless specifically prohibited, leasehold interests can be transferred freely and may be inherited. While freehold estates are considered real property, leasehold interests of the tenant are considered personal property. The leased fee estate of the lessor, however, is a freehold estate and is real property.

FORMS OF OWNERSHIP

While estates describe the degree of ownership interest, ownership can be in many forms, as discussed in the following sections (see Figure 1.9).

FIGURE 1.9
Common Ownership Forms

	Tenancy in common	Joint tenancy	Community property	Tenancy by the entirety
Parties	Any number of persons (can be husband and wife)	Any number of persons (can be husband and wife)	Husband and wife only	Husband and wife only
Division	Undivided interest (equal or unequal)	Undivided interest (must be equal)	Undivided interest (interests are equal)	Undivided interest (interests are equal)
Title	Each co-owner has a separate legal title to an undivided interest	There is only one title to the whole property	Title is in the "community" (similar to title being in a partnership)	There is only one title to the whole property
Possession	Equal right of possession	Equal right of possession	Equal right of possession	Equal right of possession
Conveyance	Each co-owner's interest may be conveyed separately by its owner	Conveyance by only one co-owner breaks the joint tenancy	Both husband and wife must join in conveyance; separate interests cannot be conveyed	Both husband and wife must join in conveyance; separate property interests cannot be conveyed
Purchaser status	Purchaser becomes a tenant in common with the other co-owners	Purchaser becomes a tenant in common with the other co-owners	Purchaser can acquire whole title of community only	Purchaser can acquire whole title only
Death	Upon co-owner's death, his or her interest passes by will to the devisees or heirs; no survivorship right	Upon co-owner's death, his or her interest ends and cannot be willed; survivor owns the property by survivorship	Upon co-owner's death, half goes to survivor in severalty; up to half goes by will or succession to others (consult attorney with specific questions)	Surviving spouse owns property in severalty; may not pass to third party by will
Successor status	Devisees or heirs become tenants in common	Last survivor owns property in severalty	If passing by will, tenancy in common exists between devisee and surviving spouse	Survivor owns property in severalty
Creditor rights	Co-owner's interest may be sold on execution sale to satisfy creditor; creditor becomes a tenant in common	Co-owner's interest may be sold on execution sale to satisfy creditor; joint tenancy is broken, and purchaser becomes a tenant in common.	Co-owner's interests cannot be seized and sold separately; the whole property may be sold to satisfy debts of either the husband or wife, depending on the debt (consult attorney with specific questions)	Co-owner's interests cannot be seized and sold separately; the whole property may be sold to satisfy debts of both the husband and wife (consult an attorney with specific questions)
Presumption	Favored in doubtful cases unless husband and wife (see Community property and Joint tenancy)	Must be expressly stated and properly formed (in some states, deed to husband and wife presumed to be joint tenancy)	Strong presumption that property acquired by husband and wife is community property in community property states	In many states, presumed if a joint tenancy between a husband and wife

Tenancy in Severalty

Tenancy in severalty is sole ownership by one individual or entity. A corporation can own property as a sole owner in the corporate name as if it were a person.

Joint Tenancy

Joint tenancy is an undivided ownership by two or more people with the right of survivorship. An **undivided interest** is a share in the whole property rather than ownership in a particular portion of the property. **Survivorship** means that on the death of one joint tenant, the deceased's interest immediately ceases and passes to the surviving joint tenants. Because the interest ceases immediately on the joint tenant's death, it cannot be transferred by will. Thus, probate procedure is not necessary for joint tenancy interests.

A joint tenancy is considered a single estate in real estate rather than separate estates for each joint tenant.

Because it can live forever, a corporation cannot hold title in joint tenancy, so survivorship is not possible.

If A, B, and C are joint tenants, the estate passes under the survivorship right, as shown in Figure 1.10.

FIGURE 1.10

Joint Tenancies

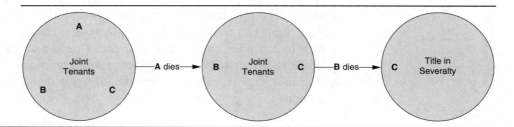

Creation.   Four unities must occur for a joint tenancy to exist:

1. *Time.* The joint tenants must have obtained their interests at the same time.

2. *Title.* The joint tenants must have obtained their interests by the same document, usually a deed.

3. *Interest.* The interests of the joint tenants must be equal.

4. *Possession.* The joint tenants must have equal and undivided rights to possession.

To create a joint tenancy, it is necessary to indicate this intent clearly. In some states, however, a conveyance to husband and wife is presumed to be as joint tenants unless the deed states otherwise. Other states require that a deed creating a joint tenancy be signed by the grantees, showing their agreement to this form of ownership.

Cessation.   A joint tenancy ceases when the four unities are no longer present as to two or more parties. For example, the sale by one joint tenant would result in a buyer who did not obtain an interest at the same time or by the same document as the other joint tenants, so the purchaser is a tenant in common, not a joint tenant. If there had been three joint tenants, the other owners would remain joint tenants as to a two-thirds interest, with the buyer having a one-third interest as a tenant in common.

Encumbering the joint tenancy.   Joint tenants can encumber their interest. While a creditor of a joint tenant could foreclose on a lien or obtain a judgment in order to break up the joint tenancy and attach the property, the death of a joint tenant before the creditor forces sale of the property would result in the property passing free of the debt or encumbrance to the surviving joint tenant(s).

Tenancy in Common (TIC)

Undivided interest by two or more parties without the right of survivorship is called a **tenancy in common (TIC).** Conveyances to two or more parties that do not specify how title is to be taken give the parties title as tenants in common. However, in some states, conveyances to spouses result in tenancy by the entirety or community property. Tenants in common may have equal or unequal ownership interests. If a deed does not specify the percentage of ownership, tenants in common are generally presumed to have equal shares.

Possession is the only one of the four unities required for joint tenancy that is also required for tenants in common. Tenants in common have equal and individual rights of possession. Because there is no survivorship, on the death of a tenant in common, the deceased's interest passes to the heirs by will, trust, or probate rather than to surviving tenants in common. Tenants in common can sell or mortgage their interest without affecting the rights of the other tenants in common.

All owners must join in encumbering or selling the entire property. The evolution of a tenancy in common from joint tenancy is shown in Figure 1.11.

FIGURE 1.11 **Tenancy in Common**	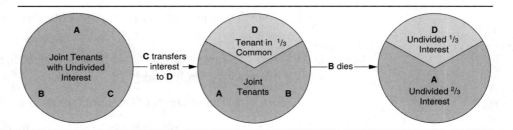

In this situation, D becomes a tenant in common because the unities of time and title do not apply to D. After C transfers interest, the four unities continue to apply to A and B until B's death which leaves A and D as tenants in common but with unequal interests.

Partition.   A court action to break up a joint tenancy or tenancy in common is called **partition.** Courts favor **partition in kind**—that is, splitting the property, but where this is not possible or would result in loss of value, the court will order a sale and a division of the sale proceeds.

Community Property

If your state is a community property state, community property questions are likely to appear on the state-specific portion of your examination rather than in the general portion of your examination.

Originally a Spanish concept, community property has been adopted by a number of states. Community property status requires that the owners be married. Property acquired during marriage is considered equally owned by both spouses. Property acquired before marriage is considered **separate property**, as is property received by either spouse as a gift or an inheritance during the marriage. Income from separate property is also regarded as separate property.

The spouses can will their individual half of the community property to third parties. When a spouse dies **intestate** (without a will), the decedent's share of the community property will go to any heirs, in accordance with state law.

Because neither spouse can partition the community property, spouses cannot separately convey their community property interest. An agreement of one spouse to sell or give community property, therefore, would not be binding on the other spouse. Separate (noncommunity) property of a spouse might become community property if **commingled** (mixed).

Tenancy by the Entirety

Like community property, questions on tenancy by the entirety are most likely to be on the state-specific portion of your examination if your state recognizes tenancy by the entirety.

In many states, when title is conveyed to a husband and wife without designating the form of ownership, each owns the entire parcel as a tenant by the entirety. Neither spouse can separately convey an interest during the other's lifetime. On the death of a spouse, the survivor owns the property. This is similar to the survivorship of joint tenancy. Divorce would change the ownership to a tenancy in common because the survivorship was based on marriage.

Generally speaking, a creditor cannot reach property held in tenancy by the entirety unless the creditor is a creditor of both husband and wife.

Tenancy in Partnership

The following material from *Partnerships Through Real Property Securities* is more likely to be on broker examinations than on salesperson examinations.

A partnership is an agreement of two or more co-owners to conduct a business for profit. Agreements to share in the profit create a presumption of a partnership. Title to partnership property may be held in the name of the partnership and can be conveyed without the signatures of the partners' spouses, although real property cannot be conveyed or encumbered without the consent of all partners.

Partners have equal rights to use partnership property for partnership purposes. In the absence of an agreement to the contrary, they share equally in the control of the partnership and in its profits.

A partnership requires consent; therefore, partners cannot assign their individual interest to another. Personal creditors of a partner cannot attach partnership property for that partner's personal debts.

General partner.   A general partner is an active partner and has unlimited personal liability for the debts of the partnership. One general partner can personally obligate the other general partners.

Limited partner.   A limited partner is an inactive partner who contributes money to the partnership. If a limited partner takes an active role in management, then that partner would lose the limited liability. States that have adopted the **Uniform Limited Partnership Act** require the filing of a certificate listing the limited partners. Limited partners have limited liability and are liable only to the extent of their investments. Limited partnerships are regarded as securities because the investors have no control over the enterprise. A limited partnership must have a general or managing partner.

Taxation of partnerships.   Partnerships do not pay separate income tax, although they must file a return. The tax is assessed directly against the partners even when profits are retained in the partnership for partnership activities.

Death of a partner.   In a general partnership, the death of a partner dissolves the partnership. The heirs of a general partner have no rights to the partnership business but are entitled to the value of the deceased partner's share in partnership assets. Limited partnership interests may be inherited.

Joint venture.   A joint venture is an association formed for a single undertaking with the joint venturers sharing in profit or loss. A joint venture is treated by the law in most cases as a partnership; however, one joint venturer cannot contractually obligate the other joint venturers to a contract.

Franchise

A franchise is an independent business that is licensed to use a designated trade name and to use a common marketing and operating plan. Many real estate offices are franchises.

Syndicate

A syndicate is made up of two or more people organized to make an investment. Although a syndicate could be a general partnership, ordinarily it is a limited partnership. The syndicator is the general managing partner, and the investors have limited liability, which means that their liability is limited to the extent of their investment. Syndicates are subject to state regulations.

Corporation

A corporation is an artificial but legal person created by state law. Because it is a separate entity, its shareholders have no personal liability for corporate debts. If individuals who control a corporation mix corporate funds with noncorporate funds, a court could "pierce the corporate veil" and hold them personally liable because they were not acting as a separate entity. Corporate profits are taxed. Dividends are taxed again as income to the stockholders who receive them. This is called **double taxation**. However, dividends are now taxed to shareholders at a reduced rate. Corporate ownership is by shares, which may be freely traded.

A **close corporation** is a corporation where the majority shareholders actively manage the corporation and there is no ready market for the shares, which are held by a small number of shareholders.

In dealing with a corporation, real estate agents should consider checking the corporate bylaws to ascertain the power of the person(s) they are dealing with. **Bylaws** are the corporation's governance rules. If an act were outside the authority of the corporate representative, the corporation would not be liable for the act.

A corporation can live forever and only ceases upon legal dissolution. Because of this perpetual life, corporations may not hold title in joint tenancy because joint tenancy is based on survivorship. **Articles of incorporation** must be filed with the state before the corporation can exist. The articles of incorporation set forth the activities the corporation will engage in.

A deed to a corporation not yet in existence is void because a deed must have a definite grantee.

S Corporation

A small closely held corporation of 75 or fewer shareholders can become an S corporation, provided all shareholders elect to be taxed as partners. Shareholders avoid the double taxation of a standard corporation but retain the protection of being exempt from personal liability for corporate debts. S corporations cannot receive more than 20% of their income from passive sources (interest, rents, royalties, dividends). Real estate investment income is considered passive income. S corporations must be incorporated in the United States and cannot be affiliated with other corporations. Stock in S corporations is freely transferable.

Limited Liability Company (LLC)

This is a business entity in which the members have limited liability, as in a corporation, but are treated like a partnership for tax purposes. A **limited liability company (LLC)** obtains the benefits offered by an S corporation without the qualifying or operational restrictions of limited partnership. Laws regarding forming or converting a business to an LLC vary by state.

LLCs have operating agreements similar to corporate bylaws. Unlike limited partnerships, management activity would not affect the limited liability of the members. Because they are less restrictive and easy to form, LLCs are replacing S corporations as a means for small businesses to avoid personal liability.

Real Estate Investment Trust (REIT)

Ownership in a **real estate investment trust (REIT)** is held in trust form for the beneficiaries by a trustee. Under federal law, a REIT must have 100 or more investors. It is taxed on retained earnings only if it distributes 90% or more of its ordinary income to the investors. Dividends received are taxed to the recipients. REITs avoid the double taxation of corporations. At least 75% of the assets must be in real estate. REITs may invest in mortgages as well as real estate.

Investors in REITs are given shares (certificates of ownership) that may be traded freely. A number of REITs are listed on the AMEX, NASDAQ, and New York stock exchanges. Interests in REITs are regarded as securities.

Trust.   Besides real estate investment trusts, property can be held in trust by a trustee for the benefit of one or more parties. The trustee may have broad or restrictive powers, depending on the restrictions set forth in the trust document.

A **living trust**, whereby the trustors give the property to themselves and others but retain the control and benefits of ownership, is used as an estate-planning tool to avoid probate.

Real Property Securities

These are investments in which investors are inactive participants, such as limited partnerships, investment contracts, and real estate investment trusts. Condominiums sold as investments with a mandatory rental pool agreement are also real property securities because the investor gives up management control to another.

When investors put up money for an investment not yet determined, it is considered a **blind pool**. Blind pools are illegal in some states.

Real property securities must be registered with the federal Securities and Exchange Commission (SEC) unless they are exempt from registration. Securities sold within a single state, or intrastate, are exempt, as are private offerings to a limited number of investors who have significant net worth. Individual states also have requirements for security registration, as well as exemptions from registration. Even though a security may be exempt from SEC registration, it is still subject to federal disclosure and antifraud legislation, as well as state regulations. Real estate licensees may need special licenses to sell real property securities, depending on state law.

Special Forms of Ownership

State and local statutes govern land divisions for the purpose of sale, lease, or financing.

Standard subdivision.   A standard subdivision is a land development with no areas owned in common.

Common interest subdivision.   Any subdivision having interests owned in common by the owners is considered a common interest subdivision.

Undivided interest subdivision.   An undivided interest subdivision is one where individual owners have an undivided interest in the entire subdivision and a nonexclusive right of occupancy. An example is a $\frac{1}{2500}$ ownership share in a campground with the right to use whatever campsite happens to be available.

Condominium.   A condominium is a development in which there is individual fee simple ownership of a unit and shared ownership of common areas with other owners as tenants in common. The developer files a master deed and condominium declaration that sets forth separate and common ownership areas, as well as the condominium bylaws and restrictions. The land is regarded as a common area. Owners pay their own mortgages and property taxes. Note that the definition of a condominium varies among states and in some states may include land ownership.

Common elements.   Common elements in a condominium are commonly owned areas for the use and benefit of all the owners. **Limited common elements** are commonly owned areas reserved for use by designated owners, such as designated parking spaces and storage lockers.

Planned unit development (planned development project).   A planned unit development (PUD) subdivision offers individual lot ownership, with common areas owned by all owners as tenants in common. An example is a subdivision with a community-owned swimming pool.

Cooperative.   In a cooperative development, each owner owns stock in a corporation and has the right to occupy a unit under a **proprietary lease**. Unlike those in condominium ownerships, co-op taxes and mortgage payments are generally made by the corporation, not by individual owners. A disadvantage is that co-op owners don't have title, so they can't mortgage their interests; however, they can borrow on their stock. Because stock rather than real estate is owned, cooperative ownership is really personal property. Most cooperatives require approval of the board to transfer the stock and possession and also may impose a stock transfer fee.

Community apartment project.   In a community apartment property, owners are tenants in common owning an undivided interest in the whole but having an exclusive right of occupancy to a designated unit.

Time-share.   Also called **interval ownership**, a time-share is an undivided interest in a unit (usually as tenants in common), coupled with the exclusive right of occupancy for either a designated or a floating period each year. Time-share owners have an undivided interest in the common area. Time-share interests can be leasehold estates, where the right of occupancy ends after a stated number of years, or fee simple ownership. Customarily, time-share properties are vacation units in which individual buyers enjoy occupancy for certain weeks each year. Some states provide a rescission period for purchasers of time-share and/or undivided interest subdivisions because of marketing practices sometimes used for these types of developments.

Homeowners associations (HOAs).   The restrictive covenants of common interest developments provide for homeowners associations to care for common elements and enforce rules and regulations. Homeowners associations customarily have the power to assess members, and unpaid assessments may become a lien on the homeowner's property.

Interstate Land Sales Full Disclosure Act.   The purpose of this act is to prevent fraud. This federal act requires disclosure of property information to buyers for unimproved land sales sold in interstate commerce. The act is enforced by the

Consumer Financial Protection Bureau (CFPB). The fraud provisions of the act apply to subdivisions of 25 or more lots. If the buyer does not receive a disclosure report, the purchaser has the right to void the agreement. If the purchaser receives the disclosure report, the purchaser has a seven-day right of rescission from the date of purchase. Some of the exemptions from the act include lots sold with structures, subdivisions where every lot is 20 acres or larger, cemetery lots, sales to adjoining property owner, sales to builders, and business and industrial property.

YOUR PERTINENT STATE INFORMATION

1.   What is the mobile home requirement for real property?

2.   Is the government survey system used in your state?

3.   What type of ownership is created when a husband and wife fail to indicate how a title should be held?

4.   May a real estate licensee sell real property securities?

5.   How is a condominium defined by your state?

6.   Does your state recognize dower and curtesy rights?

7.   Does your state recognize community property or tenancy by the entirety?

CHAPTER 1 QUIZ

1. Real property interests include
   A. cultivated annual crops.
   B. leasehold interests.
   C. mortgages.
   D. fences.

2. What is a form of ownership that is restricted to husbands and wives?
   A. Joint tenancy
   B. Tenancy in severalty
   C. Tenancy in common
   D. Tenancy by the entirety

3. What would result from a condition in a deed?
   A. Fee simple
   B. Defeasible fee
   C. Life estate
   D. Nonfreehold estate

4. A man installed central air-conditioning in his home. The compressor unit, which was located outside the home, is regarded as
   A. a trade fixture.
   B. personal property.
   C. an emblement.
   D. real property.

5. An investor's personal assets could be subject to a creditor's claim in a
   A. general partnership.
   B. syndicate.
   C. real estate investment trust.
   D. corporation.

6. How does an S corporation differ from other corporations?
   A. Its investors have no personal liability.
   B. The number of shareholders is limited.
   C. It has a separate life from that of the investors.
   D. Its tax rates are higher than those for other corporations.

7. A tenant in a commercial building installed a large sign that was anchored to the building with steel rods. Which term properly describes the sign?
   A. Fixture
   B. Trade fixture
   C. Real property
   D. Emblement

8. What type of real property description would include reference to an iron stake?
   A. Metes and bounds
   B. Informal
   C. Lot, block, and tract
   D. Government survey

9. A tenancy in common differs from a joint tenancy in that
   A. there is a survivorship right if a tenant in common dies without a will.
   B. tenants in common may have unequal interests.
   C. tenants in common have divided interests.
   D. tenants in common must acquire their interests at the same time.

10. Chattels real differ from appurtenances in that they
    A. transfer with the land.
    B. include growing trees.
    C. are personal property.
    D. are freehold interests.

11. Rights, benefits, and improvements that go with the land are called
    A. chattels.
    B. emblements.
    C. appurtenances.
    D. encumbrances.

12. Which is classified as real property?
    A. Trade fixtures
    B. Water rights
    C. Chattels real
    D. Mortgages

13. Three of the tests of a fixture are
    A. adaptability, intent, and attachment.
    B. adaptability, cost, and attachment.
    C. size, weight, and adaptability.
    D. intent, cost, and attachment.

14. All of the ownership rights that transfer with a fee simple estate are called
    A. fixtures.
    B. emblements of title.
    C. remainder rights.
    D. the bundle of rights.

15. Items that were formerly personal property but are now regarded as real property are described as
    A. emblements.
    B. fructus industrials.
    C. fixtures.
    D. trade fixtures.

16. An example of a real property security is
    A. condominiums sold with a mandatory rental pool arrangement.
    B. general partnership shares in investment property.
    C. a pur autre vie estate.
    D. a vested remainder interest.

17. Part of a legal description on a deed stated "38° 7'." What type of description was it?
    A. Metes and bounds
    B. Informal description
    C. Lot, block, and tract
    D. Government survey

18. A brother and his sister hold land as joint tenants. The sister conveys one-half of her interest to her husband. Ownership would now be held by the
    A. brother, the sister, and the sister's husband as tenants in common.
    B. brother and the sister as joint tenants and by the sister's husband as a tenant in common.
    C. brother, the sister, and the sister's husband as joint tenants.
    D. brother and the sister as joint tenants.

19. An owner granted a life estate to another but retained a future interest, which was a
    A. remainder interest.
    B. chattel real.
    C. defeasible estate.
    D. reversionary interest.

20. K, who had a life estate for the life of L, leased the property to M for five years. What would happen if K were to die?
    A. M's lease would terminate.
    B. K's heirs would be entitled to K's interest.
    C. The remainder interest holder would obtain title.
    D. L would obtain title.

21. A person other than the grantor has a future interest in a life estate. That interest is
    A. fee simple.
    B. fee simple determinable.
    C. a remainder interest.
    D. a reversionary interest.

22. A life estate was lost by merger. Merger occurred when the
    A. original grantor died.
    B. life tenant died.
    C. remainder interest holder purchased the life tenant's interest.
    D. life tenant vacated the premises.

23. The statutory right of a widow in the estate of her deceased husband is a
    A. dower right.
    B. curtesy right.
    C. tenancy at sufferance.
    D. remainder interest.

24. A man had to pay a stock transfer fee when he sold his unit. What type of development was it?
    A. Condominium
    B. Planned unit development
    C. Cooperative
    D. Time-share

25. A common feature that owners of condominium units and owners of cooperative units have is that they
    A. have individual title to the land.
    B. own their units in fee simple.
    C. own shares of stock.
    D. pay assessments to an owners association.

26. Owning property as tenants in common permits each owner to
    A. have title in severalty to half the property.
    B. have the right of survivorship.
    C. own unequal shares.
    D. avoid personal liability.

27. An example of a limited common element in a common interest subdivision is
    A. the clubhouse
    B. the gym.
    C. designated parking spaces.
    D. elevators.

28. A swimming pool in a condominium development is regarded as
    A. a common element.
    B. a limited common element.
    C. a leasehold element.
    D. an emblement.

29. L, M, and N are joint tenants. N sells his interest to O, and then M dies. Which of the following statements is *TRUE*?
    A. M's heirs, O, and L are joint tenants.
    B. M's heirs and L are joint tenants, but O is a tenant in common.
    C. L's, O's, and M's heirs are all tenants in common.
    D. L and O are tenants in common.

30. What is a partition action?
    A. A subdivision of lots by a developer
    B. A court proceeding to break up a co-ownership
    C. The conversion of rental apartments to condominiums or cooperatives
    D. The conveyance of a partial interest to form a co-ownership

31. How much fencing is required to fence the S½ of a quarter section?
    A. 1 mile
    B. 1.5 miles
    C. 4 miles
    D. 5 miles

32. A buyer of a residential unit received a share of stock and occupancy based on a lease. What type of development was the unit in?
    A. Cooperative
    B. Condominium
    C. Planned unit
    D. Time-share

33. Joint tenancy and tenancy in common are similar in that
    A. interest passes to heirs upon death of an owner.
    B. interests of owners must be equal.
    C. a sale of an interest requires approval of other owners.
    D. all owners have equal rights of possession.

34. A deed to a brother and his sister did not specify how title should be taken. Title is as
    A. joint tenancy.
    B. tenancy in severalty.
    C. tenancy by the entirety.
    D. tenancy in common.

35. J deeded property to K. The deed provided that if K ever used the property for the sale of alcoholic beverages, title would revert to J. The estate created by this conveyance is
    A. an estate on a condition subsequent.
    B. a fee simple absolute.
    C. a life estate.
    D. a nonfreehold estate.

36. The lot and block reference in a legal description relates to
    A. a metes-and-bounds description.
    B. a recorded subdivision map.
    C. the government survey system.
    D. correction lines and datum plane.

37. J and M plan to buy a home together but want to be able to will their property individually to their own children from previous marriages. They should hold title as
    A. tenants by the entirety.
    B. joint tenants.
    C. tenants in common.
    D. tenants in severalty.

38. J and his sister K were co-owners of a lot. K became the sole owner automatically when J died, because they owned the lot
    A. in severalty.
    B. in joint tenancy.
    C. as community property.
    D. in tenancy by the entirety.

39. L, M, and N owned property as joint tenants. M died, followed by the death of N. Title to the property is held by
    A. L in severalty.
    B. L and the heirs of N as tenants in common.
    C. L and the heirs of N in joint tenancy.
    D. L and the heirs of both M and N as tenants in common.

40. Interval exclusive occupancy coupled with a tenancy-in-common interest describes
    A. an estate for years.
    B. a tenancy at sufferance.
    C. a cooperative.
    D. a time-share ownership.

41. What is the highest form of ownership?
    A. Fee simple determinable
    B. Fee simple absolute
    C. Fee on a condition subsequent
    D. A nonfreehold estate

42. The court will grant a request for a partition when title is held
    A. in severalty.
    B. as community property.
    C. as a tenancy by the entirety.
    D. as a joint tenancy.

43. A property description in a deed mentions a point of beginning. Which method was the description based on?
    A. Lot and block
    B. Informal method
    C. Government survey
    D. Metes and bounds

44. An example of an estate in real property is
    A. joint tenancy.
    B. fee simple.
    C. severalty ownership.
    D. community property.

45. A legal description outlines the boundaries of a property. What type of description is it?
    A. Government survey
    B. Lot and block
    C. Metes and bounds
    D. Base line and meridian

46. J gave K a life estate, and L was named to receive the interest on K's death. Given these facts,
    A. L has a reversionary interest.
    B. L has a remainder interest.
    C. K can defeat L's interest by deed or will.
    D. K cannot borrow on her interest.

47. By purchasing the reversionary interest of the grantor, the former life tenant would now have a
    A. tenancy by the entirety.
    B. less than freehold estate.
    C. fee simple.
    D. fee simple determinable.

48. J purchased a property with K as joint tenants. When J died, it was discovered that an encumbrance had been placed against J's interest in the property and that J's will provided that the property interest should pass to L. How would title to the property be held?
    A. K in severalty free of the encumbrance
    B. K in severalty subject to the encumbrance
    C. K and L as tenants in common free of the encumbrance
    D. K and L as tenants in common subject to the encumbrance

49. A condominium is described as
    A. an undivided interest in the whole.
    B. an undivided interest in common areas and separate interest in individual units.
    C. a separate interest in the whole.
    D. a divided interest in common areas and undivided interest in each unit.

50. Homeowners associations meet the needs of
    A. common interest development.
    B. emblement ownership.
    C. metes-and-bounds descriptions.
    D. nonfreehold estates.

51. A life estate could become a fee simple estate by
    A. the sale of the property.
    B. mortgage of the property.
    C. merger of interests.
    D. leasing the property.

52. One quarter of a quarter section contains
    A. 20 acres.
    B. 40 acres.
    C. 160 acres.
    D. 640 acres.

53. Bricks are used to build a backyard barbecue. The bricks have become real property through the process of
    A. severance.
    B. annexation.
    C. easement.
    D. progression.

54. Creditors can go against the personal assets of investors in
    A. a chapter S corporation.
    B. a limited partnership.
    C. an LLC.
    D. a general partnership.

55. The maximum number of complete townships possible within a ranch that is 26 miles square is
    A. 4.
    B. 6.
    C. 16.
    D. 18.

56. What section is directly north of Section 2 in a township?
    A. 3
    B. 5
    C. 11
    D. 35

57. Where in a township would Section 18 be located?
    A. NW¼
    B. SW¼
    C. NE¼
    D. SE¼

58. How much fencing would it take to fence a township?
    A. 1 mile
    B. 2 miles
    C. 12 miles
    D. 24 miles

59. The Consumer Financial Protection Bureau is concerned with unimproved land sales in interstate commerce of
    A. any parcel.
    B. 10 or more parcels.
    C. 25 or more parcels.
    D. 50 or more parcels.

60. The south boundary line of Section 13 Township 2 North Range 3 East is
    A. 9 miles north of the base line.
    B. 15 miles east of the meridian.
    C. 3 miles east of the meridian.
    D. 9 miles east of the base line.

61. A form of ownership where one owner cannot separately convey interest is a
    A. tenancy by the entirety.
    B. tenancy in common.
    C. joint tenancy.
    D. limited partnership.

62. Which of the following rectangles is larger than an acre?
    A. 100' × 420'
    B. 90' × 450'
    C. 1 mile × 8'
    D. 209' × 209'

63. A joint venture is a form of
    A. corporation.
    B. partnership.
    C. community property.
    D. joint tenancy.

64. A woman owned an undivided half inter-
    est in a property. She now owns the entire
    property in severalty, although she did not
    buy or inherit the other one-half interest. The
    woman originally owned her undivided one-
    half interest as a
    A. limited partner.
    B. tenant in common.
    C. joint tenant.
    D. general partner.

65. A building was torn down leaving material
    that was classified as personal property. The
    act was one of
    A. severance.
    B. accretion.
    C. avulsion.
    D. reliction.

66. A vertical strip of land is six miles wide and
    is adjacent and west of a principal meridian.
    The strip is described as
    A. a section.
    B. range 1 east.
    C. range 1 west.
    D. T1NR1W.

67. The U.S. Geological Survey sets
    A. benchmarks.
    B. topographical lines.
    C. range lines.
    D. meridians.

68. The SW¼ of the SE¼ of NW¼ of SW¼ of a
    section contains
    A. 1¼ acres.
    B. 2½ acres.
    C. 5 acres.
    D. 10 acres.

69. An estate in real estate
    A. is forever.
    B. must be created by grant.
    C. must include immediate possession.
    D. can run within another estate.

70. A major difference between a planned unit
    development and a condominium is
    A. common elements.
    B. a homeowners association.
    C. land ownership.
    D. fee ownership.

71. A father wished to deed property to his son
    and daughter-in-law on a two-thirds and
    one-third basis. To do so, title is
    A. in severalty.
    B. in joint tenancy.
    C. as tenants in the entirety.
    D. as tenants in common.

72. A business that has the limited liability of a
    corporation yet is taxed as a partnership is
    A. a REIT.
    B. a joint venture.
    C. a general partnership.
    D. an LLC.

73. A city purchased land for a dump site. How
    would the city hold title?
    A. As tenants in common
    B. As joint tenants
    C. As community property
    D. In severalty

74. Four unities refers to ownership
    A. in severalty.
    B. as joint tenants.
    C. as tenants in common.
    D. in partnership.

75. If a boundary is a private road, the boundary
    line is
    A. the near edge of the road.
    B. the far edge of the road.
    C. the center of the road.
    D. three feet in from the near edge of the
       paving.

76. Areas of land enclosed by standard parallels
    and guide meridians are called
    A. sections.
    B. townships.
    C. government checks.
    D. government lots.

77. Nonstandard quarter sections resulting from land lost by rivers and lakes are designated as
    A. checks.
    B. quadrangles.
    C. government lots.
    D. plots.

78. L, M, N, and O owned property as joint tenants. L sold her interest to P, and M died. The property is owned by
    A. N, O, and P as joint tenants
    B. N and O as joint tenants and P as a tenant in common
    C. N, O, and P as tenants in common
    D. P, M's heirs, N, and O as tenants in common

79. HOAs are associated with
    A. partnerships.
    B. common interest developments.
    C. REITs.
    D. defeasible estates.

80. Which is subject to double taxation?
    A. REIT
    B. LLC
    C. Corporation
    D. Partnership

CHAPTER 1 QUIZ ANSWERS

1. **(D)** An appurtenance that goes with the land. (1)

2. **(D)** Community property also is restricted to husbands and wives. (10, 13)

3. **(B)** The estate could be lost. (7)

4. **(D)** It is a fixture. Attachment and adaptability meet two of the tests. (2)

5. **(A)** A general partner has unlimited personal liability. (14)

6. **(B)** Chapter S corporations are limited to 75 shareholders. (15)

7. **(B)** A tenant can remove a trade fixture but is liable for removal damage to real property. (2)

8. **(A)** An iron stake is referenced as a monument or point in a metes-and-bounds description. (3)

9. **(B)** Or equal interests. (10, 12)

10. **(C)** Chattels real are personal property related to real property, such as mortgages and tenant lease rights. (1)

11. **(C)** Appurtenances belong with the real estate. (1)

12. **(B)** As well as mineral rights and easements. (1)

13. **(A)** Intent is often said to be the most important of these three tests. (2)

14. **(D)** They are the rights of ownership. (1)

15. **(C)** They have been joined to the realty. (2)

16. **(A)** Owner of a security does not have any management control. (16)

17. **(A)** Degrees and minutes measure the angles between monuments. (3)

18. **(A)** There are no longer two owners possessing the four unities of joint tenancy (the brother has an undivided one-half interest, and the sister and her husband each have an undivided one-quarter interest). In some states, the sister could convey her interest to her husband and to herself as joint tenants, but in this case, she conveyed only one-half of her interest. (11)

19. **(D)** The interest reverts back to the owner. (8, 9)

20. **(B)** The life estate is based on L's life. (8)

21. **(C)** A third-party future interest is a remainder interest. An interest that reverted to the grantor is a reversionary interest. (8, 9)

22. **(C)** The life interest and remainder interests are merged into a single interest. (9)

23. **(A)** In some states, a wife is entitled to a percentage of her husband's real property and/or a life estate in a husband's home upon the husband's death. (9)

24. **(C)** The man owned a share in a cooperative. (17)

25. **(D)** HOA is required. (17)

26. **(C)** Tenant-in-common interests need not be equal. (10, 12)

27. **(C)** While owned in common, the area's use is restricted to designated tenant. Others are common elements. (17)

28. **(A)** Common areas for all owners. (17)

29. **(D)** When N sold to O, N broke the joint tenancy as to N's interest, and O had a one-third interest. When M died, L took the share by survivorship. L has a two-thirds interest and O has a one-third interest. (11–12)

30. **(B)** This is an action to divide the land of a tenancy in common or joint tenancy when the owners cannot agree. The court could physically divide the property (if feasible) or order a sale. (12)

31. **(B)** Because a ¼ section is ½ mile on each side, the S½ is ¼ mile by ½ mile. (6)

32. **(A)** Stock ownership plus proprietary lease. (17)

33. **(D)** The only one of the four unities present in tenancy in common is possession. (10, 12)

34. **(D)** TIC to other than husband and wife if not stated in deed. (12)

35. **(A)** The estate is presently valid but can be lost. (7)

36. **(B)** The legal description references the recorded map. (3)

37. **(C)** There is no right of survivorship for tenants in common. Choices (A) and (B) would go to the survivor, and (D) is ownership by one person only. (10, 12)

38. **(B)** Tenancy by the entirety and community property are only for spouses. (10, 11)

39. **(A)** On M's death, L and N held title as joint tenants. When N died, L owned the property in severalty. Interest of joint tenant passes by survivorship to remaining joint tenant(s). (11)

40. **(D)** A time-share can be a leasehold or fee simple interest for specified periods of time. (17)

41. **(B)** Fee simple ownership has no time limitation and can be freely transferred and can be inherited. (7)

42. **(D)** Or tenancy in common. (12)

43. **(D)** It measures from point to point. (3)

44. **(B)** Fee simple is the degree of ownership (estate), the others are forms of ownership. (7)

45. **(C)** It encircles the parcel from point to point. (3)

46. **(B)** L is third person. (8–9)

47. **(C)** Life estate was lost by merger into greater fee simple interest. (9)

48. **(A)** Title passes free of J's encumbrance to the survivor. It does not pass by will. (11–12)

49. **(B)** Condominium owners own their own air space, but common areas are owned with other owners as tenants in common. (17)

50. **(A)** HOAs are present and collect assessments whenever there is a common interest development. (17)

51. **(C)** When the owner of a life estate acquires the reversionary interest in the property, the interests become one and the title is no longer defeasible. (9)

52. **(B)** Because a section contains 640 acres and a quarter section is 160 acres, ¼ of a quarter section is 40 acres. (6)

53. **(B)** Personal property has become attached so as to become real property. (1)

54. **(D)** General partners are personally liable for debts of the partnership. (14)

55. **(C)** A township is six miles square, meaning it measures six miles on each side. Four complete townships can be placed in a row either vertically or horizontally in a ranch that is 26 miles square. Four rows, each containing four townships, equals 16 townships. (5)

56. **(D)** Section 2 of a township is bordered by Section 35 of the township adjoining to the north. (5)

57. **(A)** However, section 19 is in the southwest quarter. (5)

58. **(D)** Because it is six miles on each side. (5)

59. **(C)** They enforce interstate land sales disclosure that requires full disclosure to prevent fraud. (17–18)

60. **(A)** Section 13 is three miles north of its township line plus one township (six miles) north of the base line. (4, 5)

61. **(A)** Tenancy by the entirety is a joint tenancy between spouses where the spouses cannot separately convey their individual interests. (10,13)

62. **(D)** An acre is 43,560 square feet. (5)

63. **(B)** Partnership for a single undertaking. (14)

64. **(C)** Upon the death of the other joint tenant, the other half became the woman's property. (10, 11)

65. **(A)** Severed from the land. (1–2)

66. **(C)** It is the first range west of the meridian. (4)

67. **(A)** Markers showing elevation above sea level. Topographical lines follow elevation to show contour of the lands. (7)

68. **(B)** Go backwards from 640 acres. (6)

69. **(D)** Such as a leasehold interest in property held in fee simple. (7–9)

70. **(C)** In a PUD, the unit owner owns land under the unit, as well as a share in the common area. In a condominium, the land is owned in common. (17)

71. **(D)** A is one owner only, and B and C require equal ownership. (10, 12)

72. **(D)** The limited liability company description also applies to S corporations. (15)

73. **(D)** Because the city (municipal corporation) would own the property by itself. (11)

74. **(B)** The four unities are time, title, interest, and possession. (11)

75. **(C)** Similarly, the boundary is a nonnavigable river; the boundary line is the center of the river. (3)

76. **(C)** Or quadrangles. (4)

77. **(C)** Identified by lot number. (5)

78. **(B)** P has a ¼ interest as a tenant in common and N and O have the other ¾ interest as remaining joint tenants. (11–12)

79. **(B)** Homeowners associations. (18)

80. **(C)** Although S corporations also avoid the double taxation. (15)

Land-Use Controls, Restrictions, and Title Transfer

Land use is controlled by both public and private restrictions.

GOVERNMENT CONTROLS

There are local, state, and federal controls that affect land use. The purpose of government involvement is to provide for the long-term needs and welfare of an area and its population.

Planning

Planning agencies or planning commissions are responsible for determining how an area should be developed or redeveloped.

Master planning.   A master plan is a comprehensive growth and use plan for a community, indicating residential, commercial, and industrial areas. The master plan allows a community to consider its future goals. The plan is implemented through zoning.

Master planning can consider both future development and redevelopment. It takes into account housing, commercial, and transportation needs, as well as coordination of all public services; protection of the environment; and the health, safety, morals, and general welfare of the people. Master planning can encourage growth or provide for growth limitations, as well as include requirements that discourage premature development.

By allowing advantageous uses, zoning can encourage redevelopment by making it economically feasible to tear down existing structures. Redevelopment also can be pushed through special assessment districts and enterprise zones that are areas in which special tax or other benefits encourage redevelopment.

Besides providing for orderly growth and uses that are presumed to be consistent with the needs of the people, proper planning can protect property values.

Subdivision control.   Most states require approval before the sale of subdivision parcels. These requirements are intended to protect the purchasers and often require disclosures. The physical aspects of the subdivision are subject to local government approval.

Environmental impact statement.   The National Environmental Policy Act (NEPA) of 1969 calls for an **environmental impact statement (EIS)** if a federal development is likely to affect the environment.

Many states also require that the developer prepare an **environmental impact report (EIR)** for any development likely to affect the environment. The EIR may be required by a planning commission to aid in decision making. In some states, private citizens can obtain a court order to demand an EIR. The report evaluates all aspects of the proposed development: schools, services, transportation, utilities, pollution, noise, future growth effects, jobs, wildlife, and ecology. A **negative declaration** states that a development will have no significant negative effect on the environment.

Rural land planning.   Land planning can be used to protect the rural nature of an area. By **exclusionary zoning** (excluding other uses), land can be kept for agriculture. By buying an owner's development rights, it is possible for a governmental body or conservation group to ensure that property remains in a natural or an agricultural use. The same results can be obtained by purchasing an easement right that prohibits development (**conservation easement**).

Zoning

Any claim, lien, or burden on real property that affects its title, use, or value is considered an **encumbrance**. While generally beneficial, zoning is still an encumbrance.

Whereas restrictive covenants are private restrictions on land use, zoning is a public restriction that is enforceable under the **police power** of the state (to preserve the health, safety, morals, and public welfare). Zoning and planning powers have been given to cities and counties by state **enabling acts**. Even though the exercise of police power could diminish value, an owner is not usually entitled to compensation. Zoning is delegated to local, city, and/or county government. There are no federal zoning laws.

Ordinarily, a local planning commission sets zoning. An owner who objects to the zoning assigned to his or her property can appeal to the planning commission or zoning board.

Zoning variance.   A variance is a permanent exception to the zoning. For example, if an owner has a lot that is 9,800 square feet and the zoning ordinance requires 10,000 square feet, the local zoning authority might grant an exception (a variance). To obtain a variance, the owner is required to show that failure to grant the variance would deprive the owner of the reasonable benefits of use enjoyed by other owners, creating a hardship.

Conditional use permit (special use permit).   A conditional use permit is a special permission for a use otherwise not allowed under the zoning. The zoning laws must have considered the use and provided a criterion for granting such permits. A public hearing, with appropriate notice to area residents, is usually required for rezoning, zoning variances, and conditional use permits.

Rezoning.   This is an actual change in zoning. If the owner's request for zoning is turned down, the owner can appeal to the city council, the county board of supervisors, or a special zoning appeals board. After exhausting all administrative remedies, the owner can appeal to the courts. Courts will overrule the planning commission's decisions if a determination is made that the zoning was arbitrary or irresponsible.

Legal nonconforming use.   A legal use that was in existence before current zoning that prohibits the use is allowed to continue under what is called a **grandfather clause**, but it may not be expanded. Zoning will not be retroactive to completely bar a legal use previously in effect. A use, however, can be abated or eliminated if it is a nuisance.

Zoning provisions can allow a reasonable period of time in which the use must cease, allowing the owner to recoup the investment. If a nonconforming use structure is destroyed, rebuilding might be prohibited. Once a nonconforming use is abandoned, it usually cannot be reinstated.

Zoning Types and Terms

- *Downzoning.* Zoning to a more restrictive, lesser use is an act of downzoning. An example is rezoning from commercial use to single-family residential use. An owner is not entitled to compensation for loss in value suffered by downzoning the use.

- *Upzoning.* Rezoning to a less restrictive use such as from single-family use to multifamily use is called *upzoning.*

- *Cluster zoning.* Zoning that allows grouping of residences but alleviates density with green or open areas.

- *Conservation zoning.* Open zoning that excludes development to keep an area in a natural or agricultural state.

- *Aesthetic zoning.* Zoning as to architectural style so structures fit in with the neighborhood. The size and color of signs can also be regulated.

- *Incentive zoning.* Zoning that provides an incentive for a developer to include a particular feature. An example is allowing greater height of the building, or ground floor retail shops if a public plaza were included.

- *Spot zoning.* Zoning of a parcel that is inconsistent with surrounding use. Courts might refuse to permit spot zoning. (Many states consider spot zoning to be illegal.)

- *Bulk zoning.* Zoning for density using setbacks, height restriction, parking requirements, et cetera.

- *Inclusionary zoning.* Zoning that requires that something be included in a development, such as a percentage of homes for low-income buyers.

■ *Exclusionary zoning.* Zoning that specifically prohibits a use such as adult bookstores.

■ *Cumulative zoning.* Zoning that allows less restrictive use, such as apartment zoning that allows single-family dwellings.

■ *Noncumulative zoning.* Zoning that allows only the stated use.

■ *Buffer zone.* A strip of land or land use that separates different land uses such as a greenbelt between single-family residential use and multifamily structures.

Health and Safety/Building Codes

Building codes have been enacted by state and municipal governments under their police power to protect the health, safety, and general welfare of the people. Building codes, which set minimum acceptable standards, cover a wide spectrum: construction standards and methods, plumbing, electrical, heating, fire alarm, fire suppression, sewage disposal, and ventilation, to name a few.

Local building inspectors are the primary enforcers of compliance with code standards, although the local fire department might have jurisdiction over fire codes and the local health department over health codes. A building permit is issued even though a structure might have violated private restrictive covenants. Restrictive covenants are enforced privately.

Local building inspectors issue building permits, and before a new structure can be occupied, a **certificate of occupancy** must be obtained, certifying the building is fit for occupancy and complies with the codes.

Specification code.   Specification codes call for particular methods of construction or materials and can be very restrictive.

Performance code.   This code specifies performance requirements that give greater latitude to builders so long as standards of performance are met.

PRIVATE CONTROLS

Restrictive Covenants

Restrictive covenants, also called **covenants, conditions, and restrictions (CC&Rs), deed restrictions**, or restrictions on the owner's use of property, are private, voluntary agreements (contracts). Zoning, on the other hand, is a mandatory public control of land use. When the CC&Rs and zoning differ, the more restrictive of the two will prevail.

Restrictive covenants, as well as **homeowners association (HOA)** restrictions on use, are usually intended to be beneficial restrictions because they seek to enhance land value and enjoyment by setting minimum or maximum requirements. Restrictive covenants are considered encumbrances. While beneficial, they nevertheless restrict the rights that owners would otherwise have. Typically, restrictive covenants control things such as property use, single-family and other types of residences, setback, minimum lot size, minimum house size, maximum height, outbuildings, fences, the keeping of animals, and even landscaping and architectural styles.

Creation.   Although they may be placed by agreement of all the landowners subject to the restrictions, restrictive covenants are normally placed on land by subdividers who record the declaration of restrictions and then sell the parcels subject to the restrictions.

Duration.   Restrictive covenants run with the land. This means the rights and duties imposed are passed on to subsequent landowners. These rights and duties may go on forever unless state statute sets a maximum time limit or the restriction sets its own time limitation.

Enforceability.   Because covenants are promises that can be enforced by anyone who is subject to them, they are normally enforced through an injunction. An injunction is a court order that either forbids a person from performing an act or compels that person to do so. Courts ordinarily will not grant relief if any of the following circumstances are present:

- The parties have waived their rights to enforce the covenants because of failure to enforce previous breaches of the covenants.

- **Laches** would prevent a party from asserting a right. Laches is an unreasonable delay in bringing action that works to the detriment of another party. For example, if a neighbor knew your new garage would be in violation of the restrictive covenant and waited until the garage was built before seeking a court order to have it removed, the court would likely bar enforcement of the restrictions by your neighbor because of laches.

- Changes have been made in the area that would cause the enforcement to be unreasonable.

- The court determines that the restrictions are against public policy or are a violation of the law.

Racial restrictions are considered void and unenforceable (*Shelley v. Kraemer*, 334 US 1 [1948]).

Restrictions that unreasonably restrict future conveyances (alienation) will not be enforced. For example, a restriction against a transfer to other than a direct descendant of a grantor placing the restriction is an unreasonable restraint on future conveyances.

A restriction that creates a monopoly by allowing a use on a single property and prohibiting the use on similar properties would likely be declared void.

Termination.   Restrictive covenants could be terminated by any of the following:

- **Merger** of interests—one party acquiring all of the parcels covered by the restrictions

- **Quitclaim deeds**—an owner acquiring quitclaim deeds in the property from all other owners covered by the restrictions

- Agreement of termination or modification by all the parties covered, unless the restrictions allow a percentage of owners to modify or remove them

- Expiration of a set time period established in the restrictions (some states limit the time period for private restrictions)

Conditions.   A condition differs from a restrictive covenant in that it provides for forfeiture of title in the event of breach. Because courts dislike forfeiture for being too harsh, they generally will try to treat a condition merely as a covenant to avoid forfeiture.

WATER RIGHTS

Water rights are very important in many areas of the country and are based on state law. Some of the terms that are important in understanding water rights are:

- *Accretion.* The gradual buildup of land by action of water. The land added (**alluvion**) belongs to the riparian or littoral rights owner.

- *Avulsion.* The sudden tearing away of land by action of water, such as a change in a river's course. The owner retains title to land washed away by sudden avulsion and may reclaim it—for example, by returning a river to its original course (the boundary lines do not change).

- *Erosion.* The gradual loss of land by action of wind or water. The former owner loses title to land that is lost by this process.

- *Floodplains.* Level areas bordering waterways that are subject to inundation will often be subject to government restrictions on development.

- *Floodwater.* Water that overflows a defined channel. In most cases, landowners can dike property against floodwater.

- *Groundwater.* Underground, nonflowing water. The right of a landowner to the reasonable use of this underground water is called the right of correlative user. Several states follow the common-law rule that a property owner has absolute rights to water below the surface that is not in a defined channel and would not be limited by reasonable use.

- *Littoral rights.* A landowner's rights to reasonable use of water from a lake, an ocean, or a pond bordering the property (nonflowing water). In some areas, the term *riparian* is used to describe both littoral and riparian rights.

- *Ponding.* Depressions where flood water accumulates.

- *Prior appropriation.* The theory, used in several arid western states, that says the first water users have priority rights over later users of water from the same source.

- *Reliction.* Land that forms after water recedes (such land belongs to owners of waterfront property); also called *dereliction.*

- *Riparian rights.* Rights that ensure a landowner receives reasonable use of water flowing through, adjacent to, or under his or her property.

- *Sheet flooding.* Water runoff down an incline not in a water course.

- *Surface water.* Water with no defined channel. Landowners can be liable for damage caused by diverting the natural flow of surface water.

- *Wetlands.* Swampy areas and areas that seasonally are covered with water support diverse plant, animal, and bird life. Such areas are subject to federal, state, and local controls aimed at preservation. Both the Environmental Protection Agency (EPA) and the Army Corps of Engineers enforce federal regulations.

Land can be void of water despite the fact that there is water on or beneath the property as water rights can be transferred separately from the property itself.

LIENS

A **lien** is a monetary claim against a property. It is considered an encumbrance. The property is security for a debt or an obligation. The debt that gives rise to the lien may be a result of agreement between the debtor and the creditor, as in a mortgage, or it may arise as a result of operation of law, as in a tax lien. While having no right of ownership, the lienholder does have a limited right to force the sale of the secured property to pay the obligation should the owner default.

Liens intentionally placed or allowed to be placed against a property, such as a mortgage lien, are **voluntary liens**, while liens arising by action of law, such as a judgment or a tax lien, are **involuntary liens**.

Liens applying to one specific property, such as a mechanic's lien, mortgage lien, or property tax lien, are **specific liens**, while liens applying to all the property of the debtor, such as a judgment lien or an IRS lien, are **general liens**.

To be effective, a lien must be recorded in the county where the property is located.

Mechanic's Lien

A **mechanic's lien** is a specific, involuntary statutory lien (established by state law) used to secure payment for labor, services, or materials used in construction, repair, or improvement of real property. It is based on the theory that the mechanic (the supplier of material or services) has enhanced the value of the property, and to deny the mechanic's rights is to unjustifiably enrich the property owner. A mechanic's lien is specific to the property on which the work was performed. The mechanic must acknowledge the lien before a notary, file (record) the lien within a prescribed time, and generally verify that the facts stated are correct.

Verification is swearing to the truthfulness of a statement. In most states, mechanics' liens must be verified. A person whose religious beliefs will not allow oath taking may make an **affirmation**, which is a statement in lieu of an oath. Property owners can protect themselves against mechanics' liens by requiring lien waivers from contractors, subcontractors, and suppliers of material. In many states, unlicensed contractors cannot file a mechanic's lien. If a mechanic's lien is not satisfied, the lienholder can force the sale of the property affected.

Some states require that the mechanic provide a **preliminary notice** to the owner that the work will subject the property to a lien. Some states allow filing of a **notice of completion**, which sets the time period for the filing of liens.

Some states allow mechanics' liens to be placed against a property even though the owner did not consent to the work. This usually applies to work ordered by a tenant or a buyer under a contract for deed (land contract). However, most of these states allow owners to protect their interests by recording and posting a **notice of nonresponsibility** within a certain time after becoming aware of the work.

Because states allow a period after completion of work to file a mechanic's lien, a purchaser of property where work was recently completed, should make certain that mechanics have been paid in full or have signed lien waivers.

Priority of mechanics' liens.   Mechanics' liens must be filed within a time period, specified by state law, after the work is completed. In some states, mechanics' liens take priority over prior recorded mortgages, but in most states, priority is based on recording.

In some states, all mechanics' liens have equal priority; other states assign different priority based on criteria such as the following:

- Date on which the contractor started work
- Date on which the first work was performed (no matter who did it; this might include delivery of construction material to the site)
- Date of the construction contract
- Date on which the lien was filed

Know the priority of mechanics' liens in your state for the state-specific portion of your examination.

Judgment

In a lawsuit, a plaintiff brings a legal action against a defendant based on a claim. A **judgment** is a final order by a court that the defendant must pay the plaintiff an amount of money. When an **abstract of judgment** (summary of the judgment issued by the court) is recorded, the judgment becomes a general lien on all real and personal property owned by the debtor within the county where the abstract of judgment was recorded. A judgment can be recorded in more than one county. The duration of the judgment lien and renewals vary from state to state. By a **writ of execution**, the judgment creditor can have property sold by the sheriff to satisfy the judgment. State law determines priority of judgments.

Attachment

An **attachment** is a lien placed on the property of a debtor before a judgment has been rendered. The purpose of the attachment is to assure the plaintiff that, by bringing the property under custody of the court, there will be property to levy against after a judgment is rendered. An attachment is generally available only for unsecured claims based on an existing contract. Some states grant a writ of attachment only when it is believed the defendant will flee or otherwise dispose of the property. To obtain an attachment, a party might be required to post a bond.

Lis Pendens

A **lis pendens** is a recorded notice of a pending lawsuit concerning an interest in real property. It serves as constructive or public notice of an interest claimed in the subject property by a party other than the owner of record. Any purchaser of the property would take title subject to any rights the person who filed the lis pendens has against the property.

Additional Liens

Mortgages, trust deeds, and property taxes are specific liens against real estate. However, income tax liens are general liens against all of the debtor's property.

Priority of Liens

Priority of liens works similarly to priority of recordation of title. The first recorded lien generally has priority over liens placed in the public record at a later time, except for certain special cases such as tax liens and mechanics' liens. Liens for property taxes and special assessments take priority over other liens, no matter when they were incurred; however, the priority of most liens is based on time and date of recording. While property tax liens are priority liens, IRS liens do not take priority over prior recorded liens. Because a lien is secured by property, lienholders have the right to force foreclosure if owners fails to meet their obligations. In a foreclosure, liens are paid off from the sale proceeds in their order of priority. If the foreclosing lienholder buys the property at the foreclosure sale, title is taken subject to prior liens, but liens of lesser priority are lost.

EASEMENTS

An **easement** is an irrevocable right or interest one party has in another's land. A typical easement is a right of way to enter, called ingress, and exit, called egress, one property over another person's property. Easements normally run (transfer) with the land (for an exception, see "Easement in Gross" below).

Dominant tenement.   The estate that uses another's land for an easement is held by the dominant tenement holder. By using a right of way, that person "dominates" the land use of another.

Servient tenement.   The land that is used by (or that "serves") the land of another is the servient tenement. The dominant and servient tenements need not be contiguous.

Types of Easements

Easement in gross.   This is an easement without a dominant tenement (see Figure 2.1). While land of another is subject to the easement (servient tenement), no land is benefited. This is the case for easements for signs or utility lines. Because an easement in gross has no dominant tenement, the easement is personal to the easement holder and does not run, or transfer, with the land, although it can be personally transferred.

FIGURE 2.1

Easement in Gross

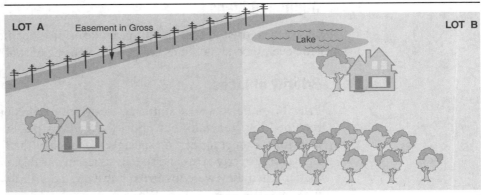

The utility company has an easement in gross across both parcels of land for its power lines.

Easement appurtenant. Any easement other than an easement in gross would transfer with the land. Such an easement is appurtenant—that is, joined to and benefiting the dominant tenement (see Figure 2.2).

FIGURE 2.2

Easement Appurtenant

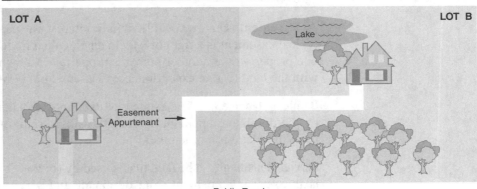

The owner of Lot B has an easement appurtenant across Lot A to gain access to his property from the public road. Lot B is dominant, and Lot A is servient.

Affirmative easement. The right to use the land of another for some stated purpose is an affirmative easement. For example, a right of entry over such land is an affirmative easement.

Negative easement. The right to prohibit an owner from a certain use, such as a height restriction to preserve light or view, is a negative easement.

Implied easement. Although not expressly stated, an implied easement can be created by intent of the parties. A grantor conveys the implied right to use those apparent and visible easements that are necessary for reasonable use of the property conveyed (see "Creation of Easements" on the next page).

Easement by necessity. In some states, an easement by necessity is an implied easement whereby the easement right is essential to beneficial use of the property. Generally, it involves a property that has become landlocked by a prior conveyance. The property of the dominant and servient tenements must have been under common ownership in the past. The courts generally take the position that a prior grantor simply neglected to provide for the easement right.

Solar easement.   A solar easement is an easement to protect an owner's access to sunlight for solar collectors. A property owner might give or sell a solar easement to a neighbor. While there is no common-law right to light, some states have enacted statutes that make plantings a nuisance if they block light to solar collectors.

View easement.   View is not a common-law right. When granted, view easements prohibit the servient tenement owner from having structures or landscaping above an agreed height so as not to obstruct the view for the dominant tenement.

Conservation easement.   A negative easement that prohibits development, it provides that land be kept in its natural state or for agricultural use only.

Creation of Easements

Easements may be created by any of the following means.

Grant or reservation in deed.   This method either conveys the easement right or conveys the land and reserves the easement. If the location of the easement is not specified, the servient tenement holder may designate a reasonable location of the easement.

Agreement.   If two neighboring landowners consent to a shared driveway or a party wall on their property line, an easement is created by agreement.

Implication.   Sometimes an easement is created by law whereby a single owner of two lots of land creates a necessary use over one of the lots and then conveys a property separately. For example, assume that the owner of lots A and B, shown in Figure 2.1, builds homes on both lots. Assume further that lot B's driveway goes across lot A. If the owner sells lot B, the court likely would determine that there was an implied easement over lot A.

Necessity.   Creating useless, landlocked property is against public policy. In many states, it is possible to obtain an easement by necessity to gain access to such property by a court action. If any other access is possible, an easement by necessity will not be granted. Should another access to the property be later acquired, this access will terminate the easement by necessity.

Prescription.   This is an easement created by adverse use that is use against the interests of the servient tenement. Generally, the use must be adverse, hostile, open, notorious, continuous, and uninterrupted for a period of time prescribed by state statute. The user can be treated as a trespasser until the easement is perfected.

In many states, **tacking on** is permitted, which means one user can use property for a period of time and a successor in interest can then use it for an additional period of time to satisfy the statutory period for uninterrupted use. In many states, nonuse of the prescriptive easement for a statutory period will terminate the easement.

A prescriptive easement cannot be taken over government-owned property. In some states, recreational users will not be granted prescriptive easements. Posting statutory notice that use is by owner's revocable permission will defeat a claim for prescriptive easements in many states. In order to perfect a prescriptive easement, the claimant could bring a quiet title action to make the right a matter of record.

Eminent domain (condemnation).   A government body can take private property or an easement for a necessary public use; however, just compensation must be given. The power of eminent domain is often given to utilities, schools, hospitals, railroads, et cetera, because they serve a public good.

Term of an Easement

Easements may be created for a specific term of years, after which they end. In some states, easements cannot exceed a statutory period, whereas in others, they can go on forever.

Easements end upon the happening of specific events, such as one of the following:

■ *Expiration*. Easement ends once a stated or statutory period ends.

■ *Agreement*. A quitclaim deed from the holder of the dominant tenement to the holder of the servient tenement extinguishes the easement.

■ *Abandonment*. In some states, intentional nonuse for a statutory period ends the easement. In other states, nonuse will only terminate an easement created by prescription.

■ *Destruction*. If the servient tenement is destroyed, so is the easement.

■ *Merger*. If one owner acquires ownership of the dominant *and* servient tenements, the easement is lost because ownership includes the lesser right of the easement.

■ *End of purpose*. An easement created for a particular purpose ends once that purpose no longer exists (easements by grant should state the purpose of the easement). Use of easement for an improper purpose may allow the easement to be terminated.

LICENSE

A license is a use granted by an owner's permission. Because it is permissive, the license grants no rights to the owner. Unlike an easement, the grantor may revoke it. Because the use is permissive and not considered an adverse use, it is not hostile; therefore, a license holder cannot obtain a prescriptive easement.

ENCROACHMENT

Encroachment is trespass by placing improvements (such as a building or fence) on or over another's land. The property owner can take court action, called **eject-ment**, to have a trespasser or encroachment removed. Inaction for a statutory period could result in the trespasser gaining a right to continued use.

Courts can order an encroachment removed, but if the encroachment is minimal and/or the cost of removal significant, a court might order money damages or even allow an unintentional encroacher to purchase the land.

NUISANCE

A person cannot use property in such a manner that it unreasonably interferes with the reasonable use of others' property. Such unreasonable use is a trespass to the senses and is known in law as a nuisance.

Normally, a nuisance is a nonphysical invasion—a smell, light, dust, vibration, radio interference, or dangerous activity. A **private nuisance** affects a relatively small area of the community, whereas a **public nuisance** affects a larger area. An **abatement action** to require removal of the nuisance or an injunction to cease the activity can be brought against a private nuisance by another property owner, but usually the city or county must bring the action against a public nuisance.

REAL PROPERTY TAX LIENS

Real property tax liens are specific liens for taxes owed. They apply to single properties. They are automatically levied. Real estate taxes are **ad valorem taxes**; that is, tax is assessed according to the value of the property. The tax assessor sets the value for each nonexempt property. Assessed value could be market value or a percentage of market value. Many states have state boards of equalization that ensure that valuations are set uniformly throughout the state. Property owners can appeal assessments, but not the tax rate, within a specified period of time through an appeal board. The total of the assessed valuations in a jurisdiction is called the assessment roll, assessment tax base, or **tax roll**.

Tax Rate

To determine the tax rate, the taxation authority divides the budgetary needs by the assessment roll:

$$\text{budget needs} \div \text{assessment roll} = \text{tax rate}$$

For example, if a community needs $850,000 and has a tax base of $20,000,000, the tax rate per dollar of assessed valuation is $0.0425:

$$850,000 \div 20,000,000 = 0.0425$$

Tax rates are often expressed in mills. A **mill** is $\frac{1}{10}$ of a cent, or $0.001. The tax rate of $0.0425 per dollar of evaluation could be expressed as 42.5 mills. To determine the taxes, simply multiply the tax rate by the assessed valuation:

$$\text{assessed value} \times \text{tax rate} = \text{annual tax amount}$$

Using the 0.0425 per dollar rate, the taxes on a home assessed at $180,000 is as follows:

$$\$180,000 \times 0.0425 = \$7,650$$

Assessed valuation is not necessarily the same as market value; it could be a much lower or even a higher figure.

Equalization factor. In some areas where assessments are not considered equitable, an equalization factor is used. The assessed value is multiplied by the factor to determine the value for tax purposes. If the equalization factor is 120%, a property assessed at $100,000 is taxed at $120,000. Similarly, if the equalization factor is 82%, then a property assessed at $100,000 would only be taxed at an $82,000 value.

Homeowner tax exemptions.   Many states allow monetary tax exemptions for homeowners and/or veterans. Some states offer increased exemptions for disabled veterans. Tax deferments for disabled and elderly homeowners, in which the tax need not be paid until the homeowner transfers the property or dies, are available in a number of states.

Special Assessments

Like property taxes, special assessments are property liens that take precedence over other liens. Special assessments cover improvements that directly benefit a property (road improvement, sidewalks, sewer, etc.). Assessments are based on benefits received and may be made on a front-foot (road frontage) or square footage basis. Because special assessments are specific liens, nonpayment can result in a public sale of the property.

Special assessments may be paid off over a number of years. Depending upon the purchase agreement, special assessments may be passed on to purchasers or paid for by sellers.

TRANSFER/ALIENATION

Alienation.   Alienation is the legal term for transferring ownership or interest in real property and is most commonly achieved as a result of a sale or lease. Transfers may be voluntary acts of the grantor or involuntary, where the property is taken away without the owner's consent.

Dedication.   Dedication is a voluntary transfer of real property or property rights to a governmental unit. Customarily, either a right-of-way (such as an easement) or an actual title is transferred. Dedication can be used for roads, school sites, parks, hospitals, and so on. Dedication might be required as a condition for approval of a development by a city or a county. The recording of an approved subdivision map showing areas dedicated to the public is regarded as **statutory dedication**.

Involuntary Alienation

Involuntary alienation refers to transfers without the owner's consent.

Tax sale.   If the taxes are not paid, they become a specific lien on the property. After a specified period, a sale at public auction is held. The tax collector issues a tax deed or quitclaim deed to the purchaser. States that allow the property owner a statutory period of redemption after the sale generally issue a certificate of the sale to the purchaser. A tax deed is not provided until the redemption period has expired.

Because real estate taxes typically are considered a priority lien, title at a tax sale passes to the purchaser, free of any mortgages, mechanics' liens, or judgment liens against the former owner.

Adverse possession.   Title can be acquired from another without permission by adverse possession. Several conditions must be met:

- The use must be continuous and uninterrupted for a period of time prescribed by statute. Some states allow continuous use by means of tacking on, in which the period of use of prior users may be added to that of a successor to satisfy the statutory possession period.

- The use must be exclusive (use need not be exclusive for a prescriptive easement).

- The use must be hostile. The owner's permission would cancel the hostile nature of the use.

- The use must be open and notorious so that a diligent owner would know that another person is in possession of the property.

Some states require that adverse possession be under some claim of right to the property or **color of title**, or provide a shorter statutory period for use when under a claim of right (e.g., a deed from a person who falsely claimed ownership).

A number of states add the requirement that the adverse user pay the taxes. Claiming rights and paying taxes generally enhance the claims of adverse users.

A new owner cannot obtain broader rights by adverse possession than the former owner had. Therefore, if former owner A had only half the mineral rights, by adverse possession, owner B would take title to the property with only half the mineral rights.

To obtain marketable title, an adverse possessor must bring a *quiet title action* that asks a court to determine ownership or obtain a quitclaim deed from the prior owner.

Title cannot be taken from the government by adverse possession, nor can it ordinarily be taken from an incompetent or a minor, because neither can properly defend property.

Sheriff's sale (judgment foreclosure).   When an abstract of judgment is recorded, it becomes a lien against real and personal property in the county where it is recorded. The creditor can get execution on the judgment. The sheriff can seize nonexempt property of the debtor and dispose of it by public sale to satisfy the judgment. Real property generally is then transferred by a **sheriff's deed**, which transfers no greater right than the debtor had. The purchaser at the sheriff's sale takes title subject to prior liens. In most cases, there is a **period of redemption** after a sheriff's sale, during which the debtor can regain the property upon payment of the sales price plus costs and interest.

Homestead exemption.   In many states, homestead exemptions protect homeowners against unsecured creditors forcing the sale of their homes. If the amount of a homeowner's equity is the same or less than the statutory exemption, the unsecured creditor cannot force the sale of the homestead. In some states, the homeowner must record a *declaration of homestead* to be protected.

Usually the homeowner must reside on the premises to file a homestead declaration (a homestead would not be possible, therefore, on a vacant parcel). In some states, lessees can file a homestead on their long-term lease rights.

Declarations of homestead do not offer protection against secured creditors, including mortgages, mechanics' liens, judgments recorded before the homestead declaration, and property tax liens.

Foreclosure.   A mortgagor or trustor (borrower) who defaults on a mortgage or trust deed may be foreclosed by the mortgagee (lender) through a public sale. The purchaser at a foreclosure sale takes title subject to all encumbrances that are senior to the foreclosing lien (priority liens such as property taxes and prior recorded liens), but junior encumbrances, recorded after the foreclosing lien was filed, are wiped out.

Condemnation.   Under the police power of the state, a property may be condemned and ordered vacated or destroyed if it is unfit or unsafe for use or occupancy. An owner whose property is so condemned is not entitled to compensation.

Another type of condemnation proceeding is the taking of private property for public use under the power of eminent domain.

Eminent domain.   A government unit may take ownership of private property for public purposes without the owner's consent but must pay just compensation. The U.S. Supreme Court has held that public purpose can include transfer to a private party for development or redevelopment. In some states, legislation has limited this expanded view of the power of eminent domain.

The power of eminent domain may be delegated to public utilities, schools, hospitals, and other institutions.

Severance damage.   When only part of the owner's land is taken by eminent domain and the taking results in a reduced value for the remaining land, the owner is entitled to compensation for this additional loss.

Inverse condemnation.   Owners can take action to force the condemnation of their property if government action has caused loss in value or the inability to use the property. Such an action might occur, for example, when a government takes away a former public access and the result is a landlocked parcel or where the government announces that it will take a property by eminent domain but then unreasonably delays in doing so.

Partition action.   As discussed in Chapter 1, a partition action is an involuntary alienation as to breaking up a joint tenancy or tenancy in common. When the parties cannot agree, a court may order that a property be divided or sold and the proceeds divided between the former joint owners.

INHERITANCE

Probate is the legal procedure for disposing of the estate of a decedent and for paying the deceased's just debts, as well as validating any will. If the decedent died **testate**, having written a valid will, the decedent would have appointed an **executor** as personal representative to administer and dispose of the estate. If there is no will, the deceased is said to have died **intestate**, and the court would appoint a personal representative called an **administrator** to administer and dispose of the estate.

An estate may be made up of two types of property:

1. *Devise*—real property given by will

2. *Bequest* or *legacy*—personal property given by will

The apportionment and division of an estate in probate, after paying costs and debts, is called **distribution**.

Wills

A **will** is a testamentary disposition determined by the deceased before death. Testators must be of sound mind and understand the nature and the disposition of their property.

A **formal will** must be signed by the testator and witnessed by a prescribed number of witnesses. A **holographic will** does not require witnesses but must be written entirely in the hand of the testator.

Nuncupative wills are oral deathbed wills and are valid in a few states as to personal property of limited value. Where valid, a nuncupative will must be reduced to writing by the witnesses.

A will can be modified or canceled at any time before the testator's death. A new will cancels a prior will. A **codicil** is an amendment to a will that requires the same formalities as a will.

In some states, a spouse can elect to take statutory dower or curtesy rights rather than what the will provides.

Ademption is the failure of a specific devise because the testator disposed of the specific property before death. The named recipient of the devise is not entitled to the property or to its cash equivalent. Some states have modified this rule allowing the devisee, in some cases, to receive proceeds of a sale closing after testator's death.

Intestate Succession

A person who dies without a will is said to have died intestate (without a testament). Property in the estate passes (is distributed) in accordance with the laws of intestate succession and distribution. Intestate succession varies among the states, with provisions for spouses and lineal descendants such as children. In the event no living descendants are found, provision is made for parents and collateral heirs, those related through a common ancestor. Intestate or hereditary succession is called **descent**.

Generally, if a blood heir is dead but has left children, the children take by **right of representation** and share equally in the share their parent would have received.

Escheat

Because all property should have an owner, when a person dies intestate and has no known heirs, after a statutory period, the title to real and personal property reverts (escheats) to the state. Abandoned personal property could also escheat to the state.

DEEDS

Deeds are voluntary transfer documents for an interest in real estate. A deed is used only once. When you buy, you receive a deed from the seller. When you sell, you give a new deed to the buyer. A deed is used to transfer only real property. Personal property is transferred by a **bill of sale**.

Requirements for a Valid Deed

Delivery. A valid conveyance or transfer of title requires that the deed be delivered to the grantee by the grantor during the grantor's lifetime. Mailing generally constitutes delivery. For delivery to occur, there must be intent to pass title immediately. A recorded deed is presumed to have been delivered.

Acceptance. Because the law does not force a person to take title, a valid deed requires acceptance. Acceptance can be any words or conduct of the grantee that indicates intent to accept. For example, a grantee offering to sell or lease the deeded property indicates acceptance of the deed. Failure to repudiate a grant within a reasonable time after learning of the grant could also indicate acceptance. Acceptance can be presumed where the grant clearly benefits the grantee.

Conveyance. A deed must have a *granting clause*, words indicating that title is to pass.

Writing. All deeds must be in writing.

Unambiguous description. The property must be described so that boundaries can be known. Although a few states require a legal description on a deed, such a description generally is not required to convey title. However, it is required to obtain title insurance.

Habendum clause. Many states require that a deed define the interest or estate granted (such as fee simple or life estate). This is the function of the habendum clause, which usually includes the phrase "to have and to hold." In some states, the deed is presumed to convey a fee simple interest if the extent of the grant is not specified.

Competent grantor. The grantor must be legally capable of conveying title. Grantees do not always have to be competent parties—for example, title can pass to a minor by gift.

Definite grantee. The grantee must be readily identifiable. Although property can be conveyed to a grantee using a fictitious name, the grantee must be a definite, specific person.

Signed. The deed must be signed by the grantor. The grantee does not have to sign. A forged deed is void and conveys nothing, nor does an altered deed.

For example, a deed in which the property description was changed without the grantor's consent is considered void.

Not Required for a Valid Deed

Witnesses.   In most states, a deed need not be witnessed (unless the grantor signs with an *X*).

Recording.   Recording a deed makes the deed a matter of public record. The recording process gives an implied notice, called constructive notice, to others of the interest conveyed. A deed must be recorded to give constructive notice of the transfer to third parties. However, recording is not required between the grantor and the grantee, who already have knowledge of the transfer.

Address of parties.   Some states require the address of the grantee to record the deed. The purpose is to determine where tax statements are to be sent, but the deed need not be recorded to be valid between the parties.

Seal.   Most states do not require a seal for a deed.

Acknowledgment.   Acknowledgment is the admission by the grantor, before a notary, that the person is the grantor and that the signing (execution) is an act of free will. Acknowledgment is not required to have a valid transfer between the parties, but in most states, it is required to record the deed.

Consideration.   In some states, the consideration must be stated in the deed, whereas in others, it need not be. Love and affection is considered to be good consideration, but it is not regarded as valuable consideration.

Date.   The deed need not be dated. It is considered dated as of the date of recording.

Types of Deeds

Warranty deed.   Under a warranty deed, the grantor personally guarantees or warrants clear title.

General warranty deed.   Grantors bind themselves and all their heirs to defend the title of the grantee (and that of the heirs) against claims of others.

There are five basic covenants, or promises, in a general warranty deed:

1.   *Covenant of seisin.* The grantor warrants that he has rightful ownership of the property and has the right to convey.

2.   *Covenant of quiet enjoyment.* The grantor warrants that the title will be good against third parties and will indemnify the grantee should any third party establish a superior claim.

3.   *Covenant against encumbrances.* The grantor warrants that the property is free of liens or other encumbrances except as stated in the deed.

4.   *Covenant of warranty forever.* The grantor promises to indemnify the grantee for any loss because of failure of title at any future time.

5.   *Covenant of further assurance.* If any further instrument or act is needed to perfect title, the grantor promises to provide it at the grantor's expense.

Special warranty deed.   The grantor warrants that he has made no undisclosed transfer of title or encumbrance (limitation on use or title). Warranty of title is limited to matters concerning title during the grantor's ownership. There is no warranty as to title defects before the grantor's ownership.

Grant deed.   Used in a few states, normally in conjunction with a policy of title insurance, the grant deed contains two warranties:

1.   The grantor has not previously conveyed the property.

2.   The grantor has placed no undisclosed encumbrances against the property.

The grant deed, as well as warranty deeds, generally convey *after-acquired title*, meaning that if, after a sale, the grantor obtains a better interest, such as a quitclaim deed from an encumbrance holder, the after-acquired interest automatically passes to the grantee.

Quitclaim deed.   This deed transfers whatever interests, if any, the grantor may have in property without making any claims of having any interest or ownership. If the grantor had good title, then a good title is conveyed to grantee. However, if the grantor had no legal interest in the property conveyed, the grantee would get nothing. Quitclaim deeds are frequently used to remove **clouds on title** (anything that appears to impair the title) or to give up an uncertain interest or an easement. Another method of removing a cloud on the title is a quiet title action, in which the court is asked to determine questions of title.

Bargain and sale deed.   This deed is similar to a quitclaim deed in that the grantor does not guarantee title, but is different because the grantor implies that she has an interest in the property. There is no such implication in a quitclaim deed.

Transfer on death deed (TOD).   Also called a beneficiary deed, 20 states and the District of Columbia now allow its use. It is a revocable transfer on death that allows real estate to go to heirs without probate or the necessity of setting up a trust. While the deed must be recorded, the transfer is not effective until the grantor dies. Grantors can, without the consent of heirs, rescind at any time before death provided they retain mental capacity.

Sheriff's deed.   Given at a sheriff's sale, the sheriff's deed carries no warranties or representations. It gives only the interest that was foreclosed. There might still be encumbrances.

Tax deed.   A tax deed is given at a property tax sale. Property taxes and special assessments generally are priority liens taking precedence over even prior recorded liens. In most states, a tax sale would wipe out liens such as mortgages.

Gift deed.   Title can pass by gift. Lack of valuable consideration will not in itself invalidate or void a transfer (while a promise to make a gift requires consideration to be enforceable, a completed transfer without consideration is valid). If it can be shown that an insolvent grantor made the gift in an effort to defraud creditors, the gift could be set aside and the creditors could seize the property. Most deeds conveying real property as a gift would describe the consideration as "love and affection."

Executor's deed or administrator's deed. This deed is given by a personal representative of a deceased owner during probate.

Cession deed. A cession deed is used to convey property to a government entity, such as a subdivider giving land to a city for streets.

Recording of Deeds

There is no time limit for recording, but no constructive notice of an interest is made until the deed has been recorded. Generally, the county recorder will time-and-date stamp the deed for recording and enter the deed alphabetically in a **grantor/grantee index**, although other forms of recordkeeping exist.

If a third party has possession of the property, that possession gives the grantee constructive notice of any interest that the possessor has (such as an unrecorded deed, option, or lease). The grantee should therefore determine what, if any, interest the possessor has.

Actual notice. **Actual notice** is when a party actually knows of an interest that another party has in a property. **Constructive notice** is where the law implies that a person should have known of an interest in property by another person (see Figure 2.3).

FIGURE 2.3

Actual and Constructive Notice

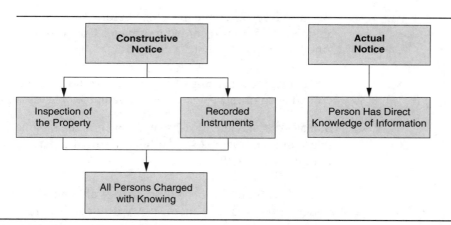

The following material on recording is more likely to appear in a broker's examination than in a salesperson's examination.

Unrecorded deed. Between the grantor and the grantee, an unrecorded deed would convey title to the grantee.

$$\text{grantor} \rightarrow \text{deed} \rightarrow \text{grantee}$$

A deed that is not recorded is considered void as to a later recorded transfer to a purchaser who acts in good faith without having any actual or constructive notice of the prior conveyance.

For example, J sells to K (the deed is not recorded). J later sells to L (the deed is recorded). If L paid value and had no actual or constructive notice of the prior sale, L would have title and K would have only a claim against J.

The reasoning for the above is that if anyone suffers, it should be buyer K who sat on his rights and failed to record, rather than diligent buyer L, who by checking the records (and property) would have no constructive or implied notice of any prior sale.

Assume that when L purchased from J, L knew of the prior unrecorded deed from J to K. In this case, K would prevail over J because of L's actual notice of K's interest.

Priority of recording.   The time and date of recording generally determine the priority of an interest. However, possession is also considered to be constructive notice. Assume the following:

$$\text{July 1: } J \rightarrow \text{ deed } \rightarrow K$$

$$\text{July 5: } J \rightarrow \text{ deed } \rightarrow L$$

If K took possession on July 3, L would have had constructive notice of K's prior interest, and the deed to L would have conveyed nothing. Assume the following:

$$\text{July 1: } J \rightarrow \text{ deed } \rightarrow K \text{ (records July 8)}$$

$$\text{July 5: } J \rightarrow \text{ mortgage } \rightarrow L \text{ (records July 5)}$$

Because L recorded the mortgage before K's recordation of the deed, K has title subject to L's prior recorded mortgage. This priority of recording is often called "the race of the diligent."

Generally, the recording of a gift deed would not take priority over a prior unrecorded deed or mortgage given for valuable consideration.

Defective recording.   If a grantor's or grantee's name is spelled incorrectly, so that a diligent records search fails to reveal a party's interest, recording would not give constructive notice.

A deed recorded in the wrong county also would fail to provide constructive notice of the grantee's interest. A **wild deed** is a deed given by a party who has no recorded interest in a property. Recording a wild deed would not give constructive notice of any claimed interest because it would not show up in a title search, which customarily is by grantor and grantee names.

DOCUMENTARY TRANSFER TAX

Most states have a transfer tax on real property sales. The tax is generally based on the seller's equity being conveyed. If there is new financing, the tax is based on the entire purchase price, but if the loan is assumed, the tax is on the seller's equity. Deeds will not be accepted for recordation without evidence that the tax has been paid.

ABSTRACT AND TITLE INSURANCE

Sellers in real estate transactions must show buyers that they are conveying marketable title. This is often accomplished through an abstract of title. An abstract is a chronological summary of every recorded document dealing with a property, prepared by an abstractor who searched the records showing the **chain of title**, which is the history of recorded ownership. An attorney then gives an opinion as to the marketability of the property. In preparing an abstract, the abstractor's only liability is failure to show a recorded document. The attorney's opinion is, therefore, based on only what is reported in the abstract.

The **Torrens system** is a method for registering title. The title is kept by a registrar and shows the owner and liens. It avoids the necessity of a title search. Title transfer requires registration and the registrar will then issue a **certificate of title**. Several states have modified versions of the Torrens system.

Title insurance is more than an opinion—it is a limited guarantee of marketable title. **Marketable title** refers to title that has no significant defect that is accepted by a prudent buyer. The title insurance company checks the records and issues a **preliminary title report**. This is not a policy of insurance but a statement of the condition of the title (setting forth liens and encumbrances); it affirms that the insurance company will issue a title policy with the noted exceptions and/or conditions. In some states, such notation is called a **title binder**. Title policies are issued at the closing of the transaction or date of title commitment.

Title policies with a one-time premium protect the purchaser and/or lender and insure against past defects in the title up to the amount of insurance purchased. Title insurance protects only the named insured or heirs. Therefore, a policy of title insurance taken out by a previous owner offers no protection to a new buyer.

Standard Policies

Standard policies of title insurance generally protect the property owner against forgery, lack of capacity, failure of delivery, recorded but unreported liens, tax liens, and undisclosed spousal interests (in some states, an extended coverage policy that covers additional risks is available for homeowners).

Lender's Extended Coverage

Because the standard policy does not cover matters not of public record, lenders frequently require an extended-coverage American Land Title Association (ALTA) policy that includes rights of parties in possession, unrecorded liens, unrecorded easements, claims that a proper survey or inspection would have revealed (the property is surveyed for this coverage), mining claims, and water rights. Because the lender's policy does not protect purchasers, separate extended coverage is available for the purchaser at an extra charge.

Lenders often insist on a spot survey as a condition of making a loan. A **spot survey** shows the location of improvements, easements, and encroachments.

Title insurance policies may take an exception to a particular problem so that coverage will not be given if the named problem results in a loss.

Title insurance does not protect the purchaser against zoning restrictions, against defects the purchaser knew of but failed to tell the insurer about, or against exceptions stated in the policy.

Figure 2.4 will help you understand the coverage of standard and lenders' extended coverage policies.

FIGURE 2.4	Standard Coverage	Extended Coverage	Not Covered by Either Policy
Owner's Title Insurance Policy	1. Defects found in public records 2. Forged documents 3. Incompetent grantors 4. Incorrect marital statements 5. Improperly delivered deeds	Standard coverage plus defects discovered through the following: 1. Property inspection, including unrecorded rights of persons in possession 2. Examination of survey 3. Unrecorded liens not known of by policyholder	1. Defects and liens listed in policy 2. Defects known to buyer 3. Changes in land use brought about by zoning ordinances

Curing Title Defects

Title problems (cloud on title) can be rectified by any one of three methods:

1. A quitclaim deed from a person who claims to or appears to have an interest to the holder of the paramount (strongest) title (thus removing any possible interest that person had)

2. An action to quiet title in which the court determines the rights of the parties and issues a declaratory judgment

3. The recording of an affidavit that clarifies or removes an uncertainty

YOUR PERTINENT STATE INFORMATION

1. What are the restrictive covenants' time restrictions?

2. What kind of priority does the mechanic's lien have in your state?

3. What are the notice requirements for mechanics' liens?

4. What are the time restrictions on filing mechanics' liens?

5. What are the requirements and applicability of your state's notice of nonresponsibility?

6. What is the duration of a judgment lien?

7. What are the attachment requirements and duration?

8. What is the statutory limit on easements?

9. Is an easement by necessity allowed?

10. What are the special requirements for a prescriptive easement?

11. Is tacking on allowed for a prescriptive easement?

12. What are your state's homeowner tax exemptions?

13. What, if any, tax deferments are offered in your state?

14. What are the redemption rights (if any) after a tax sale?

15. What is the most common deed of conveyance in your state?

16. Does your state have a documentary transfer tax? If so, how is it computed?

17. What are the special requirements for adverse possession?

18. Is tacking on for adverse possession permitted in your state?

19. What is the period of redemption after a sheriff's sale?

20. What is the amount of your state's homestead exemption?

21. What are the state's homestead requirements?

22. What are the special state deed requirements?

23. What are the requirements for a formal will?

24. Is a holographic (handwritten) will valid?

25. Is a nuncupative (oral) will valid?

26. What are the provisions for intestate succession?

CHAPTER 2 QUIZ

1. A utility company has the recorded right to erect poles on an owner's property and run electrical lines over it. The utility company has
   A. a negative easement.
   B. a prescriptive easement.
   C. an easement in gross.
   D. a license.

2. A property has an assessed value of $137,500 with an equalization factor of 117% and a tax rate of 0.037 per dollar of value. What are the taxes?
   A. $1,608.75
   B. $5,952.37
   C. $16,087.50
   D. $16,875.00

3. A lien on real property can be created by
   A. a contractor who makes improvements.
   B. restrictive covenants.
   C. an encroachment.
   D. unauthorized use.

4. T had an easement over the land of U. T purchased U's land and resold it to V without mentioning the easement. What is the result?
   A. T's easement remains intact because the easement remains once it is a matter of record.
   B. T has lost the easement rights.
   C. U now has easement rights over the land of V.
   D. V now has an easement right over the land of U.

5. Landowners who properly take water from a river flowing through the property are exercising
   A. their littoral right.
   B. their prescriptive right.
   C. their riparian right.
   D. avulsion.

6. A property has littoral rights. This means that the property
   A. is subject to restrictive zoning.
   B. borders a sea, lake, or ocean.
   C. has ownership restrictions spelled out in the deed.
   D. has oil and mineral rights.

7. A property was appraised for tax purposes at 80% of its $140,000 purchase price. The millage rate is 25.8. What will the annual taxes be on the property?
   A. $2,064
   B. $2,890
   C. $2,900
   D. $3,612

8. A lien differs from other encumbrances in that a lien
   A. is a monetary claim.
   B. can be enforced by an injunction.
   C. is a permissive right.
   D. restricts use.

9. An exception to the zoning granted by a planning or zoning commission is called
   A. a variance.
   B. a nonconforming use.
   C. rezoning.
   D. downzoning.

10. A zoning change from single-family use to multifamily use is
    A. downzoning.
    B. bulk zoning.
    C. conservation zoning.
    D. upzoning.

11. An easement that prohibits development of the servient tenement is
    A. an easement by necessity.
    B. an affirmative easement.
    C. a conservation easement.
    D. an implied easement.

12. A writ of execution is used to enforce
    A. a lis pendens.
    B. an attachment.
    C. a judgment.
    D. a zoning.

13. The term *lis pendens* refers to
    A. a valid property listing.
    B. an executory contract.
    C. construction work in progress.
    D. a recorded notice of a pending lawsuit.

14. A woman built a service station that complies with existing zoning. A subsequent change in the zoning excluded service station use on the site. What are the woman's rights?
    A. J is entitled to have the zoning changed.
    B. J's use is a nonconforming use.
    C. J has an automatic variance.
    D. The city is required to give J a conditional use permit.

15. F had an easement allowing F to place communication equipment on top of an adjacent 30-story building owned by G. The building was destroyed by fire. What are F's rights?
    A. F can force G to rebuild.
    B. F's rights terminated with the destruction of the building.
    C. If another building is built on the site, F's rights are renewed.
    D. F's rights were lost by merger.

16. K sold land to L with a restrictive covenant that the property cannot be conveyed to non-Caucasians. L wishes to sell to a buyer who is not a Caucasian. Which of the following statements describes L's rights?
    A. L can go to court to have the restriction declared void.
    B. If L sells to a non-Caucasian person, then L is liable to K for damages.
    C. If L sells to a non-Caucasian person, title would revert to K.
    D. L can ignore the restriction and sell to any qualified buyer.

17. To remove a nuisance, a property owner would bring an action for
    A. attachment.
    B. abatement.
    C. encroachment.
    D. ejectment.

18. A standard policy of title insurance covers
    A. defects that are revealed by a correct survey.
    B. rights of parties in possession.
    C. zoning restrictions.
    D. incompetent grantors.

19. A condition differs from a covenant on the point of
    A. writing.
    B. acknowledgment.
    C. forfeiture.
    D. time limitations.

20. A recorded instrument that places private restrictions on land use is
    A. a zoning restriction.
    B. a restrictive covenant.
    C. an attachment.
    D. a nuisance.

21. A lien that covers all real and personal property of the debtor within the county where it is recorded is
    A. a mechanic's lien.
    B. a judgment lien.
    C. an attachment.
    D. a lis pendens.

22. A man died intestate and without heirs. The state took title to the man's property by
    A. dedication.
    B. escheat.
    C. police power.
    D. eminent domain.

23. Restrictive covenants can be enforced by
    A. the local building inspector.
    B. anyone who knows of them.
    C. anyone who is subject to the restrictions.
    D. the local zoning commission.

24. A warranty deed contains a covenant of further assurance, which means that
    A. the grantor promises to indemnify the grantee for any loss suffered because of failure of title.
    B. the grantor warrants that the property is free of liens and encumbrances other than those stated in the deed.
    C. the grantor warrants that she has rightful ownership.
    D. if any further instrument or act is needed to perfect title, the grantor promises to provide it.

25. A woman recorded an approved subdivision map showing that certain areas of the subdivision were being dedicated to public use. This is regarded as
    A. the exercise of police power.
    B. eminent domain.
    C. statutory dedication.
    D. inverse condemnation.

26. A permissive use that gives no future rights to the user is
    A. a restrictive covenant.
    B. a nonconforming use.
    C. a license.
    D. an encroachment.

27. Which of the following is the decimal equivalent of 3 mills?
    A. 0.3
    B. 0.03
    C. 0.003
    D. 0.0003

28. After meeting the statutory requirements of adverse possession, an adverse user could obtain marketable title by
    A. tacking on.
    B. continued open notorious and hostile use.
    C. a quiet title action.
    D. inverse condemnation.

29. When J sold land to K, the deed failed to give K the right of access to the land over a road on J's land. The court later determined that K had the right to use the road because there was
    A. an express easement.
    B. an easement by reservation.
    C. a prescriptive easement.
    D. an easement by implication.

30. J uses K's land under an easement right. K's land is considered
    A. a dominant tenement.
    B. a servient tenement.
    C. a prescriptive right.
    D. an affirmative right.

31. An offensive nonphysical invasion of the land of another is
    A. an encroachment.
    B. a license.
    C. a nuisance.
    D. an abatement.

32. A recorded revocable deed that is *NOT* a present transfer is a
    A. quitclaim deed.
    B. transfer on death deed.
    C. bargain and sale deed.
    D. sheriff's deed.

33. Priority of judgment liens is based on the
    A. date of the debt.
    B. date of the lien recording.
    C. amount of the debt.
    D. reason for the debt.

34. A judgment lienholder foreclosed and purchased property at the sale. Which of the following describes the foreclosing lienholder's rights?
    A. Title is free of all but tax liens.
    B. Title is clear of all liens.
    C. Title is subject to property tax liens and prior liens.
    D. Title is subject to all liens.

35. J bought K's property but was not aware that L had filed a lis pendens action concerning the property before the purchase. The result is that
    A. L will take clear title to the property.
    B. J's title is subject to L's claim.
    C. the lis pendens is terminated by the transfer.
    D. the title is held in trust for the benefit of L.

36. The correct chronological order of events involving a judgment is
    A. judgment, lis pendens, attachment.
    B. attachment, judgment, execution.
    C. attachment, judgment, lis pendens.
    D. lis pendens, judgment, attachment.

37. G gave a deed to H for valuable consideration. Because H did not take possession or record the deed,
    A. H would have greater right than a later purchaser from G who records first.
    B. J's rights are greater than H's rights, if G later gave a gift deed to J.
    C. the deed is void.
    D. between G and H, H has good title.

38. While a lot is zoned for apartments, single-family homes can be built because the zoning is
    A. inclusionary.
    B. cumulative.
    C. exclusionary.
    D. noncumulative.

39. Which of the following liens is voluntary?
    A. Tax lien
    B. Mortgage lien
    C. Judgment lien
    D. Attachment

40. L knew that M was going to build a new structure that would be an encroachment over L's land. L waited until the structure was completed before bringing an action to remove the encroachment. A court ruling against L would be based on
    A. prior appropriation.
    B. laches.
    C. a lis pendens.
    D. M's littoral rights.

41. On the same day, J deeded the same vacant lot to K, L, and M in that order. M was the first to record, followed by K and L. Who has superior rights to the property?
    A. K because K was the first purchaser
    B. M because M was the first to record
    C. K, L, and M take equal shares as a matter of equity
    D. J retains title because J's fraud cannot pass title

42. The zoning in a subdivision allows duplexes, but the restrictive covenants restrict the use to single-family dwellings. An owner in the subdivision
    A. can build either a duplex or a single-family home.
    B. can convert a single-family home to a duplex.
    C. is restricted to single-family use.
    D. can bring an action to abate the restrictive covenants.

43. A property's tax is determined by
    A. dividing the assessment roll by the budget needs.
    B. multiplying the assessed value by the tax rate.
    C. dividing the assessed value by the tax rate.
    D. dividing the tax rate by the assessed value.

44. Tacking on refers to
    A. an addition to a structure.
    B. an additional party to a document.
    C. obtaining an easement by prescription.
    D. a codicil to a will.

45. What is required before a tenant can move into a newly completed building?
    A. The builder must supply lien waivers.
    B. The lender must approve.
    C. An occupancy permit must be obtained.
    D. The owner must post a completion bond.

46. An easement in gross differs from other easements in that it
    A. is attached to a person, not a property.
    B. is a revocable easement.
    C. has a definite termination date.
    D. is an appurtenant easement.

47. A city can enact ordinances intended to provide for health, safety, morals, and general
welfare under its
    A. injunction power.
    B. police power.
    C. power of eminent domain.
    D. riparian right.

48. The process of land being added to other
land by the gradual action of water is called
    A. avulsion.
    B. accretion.
    C. littoral rights.
    D. prior appropriation.

49. An owner who goes to court to obtain access
for landlocked property would request
    A. a negative easement.
    B. a dedication.
    C. an easement by necessity.
    D. an adverse possession.

50. A homeowner converted the basement into
a rental unit. This violated a restrictive
covenant. Another homeowner wishing to
enforce the covenant would commence an
action for
    A. liquidated damages.
    B. specific performance.
    C. forfeiture.
    D. injunction.

51. When a lake permanently recedes, the land
created belongs to the owner of the bank by
    A. avulsion.
    B. eminent domain.
    C. accretion.
    D. reliction.

52. A special warranty deed warrants that the
grantor
    A. has not made any undisclosed transfer of
title or encumbrance.
    B. will guarantee that there are no undis-
closed liens.
    C. will make good any loss suffered by the
grantee because of title defects.
    D. will provide any further instrument or
act needed to perfect title.

53. N sold a property to O before N acquired
the title from P. When N acquired the title, it
automatically went to O because the deed to
O was
    A. notarized.
    B. a quitclaim deed.
    C. a bargain and sale deed.
    D. a warranty deed.

54. A deed in which the grantor implies having an interest in the property conveyed but
offers no warranties as to title is a
    A. quitclaim deed.
    B. bargain and sale deed.
    C. warranty deed.
    D. deed of trust.

55. Under police power, a city may properly
regulate
    A. minimum sales prices.
    B. who may buy property.
    C. racial composition of neighborhoods.
    D. height of structures.

56. Real property that is transferred by will is a
    A. bequest.
    B. legacy.
    C. devise.
    D. descent.

57. Federal regulations of wetlands are enforced
by
    A. HUD.
    B. the Army Corps of Engineers.
    C. the local health agency.
    D. the Commerce Department.

58. Part of a property was taken by eminent
domain. If the owner received compensation for the reduced value of the remaining
property, it is considered
    A. severance damage.
    B. punitive damage.
    C. condemnation damage.
    D. inverse condemnation.

59. To obtain a zoning variance, an owner must show that
    A. the use sought would benefit the community.
    B. failure to grant it would create an unnecessary hardship.
    C. the variance would increase the property value.
    D. the original zoning was illegal.

60. When P died, a signed and acknowledged but unrecorded deed was found among his effects, giving his house to a local charity. P's will provide that the entire estate was to go to a nephew. The house goes to the
    A. charity because acknowledgment is a presumption of delivery.
    B. charity because his intent was clear.
    C. nephew because P died owning the house.
    D. charity because delivery is not a requirement for charitable gifts.

61. L has a right to cross M's land to get to L's property. L has
    A. a license.
    B. a dominant tenement.
    C. a servient tenement.
    D. an easement in gross.

62. A nonconforming use structure is destroyed by fire. Which of the following is *TRUE*?
    A. The owner can rebuild.
    B. The structure must be replaced exactly as it was.
    C. The state must pay damages for loss of use.
    D. The right to the use was lost.

63. Taxation according to benefits received refers to
    A. use taxes.
    B. special assessments.
    C. ad valorem taxation.
    D. income taxation.

64. Restrictive covenants are found in
    A. deeds.
    B. options.
    C. listings.
    D. easements.

65. A lien that could only cover a single property is
    A. an attachment.
    B. a property tax lien.
    C. a judgment.
    D. a lis pendens.

66. One of the differences in the requirements for obtaining an easement by prescription and a title by adverse possession is that title by adverse possession requires
    A. hostile use.
    B. open and notorious use.
    C. exclusive use.
    D. continuous use for the statutory period.

67. An ejectment action can be brought to
    A. oust a trespasser.
    B. determine water rights.
    C. obtain lateral support.
    D. evict a tenant.

68. An easement would remain valid even if
    A. the servient tenement announces cancellation.
    B. there is a merger of interests.
    C. the purpose of the easement ends.
    D. a prior lien is foreclosed.

69. Covenants, conditions, and restrictions
    A. prevail over zoning if there is a difference.
    B. are private voluntary restrictions.
    C. are illegal land control.
    D. are the exercise of police power.

70. An owner wanted a municipality to take her property because planning changes took away her only access. She would ask for
    A. severance damage.
    B. inverse condemnation.
    C. dedication.
    D. adverse possession.

71. An owner is protected against a mechanic's lien for work authorized by a tenant if the owner
    A. had title insurance.
    B. filed a notice of nonresponsibility.
    C. had a warranty deed.
    D. also authorized the work.

72. The *MOST* important element of delivery of a deed is
    A. intent.
    B. recording.
    C. acknowledgment.
    D. witnesses.

73. The covenant in a deed that the grantor has the right to sell the property is the covenant
    A. of quiet enjoyment.
    B. against encumbrances.
    C. of seisin.
    D. of quiet title.

74. A court determined that a will was invalid. In the absence of a prior will, the deceased's estate would
    A. escheat to the state.
    B. transfer by intestate succession.
    C. be distributed to charities.
    D. revert to the last prior owner.

75. After 10 years of a use that violates CC&Rs, an adjoining property owner asks the court to enforce them. The court would likely refuse because of
    A. inverse condemnation.
    B. estoppel.
    C. laches.
    D. dedication.

76. Neighbors have a right to be notified before
    A. an escheat action.
    B. a zoning variance.
    C. inverse condemnation.
    D. encroachment.

77. A certification that a structure complies with code requirements is a
    A. building permit.
    B. occupancy permit.
    C. variance.
    D. special use permit.

78. The federal case holding that deed restrictions prohibiting ownership by other than Caucasians could *NOT* be enforced was
    A. *Shelley v. Kraemer.*
    B. *Jones v. Mayer.*
    C. *Hubert v. Williams.*
    D. *U.S. v. Howell.*

79. You would never find a typed
    A. holographic will.
    B. warranty deed.
    C. codicil.
    D. mortgage.

80. To obtain the statutory use period, an adverse user of the property of another could
    A. ask for permission.
    B. claim a necessity.
    C. use tacking on.
    D. take the use by escheat.

CHAPTER 2 QUIZ ANSWERS

1. **(C)** This easement has no dominant tenement, so it is an easement in gross. It is also an affirmative easement. (37–38)

2. **(B)** To determine taxes, multiply the equalization factor by the assessed value and then apply the tax rate. (41)

3. **(A)** This is a mechanic's lien. While restrictive covenants are encumbrances, they are not liens. Liens are monetary claims. (35)

4. **(B)** The easement was lost by merger. Ownership includes the lesser interest of the easement holder. (40)

5. **(C)** Riparian rights apply to flowing water. (34)

6. **(B)** This is the reasonable right to use of a nonflowing body of water adjoining a property. (34)

7. **(B)** $0.8 \times \$140,000 = \$112,000$; $\$112,000 \times 0.0258 = \$2,889.60$. (41)

8. **(A)** With the right of foreclosure. (35)

9. **(A)** Zoning is not changed, but an exception is made. (30)

10. **(D)** Upzoning is a change to a less restrictive use. (31)

11. **(C)** A conservation easement prohibits development. (39)

12. **(C)** The sheriff would seize and sell a debtor's nonexempt property. (36)

13. **(D)** It indicates that a claim is being made against a particular property. (36)

14. **(B)** A nonconforming use is normally allowed to remain under a grandfather clause. (31)

15. **(B)** Destruction of servient tenement ends the rights of the holder of the easement. (40)

16. **(D)** Racial restrictions are void and unenforceable. (33)

17. **(B)** Abatement is a court action to remove a nuisance. (41)

18. **(D)** (A) and (B) would be covered by an extended coverage policy, but no policy covers zoning. (51–52)

19. **(C)** If the condition is breached, title could revert to the grantor. (34)

20. **(B)** Private restrictions are placed by restrictive covenant. (32–33)

21. **(B)** Judgment liens are general liens. (36)

22. **(B)** Escheats to the state. (46)

23. **(C)** Enforcement action is usually an injunction. Anyone subject to restriction can enforce it against others. (33)

24. **(D)** One of five warranties. (47)

25. **(C)** But a common-law dedication is based on agreement. (42)

26. **(C)** A license is permissive and not a right. It can be ended at will. (41)

27. **(C)** A mill is 1/10 of a cent (0.001). (41)

28. **(C)** To have a salable property, an adverse user also could obtain a quitclaim deed from the owner of records. (43)

29. **(D)** The use was intended or implied but not stated. (38)

30. **(B)** K's land serves the land of J. (37, 38)

31. **(C)** A nuisance could be smell, noise, vibration, sight, or use that endangers others. (41)

32. **(B)** Does not transfer title until the grantor's death. (48)

33. **(B)** Later lienholder's rights are subject to the rights of prior lienholders. (37)

34. **(C)** The purchaser at a foreclosure sale takes title subject to liens having priority over the foreclosing lien. (37)

35. **(B)** J had constructive notice of L's claim. (36)

36. **(B)** Lis pendens and attachment occur before a judgment. Execution follows the judgment. (36)

37. **(D)** Recording is not necessary as to rights between the grantor and grantee. (47)

38. **(B)** Cumulative zoning allows less restrictive uses. (32)

39. **(B)** The other liens are involuntary. (35)

40. **(B)** L's delay in bringing action worked to M's detriment. (33)

41. **(B)** M had no constructive notice of other buyers. (49–50)

42. **(C)** When zoning and restrictive covenants differ, the more restrictive use prevails. (32)

43. **(B)** Rate times assessed value. (41)

44. **(C)** Adverse use by two or more successors in interest may be joined to fulfill the statutory period required. (39)

45. **(C)** This is normally provided by the building inspector's office. (32)

46. **(A)** It can be personally transferred. (37, 38)

47. **(B)** Usually there is no compensation for loss in value due to exercise of police power. (30)

48. **(B)** It belongs to the littoral or riparian rights owner. (34)

49. **(C)** It may be granted when no other access is possible. (39)

50. **(D)** The homeowner would seek a cessation of rental activity. (41)

51. **(D)** The littoral rights owner gets title. (34)

52. **(A)** Others are general warranty deed covenants. (48)

53. **(D)** Warranty deed conveys after-acquired title. (48)

54. **(B)** There is no implication of having an interest in a quitclaim deed. (48)

55. **(D)** Zoning is proper exercise of police power. (30)

56. **(C)** Devise is real property. (45)

57. **(B)** The Army Corps of Engineers also enforces federal regulation of waterways. (34)

58. **(A)** To cover the value loss of the property remaining. (44)

59. **(B)** The owner is being deprived of benefits that other owners enjoy. (30)

60. **(C)** The deed was never delivered to the charity, so P died owning the property. (46)

61. **(B)** L is a dominant tenement and M is the servient tenement. Because it is a right, it is an affirmative easement and not a license. (37)

62. **(D)** The use was for that structure only. (31)

63. **(B)** For example, street improvements based on front foot. (42)

64. **(A)** Also called deed restrictions. (33–34)

65. **(B)** Each property has a separate tax lien. (35)

66. **(C)** There can be multiple users for an easement by prescription, but not for adverse possession. (43)

67. **(A)** Or to remove an encroachment. (40)

68. **(A)** The servient tenement cannot cancel as the dominant tenement has a right. (40)

69. **(B)** In case of a difference between CC&Rs and zoning, the more restrictive applies. (32)

70. **(B)** Take the property with compensation because the government made it unusable. (44)

71. **(B)** Usually posted on property and recorde(D) Also protects vendors on land contracts from work authorized by vendees. (35)

72. **(A)** Did grantor intend a present transfer? (46)

73. **(C)** The owner has possession with right to transfer. (47)

74. **(B)** To heirs as if died intestate. (45)

75. **(C)** Delay in bringing action. (33)

76. **(B)** As well as rezoning or special use permit. (31)

77. **(B)** Complete and habitable meeting health and safety codes. (32)

78. **(A)** Racial restrictions are unenforceable. (33)

79. **(A)** By definition, it must be handwritten. (45)

80. **(C)** For an easement by prescription could join prior users' time of use. (39, 43)

CHAPTER 3

Valuation, Appraisal, and Investment Analysis

VALUE

Value is worth, or the present worth of future benefits. *Appraisal* is the supported estimation of value of real estate at the time of the appraisal.

Types of Value

Market value. The cash price a willing, informed buyer would pay to a willing, informed seller in an open market, allowing a reasonable marketing time, is called **market value**. Appraisal is concerned primarily with market value (the probable sales price).

Market price is not the same as market value. Market price is the price actually paid, and it could be more or less than market value because of motivation, knowledge, or bargaining strength of the parties.

Objective and subjective value. **Objective value** is the actual market value. **Subjective value**, or utility value, is the personal use value of the benefits of ownership. The appraiser estimates the objective value that the typical buyer will be willing to pay for the benefits offered.

Book value. **Book value** is the original property cost, plus the cost of any improvements, minus any depreciation taken. It is the value carried on the owner's books; it bears no relationship to market value; and it is not used in appraising.

Assessed value. **Assessed value** is the value placed by a tax assessor. Assessed value, often influenced by the price paid, may differ from market value.

Loan value. **Loan value** is less than market value, as it is customarily a percentage of market value, leaving a margin for lender security.

Principles of Value

The following definitions briefly describe principles applied in appraising property.

Economies of scale.   A larger development or multiple units generally can be built at a lower price per square foot or per unit.

Principle of anticipation.   Value is based more on anticipated or expected future benefits than present benefits derived.

Principle of balance.   There is an optional use that creates the greatest value, such as the amount of land zoned for various uses so there will not be a surplus or shortage.

Principle of change.   Real estate value does not remain constant. An appraiser must consider how changing economic and social conditions affect the value of property.

Principle of competition.   When extraordinary profits are derived from an investment, competition will be created, which will increase the supply, thus lowering profits.

Principle of conformity.   A property will achieve and maintain its maximum value when it is in a homogeneous, or uniform, area of similar-use property, such as in a subdivision.

Principle of contribution.   Maximum value is achieved when improvements return the highest net in relationship to the investment. A decision to add amenities to a property should be based on the cost of the amenities and the anticipated increase in value that would result.

Principle of diminishing returns.   A point will be reached when additional improvements will fail to increase the value to cover the costs of the improvements.

Principle of integration and disintegration.   Property goes through phases of development (integration), stability (equilibrium), and decline (disintegration). This principle also is called the principle of the three-stage life cycle: development, maturity, and old age.

Principle of progression.   The value of a home will be increased by more expensive homes in the area. Economically, it is often desirable to have the least expensive home in an area.

Principle of regression.   The value of a home will be held down by the presence of homes having lesser value in the area. The principle of regression is the opposite of the principle of progression.

Principle of substitution.   A person will not pay more for one property than for another comparable property of equal utility and desirability.

Principle of supply and demand.   An increase in supply without a change in demand will decrease prices. A decrease in supply without a change in demand will increase prices. An increase in demand without a change in supply will increase prices. A decrease in demand without a change in supply will decrease prices.

Highest and best use.   The most profitable use to which a property can be adapted given legal restrictions is the **highest and best use**.

Assemblage and plottage.   Assemblage is the process of joining several contiguous, or touching, parcels of property together under common ownership to form one larger parcel. The larger parcel is likely to have a resulting value greater than the sum of the values of the smaller parcels because of the difficulty in assembling larger parcels in developed areas. The increase in value by assemblage is called **plottage** or plottage increment.

ELEMENTS OF VALUE

The least important factor in determining property value is **cost**, or price paid. Cost represents what was spent in the past, not the present worth. There are four essential elements of value:

1.   *Demand*. Without demand, there is no value. To be meaningful, demand must be coupled with purchasing power.

2.   *Utility*. To have value, a property must have a useful purpose; even an ornament serves a purpose.

3.   *Scarcity*. If many similar properties are on the market, the value of each will be less than if only a few such properties were available.

4.   *Transferability*. To have value, the title or possession must be capable of being transferred. An interest that cannot be transferred has no value.

Remember the acronym **DUST**: **D**emand, **U**tility, **S**carcity, and **T**ransferability.

Four Special Forces that Influence Value

1. Physical.

Topography.   Steep grades mean higher development costs. Subdividers like gently rolling land that breaks the monotony but does not result in excessive costs.

Shape.   Rectangular lots are more valuable than irregularly shaped parcels. An exception is lots on cul-de-sacs, which are valued because of diminished traffic.

Size.   The width and depth of a lot determine possible uses.

Exposure.   How a property is situated as to light, air, view, et cetera affects value. For example, the south and west sides of commercial streets generally are more valuable for foot traffic business because they offer shoppers more shade on hot afternoons.

Soil.   The ability of soil to support a structure affects construction costs. *Compaction tests* by a civil engineer would measure this ability. Fertility of soil generally has only a slight effect on value other than for agricultural land.

Corner influence.   A corner location has greater value for commercial purposes because of greater exposure for signs and displays as well as easier access.

Location.   Location is the site of a property in relationship to other uses and physical features. Appraisers often state that the three most important factors in determining value are location, location, and location.

2. Economic.   The economy affects value in that it directly affects demand. For a particular property, the local economy tends to be more important than the national economy. The economy of a particular community might run counter to the national economy. A primary measurement of the national economy is the **gross domestic product (GDP)**, which is the sum of all goods and services produced by our nation during a certain period. Changes in the GDP are indicators of changes that have occurred in the national economy.

Changes in unemployment levels indicate trends in the local economy. Real estate values tend to rise during periods of inflation, when the purchasing power of the dollar decreases. A principal measurement of inflation is the **Consumer Price Index (CPI)**.

Interest rates affect value because lower rates encourage more buyers to enter the marketplace, resulting in greater demand, which results in rising prices. The opposite can also be true as to high interest rates.

3. Political.   Government regulations (zoning, taxes, growth limitations, building codes, health codes, public housing, rent control, etc.) also affect value.

4. Social.   Social factors that influence value include population movements, size of households, attitude toward recreation, and so on.

Remember the acronym **PEPS: P**hysical, **E**conomic, **P**olitical, and **S**ocial.

Neighborhood

A neighborhood is an area characterized by social conformity. It might have defined boundaries, such as a particular street, a river, or a particular subdivision. Other neighborhoods might merge with imprecise boundaries. Similarity of interests provides neighborhood cohesiveness; similarities might include income, education, children, or recreational interests. If residents of an area have pride in their neighborhood, the neighborhood is likely to remain stable; a neighborhood that loses common interests tends to decline. A decline in the percentage of home ownership and an increase in rental units often indicate a declining neighborhood.

APPRAISAL METHODS

Three appraisal methods are used to arrive at property value:

1.   Sales comparison approach (market data or direct sales comparison)

2.   Cost approach (replacement cost)

3.   Income approach (capitalization of income)

Remember the acronym **SCI: S**ales, **C**ost, and **I**ncome.

Sales Comparison Approach

In the **sales comparison approach**, which is the oldest and easiest-to-learn appraisal method, a property's value is arrived at by comparing the sales prices of similar properties recently sold. In selecting the comparables, the appraiser considers terms of sale, special features, quality, age, size, and location, making adjustments when properties or features are not equally desirable. **Amenities** are property features that provide greater satisfaction in living or pride of ownership: a beautiful garden, mature trees, a magnificent view, a fountain, or an extra bath, for example. In the market comparison method, the amenities are considered in arriving at the value.

To calculate the value, the appraiser takes the sales price from a comparable property and then adds and subtracts based on the presence or absence of features and amenities in the property being appraised (see Figure 3.1).

FIGURE 3.1	Subject property	Comparable property	Adjustment to comparable
Sales Comparison Approach	2-car garage	3-car garage	–
	2½ baths	2 baths	+
		More desirable location	–
	12,000-sq.-ft. lot	9,000-sq.-ft. lot	+

Adjustments to Comparable Sale Price:
Comparable has advantage: deduct (–)
Subject property has advantage: add (+)

The sales price of a comparable property is adjusted upward if the comparable lacked a feature or was less desirable than the subject property and is adjusted downward if the comparable had a positive feature or was more desirable than the subject property. This adjusted price is called the **adjusted market price**. Figure 3.1 gives an example of how the adjusted selling price could be calculated in one case.

The appraiser considers depreciation as it applies to both the property being appraised and the comparables in making adjustments. There could be **physical depreciation**, such as is caused by age and wear and tear; **functional obsolescence** that is built in, such as an undesirable floor plan; and **external obsolescence**, which is forces outside the property, such as environmental or economic factors. All of these could pull value down.

Forced sales such as foreclosures bankruptcies, estate sales and short sales should be avoided as comparables because they seldom reflect market value.

The comparison method is the best appraisal method for single-family dwellings. It also can be used for land as well as improved properties where sales exhibit a high degree of similarity.

Disadvantages are the difficulties experienced in locating similar recent sales and adjusting amenities and sales terms.

Comparative Market Analysis (CMA)

A **comparative market analysis (CMA)** is not an appraisal. Licensed or certified appraisers make appraisals. The CMA is a real estate agent's tool to help the owners set a listing price for property based on comparable recently sold properties and comparable offerings currently on the market. By comparing the prices and adjusting for differences in the subject property and the comparables, an estimate is arrived at as to offering price.

While the CMA is used to help the owner understand the current market, the list price decision is made by the owner not the agent.

Cost Approach

If there are no comparables and there is no income, the **cost approach** would likely be used. The cost approach is the best method for appraising new or special use structures (e.g., library or county stadium). The cost approach tends to set upper limits on value. An exception is a market where prices are rising rapidly. Although the cost approach can be effectively used for new homes, the market comparison approach is more effective for older homes. If the cost approach were applied to an older home, an appraiser would have to determine the accrued depreciation, which tends to be subjective and reduces the reliability of the appraisal.

The cost approach is a three-step appraisal process:

1. Determine the present cost to replace improvements, that is, to build a structure of the same utility and desirability using today's material, methods, and design. *Replacement cost* differs from *reproduction cost*, the cost to duplicate the structure with exactly the same design and materials.

2. Deduct **accrued depreciation**—that is, depreciation that already has occurred; **remainder depreciation** is depreciation that will occur in the future.

3. Add the value of the land, which is arrived at by using the market comparison approach.

    This is represented with the following equation:

    cost to replace − accrued depreciation + land = value

Replacement Cost (Cost to Build)

The replacement cost can be arrived at by several different methods.

Quantity-survey method.   This is the most detailed and time-consuming method to determine replacement costs, where all costs, fees, labor, material, subcontracts, interest, and so on, are priced separately.

Builders would use the quantity-survey method when actual construction of a structure is contemplated. This is developed by considering all direct and indirect contracting costs.

Unit-in-place (segregated cost) method.   This method uses costs per unit, such as per square foot, per cubic foot, per bath, per room, per electrical outlet, and so on. Some appraisers consider price per square foot to be a separate method (the comparative unit method).

Index method.   The present cost to build is arrived at by applying increases or decreases in the construction cost index since the structure was built to its original cost to build.

Accrued depreciation.   For appraisal purposes, only improvements are depreciated; land is never depreciated. To arrive at the depreciation of a structure, the economic life of the structure must be determined. **Economic life** is the period during which the improvements contribute to the net income. **Age-life tables** provide the economic life—often 40 to 50 years—for various types of structures and construction. To determine the amount of accrued depreciation, the effective age of the structure must be estimated. **Effective age** is the structure's age for appraisal purposes. Effective age can differ from chronological age, depending on the care given to maintenance and repair. For example, an appraiser might indicate the effective age of a 10-year-old structure as 7 years because it has been well-maintained. A similar 10-year-old structure might be given an effective age of 15 years because of excessive wear and tear.

The appraiser analyzes the condition of the property, considering physical deterioration, functional obsolescence, and external factors, to determine the accrued depreciation. This is called the **observed condition method**. For example, if the economic life is determined to be 40 years, each year's depreciation amounts to 2.5% of the replacement cost.

$$100\% \div 40 = 2.5\%$$

If the property had an effective age of 10 years, it would have depreciated 25%.

$$2.5\% \times 10 = 25\%$$

For example, a 15,000-square-foot warehouse would cost $40 per square foot to build today. Its economic life is 50 years, and its effective age is 8 years. The land is valued at $170,000 (arrived at by the market comparison method). The property is valued as follows:

15,000 × $40	=	$600,000 cost to replace
50-year life	=	2% depreciation per year
8 years × 2%	=	16% depreciation
0.16 × $600,000	=	$96,000 accrued depreciation
$600,000		Cost to build today
− 96,000		Accrued depreciation
$504,000		Present value of structure
+ 170,000		Land value
$674,000		Total present value of land and improvements

Income Approach

The **income approach** is generally the best appraisal method for income-producing property. It determines the present worth of future benefits (rents). An exception is a single-family rental home, for which the market comparison method is usually preferred because of the availability of comparables.

The income approach is based on the **net operating income (NOI)** of the property being appraised. To estimate value, an appraiser determines the appropriate rate of return, the *capitalization rate*, and divides it into the NOI:

$$NOI \div \text{capitalization rate} = \text{value}$$

Annual net operating income.   To determine annual NOI, an appraiser deducts total annual expenses from the gross annual income, including an allowance for vacancies and collection losses, as well as management expenses.

$$\text{gross annual income} - \text{vacancy and bad debt} = \text{effective gross income}$$

$$\text{effective gross income} - \text{operating expensive} = NOI$$

The only costs not deducted are payments on the loan principal and interest expenses, called **debt service** and depreciation. In determining the gross income, an appraiser is more interested in anticipated future income than in past income.

Capitalization rate.   The capitalization rate is the rate of return an investor wants on a particular property. For a high-risk investment, an investor might want a 17% return, whereas a 5% return for a secure investment might be acceptable. When interest rates are high, investors use a higher capitalization rate to reflect a higher desired return on investment.

Besides indicating a return on an investment, the capitalization rate can be increased to provide for depreciation that is the return of the investment. For example, if an investor wanted an 8% return on an investment and the property was expected to have a 50-year useful life (economic life), the investor could add 2% to the rate, raising the rate to 10%. This added 2% provides for the recapture of the investment over 50 years.

Capitalization rates for comparable sales can be determined by dividing the sales price into the NOI of the comparable properties.

$$NOI \div \text{sales price} = \text{capitalization rate used}$$

For example, an appraiser anticipates that an eight-unit apartment building will have monthly rentals of $400 per unit, a 10% vacancy and collection loss factor, and total expenses of $600 per month. Find its value using a capitalization rate of 12%.

8 × $400 = $3,200	Monthly scheduled gross income
$3,200 × 12 = $38,400	Annual scheduled gross income

$38,400	Annual scheduled gross income
− 3,840	10% vacancy and collection loss
$34,560	Effective gross income (gross less vacancy and collection factors)
− 7,200	Expenses ($600 × 12)
$27,360	NOI

To determine the value after the NOI and the capitalization rate have been determined, divide the NOI by the capitalization rate.

$$\text{value} = \text{NOI} \div \text{capitalization rate}$$

$$\text{value} = \$27,360 \div 0.12$$

$$\text{value} = \$228,000$$

The value, using the income approach, is $228,000.

If the capitalization rate were 10%:

$$\$27,360 \div 0.1 = \$273,600$$

If the rate used were 14%:

$$\$27,360 \div 0.14 = \$195,428.57$$

Value moves inversely to capitalization rate; that is, value goes up if the rate goes down, and value goes down if the rate goes up. Similarly, if expenses go up, value goes down because net decreases; if expenses go down, value goes up because net increases.

Gross Rent Multiplier

A variation of the income approach multiplies the gross income by a figure called the **gross rent multiplier (GRM)** to arrive at value. If a property has a gross annual income of $10,000 and can be purchased for $70,000, the seller believes that an annual GRM of 7 is appropriate.

$$\text{sales price} \div \text{gross rent} = \text{gross rent multiplier (GRM)}$$

By knowing the average GRMs of similar properties that have sold, a prospective purchaser will have a general idea as to the value of a property being offered. Because a property might have unusually high or low expenses, a gross rent multiplier gives only a rough idea of value; it does not consider the actual net income. Because the gross rent multiplier requires comparables, it requires an active market. The GRM also can be expressed as a monthly factor, which typically is done with single-family residences.

Reconciliation (Correlation)

An appraiser might arrive at separate values using two or all three basic appraisal methods. If this happens, the appraiser will assign different weights to each method, a process called **reconciliation**. For example, an appraiser might use 80% of the value determined by market comparison, 20% of the value by the cost approach, and 0% of the value by the income approach (80% + 20% + 0% = 100% of value).

Deferred Maintenance

Owners often put off making repairs. In using the capitalization method or the gross rent multiplier, the appraiser deducts the estimated needed repair costs from the value derived to correct for the deferred maintenance.

Site Analysis and Valuation

It is often necessary to determine site value (the value of the land alone) for developed as well as vacant property. For example, the cost approach requires a separate land valuation. A number of methods can be used for site valuation.

Sales comparison. When there have been sales of similar sites, the sales comparison method can be used. The sales prices of comparable sites would need to be adjusted for factors such as size, shape, view, and topography, as well as other locational differences.

Development method. This method of appraising a site requires that the appraiser determine the highest and best use, the use that results in the greatest net attributable to the site. The appraiser determines the cost of an improvement and deducts the cost from the total value the property would have with that improvement. The balance is the site value for that use.

Sample problem. Assume that constructing a $300,000 apartment building on a site will result in a total value of $450,000 for the building and site. In this case, the site value is $150,000:

$450,000 total value – $300,000 cost of construction = $150,000

This would not be the highest and best use if $50,000 in improvements for a parking lot would give the site a value of $250,000. The value of the land is $200,000 ($250,000 – $50,000), which would make the parking lot a higher and better use.

Land residual method. The income approach can be combined with the cost approach to determine the value of the land alone when it is improved with a structure. By multiplying the applicable capitalization rate by the value of the improvements, determined by the cost approach, the appraiser finds the income attributable to the improvements. The balance of the income, therefore, is attributable to the land. By capitalizing the income attributable to the land, the appraiser determines the value of the land.

Abstractive method. By determining the value attributable to the improvements using the cost approach and then deducting this amount from the market value, an appraiser can determine the value attributable to the land alone.

Surplus productivity (principle of surplus). After deductions for labor, management, and capital investment, the balance of the value should be attributable to the land itself. It is based on the following formula:

$$land + labor + capital + management = value$$

This method is really a variation of the abstractive method.

Depth table. Appraisers use complex mathematical tables to determine value for lots of increased or decreased depth. The 4-3-2-1 approach to land value is a simplified method, where 40% of the value is in the first 25% of depth, 30% is in the next 25%, 20% is in the next 25%, and 10% is in the last 25% of depth.

Expressing land values. Land values are expressed differently for different types of property.

- *Agricultural land.* Land is priced per acre.

- *Commercial land.* Land is priced per square foot or per front foot.

- *Industrial land.* Land is priced per square foot or per acre.

- *Residential lots.* Land is priced per lot (exception: waterfront lots generally are priced per front foot).

- *100% location.* This is an idiom meaning the very best commercial location within a community for a particular type of business.

- *Excess land.* This expression refers to having more land than is economically needed for a property (land that does not contribute to value).

Depreciation

Depreciation is a loss in value from any cause. There are various types of depreciation.

Physical deterioration. Wear and tear from use, negligence, age, or other physical damage results in physical deterioration. Examples include dry rot, blistering paint, a leaking roof, or a sagging floor.

Functional obsolescence. This is loss in value that was "built into" the structure by poor design, lack of needed facilities, outdated equipment, or changes in demand. Examples include bedrooms without closets, small rooms, or an awkward floor plan. An excessively expensive improvement (overbuilding) also is functional obsolescence.

External obsolescence (economic or environmental obsolescence). This type of loss in value is caused by forces outside the property itself that negatively affect value. Examples include nearby property with an undesirable property use, such as a gravel pit, and high unemployment that reduces the demand for property. A property owner has no real control over external obsolescence.

The statement "more buildings are torn down than wear out" reflects economic obsolescence—the buildings are not worn out, but because of outside factors, they are no longer economical for their designed uses.

Curable depreciation.   Curable depreciation is loss in value that can be corrected economically. For example, if the value of a property after repair work would exceed the land value plus the cost of the repairs, the depreciation is regarded as curable because it would make economic sense. The existing improvements still have value.

Incurable depreciation.   Incurable depreciation is loss in value that cannot be reversed economically. If the value of a property after repairs were made is less than the value of the land plus the cost of the repairs, it would not be economically feasible to make the repairs. Because forces outside the property itself cause external obsolescence, an owner would ordinarily be unable to cure the problem. Therefore, external obsolescence is generally regarded as being incurable depreciation.

Computing Depreciation

The **straight-line method** of depreciation is used for appraisal purposes. With this method, an equal sum is depreciated each year over the life of the asset. Depreciation periods used for appraisal are taken from age-life tables and generally are longer than those used for income tax purposes.

APPRAISAL PROCESS

The appraisal process involves a number of steps:

- *Define the problem*. This involves determining the property and the property interest to be appraised, such as fee simple or leasehold. It also involves determining the value to be determined (market value, replacement cost, reproduction cost, etc.) and the purpose of the appraisal.
- *Determine the data needed*, and collect and verify the data.
- *Determine the highest and best use* for the property.
- *Estimate land value*.
- *Estimate the value by use of the three basic approaches to value*.
- *Reconcile the estimated values* and make a final value determination.
- *Report the value*.

APPRAISERS

The information about certified and licensed appraisers is more likely to be needed in the broker examination than in the salesperson examination.

Certified and Licensed Appraisers

Title XI of the Real Estate Appraisal Reform Amendment of the federal **Financial Institutions Reform Recovery and Enforcement Act (FIRREA)** of 1989 requires that state-licensed or state-certified appraisers be used for federally related transactions—real estate transactions involving federal financial and public policy interests. Any loan regulated or insured by a federal agency or made by a federally regulated lender, as well as transactions involving Fannie Mae or Freddie Mac, is considered federally related (this covers loans made by practically all financial institutions).

There is no certification requirement for federally related residential appraisals less than $250,000 or commercial appraisals of $1,000,000 or less. State-certified appraisers must be used for federally related complex 1-to-4-unit residential property appraisals of more than $250,000 and other transactions of more than $1 million and may be required by the particular federal agency for lower-dollar transactions.

State-licensed appraisers are required for a 1-to-4-unit residential property less than $250,000. Although states can reduce the dollar requirement for state-licensed appraisals, Fannie Mae, Freddie Mac, HUD, and VA require licensed or certified appraisers for these appraisals.

Appraiser categories are as follows:

- State-certified general appraiser
- State-certified residential appraiser
- State-licensed appraiser

Every state must enact legislation to provide for certification that is consistent with criteria established by the **Appraisal Foundation**, a private nonprofit corporation. Certification must be in residential and general categories (general level includes income as well as residential property). An examination is required, without exception, for certification. For those federally related transactions that do not require a certified appraisal, the appraiser must be licensed. Criteria for licensing must be consistent with Title XI. Every state must set minimum appraiser standards. The Appraisal Standards Board (ASB) of The Appraisal Foundation is responsible for the *Uniform Standards of Professional Appraisal Practice (USPAP)*. Appraisers are required to conform to these standards.

The **Dodd-Frank Act of 2010** provides for monitoring the activities of the Appraisal Foundation as well as existing federal legislation as to appraisers including state licensing and certification. The act also requires a national registry of certified and licensed appraisers eligible to perform federally related appraisals.

Appraisal Reports

The following sections describe various kinds of appraisal reports and report content.

Self-contained report (narrative report). Self-contained, comprehensive, and complete, this report contains the background data leading to the appraiser's supported conclusions. The report often includes photos, maps, plot plans, floor plans, community economic information, and the appraiser's credentials.

Restrictive use appraisal report.   A brief report that is limited to valuation or purpose. It includes the identity of the client, the intended use of the report and the value arrived at.

Summary report.   This report offers more details than a restrictive report but less than a self-contained report. It summarizes the market conditions and the analysis used to determine valuation. The summary report uses the three approaches to value in a simple format.

Drive-by appraisal report. An appraisal based on exterior appearance, area, and area sales figures, it provides a greater likelihood of error since interior condition, amenities, and space use are unknown. It is often used in selecting comparables.

Uniform Residential Appraisal Report (URAR). The URAR is used for most appraisals and is required by Fannie Mae, the Department of Veterans Affairs (VA), the Department of Housing and Urban Development (HUD), and Freddie Mac.

Content for appraisal reports

Federally related appraisals must conform to *USPAP*. *USPAP* requires that every written report include the following:

- Clear description of the property being appraised
- Property interest appraised (fee simple, leasehold, etc.)
- Purpose of the appraisal (insurance, loan, etc.)
- Value being appraised (market value, reproduction value, replacement value, etc.)
- Effective date of the appraisal
- Source of data gathered and confirmation of the data and assumptions that affect the appraisal conclusions
- Appraisal conclusions
- Information that was considered and the reasoning
- Procedures followed
- Highest and best use for the property
- Other appropriate information: if the appraiser has a financial interest in the property, it must be fully disclosed
- Any deviations from the *USPAP* appraisal practice
- Valuation approach used and the reasons for exclusion of any valuation approach
- Signed certification of appraiser

Neither the purpose of the report nor the sales price should influence the appraised market valuation. An appraiser should not discuss the appraisal with anyone other than the principal for whom the appraisal was performed without the permission of the principal. It is also considered unethical for an appraiser to take an appraisal that is beyond the appraiser's ability, to pay a referral fee for business, to charge a fee based on a percentage of the appraisal value, or to have any undisclosed interest in the property being appraised.

INVESTMENT ANALYSIS

Real estate investors are interested in three areas:

1. Appreciation in value
2. Present and anticipated future income
3. Use—does the property meet needs?

Investors consider all aspects of the purchase including leverage, financing terms, and anticipated economic and environmental changes. Income is analyzed as to its sustainability as well as possibilities of increases. An analysis would include alternative available investments and highest and best use analysis.

Due diligence is the process of investigation and evaluation to be expected of a reasonably prudent person in the circumstances to make certain that an investment is what it appears to be. It could include investigating and verifying facts, evaluating tenants, evaluating leases, estimating future changes, or consideration of risks, as well as consideration of alternative investments.

INCOME TAX CONSIDERATIONS

While knowledge of income tax considerations is extremely important for real estate salespersons, there will be only a few questions on the salesperson's exam relating to this subject. There will be greater emphasis on income tax matters on the broker's examination.

Income tax is an important issue for homeowners, as well as investors.

Unless subject to an exemption, gains or profit from the sale of property are taxable. While losses from the sale of business or investment property can be used as deductions against other income, a tax loss cannot be taken for the sale of a personal residence.

Determining Gain

The amount of the taxable gain is computed by deducting the seller's adjusted cost basis or book value from the net sales price. **Adjusted cost basis** is the original cost plus improvements, less depreciation.

Although improvements may enhance the value and increase the cost base, repairs will not. Repairs are considered operating expenses and are deductible expenses for income and investment property in the year expended. For example, if a rental property originally cost $100,000 and the buyer spent $10,000 in improvements, the adjusted cost basis is $110,000.

$100,000 cost + $10,000 improvements = $110,000 book value
(adjusted cost basis)

If the owner then sold the property for $150,000, there is a taxable gain of $40,000, the difference between sales price and book value (adjusted cost basis). The seller's sales costs would reduce the taxable gain. For example, if the seller incurred commission and closing costs of $8,000, the gain in the example above is reduced to $32,000. Had depreciation been taken for tax purposes, the amount of depreciation taken is deducted from the book value.

Taxpayer Relief Act of 1997

Under the Taxpayer Relief Act of 1997, homeowners were given an advantageous exemption from taxation. To be eligible for this new exemption, a homeowner must have occupied a property as a principal residence for a total of 24 months during the preceding five-year period.

Occupancy does not need to be continuous. For example, it could be for six months per year over a period of four years. Purchase of a replacement residence is not required for this exemption.

The exemption from taxation is $500,000 for married couples and $250,000 for single persons.

For example, if a married couple paid $450,000 for a home and spent $70,000 in improvements, they would have a cost basis of $520,000. If they sold the property for $1,000,000, their capital gain of $480,000 is exempt from taxation, providing they had met the two-out-of-five-year residency rule. Their gain was $480,000, and as a married couple, they have a $500,000 exemption from taxation:

Cost of home	$450,000
Improvements	+ 70,000
Adjusted cost basis	$520,000
Sales price	$1,000,000
Adjusted cost basis	− 520,000
Capital gain	$480,000

Unmarried co-owners could each claim $250,000 as an exemption to obtain a total exemption of $500,000 on a sale.

This is not a one-time exemption. For example, a couple could purchase and occupy a house for two years, sell it at a profit, repeat the process over and over again, and still be entitled to exempt gains from taxations of up to $500,000 for each sale.

Income Tax Deductions (Homeowners)

Interest is a tax-deductible expense for homeowners, with some limitations:

■ The interest limit on home-purchase loans is up to $1 million for the home loan and one second home loan, provided the loan balance does not exceed the cost of the residences plus improvements. Therefore, if a homeowner had a $2 million purchase loan, only the interest on $1 million is deductible.

■ For home equity loans, interest is deductible for loans not to exceed a total of $100,000 (principal residence plus one second home), provided that the combined home loans don't exceed the fair market value of the homes.

Discount points paid by a buyer on a home-purchase loan are considered prepaid interest and are also deductible as interest in the year paid.

Property taxes. Property taxes are a deductible homeowner expense. No other cash expenses or depreciation may be taken on a residence that is not used for business or income purposes.

INVESTMENT PROPERTY

Equity. This is an owner's interest in a property. It is the difference between the fair market value and the amount owed on the property (mortgage-trust deeds, liens).

Income. **Gross scheduled income** is the scheduled gross based on anticipated 100% occupancy. **Adjusted gross income**, also called effective gross income, is the gross income adjusted for an estimated vacancy factor and collection loss.

Net income is what an investor actually realizes from a property, considering all expenses. While interest payments are considered an expense for investment property, payments on principal are not.

Cash flow. Cash flow is **net spendable income** after all cash expenses are deducted. This would include payments on the principal.

Liquidity. Real estate investments are considered illiquid because of the relatively long time it takes to turn the investment into cash by a sale. Investors can, however, borrow on their equity.

Appreciation. Real estate values have generally increased more rapidly than the rate of inflation.

Depreciation. Investment property can be depreciated for tax purposes, which can shelter income from taxation. Depreciation is a deduction for loss in value due to wear and tear of improvements. Homeowners cannot depreciate their personal residences.

Interest and taxes. These are tax-deductible expenses for income and investment property, as well as personal residences.

Leverage. Because real estate purchases are generally financed, an investor is able to purchase property with a value far greater than the down payment. This allows the investor to take advantage of appreciation on the total value, not just the investor's equity.

Capital Gains

Information on capital gains tax and tax-deferred exchanges is more likely to be needed on the broker's than on the salesperson's examination.

A capital gain is the profit from the sale of a capital asset (such as real estate). The costs of improvements are added to the value of the property (i.e., the cost basis) for tax purposes. Repair costs are deductions from income that are taken in the year of the expenditure. Assume an investment property was originally purchased for $120,000, and the owner spent $38,000 in improvements and took $42,000 in depreciation. The cost basis is as follows:

$120,000 cost + $38,000 improvements – $42,000 depreciation =
$116,000 cost basis

If the owner sold the property for $120,000, the same price for which it was originally purchased, there still is a $4,000 taxable capital gain.

$120,000 sales price – $116,000 cost basis = $4,000 taxable gain

Inherited property receives a stepped up basis meaning the property is valued at the time of decedent's death. This means that the property is shielded from capital gains based on appreciation in value before decedent's death.

Tax Reform Act of 2003

The Tax Reform Act of 2003 reduced taxes on capital gains. For assets held for more than 12 months, the maximum **long-term capital gain** is 15% (property held for one year or less is considered a **short-term capital gain** and is taxed as regular income). For taxpayers in the 10% and 15% tax brackets, long-term capital gains are taxed at 5%. In 2008, the rate for these lower income taxpayers was reduced to zero.

The tax for long-term capital gains attributable to depreciation remains at 25%. For example, assume a property is purchased for $100,000 and the owner has depreciated it $50,000 so that the owner now has a cost basis of $50,000. If the owner sold the property for $150,000, the taxable gain to the owner would be $100,000. The portion of the gain attributable to depreciation ($50,000) is taxed at the 25% rate, while the balance of the gain ($50,000) would likely be taxed at the 15% rate.

American Taxpayer Relief Act of 2012

Under the American Taxpayer Relief Act of 2012, the capital gains has been permanently increased to 20% for single taxpayers with incomes over $400,000 and married couples filing jointly with incomes above $450,000.

In addition, there is a 3.8% Medicare surcharge for taxpayers whose income exceeds $200,000 for single filers and $250,000 for married couples. Therefore high-income taxpayers could pay 23.8% on their long-term capital gains (20% rate plus the 3.8% surcharge). Because relatively few taxpayers have incomes exceeding the higher rate or surcharge thresholds, most long-term capital gains will be subject to the 15% rate.

Capital Loss

While a homeowner who sells at a loss cannot take tax advantage of the loss, owners of investment property can use a capital loss to offset a capital gain from the sale of another property. For example, if an owner, in one year, sold one investment property at a $100,000 loss and a second investment property at a $100,000 gain, the loss would offset the gain, so no tax is due. If the taxpayer has no gain in the year of the sale to offset the loss, $3,000 of the loss can be used to offset other income and the balance of the loss can be carried forward to succeeding years each with a $3,000 deduction.

Imputed Interest

Interest received is taxable as regular income, but a capital gain is taxed at a lower rate. Some sellers who are carrying back financing will raise the sales price and lower the rate of interest to have a lower total tax liability. To discourage this attempt to avoid taxes, the IRS requires that the lender charge a minimum rate of interest, based on IRS regulations. If a lower rate is charged, then the lender will be taxed for an imputed rate of interest even though it was not received.

Tax-Deferred Exchange

By exchanging property, one can defer capital gains. A **tax-deferred exchange (1031 exchange)** can involve only property held for income and investments, and it must be like-for-like property, real property for real property.

Each party to an exchange keeps the old cost basis, increased by the amount of boot given or decreased by the amount of boot received. **Boot** is any item of personal property (usually money) given to even up a trade. Debt relief (assuming a lower indebtedness on the property received than on the property given) is considered boot. Boot is taxable as gain to the party receiving it.

Section 1031 of the Internal Revenue Code allows for a **delayed exchange** (often called a Starker exchange). A seller of property can indicate that the proceeds be held by an escrow holder to purchase another property. The property to be purchased must be designated within 45 days of the closing of the property sold, and the completion must be completed within 180 days of the closing of the property sold. In a delayed exchange, the seller must never have control of the money.

Depreciation

An owner of income or investment property can deduct depreciation as an expense for tax purposes. This deduction is based on the premise that value decreases with age and depreciation allows the owner to recoup an investment.

For tax purposes, accountants must use a 27.5-year life for residential rental property and a 39-year life for nonresidential property. Only improvements such as buildings can be depreciated; land is never depreciated. Improvements are considered to be wasting assets because value declines with age. However, land is regarded as a permanent asset. Because residential property improvements can be depreciated 100% over 27.5 years, accountants can depreciate 3.636% of the value each and every year until fully depreciated:

$$100\% \div 27.5 = 3.636\%$$

Therefore, if the value of the improvements were $100,000, we could take $3,636 in depreciation each year as an expense for tax purposes. Depreciating equal amounts each year over the life of an improvement is called the straight-line method of depreciation.

Tax Shelter

For business and income property, all expenses are deductible, including depreciation. A tax shelter reduces the income by showing a bookkeeping loss, such as depreciation.

Before the 1986 Tax Reform Act, investors could use their real estate losses to shelter other income—without limit. Noncash losses from depreciation could be used to reduce taxpayer liability to the government. Now, real estate losses, which are considered passive losses, can be used only to offset passive income (income from other real estate activities), with two exceptions:

1. Lower-income investors have retained a limited ability to shelter other nonproperty income. Investors with an adjusted gross income of less than $100,000 can use passive real estate losses to shelter up to $25,000 of other income, such as wages. For taxpayers having between $100,000 and $150,000 of adjusted gross income, this shelter has been phased out. With each $2 of adjusted gross income exceeding $100,000, the $25,000 limit is reduced by $1. Investors who do not actively manage their property (this includes real estate syndicate investors) cannot use their passive losses to shelter active income.

2. Investors who qualify as real estate professionals can use passive losses to offset other income without limitations.

Income Tax Liens

Income tax liens, when recorded, become general liens against all property of the debtor. The property can be sold at a sheriff's sale to satisfy the lien. Purchasers take title subject to all existing prior liens.

FEDERAL ESTATE TAX (INHERITANCE TAX)

The value of estate property is calculated based on the value of the decedent's interest in the property (decedent's equity) at the time of death.

After numerous adjustments, the estate tax exemption was permanently set at $5 million indexed for inflation. In 2014, it was set at $5.34 million. A married couple can combine their separate $5.34 million exemption to total $10.68 million. If one spouse inherits from the deceased spouse, there is no tax. When the surviving spouse dies, the two combined exemptions apply.

Some states also impose taxes on estates.

GIFT TAX

The federal government has a gift tax that taxes the donor. Some states also have gift taxes that tax either the donor or donee.

The federal gift tax currently has a $14,000 annual exemption per donee, so a person having five children could give each of them $14,000 per year ($70,000) without taxation. Because the $14,000 limitation applies to individual donors, the donor's spouse also could give an annual $14,000 gift to each donee, making a total of $140,000 in federal tax-free gifts each year. Real property can be conveyed by gift by giving a fractionalized interest to a donee each year. The purpose of giving gifts often is to reduce the estate so that estate taxes are reduced or eliminated.

YOUR PERTINENT STATE INFORMATION

1. What are your state's appraiser licensing requirements?

2. What are your state's appraiser certification requirements?

3. What are your state requirements for appraisal reports (if any)?

4. Does your state have special treatment for capital gains?

5. Does your state have a two-year homeowner exemption on gains from the sale of a personal residence?

6. Does your state have a gift and/or inheritance tax?

CHAPTER 3 QUIZ

1. What is the tax rate on capital gain if an investor who is in the 25% tax bracket held the property for 12.5 months?
   A. 12.5%
   B. 15%
   C. 25%
   D. 28%

2. In appraising a home for a lender who wishes to make a purchase loan, the appraiser is concerned with
   A. the amount of the loan requested.
   B. property tax assessment.
   C. the price the seller has agreed to pay.
   D. zoning changes in the area.

3. An example of external obsolescence is
   A. numerous pillars supporting the ceiling in a store.
   B. roof leaks, making the premises unrentable.
   C. an older building with very small rooms.
   D. vacant and abandoned structures in the area.

4. A woman paid $190,000 for her home in 2004. She spent $41,000 on improvements to the home. She sold the home in 2007 for $184,000 and incurred closing costs of $11,900. The woman has
   A. a tax loss of $17,900.
   B. a tax loss of $35,100.
   C. a tax loss of $47,900.
   D. no loss for tax purposes.

5. An appraiser would need to determine accrued depreciation when using the
   A. gross rent multiplier method.
   B. cost approach.
   C. income approach.
   D. sales comparison approach.

6. A high rate of inflation is of greatest value to investors who have
   A. invested in long-term, fixed-income investments.
   B. purchased property without the use of leverage.
   C. purchased property using moderate leverage.
   D. purchased property using a high degree of leverage.

7. Which of the following actions by appraisers is unethical?
   A. Refusal to make appraisals that appraisers feel are beyond their expertise
   B. Appraising properties in which appraisers have a disclosed interest
   C. Accepting an appraisal where the fee will be a percentage of the value derived
   D. Requesting payment in advance

8. An appraiser, in using the expression a "willing, informed buyer and a willing, informed seller," is referencing
   A. progression.
   B. supply and demand.
   C. the principle of highest and best use.
   D. market value.

9. Which appraisal method would tend to set the upper limit of value on a new structure?
   A. Gross multiplier
   B. Income approach
   C. Cost approach
   D. Sales comparison approach

10. The advisability of including a tennis court with a planned apartment building may be determined by the principle of
    A. contribution.
    B. progression.
    C. substitution.
    D. change.

11. A single person with an income over $400,000 had a long-term capital gain. The tax rate that applies is
    A. 3.8%.
    B. 15%.
    C. 20%.
    D. 23.8%.

12. A property has a net income of $30,000. One appraiser decides to use a 12% capitalization rate, while a second appraiser uses a 10% rate. Use of the higher rate results in
    A. a 2% increase in appraised value.
    B. a $50,000 increase in appraised value.
    C. a $50,000 decrease in appraised value.
    D. no change in appraised value.

13. An owner has a passive loss of $25,000 on an investment property. If the owner has an adjusted gross income of $125,000, how much of this loss can be used to shelter other than real estate income?
    A. $0
    B. $12,500
    C. $25,000
    D. $50,000

14. To avoid capital gains liability, J traded her commercial lot to K for raw acreage. K gave J $10,000 to balance out the trade. Based on the above,
    A. both parties will pay tax because the trade was not like for like.
    B. J will be taxed on $10,000.
    C. K will be taxed $10,000.
    D. the trade defers all taxes.

15. According to the principle of integration and disintegration,
    A. the value of a property will eventually decline.
    B. property value is best maintained in homogeneous areas.
    C. extraordinary profits will disappear with competition.
    D. the maximum value is based on cost of a comparable property.

16. The reason the gross rent multiplier is an inaccurate measurement of value is that it fails to consider
    A. depreciation.
    B. unusual expenses.
    C. location.
    D. amenity values.

17. A married couple sold their principal residence for $2,400,000. When they purchased the home seven years previously, they paid $1,200,000. Assuming no improvements were made, what is their taxable gain?
    A. $0
    B. $700,000
    C. $1,200,000
    D. $1,900,000

18. Several $250,000 homes were built in an area where the existing homes had been valued at $800,000 to $900,000. The effect was that the value of the existing homes declined. Which real estate principle applies to this situation?
    A. Regression
    B. Competition
    C. Substitution
    D. Integration and disintegration

19. With an annual net income of $40,000 and a capitalization rate of 8%, what is the value of the property using the income approach?
    A. $400,000
    B. $440,000
    C. $500,000
    D. $520,000

20. The time period during which a structure shows income attributable to the structure itself is called its
    A. economic life.
    B. effective age.
    C. diminishing returns.
    D. increasing returns.

21. A developer decided to increase the size of apartments he was building from 1,800 square feet to 2,800 square feet. While the cost of each unit increased by $180,000, the developer discovered that the market value of the larger units was only $120,000 more than that of the smaller units. This is an example of the principle of
    A. change.
    B. anticipation.
    C. diminishing returns.
    D. conformity.

22. A property being appraised has a two-car garage, while a comparable has a three-car garage. In making adjustments, the appraiser would
    A. raise the value of the comparable.
    B. lower the value of the home being appraised.
    C. lower the value of the comparable.
    D. raise the value of the home being appraised.

23. A good definition of market value is the
    A. price paid by the owner.
    B. present worth of future benefits.
    C. assessed valuation.
    D. price offered by a prospective buyer.

24. A homebuyer had a number of expenses related to closing the transaction. Which of the following could be a deduction for federal tax purposes?
    A. Appraisal cost
    B. Title insurance premium.
    C. Discount points
    D. Survey costs

25. The highest and best use is the use that provides the greatest
    A. benefit to the community.
    B. gross.
    C. value.
    D. capitalization rate.

26. Demand is *NOT* effective in determining the value of real property unless it is combined with
    A. scarcity.
    B. a use.
    C. purchasing power.
    D. access.

27. An investor making extraordinary profits from the first miniwarehouse in the area is concerned with the principle of
    A. substitution.
    B. competition.
    C. surplus productivity.
    D. conformity.

28. The principle of supply and demand predicts
    A. increasing price when supply increases.
    B. decreasing demand when supply increases.
    C. increasing demand when price decreases.
    D. decreasing price when demand increases.

29. An appraiser wanted to know the capitalization rate applicable for a recent sale. The net income was reported at $21,000, and the property sold for $300,000. What capitalization rate applied to the sale?
    A. 6%
    B. 7%
    C. 8%
    D. 9%

30. The appraiser gave greatest weight to the value arrived at by the market comparison approach, double-checked that value with the value arrived at by the cost approach, and did not consider the value arrived at using the income approach. The process the appraiser was engaged in is called
    A. the sum of the values.
    B. reconciliation.
    C. the abstractive method.
    D. the index method.

31. The appraiser could calculate the annual gross rent multiplier that applied to a recent sale by
    A. capitalizing the annual gross income.
    B. dividing the annual gross income by the price paid.
    C. dividing the price paid by the annual gross income.
    D. multiplying the monthly gross income by 12.

32. A man who paid $47,000 for a vacant parcel of land has since refinanced the property. The present balance on the mortgage is $128,000. If the man sold the property for $95,000, what is the tax consequence of the sale?
    A. Loss of $33,000
    B. Gain of $48,000
    C. Gain of $81,000
    D. Gain of $128,000

33. A property owner would have the greatest difficulty in correcting depreciation caused by
    A. chronological age.
    B. the built-in nature of the structure.
    C. forces outside the property boundaries.
    D. wear and tear due to use.

34. An appraiser sets a replacement cost of a structure at $120,000 and appraises the land value separately at $80,000. The appraiser places an economic life on the structure at 50 years and states that it has an effective age of 10 years. Using the cost approach, at what amount would the appraiser value this property?
    A. $140,000.
    B. $160,000.
    C. $176,000.
    D. $200,000.

35. In using the sales comparison approach to value to appraise a single-family residence, an appraiser might have to make adjustments for
    A. assessed valuation differences.
    B. a difference in possible rental income.
    C. date of sale.
    D. difference in the capitalization rate.

36. Each unit in a fourplex rents for $225 per month. With a sales price of $81,000, what is the gross rent multiplier?
    A. 7.5
    B. 30
    C. 90
    D. 360

37. Federal law requires that an appraiser be certified for
    A. any appraisal.
    B. any residential appraisals.
    C. any federally related appraisal.
    D. federally related residential appraisals of property valued at more than $250,000.

38. An investor has total annual cash obligations of $187,000 on a property with an annual income of $225,000. The $38,000 difference is called
    A. cash flow.
    B. equity.
    C. arbitrage.
    D. liquidity.

39. A woman intends to borrow $80,000 on her home at 7% interest to pay off credit card loans. As to this home equity loan, the woman should realize that the
    A. loan will increase her tax liability in the event of sale.
    B. interest payments on the home equity loan may be tax-deductible expenses.
    C. cost basis of the home will be increased by $80,000.
    D. $80,000 in proceeds is subject to regular income taxation.

40. With fixed rents and a capitalization rate of 8 percent, an increase in taxes of $4,000 would result in the value of a property
    A. decreasing by $5,000.
    B. decreasing by $50,000.
    C. remaining unchanged.
    D. increasing.

41. The purchaser's down payment is considered what type of funds?
    A. Borrowed
    B. Leveraged
    C. Equity
    D. Capital

42. A property being appraised had 2,400 square feet, but a comparable used by the appraiser had only 2,250 square feet. The appraiser should
    A. disregard the comparable because of dissimilar size.
    B. use the comparable but ignore the slight size difference.
    C. adjust the sales price of the comparable upward because of size difference.
    D. adjust the sales price of the comparable downward because of the size difference.

43. Which appraisal principle indicates the economic effect an improvement has on property?
    A. Progression
    B. Substitution
    C. Surplus
    D. Contribution

44. For tax purposes, residential property is depreciated based on a life of
    A. 15 years.
    B. 27.5 years.
    C. 31 years.
    D. 39 years.

45. R traded a lot to S for an apartment building. R assumed S's $86,000 mortgage, and S assumed R's $115,000 mortgage. No other consideration passed between the parties in this trade. How would this trade be taxed?
    A. R has a $29,000 taxable gain.
    B. S has a $29,000 taxable gain.
    C. S will be taxed as if he received fair market value for the lot.
    D. Neither R nor S has any taxable gain.

46. The first step in appraising an apartment building using the income approach is to determine the
    A. scheduled gross income.
    B. effective gross income.
    C. net income.
    D. vacancy factor.

47. "The whole is worth more than the sum of its parts" refers to
    A. progression.
    B. assemblage.
    C. land residual.
    D. depreciation.

48. Two adjacent residences in the center of a large development had similar values when they were built 60 years ago. They both have been maintained in similar condition and the site values are identical, but one is now worth far more than the other. The reason for the difference in value relates to
    A. physical deterioration.
    B. economic obsolescence.
    C. functional obsolescence.
    D. the principle of integration and disintegration.

49. Which appraisal method is used to determine the present value of future income?
    A. Income approach
    B. Cost approach
    C. Quantity survey method
    D. Sales comparison approach

50. A woman, who lived in her home for six years, got married last month and deeded one-half interest in the home to her new husband. Since they will move to his home, she has placed her home up for sale. What is the maximum exclusion from capital gains tax?
    A. $25,000
    B. $250,000
    C. $500,000
    D. $1,000,000

51. The federal government does NOT require a certified appraiser in a federally related transaction of less than
    A. $250,000.
    B. $500,000.
    C. $1,000,000.
    D. $5,000,000.

52. What type of appraiser is required for an appraisal where there will be a federally related loan in excess of $1,000,000?
    A. Licensed appraiser
    B. State certified appraiser
    C. Federally certified appraiser
    D. MAI

53. How many days after the transfer of a seller's property does the seller have to complete acquisition of another property to qualify for a tax-deferred exchange?
    A. 24 hours
    B. 30 days
    C. 45 days
    D. 180 days

54. Your adjusted cost basis when selling your residence is influenced by
    A. sales price.
    B. depreciation.
    C. a room addition.
    D. maintenance expense.

55. A house has been maintained like new, yet its value has gone down more than 50%. The loss in value is due to
    A. physical deterioration.
    B. plottage.
    C. external obsolescence.
    D. progression.

56. A property had net income of $71,800. One appraiser uses a 10% capitalization rate and another used an 11% rate. The higher rate resulted in a
    A. $7,180 decrease in value.
    B. 10% decrease in value.
    C. $65,273 increase in value.
    D. $65,273 decrease in value.

57. Which of these appraisal activities would occur last?
    A. Define the problem
    B. Determine the purpose of the appraisal
    C. Reconciliation
    D. Gather the facts

58. A lot increased in value because a nearby site was purchased for a university. This is an example of the principle of
    A. anticipation.
    B. change.
    C. progression.
    D. balance.

59. The value based on price paid is
    A. replacement value.
    B. market value.
    C. loan value.
    D. book value.

60. The cost approach combines the replacement cost less depreciation with the
    A. gross multiplier.
    B. abstractive method.
    C. income approach.
    D. sales comparison approach.

61. Capital gains resulting from depreciation that was taken is taxed at a
    A. 15% rate.
    B. 20% rate.
    C. 25% rate.
    D. 30% rate.

62. An appraiser using the capitalization of income approach would have to know
    A. the original construction costs.
    B. the replacement costs.
    C. accrued depreciation.
    D. property taxes.

63. An appraiser wanted to know the cost for building permits, construction supervision, and other construction costs. The appraiser was using the
    A. building residual method.
    B. quantity survey method.
    C. index method.
    D. unit in place method.

64. Licensing and certification of appraisers is required by
    A. FIRREA.
    B. RESPA.
    C. *USPAP.*
    D. Regulation Z.

65. The cost approach is to be used to appraise two homes, one of which is new and the other is 50 years old. The cost approach
    A. has no validity for either appraisal.
    B. is less effective for the 50-year-old house.
    C. is less effective for the new houses
    D. is equally effective for both houses.

66. If L hires appraiser M to appraise land owned by N, then M can discuss the appraisal with
    A. L only.
    B. L or N.
    C. no one.
    D. anyone.

67. How would you measure the quality of income?
    A. By the net spendable
    B. By the capitalization rate
    C. By the pro forma statement
    D. By the cost approach

68. In setting a capitalization rate, an appraiser could add a risk factor to the
    A. prime rate.
    B. federal reserve discount rate.
    C. ARM.
    D. no-risk investment rate.

69. Surplus utility is an example of
    A. progression.
    B. functional obsolescence.
    C. physical deterioration.
    D. economic obsolescence.

70. In a 1031 tax-deferred exchange, which of
    the following is like-for-like?
    A. A lot for an apartment building
    B. A personal residence for a commercial
       property
    C. Jewels for land
    D. A mortgage for a duplex

71. Expenses on income property increase
    $1,000 while income remains constant. With
    a 10% capitalization rate, the value would
    A. remain constant.
    B. fall $1,000.
    C. fall $10,000.
    D. increase $1,000.

72. The *MOST* expensive method of appraisal
    would likely be
    A. gross multiplier.
    B. market comparison.
    C. replacement cost approach.
    D. capitalization of income.

73. The reason that replacement cost is a better
    appraisal approach for new buildings than
    for old buildings is
    A. neighborhood influence.
    B. difficulty in determining cost when built.
    C. difficulty in ascertaining depreciation.
    D. the difference in construction methods.

74. In determining external obsolescence, an
    appraiser is interested in
    A. the management of the property.
    B. deferred maintenance of the property.
    C. development of nearby farmland for a
       shopping center.
    D. the floor plan of the property.

75. Imputed interest refers to
    A. interest charged but uncollectible.
    B. interest charged by the IRS as received
       when it was not received.
    C. usury rate.
    D. index rate.

76. Which date is *MOST* important to an
    appraiser?
    A. Appraisal
    B. Purchase agreement
    C. Loan commitment
    D. Loan closing

77. A depth table is used by
    A. surveyors.
    B. appraisers.
    C. water district.
    D. lenders.

78. The *BEST* appraisal method for appraising a
    church is the
    A. sales comparison approach.
    B. replacement cost approach.
    C. capitalization of income approach.
    D. gross multiplier.

79. Raising the capitalization rate from that used
    on similar property would imply a
    A. greater value.
    B. greater risk.
    C. higher income.
    D. stable income.

80. Which appraisal method would balance out
    amenities?
    A. Cost approach
    B. Sales comparison approach
    C. Income approach
    D. Gross multiplier

CHAPTER 3 QUIZ ANSWERS

1. **(B)** The holding period is over 12 months. Income is too low for 20% rate or surcharge. (82)

2. **(D)** This could indicate external obsolescence as well as progression or regression. The others don't affect the property's value. (69)

3. **(D)** External obsolescence deals with forces outside the property itself. (A) and (C) are functional obsolescence, whereas (B) is physical deterioration. (69)

4. **(D)** A homeowner cannot take a loss on the sale of a residence. (82)

5. **(B)** It is the cost to build today less accrued depreciation, plus the value of the land. (70)

6. **(D)** The investors get the appreciation benefits of inflation but pay back loan with cheaper dollars. (81)

7. **(C)** This could create the appearance of a conflict of interest. It is all right to have an interest in the property being appraised so long as there is open and full disclosure. (78)

8. **(D)** See the definition of market value. (65)

9. **(C)** Cost approach tends to set upper limits on value. (70)

10. **(A)** What will the tennis court contribute to the anticipated net income? (Capitalize the anticipated increase in net income to determine the value of the tennis court.) (66)

11. **(D)** 20% rate plus 3.8% surcharge. (82)

12. **(C)** Increasing the rate decreases the value. Value moves inversely to the capitalization rate: (72–73)

    net ÷ rate = value

    $30,000 ÷ 0.1 = $300,000

    $30,000 ÷ 0.12 = $250,000

13. **(B)** Each $2 of adjusted gross income over $100,000 reduces the nonproperty income tax shelter by $1. (84)

14. **(B)** The party who receives boot is taxed on the boot received. (83)

15. **(A)** Property goes through three phases—integration, equilibrium, and disintegration. (66)

16. **(B)** Because of unusual expenses, the gross may bear little relationship to the net. (73)

17. **(B)** Their gain was $1,200,000. They have a $500,000 exclusion, so $700,000 is taxed. (79–80)

18. **(A)** The new lower-value homes negatively affected the value of the more expensive homes. (66)

19. **(C)** Divide the net by the capitalization rate to determine value: (72)

    $40,000 ÷ 0.08 = $500,000

20. **(A)** When the property no longer returns an income attributable to the structure itself, it has exceeded its economic life. (71)

21. **(C)** A point was reached where the cost for additional size was less than additional value. (66)

22. **(C)** The sales price of the comparable is adjusted to the property being appraised. (69)

23. **(B)** Whereas an appraiser estimates the value, (B) is its definition. What one buyer paid does not determine a property's value. (65)

24. **(C)** Discount points paid by a buyer are considered prepaid interest (80)

25. **(C)** It is that use that will provide the greatest value attributable to the property. (67)

26. **(C)** Demand without purchasing power is only a wish. (67)

27. **(B)** Whenever extraordinary profits are being made, competition produces additional units that reduce profits. (66)

28. **(C)** When supply exceeds demand, prices drop. When demand exceeds supply, prices rise. As prices drop, there are more buyers (demand); as prices rise, there are fewer buyers. (66–67)

29. **(B)** Divide the net income by the price paid to determine the capitalization rate used. (72)

30. **(B)** Reconciliation (correlation) involves use of applicable methods, with the appraiser giving greatest weight to the approach that has the greatest relevance to the property being appraised. (74)

31. **(C)** You also can get the monthly gross rent multiplier by dividing the price paid by the monthly gross income. (73)

32. **(B)** The gain is determined by the difference between cost basis and sales price. (81)

33. **(C)** Because external obsolescence is caused by forces outside the property, it is extremely difficult for a property owner to correct it alone. (A) and (D) refer to physical deterioration and (B) to functional obsolescence. (75)

34. **(C)** Replacement cost less depreciation plus land equals value. A 50-year life means 2% depreciation per year; 2% × 10 = 20%; 0.20 × $120,000 = $24,000; $120,000 − $24,000 + $80,000 = $176,000. (71)

35. **(C)** When the market has changed since a comparable sale, an adjustment is necessary. (69)

36. **(A)** (73)

    $225 × 4 = $900 per month

    $900 × 12 = $10,800 per year

    $81,000 ÷ $10,800 = 7.5 GRM

37. **(D)** In addition, licensed appraisers must be used for federally related residential appraisals of property valued at $250,000 or less. (76–77)

38. **(A)** Spendable cash. (81)

39. **(B)** The woman can deduct interest on equity loans up to $100,000, provided all combined loans do not exceed fair market value of the home. (80)

40. **(B)** The increase in expenses of $4,000 with fixed rents will mean a $4,000 reduction in net. Capitalizing $4,000 (divided by 0.08) equals $50,000. (73)

41. **(C)** An owner's equity is the difference between value and indebtedness. (81)

42. **(C)** When the comparable has a lesser feature (or lacks a feature), raise the sales price of the comparable. If the comparable is better, lower the sales price of comparable. (69)

43. **(D)** This is used to determine the economic viability of an improvement. (66)

44. **(B)** Thirty-nine years is used for nonresidential property. (83)

45. **(A)** R's debt relief is boot and is taxable as a capital gain. Note that the property is regarded as like-for-like. (83)

46. **(A)** The scheduled gross then must be adjusted for a vacancy factor. (72)

47. **(B)** The added value due to assemblage is plottage value. (67)

48. **(C)** It is built-in obsolescence by design (outmoded or less desirable floor plan or design). Other choices are ruled out by the facts. (69, 75)

49. **(A)** Capitalizing the net determines the present value of future income. (72–73)

50. **(B)** The woman's husband does not meet the residency rule of two out of five years. (79–80)

51. **(A)** A certified appraiser is not required. (77)

52. **(B)** The state, not the federal government, certifies appraisers. (76–77)

53. **(D)** Must be designated within 45 days. (83)

54. **(C)** Adjusted cost basis is price paid plus improvements minus depreciation, but personal residences cannot be depreciated. (79)

55. **(C)** Forces outside the property. (69, 75)

56. **(D)** The 10% rate gives value of $718,000, while the 11% rate gives value of $652,727 or $65,273 less. (73)

57. **(C)** Reconciliation determines value using all appraisal methods. Final action is to report value. (74)

58. **(A)** Based on planned university's effect on value. (66)

59. **(B)** Cost plus improvements less depreciation. (65)

60. **(D)** Used to add land value. (70)

61. **(C)** The 15% capital gains rule does not apply to the portion of the gain resulting from depreciation. (82)

62. **(D)** Appraiser must determine net income. (72)

63. **(B)** To determine replacement cost for cost approach. (70)

64. **(A)** Federal Financial Institutions Reform Recovery and Enforcement Act. (76)

65. **(B)** Cost approach works well on new structures because depreciation need not be considered. (70)

66. **(A)** Only with the principal. (78)

67. **(B)** The capitalization rate is adjusted to reflect the quality of income. (72)

68. **(D)** Such as the rate paid on government bonds. (72)

69. **(B)** Such as a two-bedroom home with five baths. Extra baths would not contribute to value. (75)

70. **(A)** A real property for real property qualifies for a 1031 exchange if held for business or investment. (83)

71. **(C)** Since the capitalization rate is divided into net to determine value. (72–73)

72. **(C)** Must ascertain both cost to build today and accrued depreciation. (70–71)

73. **(C)** It tends to be subjective. (70)

74. **(C)** External obsolescence deals with matters outside the property that can affect value. (75)

75. **(B)** Interest is imputed when seller financing has unreasonably low interest rate. (83)

76. **(A)** An appraisal is valid as of the day it is made. (78)

77. **(B)** It shows the effect of additional or lesser depth. (75)

78. **(B)** Because it is a service-type building. (70)

79. **(B)** The greater the risk the higher the capitalization rate. (72)

80. **(B)** Comparables are adjusted for amenities. (69)

CHAPTER 4

Contracts and Agency

CONTRACTS

Real estate transactions are ruled by specific documents such as leases, listings, and offers to purchase. Such documents spell out the contractual rights and obligations agreed to by parties to certain transactions. Therefore, much of this chapter addresses the general area of law called contract law. An understanding of contracts is essential in dealing with real estate. In simple terms, a contract is an agreement enforceable by law.

Good faith refers to acting honestly without deception. An implied duty of good faith applies to the performance and enforcement of a contract. Parties must act in a manner consistent with the justified expectations of the other party.

Types of Contracts

Bilateral contract.   A contract that contains a promise made in exchange for a promise is a bilateral contract. Sales agreements are bilateral—promises to buy given for promises to sell. Similarly, an exclusive right-to-sell listing is a bilateral contract in which the owner agrees to pay a commission if the agent is successful and the agent in return agrees to use best efforts to locate a buyer.

Unilateral contract.   A contract that contains a promise contingent on the performance of an act is a unilateral contract. Acceptance of the promise is not in the form of another promise but in the form of an act. For example, assume a property manager promised to pay a man $100 to remove trash from a property. If the man removed the trash, he is entitled to the $100 even though he was not obligated to perform. His performance of an act made the acceptance.

Executed contract.   An executed contract is one that has been fully performed. For example, a purchase contract is executed upon closing.

Executory contract.   An executory contract has yet to be fully performed but is not in default. For example, before the closing, a purchase contract is executory.

Express contract.   An express contract is one specifically agreed to, either verbally or in writing. Because they are required by the statute of frauds to be in writing, real estate contracts are express contracts. The statute of frauds is covered later in this chapter.

Implied contract.   An implied contract is one that is understood because of actions of the parties, although a specific agreement is not stated. For example, in asking a carpenter to make repairs, you might fail to specify a fee. It is implied, however, that you will pay a fair price for the services received.

Valid Contracts

Contracts that meet all legal requirements are valid and enforceable, which means that either party can hold the other party responsible for the agreement. Four requirements must be met before a contract is valid.

1. Competent parties.   Contracting parties must have mental and legal capacity to enter into a valid contract. Persons found to be mentally incompetent cannot contract. Legal capacity is determined by legal age, which is set by law. In most states, the legal age for contracting is 18. In some states, deeds by minors are considered void, while in other states, deeds by minors are considered voidable, which means that the minor may elect to be bound by the agreement or to void the agreement at the minor's option. A minor can buy real estate from an adult; however, the minor has the option of voiding the transaction. Therefore, great care must be exercised when dealing with a minor. A minor could, of course, receive real estate as a gift. In some states, **emancipated minors**, such as married minors, are allowed to contract as adults.

Individual state laws govern the right of convicted prisoners to contract. These rights generally are restricted.

2. Mutual agreement.   To have a valid contract, there must be a meeting of the minds, that is, mutual assent, normally evidenced by an offer and acceptance. A unilateral mistake on the part of one party only will not allow that person to get out of the contract. For example, if a buyer mistakenly believed that the zoning would allow a particular use, and the seller had done nothing to indicate that the buyer's secret plans were possible, the buyer could not void the agreement because of her own error. However, a mutual mistake of fact or impossibility of performance makes the contract unenforceable. For example, assume the buyer and the seller both believed an irregularly shaped parcel contained the necessary square footage to construct a duplex. If they later discovered that the actual square footage was less than believed, so that a duplex could not be built, the buyer could likely void the agreement based on the mutual mistake.

3. Consideration.   For an agreement between two parties to be binding, the parties must give or promise something of value, called **consideration**. A promise unsupported by consideration really is a promise to make a gift and, therefore, is unenforceable. Consideration does not have to be fair, although grossly inadequate consideration could be evidence of fraud or undue influence.

Love and affection are deemed to be "good consideration." However, they are not deemed to be the "valuable consideration" required to support a contract. **Valuable consideration** is a right, an interest, a profit, or an agreement to refrain from a lawful act, any one of which the promissor considers valuable. Consideration, then, need not be money, but it must have worth.

4. Legal purpose.   To be enforceable, a contract must be for a legal purpose. A contract made for an unlawful purpose is illegal and is void and unenforceable by either party. For example, a contract in violation of state or federal antitrust laws is void and unenforceable.

Finally, some contracts have a fifth requirement: they must be in writing to be enforceable in a court of law.

Statute of Frauds

In old England, real estate was considered the basis of all wealth. Real estate transactions were so important that the statute of frauds required every real estate contract to be in writing to be enforceable. The agreement must be signed by the person who is sought to be bound. Every state has a statute of frauds that requires particular agreements to be written and to be signed by the party to be held to the agreement. Forty-seven states have passed the Uniform Electronic Transactions Act (UETA), which gives legal recognition to electronic signatures, such as email documents, in business transactions.

Verbal contracts can be valid and enforceable, unless they are required by the statute of frauds to be in writing. State statutes of fraud usually require that the following be in writing:

■   All agreements for the sale of real estate (in most states, listing agreements must be in writing because real estate is involved; however, a few states allow oral listing agreements that are one year or less in term)

■   Any lease for more than one year (however, some states allow verbal leases for more than one year)

■   Contracts that by their terms cannot be fully performed within one year of the parties entering into the agreements

■   Promises to pay the debt of another

■   Promises made in contemplation of marriage

■   Contracts for the sale of personal property for more than $500

Although executory verbal real estate contracts are unenforceable, fully executed agreements are valid transfers. For example, a verbal promise to sell a house for $300,000 cannot be enforced, but once the consideration has been paid and the title transferred, the transaction is complete and cannot be set aside because it was based on a verbal agreement.

The courts may allow enforcement of a verbal real estate purchase contract, even though the statute of frauds requires a written agreement, in cases where there has been partial performance based on the verbal agreement. This is the **doctrine of estoppel**, whereby a person is prohibited (estopped) from disavowing a verbal promise after the other party has acted to his detriment based on that promise.

For example, assume there was a verbal agreement for the sale of a lot for $30,000. Assume also that the prospective buyer, with the knowledge of the seller, spent $40,000 bringing utilities to the lot and preparing the site for construction. A court would likely determine that the seller was estopped from raising the defense of the statute of frauds because of the buyer's reliance on the verbal agreement. Of course, the buyer would have to prove the existence of the verbal agreement.

While verbal evidence may be used to show fraud, misrepresentation, or mutual mistake or to clarify ambiguities, and so on, the **parol evidence rule** prohibits the introduction of prior or contemporaneous verbal testimony to modify a written contract that appears complete upon its face.

Void Contracts

Any contract that fails to meet one or more contractual requirements is void and unenforceable by either party to the agreement.

Voidable Contracts

Voidable contracts are valid unless voided. Only one party—the innocent party to the transaction—can void the agreement or elect to be bound by it (the innocent party is the one not guilty of a wrongful act). The following factors are among those that may make contracts voidable.

Duress or menace.   Contracts entered into under force (duress) or threat of force (menace) may be voided by the injured party.

Fraud.   Fraud is an intentional statement or omission that persuades or influences another to act to that person's harm. It can also be a false statement made by a person who did not know whether it was true or false. Concealing a material defect or fact could also be fraud (negative fraud).

Fraud can be a criminal, as well as a civil, wrong. The injured party may void a contract entered into because of fraud.

Fraud as to the nature of the contract could make the contract void rather than voidable. An example is an owner representing a purchase contract as an option to buy.

Misrepresentation.   Misrepresentation is a misstatement or concealment of an important fact so that another party is led to act to her own detriment. Whereas fraud requires the element of intent to deceive, misrepresentation could be a false statement made by someone who believed it to be true. Misrepresentation also allows a contract to be voided and, like fraud, could subject the wrongdoer to civil damages.

If a person knew that a statement was false or that a material fact was being concealed, the contract would not be voidable by that person because that person was not deceived into acting to his own detriment.

Undue influence.   Undue influence exists when a person's actions are the result of an overpowering relationship rather than voluntary. If L enters into an unfair contract with M against L's own free will because of their confidential relationship (client/attorney, broker/owner, doctor/patient, parent/child), L can void the agreement.

Minor status.   A minor may generally disaffirm a contract within a reasonable period after reaching contractual age; however, a minor cannot disaffirm a contract for necessity, such as food or clothing.

Unconscionable contracts.   If a contract is so harsh that a court considers it unconscionable (shockingly unfair), the court will refuse to enforce it.

Puffing.   Puffing is merely a statement of opinion ("this is a good value"). It is not generally considered sufficient basis to void a contract, even though the statement influences another party to act to that party's detriment.

Offer and Acceptance

An offer is made by an offeror and expresses that person's willingness to enter into a particular agreement (see Figure 4.1). The offeree is the person to whom the offer is made. When the offeree accepts the offer, a contract is formed. Unless the offer specifies a particular period of time for acceptance, it is considered held open for acceptance for a reasonable time. A newspaper advertisement usually is not regarded as an offer but merely an invitation to negotiate.

FIGURE 4.1

Offer and Acceptance

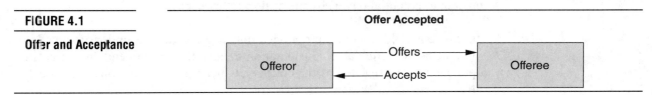

If an offer states a time for acceptance but fails to indicate that **time is of the essence**, the courts could allow acceptance after the period for acceptance expires. If "time is of the essence" is stated in the offer, acceptance must occur within the period specified or the offer is canceled automatically.

If the offer fails to specify the form for acceptance (letter, telephone call, telegram, or even performance), the offer may be accepted in any reasonable manner. Acceptance does not take place until the offeror is notified, which usually is by delivery of a signed, accepted copy of the offer to the offeror. The statute of frauds requires that offers and acceptances for the sale of real estate be in writing.

Revocation of offer.   Because the offeror did not receive any consideration for making the offer, the offeror can withdraw or revoke the offer anytime before its acceptance. This applies even when the offeror promises to keep the offer open for a specified period. The act of placing an acceptance in the mail is acceptance; however, a mailed revocation of an offer does not take effect until it is received.

Death of offeror.   The death of the offeror or offeree before acceptance voids the offer automatically. The death of the offeror or offeree after acceptance does not affect the agreement, which becomes binding on the estate of the deceased party. However, if a contract called for the personal services of one of the parties to the contract, such as the services of a well-known architect, that party's death would terminate the agreement. The death of a corporate officer of the offeror or offeree corporation does not terminate the offer because a corporation is regarded in law as a separate being.

Counteroffer. A conditional acceptance that varies from the original offer because of a new or changed requirement customarily is regarded as a counteroffer and not an acceptance (see Figure 4.2). Because a counteroffer is really a rejection of the original offer, the original offeree now becomes an offeror with a new offer. The original offeror (now the offeree) can either accept the new offer and form a binding contract or reject that offer. Once an offer is rejected, it is considered dead, and any later acceptance constitutes a new offer.

FIGURE 4.2	Counteroffer Made and Accepted
Counteroffer	

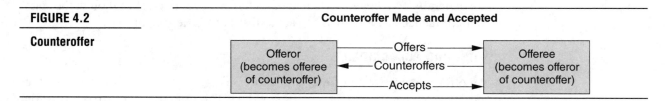

Options

An option keeps an offer open. It is a right to buy or lease property at a specified price during a designated period of time. The option right is given to the **optionee** (potential buyer) by the **optionor** (owner).

To create a valid option, the optionee must have given the optionor something of value as nonrefundable consideration to keep the offer open. Once given, an option cannot be revoked by the optionor, which makes the option an irrevocable offer.

An option is a unilateral contract until it is exercised because, while the optionor is bound by an irrevocable offer, the optionee need not exercise the option. Once the option is exercised, it becomes a bilateral contract with both optionor and optionee bound to their promises.

Right of First Refusal

A right of first refusal gives the holder the right to buy or lease a property only if the owner decides to sell or lease it to another person. It is the right to match an offer, within a designated period of time that an owner is otherwise prepared to accept. The owner, however, is under no obligation to sell or lease the property. This differs from an option, where the owner must sell or lease if the optionee wishes to exercise the option.

Rights of first refusal are often found in leases giving the tenant first chance at any purchase or later lease agreement the owner wishes to accept.

Remedies for Breach of Contract

A breach of contract is a failure to comply with a key provision of the contract, which entitles the party who is not in default to seek one of the available remedies. A **renunciation** by one party or indicating the party would or could not perform is an **anticipatory breach** that would allow legal action even if performance was not yet due. Following are some legal remedies for broken contractual promises.

Compensatory damages.   Money awarded by the court to the injured party to make up for the loss suffered is called **compensatory damages**.

Assume a seller agreed to sell a lot for $100,000 and later refused to honor the agreement. If the buyer had to pay $110,000 for a similarly desirable lot, the buyer could seek compensatory damages in the amount of $10,000.

If a buyer refused to complete a purchase, then the seller could seek to recover damages suffered. If a later sale resulted in a lower price, the seller could sue for the loss plus additional costs.

The injured party has a duty to try to keep the damages as low as reasonably possible when a contract is breached. This effort is called **mitigation of damages**. For example, if a tenant breaks a lease, the landlord has a duty to use reasonable effort to obtain a new tenant.

Punitive or exemplary damages.   Courts may award damages beyond compensatory damages to punish (punitive) or make an example of (exemplary) a party who committed a willful and/or an outrageous act or breach of an agreement.

Nominal damages.   If a breach does not result in an actual dollar loss, a token amount—called **nominal damages**—is awarded. For example, a court might award nominal damages for a wrongful trespass where no money damages occurred.

Liquidated damages.   Liquidated damages are breach-of-contract compensation agreed on by the parties at the time of their agreement. Construction contracts often include a daily liquidated damages amount if a job is not completed on time, and purchase contracts customarily provide for the buyer to give up the earnest money deposit in the event of the buyer's breach. If liquidated damages are set too high, the courts might determine that they are actually penalties, which are unenforceable.

Specific performance.   If an owner enters into a contract to sell real property and later refuses to convey the property, the buyer can request performance (specific performance) rather than money damage. Because every parcel of real estate is unique, money damages are not always an adequate remedy. Courts will, therefore, grant the remedy of specific performance for real estate contracts. Courts generally will not grant specific performance if the consideration is not considered adequate.

Injunction.   An injunction is a court order to stop doing a certain activity (cease and desist). Injunctions may be permanent or temporary.

Reformation.   An action to correct a mistake in an agreement or a deed is called **reformation**. The action amends an agreement to conform to the original intention.

Rescission.   Rescission cancels the contract and restores the parties to the positions they held before entering into the contract. One party can use a breach by the other party as the basis for rescinding the contract. **Restitution** is the return of consideration when a contract is rescinded.

Waiver.   A party to a contract can waive a contractual breach by the other party and choose to remain bound by the contract. For example, a buyer might waive the seller's failure to correct a defect and, in doing so, insist on closing.

A party also can waive any provisions for her sole benefit. For example, if an agreement was contingent upon the buyer obtaining an 80% loan at no more than 7% interest, the buyer could waive the contingency if such a loan could not be obtained and choose to go ahead with the transaction. Waiver leaves the parties as they are; rescission puts them back the way they were.

Accord and satisfaction.   Accord and satisfaction is the agreement to accept a lesser consideration than that specified in a contract. Such agreement is common in construction contracts when there is disagreement as to proper performance of the work.

Novation.   Substitution of a new contract for an old one is called *novation*. Parties to a novation agree to cancel the old contract in favor of the new agreement, as when a buyer and a builder make a contract for a model home that is different from the one originally chosen and named in a contract. Novation also is considered to occur when all parties agree to the substitution of a new party for one of the original contract parties and to the full release of the original party from all obligations under the agreement (novations may be used in loan assumptions in which the seller is released from all loan obligations by the substitution of the buyer).

Statute of limitations.   A state statute of limitations defines the period of time during which various types of legal action must be brought. The statute of limitations starts on the date an obligation is due. If no payment is made or no legal action taken during the prescribed period, the right to enforce the agreement is lost. For example, assume that your state has a four-year statute of limitations on written contracts. If a person was obligated under a written contract to pay the sum of $10,000 to another person by a specified date, the person entitled to the $10,000 is barred from forcing a collection if more than four years had elapsed from the date the money was due.

Interpretation of Contracts

Generally speaking, the courts will try to interpret contracts in accordance with the intent of the parties. Words will be given their common meaning within the trade or profession involved.

If more than one meaning is possible in interpreting a contract, the contract is ambiguous. The courts attempt to resolve ambiguities based on the intent of the parties. If the ambiguities are such that intent cannot be identified, a contract is considered unenforceable because it lacks mutual agreement.

Typed material takes priority over the printed form, and handwritten portions take priority over typed content because these additions to a printed or typed contract clearly indicate the intent of the parties.

Written words take priority over numerals. For example, if a contract states, "forty-six thousand dollars ($40,000)," $46,000, not $40,000, would stand as the contractual amount.

In the event of an ambiguity between two or more documents, a later agreement generally takes precedence over a prior agreement because it is assumed that the later, or latest one, indicates the final intent of the parties. For example, broker compensation in the purchase contract may be different from that agreed to in the agency listing. The later agreement in the purchase agreement would govern, if also signed by the broker.

Obvious typographical errors can be disregarded.

For a "take it or leave it contract," also called a **contract of adhesion**, ambiguities are resolved against the party drafting the instrument (an example of a contract by adhesion is a preprinted insurance policy).

Assignment of Contracts

Assignment of a contract is the transfer of all the interests of one of the contractual parties to a third person. Contracts that do not specifically prohibit assignment can be transferred without the approval of the other contracting party. However, contracts that are personal in nature (for particular personal services) cannot be assigned. For example, if a party contracted with a particular distinguished real estate broker to negotiate a lease, that broker could not assign the contract to another broker because the contract is considered personal in nature.

In an assignment, the assignee takes the place of the assignor and is primarily liable for the contractual duties of the assignor. The assignor, however, retains secondary liability, which means that the assignor could be held to the contract should the assignee fail to perform. This situation differs from a novation, in which a new party is completely substituted for the old party, who is released from all contract liability.

Uniform Vendor and Purchaser Risk Act

Under the **doctrine of equitable conversion**, the purchaser became the equitable owner when a purchase contract was entered into. The buyer therefore took the risk of loss. This view has been modified. A number of states have adopted the Uniform Vendor and Purchase Risk Act, which provides that

- if neither possession nor title is given to the purchaser and the purchaser is not the cause of damage to the property, then risk of loss is on the seller who cannot enforce the contract and must return any money paid; and

- if title or possession is given to purchaser and property is damaged without the fault of the seller, then the purchaser suffers the loss. Purchase contracts will often specify when risk of loss passes.

AGENCY

An **agency** is a personal relationship freely entered into whereby the **agent** acts for another, the **principal**. To appoint an agent, the principal must have contractual capacity (mental and legal capacity).

While a **client** is the principal that employs an agent to whom the agent has agency duties, the **customer** is a buyer or a seller not represented by the agent.

The principal is liable for the acts of the agent within the scope of the agency (**vicarious liability**). Vicarious liability is being liable for actions of another even when not directly responsible for the harmful act because of the relationship of the parties. Similarly an employing broker could be held liable for the wrongful act of a salesperson while acting on the broker's behalf. It does not matter whether an agent receives compensation. An agent who acts without compensation has the same duties to the parties as an agent who is paid by the principal.

Vicarious liability for actions of others is the reason that owners and brokers often elect to contract with one another as facilitators or transaction brokers rather than as an agency arrangement.

A real estate broker acts as agent of an owner or a buyer, or the broker may, in some states, even act as a dual agent. The salesperson is a subagent of the broker's principal. The listing broker is the agent of the principal. While real estate salespersons are generally regarded as agents of their employing broker and subagents of the broker's principal, in some states, real estate salespersons are considered agents rather than subagents.

Buyer agency has largely replaced subagency, where the selling agent was the agent of the listing broker rather than the seller.

Seller and Buyer Agency

Historically, real estate agents were seller agents with fiduciary duties to the seller and a duty to the buyer of fair play and to disclose negative information that they were aware of regarding the property.

There has been a significant growth of buyer agency where the broker is the agent of the buyer, regardless of who is paying the commission, and has a duty to fulfill the needs of the buyer in as advantageous a manner to the buyer as possible. Where an agent represents either a buyer or a seller, it is called a **single agency**.

Dual Agency

In some states, it is possible for a broker to elect to be a dual agent. A **dual agency** is also called a limited agency. As a dual agent, the broker would have agency duties to both buyer and seller or lessor and lessee. While dual agency agreements prohibit the broker from passing on confidential information received from one principal to the other principal, dual agencies can create a serious conflict of interest. Where dual agency is possible, the broker must obtain consent from both principals to the dual agency representation. A principal who was unaware of a broker's dual agency would likely have the right to return any compensation paid, as well as the right to void any contract entered into.

A broker could inadvertently create a dual agency if the broker's words and/or actions led a party to believe that the broker was representing her. If this should happen, the broker could be held to have agency duties to both parties to the transaction.

Designated Agency (Split Agency)

This agency relationship is not authorized in all states. It allows a listing salesperson for a firm to be the designated agent (**sole agent**) of the seller. If another salesperson from the same firm procures a buyer, that salesperson could be the designated agent of the buyer. There would then be two separate agencies under a single broker. In some states, the broker must act as a transaction broker or facilitator if licensees in the office are separately representing the buyer and the seller.

Facilitator/Intermediary/Transaction Broker

This is a relatively new concept that has been adopted in a few states. The facilitator, intermediary, or transaction broker works with both the buyer and the seller as a middleman rather than as an agent. The broker has no advocacy or fiduciary duties but must nevertheless be fair and honest with both buyer and seller. The facilitator does have a duty of confidentiality as to confidential information received from the parties. While not an advocate or agent of either party, the broker works to structure transactions to meet the needs of the parties. To avoid vicarious liability associated with agency, there has been a significant increase in the number of brokers electing a nonagency facilitator type relationship rather than the more traditional agency relationship. Some states require that the broker take an agency position, which precludes being a facilitator, an intermediary, or a transaction broker.

Agency Disclosure

To avoid accidentally creating a dual agency or allowing a party to have a misconception of the broker's role, all states require that the broker disclose agency status in writing to both buyer and seller before the signing of a purchase agreement. This disclosure generally applies to both listing and selling agents. The agency relationship specified could be buyer's agency, seller's agency, dual agency, designated agency, or even a nonagency facilitator role, where applicable.

Cooperating Broker

Some **multiple listing services (MLSs)** offer cooperating brokers subagency as an agent of the listing broker. In some states, it is possible for the cooperating broker to elect to be a dual agent.

Most cooperating brokers will represent buyers as a single agency or act as facilitators. In such cases, the cooperating broker would decline subagency, if offered.

Agreements between brokers to split commissions usually need to be in writing because they involve a dollar amount that is high enough to bring them under the statute of frauds.

Power of Attorney

A **power of attorney** is a particular written agency agreement whereby the principal authorizes another person, the agent, to act in the place of the principal as an **attorney-in-fact**. A specific power of attorney applies to one particular act, such as signing a deed in place of the principal. A general power of attorney allows the attorney-in-fact to obligate a principal in almost any way that the principal could have obligated himself. In real estate, a power of attorney is occasionally used when the principal is unavailable. A power of attorney that authorizes the attorney-in-fact to convey real property must be recorded for the attorney-in-fact to convey a marketable title. In some states, an agent cannot sign a deed.

Types of Agents

Special agent.   A real estate broker who has authority only for designated acts is a special agent. An example is a broker, who customarily has authorization to locate a buyer or a seller for a property but not to consummate a sale on the owner's or buyer's behalf.

General agent.   A general agent has all the authority necessary to conduct a business or trade. A general manager of a real estate office or a property manager might be a general agent. The term **universal agent** describes a broad general agency where the agent is appointed to do all acts a principal can lawfully delegate to another.

Agency Creation

An agency can be created in a number of ways.

Express agency.   An express (stated) agency is created by written or verbal agreement. A listing, for example, creates an express agency where the broker is the agent of the principal.

Agency by implication.   An agency that is understood by the words or conduct of the parties, although not specifically agreed to, is an agency by implication. By actions or words of an agent, a prospective buyer could reasonably be led to believe the seller's agent was representing him or her. In such a case, an implied agency could be formed that would obligate the agent to both buyer and seller (dual agency). Similarly, if a broker who wished to act as a facilitator, by words and/or actions reasonably leads a person to believe that the broker was representing her, then there could be an implied agency to that party.

Agency by estoppel.   A person might be estopped (prohibited) from denying an agency exists if that person's words or actions reasonably led a third person to act to his detriment based on the third person's belief as to the existence of the agency. For example, assume owner J told prospective tenant K that L was J's exclusive commercial leasing agent when, in fact, no agency had ever been established. Based on J's representation, K gave L a $10,000 deposit on a lease. Neither L nor the deposit can now be located. J would likely be barred from denying the existence of the agency, by estoppel, because J's words led K to act.

Agency by ratification.   An agency is created when a principal's acceptance of the benefits of an unauthorized agent's act or an act beyond the agent's authority ratifies an agency relationship. For example, assume that agent P entered into a lease claiming to be the owner's agent but had no actual authorization from the owner. If, after learning of the transaction, the owner accepts rent under the lease, the owner will have ratified the agency and will be liable for the terms of the lease.

Duties of the Agent

Fiduciary duty.   An agent has a fiduciary duty to the principal. A fiduciary duty is one of trust. There are five elements to the fiduciary duty.

1. *Care*. The agent must exercise due care, which is reasonable and diligent care, in carrying out the duties of the agency.

2. *Obedience*. The agent has a duty to obey the lawful instructions of the principal. The owner decides on list price, as well as any p rice adjustments. While the agent should make recommendations based on the principal's best interest, the principal's instructions must be obeyed. An agent who fails to obey instructions or who exceeds the authority given by the principal could be liable for resulting damages. If instructions given to the agent require that the agent perform or be an accomplice to an illegal act, the agent must withdraw from the agency.

3. *Accounting*. The agent must account for all funds received or disbursed on behalf of the principal.

4. *Loyalty*. The agent must be loyal to the principal. The agent cannot disclose to third parties any facts about the principal or the agency that are not in the principal's best interest. An agent may not act for more than one party in a transaction without the knowledge and approval of all the parties. The agent must place the interest of the principal above his personal interest should their interests conflict. Making a secret profit, regardless of amount, violates the agent's fiduciary duty. The duty to protect the interests of the principal includes warning of known risks or dangers and advising the principal to seek professional advice should the need for such assistance be indicated.

5. *Disclosure*. The agent has a duty of full disclosure and must inform the principal of any facts likely to influence the principal's decision making process. For example, if a seller's agent realizes that a buyer is willing to pay more than is being offered, a seller's agent would have a duty to inform the seller of this fact. Every offer received must be transmitted promptly to the principal. In many states, this disclosure extends to verbal, as well as written offers and even subsequent offers received after another offer has been accepted.

Remember the acronym **COALD**: **C**are, **O**bedience, **A**ccounting, **L**oyalty, and **D**isclosure.

Seller agent's duties to buyer (customer).   Even though a broker's primary duties under a sale listing are to the principal, the seller's agent has a duty to deal with buyers (customers) in good faith. All the agent's dealings must be fair and honest. Therefore, the agent must disclose to the buyer any known facts of a material nature affecting the property or title. If in doubt, disclose. The agent's creed should be "disclose, disclose, disclose."

In several states, an agent has the affirmative duty to make a reasonably diligent inspection of the property and to disclose to the prospective buyer any detrimental information discovered by the inspection. The broker must also disclose any known **latent defect** that would not be apparent from a visual inspection. An agent who knows that an intended use by a prospective buyer is not feasible or possible has the affirmative duty to disclose that fact. An agent may not disclose that a former owner or tenant had AIDS. State laws differ as to disclosure requirements regarding the violent death of a former occupant, as well as psychologically impacted **stigmatized property**, such as a haunted house or a property where a horrible crime was committed. Whenever there is any doubt as to the detrimental nature of what is known or suspected, the agent should make full and honest disclosure to the customer.

An agent cannot volunteer information as to the presence of minorities in an area because this is regarded as **steering**, which violates the Civil Rights Act of 1968.

Even when an agent only relays representations made by an owner, the agent can be held liable for misrepresentations if the agent knew, or should have known, the information to be false.

Learn your state's consumer protection laws as they relate to real estate transactions. For example, does your state require specific disclosures by agents and/ or sellers?

Secret agent.   An agent who does not reveal that she is acting in an agency capacity can be held personally liable for her actions. Third parties have the option of holding the undisclosed agent liable or taking action against the principal; they cannot do both. *Blind ads* that fail to indicate agency are prohibited.

Gifts and gratuities.   Some states specifically prohibit an agent from giving gifts of goods and services to other than the principal. The rule has been relaxed in many states, allowing an agent to give a home warranty, property inspection, title binder, and so on to a buyer.

Termination of the Agency

Agencies can be terminated in a number of ways.

Expiration.   If the agency is for a specified period of time, as in an exclusive listing, expiration of that period ends the agency.

Repudiation.   Because an agency requires consent of both principal and agent, either party can end the agreement at any time. Courts will not force an agency to continue; however, the party who wrongfully breached the agency agreement could be held liable for damages.

An exception to the principal's right to terminate an agency is an **agency coupled with an interest**. For example, if an agent advances funds to an owner in an effort to stop a foreclosure in order to obtain the listing, the agent is coupling a financial interest to the agency. Thus, the principal cannot terminate the agency.

Death. An agency is a personal service relationship; therefore, the death of either the principal or the agent terminates the agency. Because a corporation is a separate legal entity, the death of a corporate officer does not affect the agency.

Performance. The agency terminates when the agent has performed his duties, usually to procure a buyer at the price and terms stated in the listing, or at any other price and terms the principal agrees to accept, or to locate a property for a buyer.

Impossibility. Impossibility of performance, such as destruction of the property, terminates the agency.

Incapacity. If the agent becomes incapacitated and can no longer serve, the agency terminates. If the principal becomes mentally incapacitated, the agency terminates. Bankruptcy of either the agent or the principal may or may not terminate the agency, depending on the decision of the bankruptcy court.

Termination of the agency does not terminate all agency duties. For example, loyalty would prevent the former agent from disclosing to others information received in confidence and from using such information to the agent's advantage, even after the agency has ended.

LISTINGS

An agency sales listing is a contract by which a principal (an owner) employs an agent (a broker) to procure a buyer for the property. Under an agency buyer listing, a prospective buyer employs the agent to locate a property to be acquired. When a salesperson takes a listing, the listing is the property of the broker, not the salesperson. The broker, not the salesperson, is the agent. Because of the state statutes of fraud or specific rules, in most states, real estate listings must be in writing. Most verbal listings, therefore, are unenforceable although in several states, short-term verbal listings are enforceable. It may be possible to have a verbal property management contract if the agent leases for one year or less.

Listings need not be agency agreements. The listing agreement might be a nonagency agreement whereby the owner employs the broker in the position of transaction broker or facilitator to procure a buyer for the property. The differences between agency and nonagency listing agreements apply to the agency or transaction broker duties.

Listings do not give brokers rights in the listed property; therefore, listings cannot be recorded. A listing sets forth rights and obligations of the parties. For example, a listing might give the agent the right to place a sign on the property and to create subagencies with other brokers. Without this authorization, the broker could not so act.

If, after accepting an offer, the seller refuses to sell, the broker cannot force the sale. Although the broker may be entitled to sue for a commission, specific performance is a legal remedy of the buyer after the seller has accepted an offer. Because a listing requires consent, either broker or owner can cancel a listing at any time; however, that person could be liable for damages if the contract was canceled without proper cause. Similarly, a listing cannot be assigned or otherwise transferred.

Types of Sale Listings

In an **exclusive listing**, the owner agrees that only one agent will be appointed. There are two types of exclusive sale listings: exclusive-right-to-sell listings and exclusive agency listings.

All exclusive listings must have a definite termination date, and the broker must give the owner a copy at the time the listing is signed. Exclusive listings are considered bilateral contracts if a broker promises to use best efforts to obtain a buyer or a property in return for an owner's promise to pay a fee should the broker succeed.

Exclusive-right-to-sell listing. Under an **exclusive-right-to-sell listing**, the agent is entitled to a commission if, during the term of the listing or any extension thereof, the agent or anyone else procures a buyer who is ready, willing, and able to purchase the listed property under the terms of the listing or any other terms to which the principal agrees.

Because the broker is assured a commission regardless of who sells the property, this type of listing is most often sought.

Exclusive agency listing. The **exclusive agency listing** appoints the broker as the owner's sole agent to sell the property. It differs from the exclusive-right-to-sell listing in that the owner retains the right to sell the property without agent assistance without being obligated to pay a commission.

Open listing. Unless a listing agreement specifically states it is exclusive, the listing is assumed to be open. Open, or nonexclusive, right-to-sell listings may be given concurrently to more than one broker. However, only the broker who procures a buyer is entitled to a commission. If the owner sold the property independently of the agent, no commission is paid.

To earn a commission under an open listing, the broker must be the **procuring cause** of the sale; that is, the broker's efforts must have started an uninterrupted chain of events that resulted in the sale. An open listing can simply be a letter from an owner. It is not necessary for the owner to receive a copy or for the listing to contain a definite termination date. Either principal or agent can cancel an open listing at any time. An open listing is regarded as a unilateral contract if the broker is not obligated to use any effort to locate a buyer. The broker's act of obtaining a buyer forms the acceptance of the offer.

Net listing. A net listing can be an exclusive or an open listing. The term *net* refers to the broker's fee. Under a net listing, the broker gets all the money exceeding a net amount that the owner is to receive. Because the agent is likely to be more interested in profit than in the owner's best interests, net listings are considered by many to be unethical. In a number of states, they are illegal. Even where legal, they should be avoided because any extraordinary broker profit will likely result in a lawsuit by the seller.

Buyer Agency Listing

Representing a buyer rather than a seller has become an important aspect of real estate agency. In a buyer agency agreement, the agent agrees to use effort to locate a property that meets the needs of the buyer at the best price. Buyer listings may be exclusive-right-to-locate-property listings, exclusive agency listings, or open listings.

Broker compensation may be based on a set percentage of purchase price, a fixed fee or some variation. The agreement usually provides that if anyone else compensates the broker (a commission split with another broker), then that amount is credited to the buyer's obligation. If a buyer's broker locates a property listed by another broker, then the split commission will normally fulfill the buyer's obligation. However, if the broker locates a property for the buyer where the seller is not paying any selling fee, such as a for-sale-by-owner situation, then the buyer would pay the fee.

Like seller listings, buyer listings usually provide a safety clause where the broker is entitled to compensation should the buyer buy a property the broker introduced the buyer to within a stated period after the expiration of the listing.

Brokers who are buyer agents have the same agency duties to their principal as do seller's agents.

Buyer agency has pretty well replaced subagency where the selling agent was considered to be the subagent of the listing broker, therefore representing the seller rather than the buyer.

Multiple Listing Services (MLSs)

Listings that authorize brokers to cooperate with other brokers may be submitted to MLSs that publish and distribute listings. MLSs are usually associated with the local board of REALTORS®. In the absence of any authorization to cooperate with others, the broker has no right to share the listing with other agents.

It is considered a restraint of trade for listing organizations to set minimum commissions, to exclude brokers from access to their services, or to conspire to participate in these activities. In some states, an MLS cannot exclude an open listing.

Listing Provisions

Provisions that may be included in a listing include the following:

- *Relationship of the parties.* Type of agency. (Most states require that the agent disclose the type of agency for the transaction.)
- *Description.* While a legal description of the property is not required, the description of the listed property must be clear and unambiguous.
- *Price.* The owner determines the price at which the property is to be offered. However, the agent generally recommends an offering price based on an informed analysis of the market.
- *Commission.* The commission must be negotiated between owner and agent and clearly set forth in the listing. While commission is generally stated as a percentage of sale price, it may be a fixed price or a formula based on service.

■ *Safety or protection clause*. This clause provides that the agent is entitled to a commission when the owner sells to a buyer after the expiration of the listing in cases where the agent negotiated with that buyer and provided the buyer's name to the owner within a stated time period. Safety clauses may provide that the owner is relieved of liability if the property is relisted with another broker.

■ *Buyer damages*. This clause may provide for a division of damages received between owner and broker when a buyer defaults on a purchase.

■ *Hold-harmless clause*. This clause provides for owner reimbursement to the agent for the agent's liability when the agent repeats false or incomplete information furnished by the owner.

■ *Title*. The listing specifies how evidence of a marketable title will be shown.

■ *Attorney's fees*. Listings frequently provide that in the event of a legal action between the parties, the prevailing party will be entitled to attorney's fees.

■ *Disclosures*. To be made by seller to buyer.

■ *Arbitration*. Arbitration clauses provide for either voluntary or mandatory arbitration of broker/owner disputes.

PURCHASE CONTRACTS

Real estate purchase agreements are offers by the purchaser (**offeror**) to buy at definite prices and terms. Like any offer, a purchase offer can be revoked before acceptance, but if accepted by the seller (**offeree**) during the period designated for acceptance, a binding contract is formed.

Purchase Deposits

While a deposit is not necessary to have a valid purchase contract, deposits called **earnest money** normally accompany offers to purchase (sales requiring court approval, such as estate sales, normally have deposit requirements). Because the amount of earnest money is not set by statute, it is determined by the purchase contract as agreed by buyer and seller. A deposit indicates good faith on the part of the purchaser and may provide readily available damages for the seller should the buyer default on the purchase agreement.

If the deposit is in a form other than cash or check, the owner must be informed as to the form of the deposit.

The purchase agreement must contain an unambiguous description of the property, and the price to be paid or a formula to determine the price. If payment terms are not specified, it is understood that payment will be at time of closing.

OFFER-TO-PURCHASE PROVISIONS

Some of the provisions that may be found in offers to purchase include the following:

Liquidated damages.   The agreement may provide for the forfeiture of the buyer's deposit as the seller's sole remedy should the buyer default on the agreement. By agreeing to liquidated damages, the seller gives up the right to sue for actual damages sustained due to the buyer's breach, should it occur. If liquidated damages agreed to are excessive, a court could consider the damages to be penalties, which are unenforceable.

Contingencies.   Frequently, purchase agreements are contingent upon financing or other conditions, such as completion of the sale of another property, zoning changes, or other requirements.

Time is of the essence.   This clause provides that failure to accept or perform under the agreement by the specified date(s) will be a breach of the contract. Without this clause, the courts might excuse reasonable delays. If the words **"time is of the essence"** are used without a date specified, it would likely be interpreted to mean as soon as reasonably possible.

Closing/possession.   Unless a date for closing is set, closing must occur within a reasonable time. If a date for possession is not given, possession is upon closing.

Condition of property.   Purchase agreements normally provide that the owner properly maintain the property until closing and warrant that appliances and systems are in proper working order. The agreement usually allows the buyer a final walk-through inspection before closing.

Some states require the listing agent to make a visual inspection of the property in readily accessible areas. **Red flags** are visual signs of possible problems, such as water stains in ceilings, cracks in the foundation, or uneven floors.

As is.   An as-is provision means that there are no warranties. It is common in selling foreclosed property because it does not excuse failure to disclose a known problem.

Costs and prorating.   The contract would specify who is responsible for what costs, as well as costs that will be prorated.

Title.   The contract would specify how title is to be taken and how evidence of marketable title will be provided.

Fixtures/inclusions/exclusions.   The contract would specify items to be considered fixtures so as to be included in the sale. Items of personal property to be included or excluded could also be specified.

Inspection/testing.   Provision is set forth for buyer's inspection and testing of the structure, soil, systems, and so on.

Provisions may be made for the seller to be able to correct defects revealed by a professional inspection or allow the buyer the right to rescind the agreement.

Dispute resolution.   Provision might be included for mediation and/or arbitration of disputes.

Disclosures.   Federal and state mandated disclosures could be set forth in the purchase contract.

YOUR PERTINENT STATE INFORMATION

1. What is the contractual age in your state?

2. Can minors purchase real estate (void or voidable)?

3. Describe an emancipated minor in your state.

4. What are the rights of prisoners to contract?

5. What special provisions relate to the statute of frauds?

6. What is the statute of limitations on written contracts?

7. What is the statute of limitations on verbal contracts?

8. May a broker be a dual agent?

9. May a broker be a facilitator in your state?

10. Does your state allow the designated-broker concept?

11. What are your state's special agency provisions?

12. Are verbal listings allowed in your state?

13. What are your state's requirements for listing provisions?

14. Are net listings legal?

15. What, if any, are your state's special requirements for real estate purchase contracts?

CHAPTER 4 QUIZ

1. Mutual assent to a real estate contract is indicated by
   A. attestation.
   B. offer and acceptance.
   C. acknowledgment.
   D. seals.

2. An example of an executory oral contract that is enforceable is a
   A. lease for six months starting in six months.
   B. sale of a lot for less than $500.
   C. lease for two weeks starting in 12 months.
   D. sale of drapes for $600.

3. A contract of adhesion is a contract that
   A. is impossible to perform.
   E. has no offeror.
   C. is offered as "take it or leave it."
   D. cannot be breached.

4. After an offer is accepted, the seller finds out that the broker was the undisclosed agent for the buyer, as well as the agent for the seller. What are the seller's rights?
   A. The seller can withdraw without obligation to broker or buyer.
   B. The seller can withdraw but is subject to liquidated damages.
   C. The seller can withdraw only with concurrence of the buyer.
   D. The seller is subject to specific performance if refusing to sell.

5. A voidable contract could be described as
   A. valid unless voided.
   B. void unless validated.
   C. illegal.
   D. unenforceable by either party.

6. A remedy that puts the parties back in the positions they were in before entering into a contract is
   A. specific performance.
   B. waiver.
   C. rescission.
   D. accord and satisfaction.

7. By agreement, one party to a contract was discharged and another party took her place. This is an act called
   A. a rescission.
   B. a reformation.
   C. a novation.
   D. an accord and satisfaction.

8. Which of the following is regarded as a customer of a broker?
   A. A property owner under an open sale listing
   B. A property owner under an exclusive sale listing
   C. A buyer under an exclusive buyer listing contract
   D. A buyer who is not represented by an agent

9. In an assignment of a contract,
   A. the old party is relieved of all contractual obligation.
   B. the assignor remains primarily liable for the contract.
   C. the assignee assumes contractual liability.
   D. a new agreement is substituted for the old agreement.

10. An anticipatory breach of contract is
    A. a statement by a party that they would not perform.
    B. a request for extension of time.
    C. failure to perform by date set for completion.
    D. a request for contract reformation.

11. Under the Uniform Vendor and Purchaser Act, the buyer is responsible for property loss
    A. after purchase contract is entered.
    B. only after title passes to the buyer.
    C. when taking possession.
    D. only if the buyer caused the loss.

12. M and N agreed that M would buy N's lot for $68,000, with the settlement scheduled for next Thursday. What type of contract was made?
    A. Bilateral, express, and executory
    B. Implied, express, and executed
    C. Unilateral, express, and executory
    D. Bilateral, implied, and executed

13. M agreed to buy N's lot, which was represented by N as being zoned for a duplex. After closing, M found that the lot had single-family zoning and was not suitable for M's needs. M should seek the remedy of
    A. specific performance.
    B. liquidated damages.
    C. reformation.
    D. rescission.

14. A seller's agent owes the buyer the duty of
    A. loyalty and obedience.
    B. confidentiality and accounting.
    C. fairness and honesty.
    D. disclosure and due care.

15. A deed given to a buyer left out a paragraph. Because of this error, the buyer received 20 acres less than bargained for. When the buyer discovers the error, what remedy should be sought?
    A. Punitive damages
    B. Injunction
    C. Waiver
    D. Reformation

16. L promised to give M a condominium for her birthday. L had a change of mind and refused to do so. Based on these facts, in a lawsuit brought by M, the primary concern of the court is
    A. the legality of the promise.
    B. consideration for the promise.
    C. mutuality of the agreement.
    D. competency of the parties.

17. A real estate broker who has a sale listing is normally a
    A. buyer's agent.
    B. special agent.
    C. general agent.
    D. universal agent.

18. An agent indicated he was acting as a principal. A third party suffered damages because of the agent's action. The person liable for the loss is
    A. only the agent, because the agency was not revealed.
    B. only the principal, because the principal bears ultimate responsibility.
    C. both the agent and the principal.
    D. either the agent or the principal.

19. In most sales, the buyer's agent is *NOT* paid a commission by the buyer because
    A. commissions are never paid by buyers.
    B. the buyer's agent receives a commission split from the seller's agent.
    C. the buyer's listing requires the sellers to pay the buyer's broker fee.
    D. the broker acts as a dual agent.

20. An oral contract for the sale of real property was consummated. After the sale, the seller wants to rescind. Which of the following is *TRUE*?
    A. The contract is binding upon buyer and seller.
    B. Only the buyer can rescind.
    C. Only the seller can rescind.
    D. Because the contract was oral, the sale was void.

21. A requirement of a valid purchase agreement is
    A. liquidated damages.
    B. earnest money.
    C. "time is of the essence" clause.
    D. offer and acceptance.

22. An agent made a secret profit while acting for the principal. This violated the agent's duty of
    A. care.
    B. loyalty.
    C. obedience.
    D. accounting.

23. Which of the following would make a contract voidable?
    A. A contract for an illegal purpose
    B. A contract by a person adjudged insane
    C. A contract to make a gift in the future
    D. A contract entered into because of fraud

24. A purchase contract provision stating that the buyer, if failing to complete the purchase, will forfeit the deposit is called
    A. liquidated damages.
    B. the safety clause.
    C. punitive damages.
    D. the subordination clause.

25. Failure to include a time period for acceptance in an offer to purchase would
    A. void the offer.
    B. keep the offer open for acceptance during a reasonable period of time.
    C. allow the offer to be accepted anytime before revocation.
    D. require immediate acceptance or the offer will expire.

26. A court ordered L to pay M $100,000 in excess of M's out-of-pocket damages that resulted from L's breach of a contract with M. What is this $100,000 called?
    A. Liquidated damages
    B. Compensatory damages
    C. Punitive damages
    D. Nominal damages

27. L purchased a commercial lot from M based on M's fraudulent representation as to lot size, zoning, and sewer connections. L cannot use the parcel purchased. What remedy should L seek?
    A. Reformation
    B. Waiver
    C. Rescission
    D. Specific performance

28. S's offer to purchase states that it will be kept open three days for acceptance. One day after making the offer, and before acceptance, S wants to withdraw it. The real estate agent should inform S that
    A. the offer may be withdrawn without penalty.
    B. revocation means the forfeiture of earnest money.
    C. only in the event of death can the offer be revoked before acceptance.
    D. the offer is irrevocable.

29. An owner died one month after signing a six-month exclusive-right-to-sell listing. The day after the owner's death, the listing agent procured a buyer for the full list price. The administrator of the owner's estate does not wish to sell. What are the rights of the parties?
    A. The buyer can obtain specific performance.
    B. The listing broker has earned a commission.
    C. The listing broker can obtain specific performance.
    D. The administrator need not sell and is not liable for a commission.

30. A prospective buyer sued a seller for specific performance. While the purchase agreement was a valid contract when entered into, the buyer discovered it was unenforceable because of
    A. the seller's death.
    B. the statute of frauds.
    C. the statute of limitations.
    D. an assignment of interests.

31. An owner listed the same property with three separate agents. The owner gave an exclusive-right-to-sell listing to broker L, an exclusive agency listing to broker M and an open listing to broker N. Broker N sold the house and collected a commission while the other listings were still in effect. What are the rights of L and M as to a commission?
    A. L and M both are entitled to a split of the commission from N.
    B. L and M are entitled to a second commission to be split between them.
    C. L and M are each entitled to a full commission.
    D. L and M are not entitled to any commission.

32. On June 1, J mailed K an offer to buy K's property. J gave K 15 days for acceptance. On June 3, J mailed a letter to K revoking the offer. On June 4, before receiving the revocation, K mailed a written acceptance of J's offer. Based on these facts,
    A. a valid contract was formed because the offer was irrevocable for 15 days.
    B. J is bound to the purchase agreement because the offer was accepted before revocation.
    C. the offer cannot be accepted because the acceptance was mailed after the revocation was mailed.
    D. if the revocation is received before receipt of the acceptance, no contract will be formed.

33. One salesperson in a brokerage office is serving as an owner's agent, while another salesperson in the same office is serving as the buyer's agent for the same transaction. This is an example of a
    A. limited liability transaction.
    B. facilitator transaction.
    C. designated agency.
    D. controlled business arrangement.

34. An agency that may *NOT* be terminated by an owner is
    A. an exclusive listing.
    B. an agency coupled with an interest.
    C. a power of attorney.
    D. an express agency.

35. J agreed to sell a lot to K. J mistakenly believed the lot was zoned for multifamily apartments and told K that the lot was zoned for a 16-unit apartment building. However, K knew the correct zoning and nevertheless entered into the purchase agreement. Before closing, what are the rights of the parties?
    A. Either J or K can void the contract.
    B. Only K can void the contract.
    C. The contract is void because of the misrepresentation.
    D. The agreement as made is enforceable by either J or K.

36. A contract is void if it involves
    A. misrepresentation of the purchaser's intentions.
    B. an illegal purpose.
    C. duress.
    D. undue influence.

37. In interpreting a contract, a court would consider that
    A. a contract should be interpreted in favor of the party drafting the instrument.
    B. a later document takes precedence over an earlier document.
    C. numerals take precedence over written words.
    D. a printed clause would take precedence over a handwritten portion of an agreement.

38. J agreed to sell K a lot for $6,000. J later refused to sell, and K purchased a similar lot for $8,000. A court awarded K $2,000 in damages. Which term describes the damages?
    A. Nominal
    B. Punitive
    C. Compensatory
    D. Liquidated

39. The amount of commission is determined by
    A. local custom.
    B. the multiple listing service.
    C. the department of real estate.
    D. negotiation.

40. A broker obtained an offer on an apartment building from a syndicate. The broker was a member of this syndicate but had not informed the seller of this interest. Before the closing of the accepted offer, the owner discovered the broker's interest and refused to sell. If the broker sued the owner for the commission, the court would
    A. order revocation of the broker's license.
    B. order payment of the commission to the broker.
    C. release the owner from the obligation to pay the commission.
    D. order that the buyer obtain specific performance.

41. L and M agree that L will buy M's farm for $400,000 cash, with the sale to take place in three months. This is an example of what type of contract?
    A. Bilateral, express, executed
    B. Bilateral, express, executory
    C. Unilateral, express, executory
    D. Unilateral, implied, execute

42. A clause requiring punctual performance of a contract is called the
    A. "time is of the essence" clause.
    B. contingency date clause.
    C. reasonable time for performance clause.
    D. excusable delay clause.

43. J, who operated his brokerage office as a sole proprietorship, died. His daughter K, also a broker, wishes to take over all her father's listings. She should
    A. inform all the owners that she is the successor in interest to her father.
    B. obtain the approval of the probate court.
    C. inform the state that she has taken over responsibility for the listings.
    D. renegotiate all the listings.

44. A right to buy a property at a yet undetermined price, where the seller is free not to sell, is a
    A. lease option.
    B. right of first refusal.
    C. purchase contract.
    D. sale-leaseback.

45. A builder failed to follow the agreed landscaping plans. The purchaser decided to accept the variance and pay the full contract price. This is called
    A. accord and satisfaction.
    B. waiver.
    C. novation.
    D. reformation.

46. A contractual disagreement led to a builder's reduction of the contract price by $1,000. This agreement is
    A. unenforceable because of a lack of consideration.
    B. an accord and satisfaction.
    C. a novation.
    D. a waiver.

47. An owner refuses an offer, even though it is exactly in accordance with a valid exclusive-right-to-sell listing. What are the owner's rights?
    A. The owner does not have to sell.
    B. The owner is liable to the buyer for money damages.
    C. The owner likely will be sued by the broker for specific performance.
    D. The owner is liable to the buyer for specific performance.

48. Broker M told buyer N that a home was in a "great neighborhood." After purchasing the home, N found out that there had been several recent crimes in the area. The statement of broker M is regarded as
    A. misrepresentation.
    B. a mutual mistake.
    C. fraud.
    D. puffing.

49. An oral contract for the sale of real estate is
    A. illegal.
    B. unenforceable.
    C. valid for property of low value.
    D. enforceable if witnessed.

50. Broker L works with both buyers and sellers to complete sales transactions but does not have any agency obligations. Broker L
    A. is a dual agent.
    B. is acting as a facilitator.
    C. still has a fiduciary duty to both parties.
    D. has no disclosure duties to either party.

51. In order to obtain a sale listing, the agent loaned the owner money to avoid foreclosure. The agency is
    A. illegal.
    B. coupled with an interest.
    C. implied.
    D. by estoppel.

52. A broker has a single agency with a seller. Nevertheless, the broker has a duty to
    A. disclose to a buyer detrimental facts about the property.
    B. obtain the best possible deal for a buyer.
    C. tell a buyer why the seller is selling.
    D. tell a buyer about any previous offers received that failed to close.

53. A broker never saw, talked to, or corre-
    sponded with a buyer, yet the broker earned
    a commission when the buyer made an
    accepted offer to the owner. What kind of
    listing was it?
    A. Open
    B. Exclusive right to sell
    C. Exclusive agency
    D. Buyer

54. In a buyer brokerage situation, who pays the
    salesperson's commission?
    A. Buyer only
    B. Seller only
    C. Buyer and seller
    D. Salesperson's broker

55. The principle that verbal evidence cannot be
    used to modify a written document that is
    complete on its face is
    A. the statute of frauds.
    B. the statute of limitations.
    C. the parol evidence rule.
    D. laches.

56. Which listing would raise an ethical ques-
    tion because of the owner's and the broker's
    differing interests?
    A. Buyer listing
    B. Net listing
    C. Open listing
    D. MLS listing

57. At an auction, the
    A. person bidding is the offeror.
    B. auctioneer is the offeror.
    C. owner is the offeror.
    D. buyer is the offeree.

58. Which of the following would constitute an
    acceptance to a purchase offer?
    A. An acceptance where the closing date
       was changed
    B. An acceptance that required an increase
       in earnest money
    C. A verbal acceptance with a promise of a
       written confirmation
    D. An acceptance that requests a change in
       closing date

59. When presenting multiple offers to purchase,
    the agent should
    A. present the offers in the order received.
    B. present the agent's offer first before
       offers from other firms.
    C. inform the owner that one of the offers
       must be accepted.
    D. present all offers together.

60. A buyer asks for specific performance. The
    buyer wants the seller to
    A. pay compensatory damages.
    B. pay punitive damages.
    C. convey in the manner agreed.
    D. insure the title.

61. An owner refuses a full price offer on
    a property for which the broker has an
    exclusive-right-to-sell listing. The broker is
    entitled to
    A. monetary damages.
    B. specific performance.
    C. waiver.
    D. novation.

62. A listing stated that commission would be
    "five percent (5%) of the sales price." The
    purchase contract signed by the buyer and
    the listing agent and accepted by the owner
    said that the broker's commission would be
    4.5%. What is the broker entitled to?
    A. 6%, because it is stated as a number in
       the listing
    B. 5%, because it is stated in words in the
       listing
    C. 4.5%, because it is in the purchase
       agreement
    D. Nothing, because there is no meeting of
       the minds

63. A tenant took possession under an oral
    10-year lease. One month later, the lessor
    gave the tenant a notice to vacate. As to the
    tenant's rights,
    A. the tenant has no enforceable lease.
    B. the tenant is entitled to one year tenancy
       at agreed rent.
    C. the tenant must vacate but is entitled to
       damages.
    D. the tenancy is for 10 years as possession
       passes.

64. A requirement of any valid purchase contract is
    A. earnest money.
    B. liquidated damage provision.
    C. description of the property.
    D. date of closing.

65. The owner wishes to cancel an exclusive-right-to-sell listing before its expiration. Which of the following statements is *TRUE*?
    A. The broker can disregard the owner's request, and if a full price offer is received, the owner must accept.
    B. The owner is liable for punitive damages.
    C. The owner can cancel the listing if reasonable notice is given.
    D. The owner can cancel the listing immediately.

66. A transaction broker has duties to both buyer and seller. These duties constitute
    A. dual agency.
    B. separate but equal agencies.
    C. fair and honest dealing.
    D. the same as an agent's duties.

67. An agent rented property to a tenant without checking the tenant's credit. A credit report would have shown a history of repeated evictions for nonpayment of rent. The agent breached a duty of
    A. loyalty.
    B. obedience.
    C. financial trust.
    D. due care.

68. Damages greatly in excess of losses suffered were awarded by a court. These were *MOST* likely
    A. liquidated damages.
    B. liquidated damages.
    C. punitive damages.
    D. compensatory damages.

69. Which of the following is considered an invitation to negotiate?
    A. A bilateral contract
    B. An exclusive-right-to-sell listing
    C. A newspaper advertisement
    D. A net listing

70. A prospective buyer gave an owner $500 to keep an offer to sell open for 30 days. The agreement was reduced to writing and signed by the parties. Ten days later, the owner indicated that she would not sell. Which of the following is *TRUE*?
    A. While the owner need not sell, the $500 must be returned.
    B. The owner must sell as well as return the $500.
    C. The buyer is not obligated to buy.
    D. The agreement can be enforced by the owner.

71. The difference between rescission and waiver is that
    A. rescission may be assigned.
    B. waiver is retroactive.
    C. waiver leaves parties as they are.
    D. waiver allows specific performance.

72. A broker was sued for reporting false information supplied by an owner. The owner has a liability to the broker for broker loss based on the
    A. habendum clause.
    B. safety clause.
    C. hold-harmless clause.
    D. arbitration clause.

73. An exclusive agency listing states "6¢" rather than "6%" commission. The owner sells the property. The broker is entitled to
    A. a 3% commission.
    B. a 6% commission.
    C. a 6¢ commission.
    D. nothing.

74. A nurse persuaded her long-term patient to sell the house to the nurse at a small fraction of its value. Based on these facts, to set aside the transaction, the patient's children would allege
    A. fraud.
    B. undue influence.
    C. an illegal contract.
    D. menace.

75. Which of the following is *FALSE* regarding an assignment of a contract?
    A. The assignee is primarily liable on the contract.
    B. All of the assignor's interests are transferred to the assignee.
    C. All contracts are assignable.
    D. The assignee assumes the duties of the assignor.

76. An exception to the statute of frauds requiring real estate sales agreements to be in writing is
    A. where the value is insignificant.
    B. when a broker is not involved.
    C. when the buyer takes possession and makes improvements.
    D. a verbal sales agreement where the seller is a government agency.

77. After an offer is accepted, but before closing, a broker notices evidence of termite infestation. The broker should
    A. remain silent as the contract has been entered into.
    B. inform the buyer only.
    C. inform the seller only.
    D. inform the buyer and the seller.

78. A right that does not exist until an owner makes a decision is
    A. an option.
    B. a right of first refusal.
    C. a license.
    D. an easement in gross.

79. An optionor is
    A. a tenant.
    B. the person receiving the option.
    C. the person exercising the option.
    D. the person giving the option.

80. A seller did not evict a tenant before closing as agreed. Knowing of the failure, the buyer elects to complete the transaction. This is regarded as
    A. accord and satisfaction.
    B. waiver.
    C. reformation.
    D. substantial performance.

CHAPTER 4 QUIZ ANSWERS

1. **(B)** This indicates a meeting of the minds. (98)

2. **(A)** A lease for one year or less that can be fully performed within one year can be oral. (99)

3. **(C)** In a case of ambiguity, contracts of adhesion are interpreted against the party drafting it. (105)

4. **(A)** Because of the undisclosed agency, the seller can withdraw without obligation and the broker could be subject to disciplinary action. The seller would also be entitled to the return of any commission paid. (106–107)

5. **(A)** Only one party can void it at that party's option. (100)

6. **(C)** Waiver, however, leaves them as they are. (103)

7. **(C)** This is a substitution of parties to a contract or of contracts. (104)

8. **(D)** The others are clients with agency duties. (106)

9. **(C)** The assignor remains secondarily liable. (105)

10. **(A)** This is a renunciation of the agreement and can be treated as a breach even if performance is not yet due. (102)

11. **(C)** Or when title passes. (105)

12. **(A)** Mutual promise that was expressed but not yet performed. (97)

13. **(D)** Contract based on mutual mistake of fact. (98, 104)

14. **(C)** The others are fiduciary duties owed to the principal. (109)

15. **(D)** To reflect the actual agreement. (103)

16. **(B)** If there was no consideration for the promise, it is not enforceable. (98)

17. **(B)** A special agent with the powers designated. (108)

18. **(D)** Cannot hold both liable if a secret agency; must decide who to go against. (110)

19. **(B)** Most sales are co-operative where buyer's broker finds listing of a seller's agent. (113)

20. **(A)** While oral contracts to sell may not be enforceable because of the statute of frauds, completed property sale is valid. (99)

21. **(D)** Shows mutuality, a requirement of a valid contract. (98)

22. **(B)** Duty to the principle of disclosure. Failure was disloyal. (109)

23. **(D)** Others make contract void not voidable. (100)

24. **(A)** The parties agreed in advance what the seller's damages would be in the event of a buyer breach. (103)

25. **(B)** The offer can still be revoked before the acceptance. (101)

26. **(C)** This punishes L for outrageous conduct. (103)

27. **(C)** The other remedies would not benefit L. (103)

28. **(A)** An offer can be withdrawn any time before acceptance unless consideration was given to keep it open. (101)

29. **(D)** The death of the principal terminated the agency. (111)

30. **(C)** While the contract is valid, the statute of limitations makes it unenforceable because of delay in bringing the action. (104)

31. **(C)** By signing the two exclusive listings, the owner became obligated to both for a full commission if a sale was consummated in accordance with the listings. (112)

32. **(B)** Acceptance takes place upon mailing, but revocation takes place upon receipt. (101)

33. **(C)** This concept allows for separate agency representation of buyer and seller within the same office. (107)

34. **(B)** The agent has an interest in the property. (110)

35. **(D)** Because K knew of the false statement, it was not relied on. (100)

36. **(B)** Answers (C) and (D) would make the contract voidable. (99)

37. **(B)** It shows the final meeting of the minds. (105)

38. **(C)** This makes up the actual cash loss to K. (103)

39. **(D)** Owner and broker are free to agree on commission. It is considered an illegal restraint on trade for brokers to agree as to minimum commissions. (113)

40. **(C)** The broker could also be disciplined by the state licensing authority but not as a decision in a civil suit. (109)

41. **(B)** It is bilateral, a promise for a promise, stated so it is express and executory because it has yet to be performed. (97)

42. **(A)** A delay in performance would place the delaying party in default. (101)

43. **(D)** The listings ended with the death of the agent. (111)

44. **(B)** The right to buy is triggered only if the owner wishes to sell to another. (102)

45. **(B)** The purchasers waived the breach by the builder. (104)

46. **(B)** The builder agreed to accept a lesser consideration. (104)

47. **(A)** The owner could be liable to the broker for a commission, but there is no contract with the buyer. (111)

48. **(D)** This was a statement of opinion, not a warranty. (101)

49. **(B)** It is not a violation of the law (illegal), but it cannot be enforced. (99–100)

50. **(B)** But has duties of fair dealing, which would require disclosure of material facts to both parties. (107)

51. **(B)** Because broker has a financial interest in property, the agency cannot be unilaterally terminated by the owner. (110)

52. **(A)** Duty of fair and honest dealing. (109)

53. **(B)** If anyone sells it, including the owner, the listing broker earns a commission. (112)

54. **(D)** Only a salesperson's broker can compensate a salesperson. (106, 111)

55. **(C)** However, verbal evidence can be used to clarify ambiguities. (100)

56. **(B)** The broker would want a sale at the highest price possible, while the owner wants a quick sale that meets net amount. (112)

57. **(A)** The bidder makes an offer that is accepted by the auctioneer (offeree's agent). (101)

58. **(D)** A request is not a condition, so it is not a counteroffer. (102)

59. **(D)** Agent's duty of fairness requires all offers to be presented together. (109)

60. **(C)** Perform as agreed. (103)

61. **(A)** The broker can get damages because the broker has fully performed on the listing but cannot force the owner to sell. (111)

62. **(C)** Which was signed after the listing. (105)

63. **(A)** Statute of frauds is not enforceable for oral lease exceeding one year. (99)

64. **(C)** Property must be identified. (98)

65. **(D)** However, the owner could be liable to the broker if the cancellation was not justified. (110)

66. **(C)** A transaction broker has no agency duties but must treat both parties fairly and honestly to meet their needs. (107)

67. **(D)** Agent was negligent in performing agency duties. (109)

68. **(C)** To punish a wrongdoer for outrageous conduct. (103)

69. **(C)** It is not an offer that can be accepted. (101)

70. **(C)** It is an option. Only the optionee can enforce it, but the optionee need not do so.. (102)

71. **(C)** And rescission puts them back the way they were. (103–104)

72. **(C)** Agrees to indemnify broker for false information. (114)

73. **(D)** Because it was an exclusive agency listing and the owner made the sale (normally obvious typos can be disregarded). (112)

74. **(B)** The nurse took advantage of the nurse-patient relationship, so the patient was not acting under his own free will. (101)

75. **(C)** Contracts for personal services and contracts that prohibit assignment cannot be assigned. (105)

76. **(C)** The seller is estopped from raising defense of statute of frauds. (99)

77. **(D)** Duty of disclosure to principal, as well as fair and honest dealings with all parties. (109)

78. **(B)** When the owner decides to accept an offer, the rights holder has the right to buy at a price the owner will sell at. (102)

79. **(D)** Optionor (owner) gives option to optionee. (102)

80. **(B)** The buyer elected to excuse the seller's breach and go through with the purchase. (104)

CHAPTER 5

Environmental Regulations, Disclosures, Risk Management, and Federal Laws

ENVIRONMENTAL REGULATIONS

Both state and federal laws and regulations deal with protecting the public from toxic substances.

Lead Paint

For housing built before 1978, sellers and lessors must disclose any known lead paint hazards to buyers or lessees. The lead paint disclosure booklet *Protect Your Family from Lead in Your Home* must be given to buyers and lessees.

Buyers of residential property must be given a 10-day period to inspect and assess risks associated with lead-based paint and to inform the seller of any deficiencies and corrective action required. If the seller refuses to correct lead paint problems, the buyer may terminate the contract and be entitled to the return of all earnest monies.

The EPA certifies contractors for lead paint removal. Employees must be trained to follow protective standards in working in pre-1978 structures.

 Federal law does not require testing for or removal of lead paint; however, either or both may be the subject of negotiations between buyer and seller.

Renovate Right Program.   The **Renovate Right Program** requires contractors who disturb paneled surfaces in homes built before 1978 to be certified and follow EPA-specific work practices to prevent lead contamination. Restorers must give an information pamphlet, as to lead paint hazards, to owners and tenants if renovations cover 6 square feet or more of painted surfaces or more than 20 square feet of exterior surfaces.

Comprehensive Environmental Response Compensation and Liability Act (CERCLA)

The federal **Comprehensive Environmental Response Compensation and Liability Act (CERCLA)** of 1980 (Superfund) enforced by the Environmental Protection Agency, provides for strict liability of owner, operator, and lessee for cleanup of hazardous substances generated, transported, or disposed of. A defense of innocence is possible for an owner as to a preexisting problem only if appropriate inquiry was made before acquiring the site.

Other hazardous substances.   The owner must disclose known environmental hazards (see Figure 5.1). Hazardous substances can include the following:

- *Asbestos*. This fire-resistant material was at one time extensively used in insulation, floor and ceiling tile, and roofing. Asbestos dust has been found to cause respiratory problems, including lung cancer. Asbestos that is friable (easily crumbled) is exceedingly dangerous. Federal, as well as state, regulations set standards for asbestos removal. The discovered presence of asbestos often leads to failure to close sale transactions.

  Removal of asbestos requires great care because removal can result in asbestos dust. An alternative to removal is encapsulation, where the asbestos material is sealed.

- *Lead*. This substance was commonly used in oil-based paint and in plumbing solder. The greatest household danger is from lead dust caused by deteriorating paint. Lead poisoning can result in brain, kidney, and nervous system damage.

- *Radon gas*. This is a naturally occurring colorless, odorless gas that can enter homes through cracks in foundations or basements. Radon is considered carcinogenic. Dangerous levels can be detected by a spectrometer.

- *Mold*. Mold has been discovered to have serious health effects. Causes of mold include floods, roof and wall leaks, and high humidity levels. The presence of mold is not always readily apparent because mold can exist inside walls. Test kits are available to test for mold. Corrective action can be very expensive

- *Electromagnetic fields (EMFs)*. EMFs are generated by the movement of electrical currents. The major concern involves high-tension power lines. There is a great deal of controversy about alleged cancer dangers from EMFs.

- *Protected species*. Under the Endangered Species Act (ESA), species (plant or animal) can be designated "threatened" or "endangered" and critical habitat is designated. The critical habitat designation curtails government interference with the habitat. The act also covers private owners who might engage in acts that harm threatened or endangered species. Removing, malicious damage to, or harming protected species can be illegal under ESA as well as state law.

■ *Underground storage tanks (USTs).* Leakage of fuel or chemicals from these often-forgotten tanks can result in soil and water contamination. Owners of commercial tanks must register tanks and make them leakproof (farm and residential tanks holding less than 1,100 gallons are exempt). Responsible parties are liable for cleanup of contaminated soil.

■ *Waste disposal sites.* Unless property used as a dumpsite is properly capped and lined, dumped substances might endanger persons living in the vicinity and leach into the underground water supply.

■ *Fertilizers and pesticides.* Agricultural chemicals could present a health risk to current users of the land, as well as present a problem to others because of runoff and pollution of groundwater.

■ *Perchlorate.* A dangerous substance found in rocket fuel, explosives, and some fertilizers. It has contaminated some water supplies.

■ *Polychlorinated biphenyls (PCBs).* PCBs were formerly used in electrical transformers and other electrical equipment. PCB leakage can create a serious health hazard. PCBs are considered carcinogenic.

■ *Urea-formaldehyde foam.* Formerly used as insulation (or as a binder material in some particle board), this substance emits an irritating gas as it deteriorates.

■ *Chemical discharge.* Spills and careless disposal of various chemicals from commercial and industrial sources have created many significant environmental problems. Contaminated land is called *brownfields*. Additional common hazardous substances include arsenic, mercury, vinyl chloride, and benzene.

■ *Wetlands.* While there is no single comprehensive federal wetlands protection act, a number of federal laws and regulations affect wetland use. In addition, most states regulate any wetland development. Wetlands refer to land seasonally or permanently inundated with water. Wetlands are important in that, in addition to being habitat for many species, they serve to protect shorelines from erosion, aid in flood control and serve a role in the water purification process. Federal regulations are enforced by the Corp of Engineers, the Environmental Protection Agency, the National Oceanic and Atmospheric Administration, the National Resources Conservation Service, and the U.S. Fish and Wildlife Service.

FIGURE 5.1

Environmental Hazards

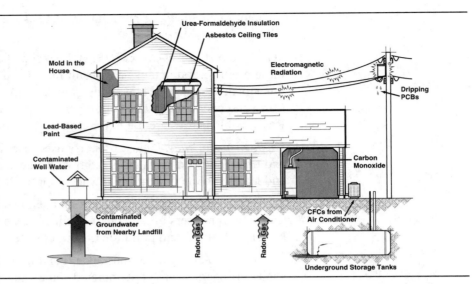

Flood Hazard Area

The seller must disclose to the buyer that improved real estate (or mobile home) is located in a flood hazard zone as indicated on maps published by the Federal Emergency Management Agency (FEMA). Once FEMA declares a flood hazard area, the community is required to adopt floodplain management regulations that take flood hazards into account. A **floodplain** is a flat area along a waterway subject to flooding.

Flood Insurance

Where a seller has previously received federal flood disaster assistance, the seller must notify the buyer about the requirement to obtain and maintain flood insurance. If the seller fails to notify the buyer and the property is damaged by flood requiring federal disaster relief because of failure to insure, then the seller will be required to reimburse the federal government.

DISCLOSURES

In addition to agency duty disclosures, you should disclose to a buyer anything you would conceivably want to know if you were a buyer. The following sections discuss mandated disclosures.

Property Condition or Disclosure Report

Besides broker disclosure of known detrimental facts, most states now require the seller to also disclose known problems concerning the property and even the area. The concept of *caveat emptor*—let the buyer beware—has been replaced by full disclosure. Generally, seller disclosures are only required for residential property of stated size, such as one-to-four residential unit buildings. Currently, 34 states and the District of Columbia require a mandatory property condition disclosure that includes all known facts that can affect the value and desirability of a property. Typically, a seller must notify the buyer about the home's physical condition, material defects, or major repairs that might affect the buyer's decision to purchase.

Even if your state law does not require a mandatory property condition report, disclosures should be made because it is simply good business and an indication of fair and honest dealing.

Home Inspection Notice

For the sale of one-to-four residential unit buildings, including mobile homes, that involve FHA financing or are HUD owned, the borrower must sign a notice titled *For Your Protection: Get a Home Inspection.*

Consumer Caution and Homeownership Counseling Notice

The Federal Trade Commission requires that this notice be given to loan applicants no later than three days before signing loan documents. It warns borrowers that they're placing a lien on their home and could lose their home and all of their equity.

Megan's Law

Megan's Law is a federal law that allows the release of information to the public about convicted sex offenders. Various states have adopted and implemented statutes that allow the public to call and obtain information about child molesters and other sex offenders living in their area. States may require that buyers and lessees of real property be informed as to where such information can be obtained.

Elder Abuse Laws

A number of states have elder abuse laws that require broker and closing agents to report cases where parties appear to be acting against their best interests because of coercion or undue influence.

Stigmatized Property

An agent need not disclose natural death or death by AIDS on the property. State law might require disclosure of a murder or other violent death within a stated time period. If you feel that a fact will affect a buyer's purchase decision, you should disclose.

Miscellaneous Disclosures

In addition to the fiduciary duty disclosures that must be made to the seller and the disclosures of known defects that must be made to the buyer, many states have mandated disclosures concerning financing, environmental hazards, state subdivision, and so on. In addition to state disclosures, federal disclosures are required under the Real Estate Settlement Procedures Act (RESPA) (covered later in this chapter and in Chapter 6).

RISK MANAGEMENT

Risk management is dealing with occurrences of an uncertainty. There are three basic steps to managing risk: identify, evaluate, and mitigate. You should consider possible risks (identify) and the likelihood of an effect if the risk occurred (evaluate) and then determine how to deal with the risk to minimize the consequences of the happening of the uncertainty.

The form of business is important in risk management. A corporate or limited liability company (LLC) will protect personal assets of owners from liabilities of the business.

In risk mitigation, screening, training, and supervising employees will reduce the likelihood of many uncertainties happening. Nevertheless, unforeseen events occur that could seriously affect the financial well-being of an individual or business. By transferring risk to an insurer for the payment of a premium, the insured can protect their financial viability.

To reduce risk, many real estate brokers have adopted a number of strategies:

- Disclose anything that could remotely affect the property use or value, even if it is hearsay.
- Carry adequate errors and omission insurance coverage for the broker and all employees, as well as auto liability.
- Obtain signed disclosures from sellers as to all known defects, as well as area problems.
- Conduct comprehensive visual physical inspection of properties, being alert for "red flag" issues.
- Strongly recommend a professional property inspection to buyers.
- Obtain home warranty insurance.
- Notify both buyer and seller immediately of any problems or delays.
- Adopt safety procedures for client and personnel protection.

INSURANCE

Insurance is a personal contract whereby an insurer agrees to indemnify and protect an insured in the event of a specified loss. In exchange for payment of a premium, the risk of loss is shifted from the insured to the insurer. An agent should have an understanding of the following insurance types and terms.

Basic fire policy.   This hazard policy covers loss by fire, lightning, and smoke from a hostile fire.

Extended coverage policy.   This includes coverage for wind, hail, water damage, and other specified perils.

Homeowners policy.   This provides a package of protection from losses beyond the extended coverage policy, including vandalism and theft coverage, personal property protection, and liability coverage.

Rental policy.   This provides a package of protection for tenants' personal property and also may include liability protection

Condominium owner policy.   Similar to a tenant policy, this includes most of the general homeowners coverage except for loss of the structure, which is covered by a separate policy of the condominium owners association.

Public liability.   This protects an owner as to members of the public who may enter the premises and be injured because of the condition of the premises. Lessors frequently require commercial tenants to carry such coverage with the lessor as a named insured. Business liability insurance will protect a business from specified perils.

Automobile insurance.   While an agent might be concerned with collision coverage covering the agent's vehicle in an accident, as well as comprehensive coverage that covers flood, fire, theft, and vandalism, the agent's broker is most concerned with liability coverage. A court could determine a broker liable for injury to persons or property resulting from the agent's negligence. To minimize risk, many brokers insist that salespersons carry a minimum liability protection, receive copies of the policy and are named on the policy as an additional insured.

Workers compensation insurance.   This insurance provides wage replacement coverage, as well as medical benefits to employees injured in the course of employment. The worker gives up the right to sue the employer for negligence. State statute governs this coverage. It is generally required for all employees.

Medical pay.   This coverage covers medical expenses of persons injured on the premises regardless of liability.

Flood insurance.   The National Flood Insurance Program makes flood insurance available through private insurance carriers under a government-subsidized program.

Government-regulated lenders within flood-prone areas (identified on FEMA maps) require flood insurance as a condition of the loan. Owners not required to have flood insurance may also apply for this insurance. For a community to be eligible for the flood insurance program, it must adopt a floodplain management ordinance to reduce flood damage and ascertain that elevations of new buildings meet required standards. FEMA issues a certification of building elevations.

Earthquake insurance.   Although earthquake coverage can be included as part of another policy, it usually requires a separate policy.

Boiler insurance.   Boiler explosions are not normally covered by fire policies. Hartford Insurance provides a boiler inspection and insurance policy. The policy also covers equipment breakdowns. A benefit of Hartford policies is periodic professional inspections by trained engineers that serve to prevent losses.

Errors and omissions (E&O) insurance.   A real estate brokerage or property management office would carry this type of policy. It is similar to medical malpractice coverage in that it protects the insured from liability based on negligence or failure to perform. It customarily covers defense costs. It does not protect the insured from their own fraudulent acts.

Umbrella policy.   Umbrella insurance is an insurance policy that provides excess coverage beyond the basic insurance policies. The policy requires the insured to carry set limits on other policies. For example, an insured might have liability coverage on real estate and automobiles with a $1 million limit on each policy. An umbrella policy of $1 million would add $1 million additional coverage to the other limits.

Home warranty plans.   This buyer insurance plan covers structural, mechanical, and electrical problems over a stated period of time. It is issued to a buyer at the time a home is purchased.

Rent insurance.   Rent insurance protects the owner against lost income while a property is being repaired or rebuilt as a result of a casualty (an accidental) loss.

Mortgage life insurance.   Mortgage life insurance is a term life insurance policy, or life and disability insurance, that pays off the mortgage if the insured dies or becomes disabled. It is really declining term insurance because coverage decreases as the mortgage is paid off.

Deductibles.   Premiums can be reduced by having a deductible amount withdrawn from the coverage. The higher the deductible, the lower the premium.

Assumption.   In some states, property insurance policies can be assumed, with approval from the insurer. An insured that cancels a policy gets a **short rate refund**, which is less than a prorated refund. If the insurance company cancels the policy, the insured is entitled to a **full-prorated refund**. To get full credit for the insurance, it is in the best interest of the seller for the buyer to assume the insurance policy where possible.

Coinsurance.   Coinsurance requires an insured to carry a particular percentage of the replacement value, usually 80%, in order to be fully reimbursed for a loss. An insured who carries less than the required percentage coverage can collect only that percentage of any loss suffered up to the amount of coverage.

Riders.   These are amendments to policies that usually exclude or increase coverage.

Fidelity bonds.   By bonding an employee, an employer is protected against employee's dishonesty.

Performance bonds.   These bonds guarantee completion of a contract should a contractor be unable to complete the work.

Protecting the Public and Staff

The public should be protected by ensuring the safe condition of both office and vehicles used as well as ascertaining that drivers are licensed and capable. Checking for unsafe conditions of properties and warnings where required further insures personal safety.

To reduce risk, many real estate broker have adopted a number of strategies:

- Meeting new prospective buyers at their office
- Telling others where they will be and always leaving door unlocked while showing property
- Not leaving a car where it can be blocked
- Avoiding the wearing of expensive jewelry

Recordkeeping

State law sets minimum standards for keeping records. You should keep records pertaining to transactions, even if they fail to close. Today, most records are kept on computers. Your computer should be password protected and have a backup storage either on offsite duplicate disks or a cloud storage system.

Paper records, such as correspondence, closing statements, and memos, should be kept locked in a fire-resistant file cabinet. Paper records should include copies of important email messages.

Many software programs are available for office management, finances, trust accounts, and client management. Records should be kept as to property and client. Financial records should be audited on a regular basis.

Privacy

Never discuss any personal data regarding a client or a customer with other clients or customers without express permission of that party. This duty as to privacy protection extends beyond any working relationship with the party. Unless you have permission to disclose details of a sale to the public, it should be considered a matter for privacy.

Never discuss a customer or client in a social media.

FEDERAL FAIR HOUSING

Civil Rights Act of 1866

The **Civil Rights Act of 1866** gave all citizens the same rights as those enjoyed by white citizens—to inherit, purchase, lease, sell, or hold real and personal property.

For many years, this act was ineffective because of narrow court interpretation. *Jones v. Mayer* (U.S. Supreme Court, 1968) held that based on the 13th Amendment, the act was valid. A victim of racial discrimination in the sale of housing can take the case to federal court for damages, obtain an order that prohibits sale to another, or force the owner to sell to the plaintiff. There is no limit to punitive damages under this act.

Civil Rights Act of 1964

This very limited act prohibited discrimination in housing wherever there was government assistance. It applied to Federal Housing Administration (FHA) and Department of Veterans Affairs (VA) programs, as well as other government assistance programs, such as urban renewal.

Civil Rights Act of 1968

Title VIII of the Civil Rights Act of 1968 is called the **Fair Housing Act**.The act prohibits discrimination based on national origin, color, religion, and race when selling or leasing residential property. A 1974 amendment extended protection based on sex, and in 1988, the act was expanded to include familial status and the handicapped (now termed disability).

Exemptions

■ Religious groups having nonprofit housing may limit sale or lease to members of their religious group, providing the religion is open to others without discrimination.

■ Private clubs can discriminate in favor of their members in the sale or lease of housing for noncommercial purpose and limit sale or leasing.

■ Owner-occupants of one-to-four residential unit buildings can discriminate in renting rooms or units if no agent is involved and no discriminatory advertising is used.

■ Owners of single-family homes who own three or fewer rental units can discriminate if they are not in the business of renting and neither an agent nor discriminatory advertising is used. Owners who occupy a home at the time of the transaction are limited to the exemption of one sale within any 24-month period.

The *Jones v. Mayer* decision held that without exception, the Civil Rights Act of 1866 prohibits all racial discrimination. Therefore, a person discriminated against may seek remedy under the 1866 act, or state law, even though the discriminatory acts were among those covered by the exemptions in the 1968 law.

Prohibitions.   The federal Fair Housing Act prohibits these activities:

■ Broker discrimination as to clients and customers

■ Refusal to show, rent, or sell by falsely claiming that a property is not available

■ Discrimination in access to multiple listing services

■ **Steering**—that is, directing people of certain races, religions, and such away from (or toward) particular areas

■ Discriminatory advertising (prohibited even for those exempt from the act); discrimination includes ads that indicate a property is close to a religious institution or area with residents of a particular ethnic or racial group, as well as ads that indicate a preference, which would discriminate against any protected group

■ Retaliatory acts against those making fair housing complaints, or intimidation to discourage complaints

■ Discriminatory sale, lease, or loan terms

■ **Blockbusting**, which induces panic selling by claiming that prices will drop or crime will increase as a result of certain groups entering the area

■ **Redlining**—that is, refusing to loan or insure within a certain area

■ Coercion, intimidation, or other interference with a person's rights in buying, selling, or leasing

■ Falsely indicating to a prospective buyer or lessee that a property is not available

Enforcement.   The Department of Housing and Urban Development (HUD) may initiate complaints on its own, or aggrieved parties can take the following actions:

■ Parties can bring a complaint to HUD within one year of the discriminatory action (the 1968 act is administered by the secretary of the Department of Housing and Urban Development).

■ A hearing on the complaint is held before an administrative law judge, who can assess civil penalties from $16,000 to $70,000, as well as actual damages and compensation for humiliation suffered because of discriminatory practices.

■ Parties can bring a civil action in a state or federal district court within two years after the alleged occurrence. The court could award actual damages plus punitive damages, as well as court costs and attorney's fees and/or a permanent or temporary injunction or restraining order to cease or refrain from an activity.

■ HUD may use minority, as well as nonminority, testers to determine whether the treatment of buyers and renters is equal.

Many states also have fair housing laws that provide remedies in state courts. A single discriminatory act could violate one or more state laws, as well as federal laws.

Fair Housing Amendments Act of 1988

The **Fair Housing Amendments Act of 1988** added fair housing protection for persons with a physical or mental handicap (now termed disability), as well as protection based on familial status.

Disability.   The term *disability* refers to mental as well as physical disabilities affecting one or more major life functions. While drug addiction is not regarded as a disability, alcoholism, cancer, and speech, vision, hearing, and mobility impairments, as well as AIDS and HIV infection, are regarded as disabilities.

Modification of a unit.   Tenants with a disability may modify a unit at their own expense to allow reasonable use of the premises. Tenants may also make alterations to common areas for access. While the landlord may require restoration, at the tenant's expense, of internal alterations, tenants need not restore the common areas to their previous condition upon vacating the property.

Support animals.   Rules against pets cannot be applied to seeing eye dogs or support animals. A tenant with a disability cannot be charged an increased security deposit because of a Seeing Eye dog or support animal or because the tenant altered the unit to obtain reasonable benefits of use. However, a tenant is liable for any damage done to the property by a Seeing Eye dog or support animal.

Prohibited acts.   It is illegal to ask whether an applicant has a disability or to question the severity of a disability.

It is unlawful for a landlord to refuse reasonable accommodation in terms of rules, policies, practices, or services necessary to ensure equal enjoyment opportunity for a unit. For example, a landlord may have to provide special parking access for a disabled tenant for that person's reasonable enjoyment of a unit.

Landlords may not advertise that a particular unit is unavailable to a person with a disability or those with familial status. Landlords may, however, advertise a unit's accessibility features, as well as its family benefits.

New units. The 1988 law requires that new multifamily units (four or more) be readily accessible in public and common areas for use by individuals with a disability.

Familial status. The term *familial status* refers to persons younger than age 18 living with a parent or guardian, to persons in the process of obtaining legal custody of a person younger than age 18, or to pregnant persons.

Apartments that have sections designated "adults only" or "family section" are in violation of the law because they would still be discriminating as to familial status regarding particular units. Steering prospective tenants toward a family or an adult area in an apartment complex and away from another area also violates the act.

Apartments can have rules for children's use of facilities if there is a nondiscriminatory reason for the difference in rules. The act does not prohibit owners from setting maximum occupancy of units so long as the rule is reasonable and enforced without discrimination.

Exemptions. There are several exemptions to the prohibition of refusing to rent or sell based on familial status:

- Housing provided under any state or federal program that the secretary of HUD determines is specifically designed and operated to assist elderly persons
- Housing having at least 80% of the units occupied by at least one person aged 55 or older
- Housing intended for and occupied solely by persons aged 62 and older

While gay, lesbian, bisexual, and transgender persons are not specified as being covered by the fair housing laws, in 2012, HUD stated that HUD programs must be offered regardless of sexual orientation, gender identity, or marital status.

Americans with Disabilities Act (ADA)

The **Americans with Disabilities Act (ADA)**, which applies to both physical and mental disabilities, prohibits any discrimination that would deny the equal enjoyment of goods, services, facilities, and accommodations in any existing **place of public accommodation** (defined as nonresidential facilities that affect commerce). Owners and operators (including management companies) of commercial facilities must make the facilities accessible to the extent readily achievable. **Readily achievable** is defined as easily accomplished, without a great deal of expense. This is based on costs of compliance when related to property value and the financial ability of the property owner.

New construction must be readily accessible and usable unless it is structurally impractical (practicality relates to the cost of making access possible); alterations must also comply with the guidelines.

Elevators are not required for either new or existing structures having fewer than three stories or fewer than 3,000 square feet per story.

The act also applies to employment discrimination if there are 15 or more employees. The employer must alter the workplace to provide reasonable accommodations for an employee with a disability unless it creates an undue hardship on the business.

The act can be enforced either by an action by the U.S. attorney or by a civil action by a private citizen and could result in

- $55,000 in civil penalties for the first discriminatory act,
- $110,000 for each subsequent violation,
- compensatory damages, and
- attorney's fees.

Equal Housing Opportunity Poster

A current equal housing opportunity poster (supplied by HUD) must be exhibited prominently in every broker's place of business. Failure to display the poster shall be deemed prima facie evidence of discriminatory housing practice. A sample poster is shown on the next page in Figure 5.2.

Discriminatory Advertising

The Civil Rights Act of 1968 prohibits discriminatory advertising. Discriminatory advertising includes advertising that indicates any preference, limitation, or discrimination because of race, color, religion, sex, handicap, familial status, or national origin.

Some discriminatory words and phrases are not readily recognized by many as being discriminatory. In addition, some words carry different connotations among different social, ethnic, and economic groups. Words also have different meaning based on geographic location.

HUD seems to indicate that the rule is one of reasonableness. If an ordinary person would feel an ad favored or disfavored a protected group, it is discriminatory.

Bear in mind that state and local laws may be more restrictive than federal law and may prohibit language that would not be objectionable to HUD.

FIGURE 5.2

Equal Housing Opportunity Poster

U. S. Department of Housing and Urban Development

EQUAL HOUSING OPPORTUNITY

We Do Business in Accordance With the Federal Fair Housing Law

(The Fair Housing Amendments Act of 1988)

It is illegal to Discriminate Against Any Person Because of Race, Color, Religion, Sex, Handicap, Familial Status, or National Origin

---

■ In the sale or rental of housing or residential lots

■ In advertising the sale or rental of housing

■ In the financing of housing

■ In the provision of real estate brokerage services

■ In the appraisal of housing

■ Blockbusting is also illegal

Anyone who feels he or she has been discriminated against may file a complaint of housing discrimination:
    1-800-669-9777 (Toll Free)
    1-800-927-9275 (TTY)
    www.hud.gov/fairhousing

U.S. Department of Housing and Urban Development
Assistant Secretary for Fair Housing and Equal Opportunity
Washington, D.C. 20410

Previous editions are obsolete   form HUD-928.1 (6/2011)

ANTITRUST LAWS

Antitrust laws were developed because of abuses that were prevalent when a business became a monopoly, thus controlling a marketplace, or where groups of businesses conspired to control prices and/or competition. The principal antitrust law is the federal **Sherman Antitrust Act** (there are also state antitrust acts). Violation of the Sherman act can result in a fine up to $100,000 (up to $1,000,000 for corporations) and up to three years in prison. An individual injured by an antitrust violation is entitled to triple the amount of actual damages plus costs and attorney fees.

Sherman Antitrust Act violations include the following actions:

■ *Price-fixing*. Setting prices is illegal. For example, it is illegal for a group of brokers to agree on minimum commissions or to withhold cooperation from brokers who did not abide by these rules.

■ *Market allocation*. Agreements of firms to divide the marketplace on a geographic or type-of-service basis are illegal because they reduce or eliminate competition.

■ *Group boycotting*. Agreeing to not do business with another business to reduce competition is illegal. For example, if a group of brokers agree that they will not allow a particular broker to show their listings, it is a group boycott.

■ *Tie-in agreements*. These illegal agreements require that a business buy goods or services in order to obtain other goods or services. If a builder wished to buy a lot to build a home and the broker required the builder to list the home with the broker as a condition of lot purchase, it would likely be an illegal tie-in sale.

TRUTH IN LENDING ACT (REGULATION Z)

Regulation Z, a part of the federal Consumer Credit Protection Act of 1968, requires that the lender provide the borrower with a **disclosure statement** showing credit costs in percentage as well as total finance charges. The act applies to credit secured by a residence, as well as personal property credit loans of $25,000 or less. It is enforced by the Federal Trade Commission.

Note that the Good Faith Estimate required by RESPA can be combined with the truth-in-lending disclosure.

Finance charges include interest, loan fees, finder's fees, any price differential for buying on credit, points, service fees, and premium for credit life insurance (if a condition of the loan). Disclosure also must include late payment charges and prepayment penalties. Not included in finance fees are title insurance costs, credit report costs, legal and recording fees, and tax and insurance impound accounts.

Truth in lending applies to loans where credit is extended with a finance charge or credit payable in more than four installments. If the amount or percentage of down payment, the number of payments or period of repayment, or the amount of payment or finance charges is included in any advertisement, the ad must include three elements:

1. Amount or percentage of down payment

2. Terms of repayment (number, amount, and due dates of payments)

3. **Annual percentage rate (APR)** (the true interest rate considering points and other loan costs; the nominal rate is the rate stated on the note)

Advertising the APR alone will not trigger the above disclosure requirements.

Truth in lending makes **bait-and-switch advertising** a federal offense. This is advertising property that agents don't intend to sell or that is not available in order to attract buyers for other property.

The requirement to supply the borrower with a truth-in-lending disclosure statement showing all loan facts applies to creditors that regularly extend credit. This means creditors extending credit more than 25 times, or more than five times if the loan is secured by a dwelling, within the preceding year.

Three-day rescission right.   If the loan is for consumer credit secured by the borrower's residence, the borrower has the right to reconsider and cancel. This right is valid until midnight on the third business day following loan completion. The rescission right does not apply to home-purchase mortgages but does apply to refinancing and home equity loans.

Penalties.   A penalty may be assessed of up to $10,000 per day if a violation continues, as well as up to $10,000 for an unfair or deceptive practice. Creditors may also be penalized twice the amount of the finance charge (minimum $100, maximum $1,000 plus costs) and actual damages. Willful violation of the act could subject the creditor to a criminal penalty of up to $5,000 and/or one year in jail.

Dodd-Frank Act changes.   The Dodd-Frank Act has expanded and modified truth in lending. It applies to any dwelling, not just a principal residence. Provisions added by Dodd-Frank include the following:

- Delivery or mailing of truth-in-lending disclosures within three business days of receiving mortgage loan application.

- If the APR changes, a three-day waiting period is tacked on before loan can close.

- Any fee other than a credit report charge may not be assessed until truth-in-lending disclosures are provided.

- A you-are-not-committed statement must be included to inform consumers that they are not required to complete the loan because the consumers applied for the loan or received early disclosures.

- Home loans are not allowed to close until seven business days after the borrower receives truth-in-lending disclosures. However, a consumer can request an expedited closing in case of an emergency need.

In 2014, the Consumer Finance Protection Bureau amended Regulation Z to prohibit a creditor from making a high-price mortgage loan without regard to the consumer's ability to repay the loan.

Predatory lending.   Predatory lending refers to unfair, abusive, and fraudulent loan practices. Amendments to the Truth in Lending Act have been enacted to curb predatory lending such as repeated refinancing over a short time period, which fails to benefit the borrower, or extending credit without regard to a borrower's repayment ability. Many states have also enacted legislation to protect homeowners from sharp practices of lenders targeting the elderly and minorities with high-cost home-secured credit, loans with exorbitant prepayment penalties, and **flipping** (persuading borrowers to regularly refinance).

Telephone Consumer Protection Act

Unless the recipient has given prior express consent, the act provides the following:

- Calling residences before 8 am or after 9 pm is prohibited.

- Solicitors must honor the do-not-call registry and maintain a company-specific list of consumers who ask not to be called.

- Solicitors must provide the name of the person on entity on whose behalf the call is made and contact information.

- Solicitations using an artificial voice or recording are prohibited.

- Unsolicited advertising faxes may not be sent.

Fines may be up to $1,500 for each violation.

CAN-SPAM ACT OF 2003

The Controlling the Assault of Nonsolicited Pornography and Marketing Act of 2003 (**CAN-SPAM Act**) protects consumers from being assaulted by misleading emails.

Unsolicited emails must include the following:

- An opt-out mechanism where the recipient can indicate no more emails are to be sent

- A functioning return email address

- A valid subject line indicating the message is an advertisement

- The legitimate physical address of the sender

Text messages, prerecorded messages, and emails may only be sent to mobile phones if the recipient previously agreed to receive them.

It is a misdemeanor to send spam with falsified heading information. Each violation is subject to a fine up to $16,000.

FAX SOLICITATIONS

The federal Telephone Consumer Protection Act prohibits sending unsolicited advertisements to fax machines. Permission to send fax solicitations requires a signed statement that includes the fax number where the fax may be sent. An exception to the rule against sending unsolicited fax advertisements is where there is an established business relationship. Such fax solicitations must include an opt-out mechanism, as well the identity of the sender and the sender's phone or fax number. Violators could be liable for $500 to $1,500 to the recipient for each junk fax sent.

REAL ESTATE SETTLEMENT PROCEDURES ACT

The **Real Estate Settlement Procedures Act (RESPA)** requires lender disclosure of loan costs (separate from financing costs) to buyers and sellers for federally related real estate purchase loans of one-to-four residential unit buildings involving a new first loan. Federally related loans are loans made by a federally insured or federally regulated lender and to federally guaranteed or insured loans, as well as to loans that are to be resold to Fannie Mae, Freddie Mac, or Ginnie Mae, or administered by HUD (like Regulation Z, escrow impounds for taxes and insurance are not considered loan costs so need not be listed). The act is administered by the Consumer Financial Protection Bureau.

RESPA requires that the HUD information booklet *Shopping for Your Home Loan* be given to the borrower, generally at the time of loan application. The borrower also must be given a **good-faith estimate** of settlement costs within three business days of loan application. If the lender or the broker requires the use of a particular service provider (required provider), such as an insurance company, attorney, title company, and so on, the lender or the broker must disclose its relationship with that service provider and estimate the costs involved. Where a broker has more than a 1% interest in a service provider, that interest must be disclosed (affiliated business disclosure) and the borrower must be allowed to obtain the services from another provider.

HUD's **Settlement Statement (HUD-1)**, which covers all loan costs and fees, specifies the following:

- While the HUD-1 is required for all federally related purchase loans for one-to-four residential unit buildings, it is not required for other loans.
- The purchaser has a right to review the statement on the business day before closing.
- Every charge must be justified by a service rendered.
- The buyer cannot be required to purchase title insurance or other services from a particular company.
- The lender cannot give or accept kickbacks for referring a service. An exception is referral fees to a genuine employee.
- Federal law prohibits kickbacks and referral fees from a service provider when no service was rendered by the broker, but it does not prohibit referral fees between brokers.
- The lender cannot charge for preparing the disclosure statement.
- Limits are placed on the amount of advance taxes and insurance payments the lender can collect. The lender cannot collect more than two months' advance taxes and insurance, in addition to prorated amounts based on date of closing.

The law does not apply to business property, vacant land, dealers buying for resale, or seller financing where the seller takes back a purchase money mortgage or uses a land sales contract or for loan assumptions unless the contract is modified or the lender charges more than $50 for the assumption.

Servicing disclosure.   The lender must disclose to the borrower if the loan is to be assigned or sold and the fact that the right to service the loan may be assigned.

The borrower who believes there is an error in an account can make a qualified written request to correct the error. Loan service must acknowledge the receipt of the request within five business days and provide names and numbers of persons who can discuss the matter.

Controlled business arrangement (CBA).   A real estate company can offer a package of services to a customer, such as title insurance, property insurance, mortgage banking, and home inspection service (one-stop shopping). RESPA allows such a package provided that the borrower understands the relationship between the service providers and that other service providers are available. However, fees may not be exchanged for referrals. While the broker may have an ownership interest in a service provider, the broker may receive compensation only on a profit-sharing basis. The controlled business arrangement must function as a separate business.

Computerized Loan Origination (CLO)

When a fee is charged to a borrower for access to computerized loan origination (CLO) services, a disclosure must be provided to the borrower in a format set forth by RESPA. The disclosure must inform the borrower that the fee can be avoided by directly approaching lenders.

Adjustable Rate Loan Disclosure

For adjustable rate loans, the lender must provide a copy of the Federal Reserve Board booklet *Consumer Handbook on Adjustable-Rate Mortgages* to the borrower. The booklet explains the various loan terms and how the caps work. The consumer is warned about payment shock at the first adjustment period after the initial rate.

The Dodd-Frank Act expanded and modified RESPA. Under the act, servicers of mortgage loans may not

- obtain force-placed hazard insurance unless there is a reasonable basis to believe the borrower has failed to comply with the loan insurance requirements;

- charge fees for responding to valid written requests;

- fail to act timely to borrower's request to correct errors relating to allocation of payments, as well as to provide a final balance for purpose of loan payoff or avoiding foreclosure;

- fail to respond within 10 business days to a request for contact information about an owner or assignee of a loan; or

- fail to comply with any other regulation mandated by the Consumer Finance Protection Bureau.

Dodd-Frank increased penalties for RESPA violations from $1,000 to $2,000 and class action penalties from $500,000 to $1 million.

Dodd-Frank requires servicers to return the balance of escrow accounts to borrowers within 20 days of the loan being paid off. Dodd-Frank also requires lenders to acknowledge receipt of a qualified written request within 5 days and respond within 30 days.

Reporting cash transactions.   Real estate professionals are required to report any single or series of related transactions in excess of $10,000 in cash (use IRS Form 8300), as well as check a list maintained by the Office of Foreign Assets Control of the U.S. Department of the Treasury. The list is of individuals and companies owned and controlled by targeted countries. The list can be found at www.treasury.gov/sdn. If a party is on the list, the USA PATRIOT Act requires the broker to report to the Department of the Treasury's Office of Foreign Assets Control.

NATIONAL DO NOT CALL REGISTRY

The Federal Trade Commission has established the National Do Not Call Registry to protect consumers from unwanted commercial solicitations. The fine for calling someone whose name appears on the list is up to $16,000 per call. If you make calls seeking buyers, sellers, lessees, or lessors or solicit any service, you should do so only after consulting the registry.

Exceptions to the do-not-call rule include the following:

- You may call a listed party if you have an existing business relationship (within 18 months) of a purchase, sale, or lease.
- You may call a party within three months of an inquiry.
- You may call persons who have given you permission to call.
- You may call commercial numbers (the registry only applies to residential telephone numbers).
- You may call on for-sale-by-owner signs and ads as a buyer representative, but not for the purpose of obtaining seller representation.
- You may call for survey purposes but no solicitation can be included in the call.

FTC has telemarketing sales rules that prohibit a telemarketer from making abandon calls. An abandonment call is dead air in which the telemarketer fails to connect the consumer with a live sales agent within two seconds of answering the phone.

EQUAL CREDIT OPPORTUNITY ACT

The **Equal Credit Opportunity Act (ECOA)** prohibits discrimination against any loan applicant on the basis of race, color, religion, age, national origin, sex, marital status, or dependency on public assistance (source of income).

Lenders cannot ask questions concerning marital status, pregnancy, plans to have children, or divorce. Lenders cannot arbitrarily reject secondary income. Lenders may not discount income because of sex or marital status or discount or refuse to consider income from part-time employment, Social Security, pensions, or annuities. Lenders must consider reliable alimony, child support, or separate maintenance income. A lender must notify the applicant within three days of action taken on a loan request. If the loan is denied, the reason for denial must be listed. The borrower has the right to rebut (appeal) the reasoning for loan denial. The act also provides that borrowers on a first lien must be told they can receive a free copy of the appraisal report plus the documentation used to determine the amount of the loan, as well as significant information integral to the evaluation of the property.

SAFE LICENSING

The Federal Secure and Fair Enforcement Mortgage Licensing Act of 2008 (SAFE Act) was enacted to protect consumers and reduce fraud in mortgage loan transactions. Every state is required to have a licensing system for residential loan originators. Every licensee must have a national identification number, and a registry of licensees is maintained by the Nationwide Mortgage Licensing System and Registry.

Mortgage loan originators (MLOs) must meet minimum standards of licensing and registration. They must pass a written test that covers both federal and state laws, complete an educational requirement, be fingerprinted, and meet net worth and bonding requirements.

COMMUNITY REINVESTMENT ACT

This act was enacted to prevent redlining and to encourage lenders to meet the needs of lower income borrowers. Lenders must publicize their programs to make loans to lower income borrowers.

YOUR PERTINENT STATE INFORMATION

1. What are your state regulations regarding environmental hazards?

2. What are your state regulations regarding wetlands protection?

3. What are your state seller/broker disclosure requirements?

4. What are the provisions of your state's fair housing law(s)?

5. Which, if any, of your state's antitrust laws would apply to real estate activities?

6. Which, if any, state regulations govern unsolicited phone calls and fax solicitations?

7. What are your state's antidiscrimination regulations as to advertising?

CHAPTER 5 QUIZ

1. The Americans with Disabilities Act prohibits employment discrimination by
   A. all employers.
   B. employers having 5 or more employees.
   C. employers having 10 or more employees.
   D. employers having 15 or more employees.

2. Failure of a broker to post an equal housing opportunity poster could result in
   A. automatic revocation of the broker's license.
   B. evidence of broker discrimination.
   C. suspension of the broker's license.
   D. criminal penalties.

3. In renting residential units, a property manager may properly
   A. charge families higher security deposits than single renters.
   B. require tenants with a disability who remove interior doors for accessibility to restore the premises at the end of a lease.
   C. refuse to rent to pregnant women.
   D. designate adult and family sections in an apartment complex.

4. Owners wish to list an expensive home but insist that the home be sold to Caucasians only. The agent should
   A. refuse the listing.
   B. explain that it is unlikely that non-Caucasians can afford the house.
   C. advise the owners to sell it themselves.
   D. accept the listing and ignore the owner's request.

5. An owner may properly refuse to rent to a prospective tenant because the prospective tenant
   A. has AIDS.
   B. has a mental disability.
   C. is an alcoholic.
   D. is a drug addict.

6. In order to force a broker to increase commissions, several brokers agreed that they would refuse to cooperate with the offending broker. Their action is regarded as
   A. price-fixing.
   B. market allocation.
   C. group boycotting.
   D. a tie-in arrangement.

7. Persons or groups specifically exempted from discriminatory practices by the Civil Rights Act of 1968 include
   A. all nonprofit groups.
   B. religious groups limiting leases on nonprofit housing to members of its religion.
   C. owners of furnished units.
   D. hotel and motel operators.

8. A white couple responded to a broker's ad for a property in a predominantly minority neighborhood. The broker should
   A. try to direct them to another property in a white neighborhood.
   B. explain that the neighborhood is predominantly minority.
   C. tell the prospects they are uncomfortable in the neighborhood.
   D. show the property.

9. A biracial family inquires about a home in a predominantly white area. The agent should
   A. explain the problems their presence in the neighborhood could cause.
   B. inform the owners of the buyers' racial status before showing.
   C. treat the prospective buyers the same as anyone else.
   D. attempt to interest the prospects in homes in integrated areas.

10. In determining rental rates and security deposit requirements, a landlord may properly
    A. require an increased security deposit for tenants with pets.
    B. require an increased security deposit for tenants with children.
    C. provide that single-person occupancy will be entitled to a $100 reduction in rent.
    D. have a monthly surcharge of $25 above the basic rent per resident.

11. Lead paint disclosure must be provided to a buyer of a residential property built before
    A. 1966.
    B. 1978.
    C. 1992.
    D. 2000.

12. Under the 1988 amendment to the Civil Rights Act of 1968, an apartment owner is acting within the law by
    A. refusing to pay for modifications to an apartment that would allow a person with a disability the full enjoyment of the unit.
    B. asking whether a renter has a disability and attempting to determine its severity.
    C. refusing to make reasonable accommodations in rules, policies, practices, or services to allow a person with a disability equal opportunity to use a dwelling.
    D. refusing to rent to a person whose disability is mental rather than physical.

13. A broker has installed ramps over stairs to her office, moved furniture for easier access within the office, and installed a paper-cup dispenser by the water fountain. She performed these actions to comply with
    A. Title VIII of the Civil Rights Act of 1968.
    B. the Americans with Disabilities Act.
    C. the Civil Rights Act of 1964.
    D. the 1988 Fair Housing Amendments Act.

14. In soliciting listings of homes in an area where minorities had recently purchased homes, a broker told his salespeople to solicit only Caucasian owners for listings because they will likely want to leave the area. This action is regarded as
    A. steering.
    B. blockbusting.
    C. redlining.
    D. intimidation.

15. If members of a minority racial group live next door to the home that prospective buyers are interested in, you should
    A. inform the prospective buyers.
    B. inform the prospective buyers only if they indicated an animosity to the group.
    C. treat it as a benefit and tell the buyers of the advantages of living in a mixed racial area.
    D. ignore the presence of a minority neighbor.

16. Redlining refers to a refusal to
    A. advertise in designated areas.
    B. loan in designated areas.
    C. list in designated areas.
    D. cooperate with other agents in designated areas.

17. A protected group under federal fair housing law is
    A. poor people.
    B. blue collar workers.
    C. drug addicts.
    D. alcoholics.

18. A woman's rental ad stated, "No communists, tall people, night watchmen, or disabled need apply." Which exclusion specifically violates the fair housing law?
    A. Communists
    B. Tall people
    C. Night watchmen
    D. Disabled

19. The Civil Rights Act that applied only to race was the
    A. Civil Rights Act of 1968.
    B. Civil Rights Act of 1866.
    C. Equal Credit Opportunity Act.
    D. Civil Rights Act of 1964.

20. The borrower must sign the notice titled *For Your Protection: Get a Home Inspection* when purchasing
    A. any property.
    B. a one-to-four residential unit building.
    C. a home with FHA financing.
    D. home insurance.

21. A broker may properly
    A. advertise a property only in a paper sold to a particular racial group.
    B. refuse to handle mortgage loans in a designated area.
    C. quote different terms to prospects of different ethnic backgrounds.
    D. refuse to rent to families with minor children in senior citizen communities that are limited to residents age 62 or older.

22. An owner of a desirable housing complex has a long waiting list of prospective tenants. The owner has a policy where widows of veterans who were killed in action are moved to the top of the list. The owner should be concerned with which of the following laws?
    A. Soldiers and Sailors Civil Relief Act
    B. Americans with Disabilities Act
    C. Civil Rights Act of 1968
    D. Civil Rights Act of 1866

23. The Federal Do Not Call Registry allows calls to residential numbers to solicit sellers when
    A. the person is not listed on the registry.
    B. the agent is seeking commercial listings.
    C. the calls are made intrastate.
    D. the agent has not previously called the party.

24. Brokers would not be limited in calling for-sale-by-owner ads when they
    A. are seeking a sale listing.
    B. are seeking a rental listing.
    C. are representing a buyer.
    D. have previously called the owner.

25. You can protect yourself from unsolicited emails by
    A. placing your name on the do-not-contact email registry.
    B. exercising the opt-out option for further emails.
    C. not opening emails.
    D. notifying the attorney general.

26. The CAN-SPAM Act applies to unsolicited
    A. faxes.
    B. emails.
    C. telephone calls.
    D. mailings.

27. You may send unsolicited fax solicitations if you
    A. include a return physical address.
    B. have a valid subject heading.
    C. have signed permission, including the fax number.
    D. include an opt-out mechanism for further fax solicitations.

28. You may properly solicit a listing by telephone when
    A. the person's name is on a national registry.
    B. the party contacted you for listing information within the prior three months.
    C. calling a residence.
    D. you have no prior relationship with the person called.

29. Unsolicited emails must include
    A. the sender's Social Security number.
    B. an opt-out mechanism.
    C. the fact that the recipient is not required to respond.
    D. reference to applicable statute.

30. Unsolicited fax solicitations to strangers
    A. may not be sent.
    B. require an opt-out mechanism.
    C. must include a valid return fax number.
    D. must include a subject line indicating it is a solicitation.

31. Brownfields are
    A. vacant farmland.
    B. contaminated soil.
    C. redevelopment.
    D. arid land.

32. What is the maximum fine for calling a person whose name is on the National Do Not Call Registry?
    A. $1,000
    B. $11,000
    C. $16,000
    D. $100,000

33. A broker made an unsolicited call to a person who was on the do-not-call registry for a listing solicitation. The call was *NOT* in violation of the law because the broker
    A. knew the person.
    B. called a business number.
    C. used an automatic message machine.
    D. did not know the party was on the registry.

34. An owner contacted a broker for listing information. If the owner is on the National Do Not Call Registry, how long after the inquiry can the broker make solicitation calls to the owner?
    A. 3 days
    B. 10 days
    C. 30 days
    D. 3 months

35. A broker was *NOT* required to check the National Do Not Call Registry when making random calls for
    A. listing solicitation.
    B. referrals.
    C. survey purposes.
    D. buyer representation.

36. Which of the following statements regarding unsolicited emails is *TRUE*?
    A. They are illegal.
    B. They may not be used for solicitation purposes.
    C. They must include a functioning return email address.
    D. They may not be sent to a home if the person is on the do-not-call registry.

37. The fine for falsified subject information on an email can be up to
    A. $11,000.
    B. $12,000.
    C. $16,000.
    D. $20,000.

38. The fine for sending an unsolicited fax advertisement can be up to
    A. $1,000.
    B. $1,500.
    C. $10,000.
    D. $11,000.

39. Ventilation will mitigate
    A. lead paint.
    B. PCBs.
    C. radon gas.
    D. EMFs.

40. A brokers' organization agreed that commissions for single-family homes be set at 6%. This agreement is called
    A. price-fixing.
    B. redlining.
    C. boycotting.
    D. market allocation.

41. Two brokers agreed that they would divide an area geographically and would not do business in each other's territory. This is called
    A. price-fixing.
    B. redlining.
    C. boycotting.
    D. market allocation.

42. A broker refused to accept a buyer's offer on a house until the buyer agreed to list her present home with his office. This action is called
    A. price-fixing.
    B. market allocation.
    C. group boycotting.
    D. tie-in agreement.

43. A mineral formerly used in home construction that can cause lung cancer is
    A. asbestos.
    B. radon.
    C. lead.
    D. urea-formaldehyde foam.

44. It is proper to advertise an apartment with the restriction of
    A. nonsmoking.
    B. no alcoholics.
    C. no smokers.
    D. Christians only.

45. A For Rent advertisement may properly state
    A. "adults preferred."
    B. "children under five years of age welcome."
    C. "retired lady preferred."
    D. "walk to work."

46. The effective rate of interest describes
    A. APR.
    B. the nominal rate of interest.
    C. compound interest.
    D. the usury rate.

47. How many installment payments must there be before truth-in-lending disclosure is required?
    A. Two
    B. Three
    C. Four
    D. Five

48. A broker offers buyers one-stop shopping by handling title insurance, home inspection, mortgage origination, and other services to buyers. This is an example of
    A. a limited liability company.
    B. a controlled business arrangement.
    C. designated agency.
    D. dual agency.

49. An ad used a term that triggered full disclosure of loan terms. The ad stated
    A. "low down payment."
    B. "payments like rent."
    C. "$10,000 down."
    D. "8% APR."

50. What law requires that a good-faith estimate be given to a borrower for a federally related loan?
    A. Truth in Lending Act
    B. Real Estate Settlement Procedures Act
    C. Equal Credit Opportunity Act
    D. Fair Credit Reporting Act

51. The Truth in Lending Act provides that
    A. ads must show prices.
    B. use of the APR in ads requires full disclosure.
    C. ads must indicate advertiser is an agent.
    D. bait and switch ads are a federal offense.

52. Which of the following is allowable by RESPA?
    A. Broker kickbacks for referrals
    B. Unjustifiable charges by service providers
    C. A $25 charge for preparing the disclosure statement
    D. A computerized loan origination fee

53. A home sale ad indicated the amount of down payment required. The ad must also include
    A. the name of the lender.
    B. terms of repayment.
    C. size of the home.
    D. property zoning.

54. Bait and switch advertising is prohibited by
    A. RESPA.
    B. the Truth in Lending Act.
    C. the Civil Rights Act of 1950.
    D. the CAN-SPAM Act of 2003.

55. RESPA is applicable to
    A. loans for large apartment complexes.
    B. federally related loans.
    C. commercial loans.
    D. refinancing loans.

56. A broker has protection as to a client's slip and fall in her office under her
    A. errors and omission insurance.
    B. workers compensation coverage.
    C. public liability coverage.
    D. extended coverage fire policy.

57. How long after the loan application does the lender have to give a good-faith estimate of settlement costs?
    A. 24 hours
    B. 3 business days
    C. 5 business days
    D. 7 days

58. When must the Settlement Statement (HUD-1) be given to the borrower?
    A. On business day before closing
    B. Within 3 days of the loan application
    C. Within 3 days of the settlement
    D. Within 30 days of the settlement

59. RESPA requires broker disclosure of an interest in a service provider if the broker's interest is
    A. over $1,000.
    B. more than 1%.
    C. more than 3%.
    D. more than 10%.

60. The Settlement Statement (HUD-1) is required for purchase loans of
    A. improved lots.
    B. one-to-four residential unit buildings.
    C. more than $240,000.
    D. more than $407,000.

61. Megan's Law requires a disclosure as to
    A. lead paint.
    B. property condition.
    C. sex offenders.
    D. negative amortization.

62. The term *one-stop shopping* for real estate services relates to
    A. brokers with offices servicing a large area.
    B. brokers belonging to multiple listing services.
    C. controlled business arrangements.
    D. virtual internet tours.

63. A broker who offers computerized loan origination (CLO) services
    A. must provide the services at no cost.
    B. is limited to lenders where there is a controlled business arrangement.
    C. is in violation of the Sherman Antitrust Act.
    D. must inform borrowers that they can contact the lender directly.

64. Prohibitions against price-fixing are set forth in the
    A. Truth in Lending Act.
    B. Sherman Antitrust Act.
    C. Procedures Act.
    D. CAN-SPAM Act.

65. The Supreme Court case *Jones v. Mayer* upheld the validity of the
    A. Civil Rights Act of 1866.
    B. Civil Rights Act of 1964.
    C. Civil Rights Act of 1968.
    D. 1988 Fair Housing Amendments Act.

66. An MLO license is sought by
    A. an appraiser.
    B. a mortgage broker.
    C. a property manager.
    D. a telemarketer.

67. The Civil Rights Act of 1964 had limited effect because
    A. of narrow court interpretation.
    B. it was limited to housing where there was government assistance.
    C. it only applied to racial discrimination.
    D. it was limited to commercial property.

68. Which of the following is regarded as the federal Fair Housing Act?
    A. Civil Rights Act of 1866
    B. Civil Rights Act of 1964
    C. Civil Rights Act of 1968
    D. Americans with Disabilities Act

69. A buyer may be held responsible for cleaning up contamination caused by a prior owner under
    A. CERCLA.
    B. the Sherman Antitrust Act.
    C. SAFE.
    D. MLO.

70. An African American was denied a rental in an owner-occupied duplex that the owner was advertising for rent. The owner indicated that he would only rent to Caucasians. Which federal law did the owner violate?
    A. Civil Rights Act of 1866
    B. Civil Rights Act of 1964
    C. Civil Rights Act of 1968
    D. 1988 Fair Housing Amendments Act

71. The Civil Rights Act of 1968 prohibits
    A. retaliating acts against those making fair housing complaints.
    B. premises that have barriers to persons with a disability.
    C. controlled business arrangements.
    D. kickbacks.

72. The purpose of the SAFE Act is to
    A. protect homes from flood damage.
    B. provide uniformity to state real estate licensing.
    C. protect consumers.
    D. require smoke alarms in new construction.

73. According to the Americans with Disabilities Act, a place of public accommodation refers to
    A. one-to-four residential unit buildings.
    B. any residential unit.
    C. nonresidential facilities.
    D. government-owned properties.

74. To accommodate a person with a disability, the term *readily achievable* means if
    A. at all possible.
    B. possible at no additional cost.
    C. possible without a great deal of expense.
    D. the cost is less than ½% of the property value.

75. Which of the following terms in an advertisement would violate the Civil Rights Act of 1968?
    A. Master bedroom
    B. One child OK
    C. Mother-in-law suite
    D. Bachelor apartment

76. A broker advertised a four-bedroom, handicap-accessible home in a desirable neighborhood at a low price. While he did not have such a home available, he intended to direct inquiries to similar properties in other areas. What law did the broker violate?
    A. Civil Rights Act of 1968
    B. American with Disabilities Act
    C. Truth in Lending Act
    D. Real Estate Settlement Procedures Act

77. Under RESPA, a lender must disclose to a borrower
    A. how much profit will be made if the loan is resold.
    B. if the loan is to be assigned or sold.
    C. the reason the loan was approved.
    D. what other lenders are charging in loan costs for similar loans.

78. A broker need not report to the IRS when a buyer
    A. is a foreign national.
    B. pays $80,000 cash for a lot.
    C. has a series of cash transactions each for $9,5000.
    D. makes a $20,000 cash earnest money deposit.

79. The *Consumer Handbook on Adjustable-Rate Mortgages* warns borrowers as to
    A. costs associated with home ownership.
    B. payment shock when rate is adjusted.
    C. settlement costs.
    D. dangers of debt.

80. An apartment owner was in violation of the Fair Housing Act because
    A. there were no specific accommodations for children.
    B. children were excluded from the pool without adult supervision.
    C. there was one section for adults and another section for families.
    D. all residents were over 55 years old.

CHAPTER 5 QUIZ ANSWERS

1. **(D)** Smaller-business employers are excluded from the act's requirements. (146–147)

2. **(B)** The broker would have to prove she did not discriminate. (141)

3. **(B)** If a person with no disability would not want the alteration, the tenant can be required to restore the premises. (139)

4. **(A)** If the owner or another agent sold based on racial exclusion, they would violate the fair housing laws. (138)

5. **(D)** Drug addiction is specifically excluded from protection for those with a disability. (139)

6. **(C)** A Sherman antitrust law violation. (143)

7. **(B)** However, religious groups are not exempt under the 1866 act and many state fair housing laws. (138)

8. **(D)** The other actions listed are steering, which are prohibited by the Civil Rights Act of 1968. (138)

9. **(C)** The other actions are steering. (138)

10. **(A)** The others discriminate based on familial status. (140)

11. **(B)** The *Protect Your Family from Lead in Your Home* booklet must be provided to buyers and lessees. (129)

12. **(A)** It is the disabled person's responsibility to modify the unit. (139)

13. **(B)** The ADA requires access to places of public accommodation. (140–141)

14. **(B)** While subtle, the broker is nevertheless inducing owners to sell based on entry of minority groups to the area. (138)

15. **(D)** To mention the minority neighbor would likely be regarded as steering, a violation of the Fair Housing Act of 1968. (138)

16. **(B)** Violation of Civil Rights Act of 1968. (138)

17. **(D)** Alcoholism is a covered disability. While owners can prohibit intoxication, they cannot refuse to rent to an alcoholic. (139)

18. **(D)** Persons with a disability are protected under the 1988 Fair Housing Amendments Act. (139)

19. **(B)** All citizens have the same rights to housing, regardless of race. (137)

20. **(C)** Also for HUD-owned property (applies to one-to-four residential unit buildings). (137)

21. **(D)** Senior housing exception to fair housing act. (138, 140)

22. **(C)** Appears to be giving preference based on familial status and sex, which also means discrimination. (140)

23. **(A)** The act only applies to residential telephone numbers listed on the registry. (148)

24. **(C)** Calling as a buyer agent is proper, but not to solicit a listing. (148)

25. **(B)** Solicitation emails must include an "opt-out" mechanism for future solicitations. (145)

26. **(B)** Controlling the Assault of Non-Solicited Pornography and Marketing Act of 2003. (145)

27. **(C)** Otherwise you violate the Federal Telephone Consumer Protection Act. (145)

28. **(B)** They must have made the inquiry. (148)

29. **(B)** The recipient must be able to stop future solicitations. (145)

30. **(A)** They are prohibited. (145)

31. **(B)** Soil contains toxic material. (131)

32. **(C)** Fine per call. (148)

33. **(B)** The National Do Not Call Registry only applies to residential telephones. (148)

34. **(D)** Three months after inquiry. (148)

35. **(C)** Survey calls with no solicitation involved are exempt from do-not-call restrictions. (148)

36. **(C)** As well as a valid subject heading indicating it is a solicitation and an opt-out mechanism. (145)

37. **(C)** For each violation. (145)

38. **(B)** For every unsolicited fax. (145)

39. **(C)** Naturally occurring that rises through the soil. (130)

40. **(A)** A Sherman Antitrust Act violation. (143)

41. **(D)** A Sherman Antitrust Act violation. (141)

42. **(D)** A Sherman Antitrust Act violation. (141)

43. **(A)** Was used in insulation, roofing, and flooring. (130)

44. **(A)** Can prohibit smoking on the premises but cannot refuse to rent to smokers. (139)

45. **(D)** Stating preferences is considered discriminatory. (141)

46. **(A)** True rate considering all loan costs. (143)

47. **(D)** Disclosure is required only for loans having more than four payments. (143)

48. **(B)** The buyer must be told that other service providers are available. (147)

49. **(C)** Amount of payments or down payment trigger full disclosure. (143)

50. **(B)** Estimates of settlement costs must be given within three business days of loan application. (146)

51. **(D)** Advertising an item that is not available or won't be sold. (144)

52. **(D)** However, disclosure must be made that fee can be avoided by going directly to lender. (147)

53. **(B)** As well as the APR. (143)

54. **(B)** Advertising product that will not be sold or is unavailable. (144)

55. **(B)** New first loans for 1–4 residential units. (146)

56. **(C)** Covers premise injuries by the public. (134–135)

57. **(B)** Required by RESPA. (146)

58. **(A)** Required by RESPA. (146)

59. **(B)** Insignificant interest need not be disclosed. (146)

60. **(B)** Does not apply to nonresidential loans. (146)

61. **(C)** Availability of list of those living in the area. (133)

62. **(C)** Broker provides services with firms broker has an interest in. (147)

63. **(D)** And avoid broker fees for the service. (147)

64. **(B)** Antitrust act. (142–143)

65. **(A)** The 1968 case decision was same year as the Fair Housing Act. (137)

66. **(B)** Mortgage loan originator. (149)

67. **(B)** It was a first step toward enforceable fair housing legislation. (137)

68. **(C)** This was a comprehensive fair housing act. (137)

69. **(A)** Comprehensive Environmental Response Compensation and Liability Act. (130)

70. **(A)** While an exemption from the 1968 Fair Housing Act, it is covered by the 1866 act that offers no exemptions for racial discrimination. (137)

71. **(A)** Landlord cannot retaliate by eviction or cutting service for fair housing complaints. (138)

72. **(C)** And reduce fraud in mortgage transactions. (149)

73. **(C)** Open for business to the public. (140)

74. **(C)** What is reasonable considering the value of the property and the expense in compliance. (140)

75. **(B)** Limiting family size to a single child but not total occupancy based on reasonable use. Others have been deemed by HUD to be acceptable. (141)

76. **(C)** The Truth in Lending Act prohibits bait and switch ads. (144)

77. **(B)** Or the loan servicing is to be assigned. (147)

78. **(A)** Cash transactions of $10,000 or more or series of transactions. (148)

79. **(B)** And warns about payment increases. (147)

80. **(C)** Discrimination applies to every unit; it does not matter that housing was available in another section. (140)

C H A P T E R

6

Financing and Settlement

FINANCING INSTRUMENTS

For financing purposes, real estate typically is **hypothecated**—that is, the borrower retains possession while the lender holds security interest. The three basic instruments used to finance real estate are

1. the mortgage,

2. the trust deed or deed of trust, and

3. the land contract, also called the contract for deed (there are regional differences in terminology).

A **note** is the primary evidence of the debt. It is a promise to pay a sum of money. The note includes all the terms of the borrower's promise to pay, including loan amount, interest rate, and time and method of payment. The security for the note is the financing instrument (mortgage/trust deed).

MORTGAGES

The mortgage is a two-party instrument whereby the **mortgagor** (the borrower) gives an interest and a note to a **mortgagee** (the lender) in exchange for a loan. The promissory note is the evidence of the debt, and the real estate interest (the mortgage) is given as security for that debt. The mortgage is regarded as personal property (**chattels real**) and while the mortgagee's interest can be transferred, it must be transferred with the debt (note) (see Figure 6.1).

FIGURE 6.1

Mortgage—Two Parties

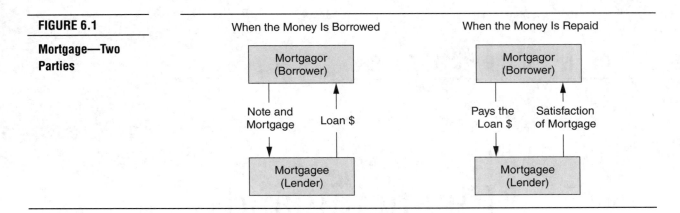

Mortgage Theories

Lien theory.   In the majority of states, the borrower retains title and gives the lender a lien on the property. The lien is perfected when the mortgage is recorded in the county where the real estate is located. When the borrower has paid off the loan, the lender gives the borrower a **satisfaction of mortgage**, which, when recorded, removes the lien.

Title theory.   In title theory states, the borrower transfers title to the lender on a condition subsequent, usually by a trust deed. This means that when the condition is met (payment of the mortgage note), title reverts back to the borrower.

Intermediate theory.   Under the intermediate theory, title remains with the borrower, as in the lien theory, but it automatically transfers to the lender in the event the borrower defaults.

No matter what mortgage theory is used, the borrower has the right to convey the property. However, this might require that the mortgage note be paid off.

DEED OF TRUST

A **deed of trust**, also called a **trust deed** or **trust indenture**, is a three-party instrument whereby the trustor (borrower) gives a note to the **beneficiary** (lender) and, as security for the note, conveys a bare legal or naked title and/or a power of sale to a **trustee** (third person) (see Figure 6.2). The trustor retains possession of the property.

FIGURE 6.2

Trust Deed—Three Parties

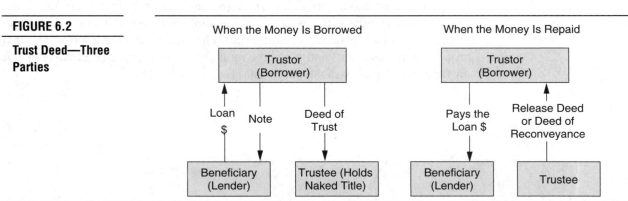

When the trustor has paid the note in full, the beneficiary directs the trustee to return the interest held to the trustor, generally accomplished with the trustee's **deed of reconveyance**. Should the trustor default on the note, the beneficiary would order the trustee to conduct a sale. The purchaser at such a sale would receive a **trustee's deed**. The trustee is said to hold only a bare, or naked, legal title because the trustee's rights are so limited.

Many lenders prefer trust deeds to mortgages because they generally provide for a quick and inexpensive sale and, in most states, avoid lengthy mortgage redemption periods.

Trust deeds are used in more than half the states, although mortgages are also allowed in many of these same states.

LAND CONTRACTS (SALES CONTRACTS)

Land contracts (also called land sales contracts or contracts for deed) are financing agreements whereby the seller retains the legal title as security for the borrower's promise to pay. Under a land contract, the borrower has an interest called **equitable title**. The contract is signed by both **vendor** (seller) and **vendee** (buyer) (see Figure 6.3). Unlike mortgages and trust deeds, a land contract generally does not require a separate note.

FIGURE 6.3

Land Contract

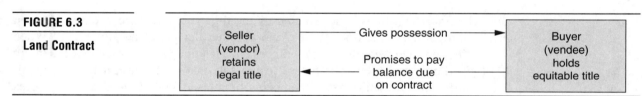

Because land contracts provide for relatively quick forfeiture of the buyer's interests in event of default, they often are used in sales with low down payments.

A deed is not given until the property is paid for or the loan balance is reduced to an agreed amount. This can create a danger to the buyer in that the seller might be unable to provide good title. Land contracts could provide that the deed be given to an escrow, which would offer the purchaser some protection.

Courts in many states have placed restrictions on the quick and easy forfeiture provisions of land contracts, and in some cases, judicial foreclosure is required. Land contracts should be recorded to protect the buyer's interests, but often they are not. They must be acknowledged by the vendor to be recorded.

SHORT SALE

When property values decrease to a point where property value is less than mortgage indebtedness, the loan is said to be upside down. The loan exceeds the value so that the mortgagor has no equity in the property.

To avoid the time and expense associated with foreclosure should the borrower default, lenders will often agree to a **short sale**, in which the lender accepts the sale proceeds as settlement of the loan indebtedness.

Debt relief is normally taxed as income to the taxpayer, but the **Mortgage Forgiveness Debt Relief Fact of 2007** provided that mortgage forgiveness would not be taxed as an imputed gain to the taxpayer for purchase money loans to purchase a principal residence. This exemption applied to debt relief through 2013. While the act has expired, as of this writing, it may be extended.

The **equator platform** is a standardized short save system used by many lenders. An agent can log in to the equator platform and initiate a short sale online.

FORECLOSURE

The Dodd-Frank Act provides that the lender's first notice of residential foreclosure cannot be sent until the homeowner is at least 120 days delinquent.

If the borrower defaults on a note, mortgage foreclosure normally involves a public auction after statutory notice is given (**judicial foreclosure**). The lender could bid the amount owing on the foreclosing loan; other bidders would have to bid cash. Should the sale bring more than the amount owed on the foreclosing loan, the balance would go to pay off junior encumbrances in the order of their priority. Any further excess is paid to the borrower. In some states, money received from a foreclosure sale must be applied first to delinquent property taxes because taxes are priority liens.

The priority of liens is determined by the time and date of recording—the first recorded lien is the priority lien, and all other liens become junior to it. When a lien is foreclosed, the encumbrances (liens) junior to the foreclosing lien are wiped out. A purchaser at a foreclosure sale takes title subject to the encumbrances that are senior to the loan being foreclosed, but all junior encumbrances are eliminated.

For example, suppose there were five mortgages on a property:

1. Mortgage 1—recorded September 1, 1986

2. Mortgage 2—recorded August 3, 1990

3. Mortgage 3—recorded May 15, 1992

4. Mortgage 4—recorded July 9, 1994

5. Mortgage 5—recorded December 24, 1999

If mortgage 3 foreclosed, the purchaser would take title subject to mortgages 1 and 2, and mortgages 4 and 5 would be wiped out.

The lender on a junior lien that contains a **default clause** could protect its interest before foreclosure by making the payments on the senior lien in default and then foreclosing on the junior lien. This would leave the former junior lienholder as the owner, subject to any senior encumbrances. Because unpaid property taxes and special assessments are priority liens, they are not affected by a foreclosure.

Redemption. In some states, after a judicial foreclosure (foreclosure by court action), borrowers have a statutory period for redeeming the property by paying the foreclosure sales price plus interest and penalties. In some states, the borrower is allowed possession during the redemption period, which can be as long as one year. In other states, redemption must occur be before the foreclosure sale. Redemption after the foreclosure sale requires paying off the lien in full. Some states allow the borrower to reinstate the loan before the foreclosure sale by making the loan current and paying costs and interest.

Mortgage Electronic Registration System (MERS).   The Mortgage Electronic Registration System (MERS) is a private national mortgage database that provides services and acts as noteholder. MERS keeps records of the lenders when loans are sold. MERS holds the mortgage note. Some states allowed MERS to foreclose on a delinquent mortgage as the owner of record, while others did not. MERS no longer forecloses in its own name but as an assignee.

Deficiency judgments.   If the amount realized at a foreclosure sale is not sufficient to satisfy the debt owed to the foreclosing mortgagee, it is possible for a deficiency judgment to be granted for the difference between the sales price and the amount owing. The foreclosed mortgagor not only loses the property that secured the mortgage but is still liable for the deficiency. Several states prohibit deficiency judgments, and many others place strong limitations on their use.

Deficiency judgments generally are not allowed where the foreclosing mortgagee purchases the property for less than its fair market value or where the foreclosing mortgagee is the seller (purchase-money loan) who is simply taking the property back by bidding at the foreclosure sale.

In cases of trust deeds, deficiency judgments generally are not allowed when foreclosure is by exercising the power of sale in the trust deeds (nonjudicial foreclosure).

A loan for which a deficiency judgment is not possible is considered **nonrecourse financing**, which means the borrower has no personal liability under the loan. The lender's sole remedy is to foreclose on the property.

Strict foreclosure.   In several states, strict foreclosure is allowed, whereby the court orders the borrower's interest to be terminated without a sale. Some New England states allow **foreclosure by entry**. If the lender can peaceably take possession, after a required period, the borrower's interests are terminated. Deficiency judgments are not allowed in cases of strict foreclosure or foreclosure by entry.

Deed in lieu of foreclosure.   To avoid the credit stigma of a foreclosure sale, an owner sometimes deeds her interest to the lender. Although a foreclosure sale wipes out junior liens, accepting a deed in lieu of foreclosure could give title to the lender with the subsequent liens intact.

Nonjudicial foreclosure.   In some states, mortgages can provide for a nonjudicial foreclosure procedure similar to the trust deed foreclosure sale described earlier.

Service Members Civil Relief Act of 2003. This act expanded the protection granted service personnel in the Soldiers and Sailors Civil Relief Act of 1940. Key points of the act include the following:

- If the rent is $2,400 per month or less, no eviction without court approval (since the amount is adjusted for inflation; in 2013, it was $3,139.35 per month).

- No interest can be charged on credit obligations above 6% for loans entered into before active duty. This applies to mortgages as well as credit cards. Interest over 6% is permanently forgiven.

- Residential and business property leases can be terminated without penalty when they began before active duty.

- A service member who is deployed to a new permanent station (for 90 days or more) may terminate a housing lease without penalty.

- Mortgage or trust deed foreclosures are stayed for a period of 90 days after the end of active duty service.

This act does not apply to career military.

Helping Families Save Their Home Act of 2009. The Helping Families Save Their Home Act of 2009 allows HUD to modify federal housing authority loans by paying off the balance due in excess of market value.

Protecting Tenants at Foreclosure Act of 2009. The Protecting Tenants at Foreclosure Act of 2009 protects residential tenants from eviction at foreclosure. There is a 90-day notice period required to vacate if there is no lease. Tenants who have a lease can remain until the lease has expired unless the owner intends to occupy the unit in which case a 90-day notice is required.

Mortgage Assistance Relief Services Rule (MARS). This rule applies to deceptive acts or practices involving loan modifications and foreclosure rescue services, such as arranging short sales. The rule prohibits deception and mandates disclosures and retention of records, including sales scripts. Service providers may not tell clients not to contact the lender directly. The rule does not apply to a real estate licensee working in a licensed capacity to obtain short sale approval.

The rule prohibits collecting advance payments.

FEDERAL RESERVE

The Federal Reserve is our nation's central bank and responsible for our **monetary policy** (controls money supply). They seek to adjust availability and cost of funds so we can have a strong economy with minimum unemployment and also keep inflation in check. The Federal Reserve has four basic controls:

1. *Discount rates.* By raising and lowering the discount rate, that is, the interest rate charged to member banks to borrow funds, the Fed affects the long-term interest rates charged by lenders. Lowering mortgage interest rates means lower mortgage payments and is conducive to a healthy real estate market. Raising interest rates means higher mortgage payments and fewer potential borrowers being able to qualify for home loans, which would have a negative effect on the real estate market.

2. *Reserve requirements.* By lowering reserve requirements of member banks, banks can lend a greater portion of their assets. Raising reserve requirements means less money available to loan.

3. *Open market transactions.* The Federal Reserve can buy and sell federal securities (bonds) in the open market. Buying securities puts more money into the economy, while selling securities takes money out of the economy.

4. *Money supply.* The federal reserve can create money to match the supply of currency in circulation to the growth needs of the economy.

Expansionary policies to promote growth include lowering the discount rate, lowering reserve requirements, buying government securities, and placing more currency in circulation.

Contractionary policies to slow the economy and fight inflation include raising the discount rate, raising the reserve requirements of lenders, selling government securities on the open market, and restricting the supply of new currency.

The Federal Reserve does not control the government's *fiscal policy*, which is governmental taxation and governmental spending.

LOAN TYPES, TERMS, AND PROVISIONS

Loans are categorized in a number of ways so that a single loan might be called more than one loan type.

Loan Types

Purchase money loan. With a **purchase money loan**, the seller finances the buyer. No money changes hands, and the interest rate is often less than for *hard-money loans* where cash is involved. The term is used in some areas to denote any loan made for the purpose of purchase.

Home equity loan. This is a second mortgage taken out on the equity a home-owner has in her home. It is usually at a higher rate of interest than a home purchase loan.

Amortized loan. This is a loan in which the regular equal payments fully pay the loan during the period of the loan. Each payment on an amortized loan applies a greater amount to principal and a lesser amount to interest than the prior payment.

Partially amortized loan. This is a loan whose payments do not fully liquidate the loan and that thus requires a final large balloon payment

Straight or term loan. This is a loan where interest only is paid. The principal is due in full on the due date.

Negative amortization. When the loan payments fail to pay the interest due, the principal increases. This is called **negative amortization**. Under the Dodd-Frank Act a negative amortized loan secured by a dwelling requires specified disclosure and, in some cases, homeownership counseling. A number of states now prohibit negative amortization loans.

Graduated payment mortgage (GPM).   These mortgage loans have lower payments during the early years. The payments, which are not sufficient to pay the interest, result in a negative amortization during the early years. This means that the amount owed actually increases. These loans are well suited to young buyers with rising incomes because low initial payments allow the buyers to qualify for a larger loan than would otherwise be possible.

Growing equity mortgage (GEM).   These loans have initial payments based on a long-term amortization schedule, such as 30 years. They provide for periodic payment increases that apply directly to the loan principal, allowing the GEM to be paid off in a relatively short period.

Biweekly mortgage.   This type of mortgage loan provides for half of the monthly payment to be made every two weeks. The result is that 26 payments are made every year (13 months), which shortens the amortization period.

Renegotiable rate mortgage (RRM).   Also called a rollover or two-step loan, this instrument is short term (usually five to seven years), with payments based on a 25-year or 30-year period. When the term expires, the lender rewrites the loan at the then-current interest rate or the loan may be paid off.

Adjustable-rate mortgage (ARM).   With ARMs, the interest rate can be adjusted up or down during the loan term. Special terms that apply to ARMs are as follows:

- *Index*. The index is the interest indicator that the loan interest is based on, such as federal cost of funds or LIBOR rate.

- *Margin*. The margin is an amount added to the index to determine the rate of interest for the loan, such as 2.5%.

- *Adjustment period*. Loans often set the frequency of interest adjustments to every six months or annually.

- *Cap (rate cap)*. The cap is the maximum amount of an interest increase or decrease. There is usually a payment cap on a periodic adjustment (such as 1%), as well a lifetime cap over the period of the loan (maximum cap is generally 5%).

- *Introductory rate*. This rate, also called a teaser rate, is generally set below the index rate plus the margin. It allows a lower qualifying income for borrowers and lower initial payments. One problem with the low introductory rate is that borrowers frequently experience payment shock at the first adjustment to their payments.

- *Negative amortization*. Some ARMs allow negative amortization when the payment is kept to less than the interest because of caps on payments. Most ARMs do not allow negative amortization. If there is negative amortization, the loan principal increases rather than decreases.

A variation of an adjustable-rate mortgage is a two-step, 30-year loan with a fixed rate for a period, such as 5 years followed by a 25-year adjustable-rate loan. Such a loan might be called a 5–30 loan.

Reverse-annuity mortgage (RAM) or reverse mortgage.   With RAMs, owners borrow against the equity in their homes by receiving monthly payments. This mortgage provides a means for elderly people to keep their homes. The mortgage is paid off when the mortgagors die or when the property is sold.

Blanket mortgage.   A blanket mortgage is secured by more than one property. Normally it would include a **release clause**, providing for the release of parcels from the mortgage upon the payment of stated amounts.

Open-end mortgage.   An open-end loan can be increased to an agreed-on ceiling.

Open mortgage.   An open loan can be prepaid without penalty.

Package mortgage.   A package mortgage is secured by both personal property and real property. A mortgage on a hotel might be secured by both the real property and the furnishings.

Construction mortgage.   The payments that are made as work progresses are called **obligatory advances**. The final payment usually is not made until the lien period expires. Construction loans are made at a higher interest rate than permanent financing. Construction loans are usually first loans.

Subprime loan.   These are higher-risk loans because of the structure of the loan, borrower's credit, size of loan, income documentation, type of property, or loan-to-value ratio. They generally bear higher rates of interest to compensate for the greater risk.

Convertible mortgage.   This is an adjustable-rate loan where the borrower may convert the loan to a fixed-rate mortgage at a later date.

Option ARM.   An option ARM is an adjustable-rate mortgage where the borrower has the option of making a payment less than is necessary to amortize the loan. The lowest payment is likely to be even less than the interest. Because the loan has negative amortization, a much larger payment is required when the option period ends, which could be after three to five years. The option arm allows buyers to qualify for larger loans than they would otherwise be eligible for.

Borrowers often encountered difficulties when the option period expired and payments increased for loan amortization leading to loan default and foreclosure.

Interest-only loan.   Because payments of interest only for a number of years are required, the borrower can qualify for a larger loan. At the end of the interest-only period, payments that will amortize the loan will have to be made.

Participation mortgage.   On large commercial projects, lenders may insist on sharing ownership, as limited partners, as well as receive interest on the loans. The participation loan may carry a lower interest rate than otherwise required.

Shared appreciation mortgage (SAM).   This is an amortized loan in which the investor or the lender makes the down payment for a buyer or gives the borrower a lower rate of interest in exchange for an agreement whereby the investor will share in the appreciation of the property value. The agreement usually sets a date for the property to be sold.

Wrap-around mortgage or all-inclusive mortgage.   This is a second loan written to cover the amounts of a first and second loan. The buyer makes the total payment to the seller, who then makes the payment on the first loan. This arrangement allows the seller to make money on the interest differential between the rate on the first loan and the rate on the second loan, as well as to get the interest on the equity. The income resulting from the difference in interest rates is called **arbitrage**.

Take-out loan. This is the permanent financing that "takes out" the construction loan.

Bridge loan (swing loan or gap loan). A bridge loan is a short-term loan between other loans—for example, a loan between the construction loan and suitable permanent financing (take-out loan). Bridge loans have higher interest than permanent financing.

Seasoned loan. A seasoned loan is an existing loan with a payment history. On the secondary mortgage market, it might sell at a premium when compared with a similar new loan.

Nonrecourse loan. Under a nonrecourse loan, the borrower is not personally liable on the loan, so a deficiency judgment is not possible.

Personal property loan. The Uniform Commercial Code (UCC) provides that recording a **financing statement** creates a lien against personal property, including property that becomes a fixture.

Loan Terms

Loan terms define common loan expressions.

Interest. Interest is the charge paid to borrow money. The interest rate is a percentage of the amount borrowed.

Compound interest. This is interest computed on the principal plus accrued interest. An amortized mortgage carries *simple interest*—the only time the interest is compounded is when payments are not made.

Usury. State law regulates maximum interest rates that can be charged by various categories of lenders. Interest charged in excess of the maximum rate is usurious and cannot be collected because the practice is illegal. Usury is treated as a misdemeanor or a felony. In most states, however, a loan with usurious rates is not invalid; the loan must still be repaid, although state law might prohibit interest, limit interest to the amount legally collectible, and/or provide penalties for usurious interest already collected.

Discounting a mortgage. Selling an existing mortgage for less than its face value results in discounting the mortgage.

Compensating balance. Banks might require that a borrower maintain a balance of a percentage of the loan in a savings or checking account at the bank. The net effect of maintaining such an account at a relatively low or no interest rate is to raise the effective rate of interest on the loan.

Mortgage warehousing. This is interim financing by a mortgage company. Mortgage bankers borrow on their inventory of loans rather than sell the loans when they believe interest rates will fall (thus increasing the resale value of their inventory).

Points. Points are units of measure (one point equals 1% of the loan). Points are charged by lenders to cover lender expenses, increase lender yield, and/or allow a lower mortgage rate.

As a rule of thumb, each point increases the lender's yield by approximately ⅛ of 1% in interest. Although this one-time charge is considered interest when paid by a buyer, points paid by a seller may be considered a sales cost that is reflected in any capital gain.

Buydown loans.   In a buydown loan, the seller pays discount points to a lender so that the lender can offer the buyer a below-market rate of interest. Developers will offer buydown loans to obtain a competitive advantage for home sales. Zero interest loans are short-term loans where the seller pays points in order to reduce the interest rate to zero.

Loan assumptions.   A buyer who assumes a loan agrees to be primarily liable for payment of the loan; the seller remains secondarily liable. Because the buyer has agreed to pay, a deficiency judgment is possible against the buyer in event of default.

A loan without a *due-on-sale clause* does not prohibit assumption, so it may either be assumed or the buyer could take "subject to" the loan.

"Subject to" loan.   When a buyer purchases "subject to" an existing loan, the buyer acknowledges the existence of the loan but does not agree to accept liability for the loan if the loan payments are not paid. In the event of foreclosure, the buyer loses the property but is not liable for a deficiency judgment. In a "subject to" sale, the seller remains primarily liable on the loan and could be held liable for a deficiency judgment. If a loan contains a due-on-sale clause, a buyer cannot take title with the loan remaining.

Predatory lending.   While a number of federal laws require disclosures and Dodd-Frank requires lenders ascertain borrower's ability to repay, there is no comprehensive federal predatory lending law. However, many states have predatory lending laws to protect consumers against loan originators taking unfair advantage of borrowers.

Loan Provisions

Loan provisions are conditions included in the loan documentation and/or note. Basic loan provisions include amount of loan, interest rate, monthly payments, term of the loan, and so on. The following are some of the additional provisions that may be included in a loan.

Late charges.   Grace periods (the number of days allowed for a late payment), as well as charges for late payments, generally are set forth in the loan agreement and may be regulated by state statutes. Courts will not allow excessive late charges.

Defeasance clause.   The defeasance clause provides for the release of the lien when the obligation under the note is discharged by payment.

Prepayment penalty.   Without special authorization or state statute to the contrary, the borrower has no right to repay a loan in any manner other than as set forth in the note. Prepayment clauses allow early repayment but may specify a penalty—for example, "six months' interest based on the amount prepaid." Prepayment penalties cannot be charged if an early payment is required under a due-on-sale clause. Many states regulate prepayment penalties.

"Or more" clause.   The use of words such as "payments of $550 or more per month" allows the mortgagor to prepay a loan without penalty.

Lock-in clause.   A lock-in clause allows prepayment but requires that all interest be paid as if the original loan schedule were followed (actually a severe prepayment penalty). Many states strictly regulate or prohibit the use of such clauses. Where lock-in clauses are permitted, they generally are used in commercial loans by long-term lenders (such as insurance companies and pension funds that want the long-term interest).

Due-on-sale (alienation) clause.   A loan with a due-on-sale clause must be paid in full if the property is sold; therefore, such a loan cannot be assumed. If the lender discovers that title has been passed, the lender can accelerate the payments.

A lender often will allow an assumption rather than accelerate the payments if the interest rate is favorable to the lender or if the loan is assumed at a higher rate of interest.

Acceleration clause.   This clause accelerates all loan payments (entire amount due) if a borrower defaults—for example, fails to make payments by a given date. The entire loan can be declared due and payable immediately, which will often lead to foreclosure (there may be state restrictions on accelerating payments). A due-on-sale clause is a type of acceleration clause.

Nondisturbance clause.   This clause is an agreement by the mortgagee to honor subsequent leases should the mortgagee foreclose.

Assignment of rents.   This clause provides that the lender will have the right to collect rents and apply them to the debt should the borrower default. Otherwise, the borrower could collect and keep the rent receipts until the foreclosure sale.

Balloon payment.   A balloon payment is a large payment, often at the end of an unamortized or partially amortized loan. Although a loan payment might be based on a long amortization period, the loan might state "balance all due and payable seven years from date hereof," which would require that the buyer either come up with cash or be able to refinance the loan. A balloon payment could also be used for a deferred down payment. Many states have restrictions on balloon payments.

Power-of-sale clause.   This clause allows for a relatively quick nonjudicial foreclosure should the borrower default (not allowed in all states).

Release.   If a mortgage or trust deed covers more than one property (blanket mortgage), release clauses allow individual properties to be freed from the lien on payment of specified sums. Without a release clause, the entire loan balance must be paid off to sell one parcel.

Subordination.   This clause changes the priority of a loan, making it secondary to a later recorded loan. It is often used with land sales where the seller agrees to take a lien that will be subordinate to a later recorded construction loan. Subordination clauses subject the seller to great risks.

Impound account. Also called a borrower's escrow account or reserve account, an impound account is a trust account kept by the lender for taxes and insurance when taxes and insurance are part of the borrower's payment to the lender. In some states, these accounts are required to bear interest. FHA loans, VA loans, and many state loan programs require impound accounts.

Default clause. This clause allows a junior lienholder to cure a default of the borrower on a prior lien. If the prior lien had foreclosed, the junior lien would be wiped out.

PRIMARY AND SECONDARY FINANCING

Most funds for real estate financing come indirectly from private and business savings deposited with institutional lenders.

Primary financing refers to the first loan on a property, such as a first mortgage. **Secondary financing** refers to second mortgages.

Characteristics of secondary financing often include the following:

- Shorter term compared with primary financing
- A greater likelihood of having a balloon payment with a large final balance
- Higher interest rate compared with primary financing, because of greater lender risk

As a rule, primary financing uses amortized loans—that is, loans that are paid off over the loan period with equal monthly installments applying to principal and interest.

Do not confuse primary and secondary financing with the primary and secondary mortgage markets. Key distinctions are as follows:

- *Primary financing*—first loans
- *Secondary financing*—second or junior loans
- *Primary mortgage market*—loans made directly to borrowers
- *Secondary mortgage market*—the purchase and sale of existing loans

Seller financing can be primary or secondary financing. Land contracts are often used because the seller retains title and ease of foreclosure.

Lenders

Besides individual lenders, there are a number of institutions and businesses that engage in arranging or making loans secured by real estate.

CONVENTIONAL LOANS

Loans made without government guarantees or insurance are conventional loans. They often have a lower **loan-to-value ratio (LTV)** than government-insured or government-guaranteed loans, which means that larger down payments are required.

Commercial Banks

Commercial banks use demand deposit funds to make loans. They will usually sell their loans to Fannie Mae or Freddie Mac or other institutions to maintain liquidity. Loans that banks keep are called **portfolio loans**. These are often loans at higher interest rates. Commercial bank deposits are insured by the Federal Deposit Insurance Corporation (FDIC).

Insurance Companies

Insurance companies prefer large commercial and industrial loans and some new-home loans. They seldom make individual loans on older homes and generally do not make construction loans. Insurers often purchase loans from mortgage bankers and/or make loans through mortgage brokers.

Mortgage Bankers

Mortgage bankers (mortgage companies) use their own funds to make loans, which they usually sell to institutions and lenders. They make money on origination fees and loan servicing fees. They frequently service the loans they sell. Mortgage bankers are currently the largest source for mortgage loan origination.

Mortgage Brokers

Mortgage brokers are middlemen who arrange loans between borrowers and lenders. They do not use their own funds. They make money on relatively high loan origination fees. The loans they make are generally at higher interest rates to borrowers who fail to qualify for loans from institutional lenders. The lenders who make the loans they arrange are generally individuals or *subprime* lenders. Mortgage brokers seldom service the loans that they arrange.

Private Mortgage Insurance (PMI)

Several firms offer lenders mortgage protection coverage (similar to FHA insurance) against the default of the mortgagor. Lenders will require private mortgage insurance for conventional loans where down payments are less than 20%. Under federal regulations, a borrower may request cancellation of PMI when the principal balance reaches 80% of the original value. The lender must automatically terminate PMI when the balance reaches 78% of value and the borrower is current on payments.

GOVERNMENT LOANS

The government does not make **government loans**. Most of what are called government loans are government-insured or government-guaranteed loans. Federal Housing Administration (FHA) and Department of Veterans Affairs (VA) loans are made by lenders subject to government supervision. FHA loans are government-insured, whereas VA loans are government-guaranteed.

General information about FHA and VA loans is outlined in Figure 6.4.

FIGURE 6.4		FHA	VA
FHA and VA Loan Information	Government involvement	FHA insured—mutual mortgage insurance premium (MIP) paid by borrower; up-front premium paid on closing, as well as a fee with payments	VA guarantee
	Who is eligible?	Anyone who qualifies	U.S. veterans who will be owner-occupants
	Who makes the loans?	Approved lending institutions	Approved lending institutions
	Loan costs	1% loan origination fee plus mortgage insurance premium	1% loan origination fee plus funding fee to VA
	Loan purpose	Housing only (includes mobile homes and 1–4 unit apartments)	Farm, home (1–4 units), or business (if for a home, it must be owner-occupied)
	Maximum loan allowed (subject to change)	Varies by county—may be below $300,000 or over $700,000	No limit to loan, but loan can't exceed CRV (appraisal)
	Interest rates	Negotiable	Negotiable
	Term of loan	Usually 30 years	Maximum 30 years
	Down payment	Minimum 3.5%	No down payment required for loans up to $417,000 (lender can require down payment)
	Prepayment penalty	None	None
	Secondary financing	Not allowed at time of sale	Not allowed at time of sale
	Assumable (loans made before specified dates are assumable by anyone)	Loans made after December 15, 1989, assumable only by owner-occupants who qualify for the loans	Loans made after March 1, 1988, assumable only if buyers qualify for the loans

Qualified Mortgage Rule

The Dodd-Frank Act required HUD to define qualified mortgages. A qualified mortgage is a mortgage insured, guaranteed by or administered by HUD. Lenders making qualified mortgages are presumed to have met the ability-to-repay provisions of the Dodd-Frank Act. To be a qualified mortgage, the following requirements must be met:

■ Loans for 30 years or less

■ 3% limit on upfront points and fees

■ Periodic payments without toxic loan features such as interest-only loans, negative amortization, loan terms beyond 30 years, or balloon payments

■ Be insured or guaranteed by FHA or HUD

Generally, a qualified mortgage limits the debt-to-income ratio at no more than 43% of income.

Federal Housing Administration (FHA) Loans

The FHA was established in 1934 to encourage improvements in housing and to encourage home ownership through its home financing programs.

Title I loans are home improvement loans with a maximum term of 15 years.

Title II loans are home purchase loans limited to one-to-four residential unit buildings. Generally, they are 30-year loans but can be up to 40 years.

FHA loans include the following characteristics:

1. FHA loans are government-insured. A one-time **mortgage insurance premium (MIP)** of 1.75% of loan amount is collected at settlement or added to the mortgage. There is also a monthly insurance premium that is based on the amortization period and the loan-to-value ratio. FHA insurance insures the lender against losses suffered if the borrower defaults.

2. The loans cover housing only, including mobile homes and apartments (one to four residential units).

3. An FHA appraisal is required.

4. The property must meet **minimum property requirements (MPRs)**.

5. They are high loan-to-value-ratio loans. The maximum FHA loan percentages are based on purchase price and are subject to change. The purchaser must, however, have a minimum cash investment of 3%, but it can come from a gift.

6. One hundred percent of reasonable closing costs may be financed.

7. FHA local field offices set a maximum loan amount on single-family dwellings based on the region.

8. Secondary financing is not allowed at time of loan origination.

9. Loan discount points may be paid by the buyer, the seller, or both and are subject to mutual agreement.

10. They are fully amortized loans. Balloon payments are not allowed.

11. They are long-term loans and, therefore, require lower monthly payments than many shorter-term conventional loans.

12. No prepayment penalty is allowed.

13. Taxes and insurance are included in the payments.

14. The assumability of FHA loans depends on the origination date of the loans:

    ■ Loans made before December 15, 1989, are fully assumable without qualifying by the purchaser.

    ■ Loans made after December 15, 1989, are assumable only by owner-occupants who qualify for the loans (investors cannot assume loans). Unless there is a novation (substitution of liability), a seller could be held liable on a loan.

    ■ The FHA cost for loan assumption without buyer qualification is $125. Loans assumed with buyer qualification requirements incur FHA costs of actual costs or $500, whichever is less.

15. The loans are made by institutional lenders. The FHA will issue a six-month conditional commitment to insure a loan for a property, provided the buyer, when found, qualifies for the loan. A firm commitment to insure may be obtained for a property when there is a definite buyer.

16. Lenders may be allowed to determine whether a loan qualifies for FHA insurance. This process, called direct endorsement, speeds up loan processing.

Department of Veterans Affairs (VA) Loans

These loans may be called DVA loans.

VA loans include the following characteristics:

1. The veteran, if not on active duty, must submit a copy of discharge papers and obtain a **certificate of eligibility**. National Guard and reservists with at least six years of service are also eligible.

2. An appraisal and a **certificate of reasonable value (CRV)** are required. The veteran is not obligated to complete the purchase if the sales price exceeds the CRV. The veteran can, however, pay the difference in cash.

3. Institutional lenders usually make the loans.

4. Figure 6.5 outlines the VA's guarantees.

FIGURE 6.5	Loan Amount	Guarantee
VA Guarantees	Up to $45,000	50% of loan
	$45,000–$144,000	Minimum guarantee of $22,500, maximum guarantee is 40% of loan up to $36,000
	More than $144,000	25% of loan up to $104,250

5. There is no limit on the amount of a VA loan, so long as it does not exceed the CRV. The limit is on the guarantee. However, lenders will generally limit their loans to the loan purchase limit set by Fannie Mae.

6. VA loans can be for farm, home, or business. VA housing loans are limited to one to four residential units, and residences must be owner occupied.

7. Loans up to $417,000 do not require a down payment in most parts of the country. In high-cost areas, the limit is higher.

8. Secondary financing is not allowed at the time of purchase.

9. The loans are long term (30 years for home).

10. The loans are amortized (no balloon payments).

11. The veteran may pay a 1% loan origination fee. Payments of points are negotiable between the buyer and the seller. While the veteran can pay points, unlike FHA loans, points (and origination fee) may not be financed as part of the loan.

12. The veteran pays a percentage of the loan as a *funding fee* and reasonable loan costs to the VA at the time of the loan (the fee can be included in the loan). The funding fee varies from 1.25% to 2.4%, based on type of service and down payment.

    The funding fee may be waived for disabled veterans and widows whose spouse's death was service connected.

13. VA loans made before March 1, 1988, are fully assumable by anyone, without qualification.

    Loans made after March 1, 1988, are assumable only if the buyer qualifies for the loan. The veteran is no longer liable for any deficiency judgment should the qualifying buyer default, except in the case of fraud.

14. Restoration of loan benefits is possible. A veteran can restore loan eligibility by paying off the loan upon sale or can ask for a substitution of entitlement if another veteran assumes the loan. A processing fee can be charged for loan assumptions.

15. VA loans charge no prepayment penalty.

16. Prepayment can't be less than $100 or one installment.

17. Payments include taxes and insurance.

18. No buyer loan broker fee (commission) can be charged to the veteran buyer.

SECONDARY MORTGAGE MARKET LOANS

There are a number of organizations and individuals engaged in the secondary mortgage market, which involves the buying and selling of existing mortgages.

Fannie Mae. Fannie Mae (formerly called Federal National Mortgage Association, or FNMA) was a private corporation, presently under federal conservatorship, that creates a marketplace for existing mortgages by buying FHA, VA, and conventional mortgages in the secondary mortgage market. The loan limit for the purchase of single-family homes is $417,000 at the time of printing, but the limit is subject to annual adjustment. Several states have higher limits. To raise funds, Fannie Mae sells securities backed by pools of mortgages. **Participation certificates (PCs)** are one of the forms of securities issued.

Fannie Mae's *Desktop Underwriter* computer application allows mortgage loan applications to be processed in 15 minutes or less.

Freddie Mac. Freddie Mac (formerly called Federal Home Loan Mortgage Corporation, or FHLMC), a private government-chartered corporation now under federal conservatorship, was established to provide a secondary mortgage market for federal savings associations. It now buys FHA, VA, and conventional mortgages and uses them as security to sell bonds and participation certificates. Freddie Mac dollar limits are the same as for Fannie Mae.

Farmer Mac (Federal Agricultural Mortgage Corporation). Federally chartered, Farmer Mac provides a secondary mortgage market for agricultural and rural housing loans by purchasing qualified loans from lenders and issues government guaranteed securities.

Ginnie Mae. Ginnie Mae (formerly called Government National Mortgage Association, or GNMA) is a division of the Department of Housing and Urban Development (HUD). It guarantees government-assistance loans where other financing is unavailable and uses **mortgage-backed securities (MBSs)**.

Ginnie Mae increases liquidity in the mortgage market by its MBS program. It will guarantee securities issued by private intermediaries such as banks or mortgage companies that are backed by pools of mortgages.

Conforming and nonconforming loans. Conforming loans are conventional loans that meet the purchase standards of Fannie Mae or Freddie Mac. Because of strict underwriting requirements and the fact that there is a ready market to resell these loans, the interest rate for conforming loans may be less than the rate for nonconforming loans.

Nonconforming loans don't meet Fannie Mae or Freddie Mac purchase requirements, so sometimes they are held by the lender (portfolio loans) rather than resold in the secondary mortgage market. Single-family home loans over $417,000 are called **jumbo loans** (this amount may be revised annually based on housing costs).

LENDER REQUIREMENTS

In evaluating borrowers, lenders are interested in the four Cs: *collateral*, *capacity*, *character*, and *capital*.

Collateral. The value of the collateral (security for the loan) is crucial. The lender wants a margin for safety in its loan-to-value ratio (LTV). A lower LTV might mean better loan terms. A higher loan-to-value ratio is possible with government-insured or government-guaranteed loans, as well as with loans having private mortgage insurance (PMI).

The value of the collateral is determined by a lender appraisal, which is paid for by the borrower.

Capacity. Capacity deals with a borrower's income and indebtedness; the incomes of both spouses and joint borrowers are considered. Generally, lenders will not consider overtime earnings, and only a portion (usually 50%) of dividend income from stocks will be considered. In qualifying borrowers for home loans, lenders generally use two ratios—the **front-end ratio**, which is the ratio of the borrowers' gross monthly income to the **principal, interest, taxes, and insurance (PITI)** loan payment, and the **back-end ratio**, which is the ratio of gross monthly income to the PITI loan payment plus all monthly long-term credit obligations (beyond 10 months). The front-end ratio is generally 28%, which means the borrower cannot pay more than 28% of gross monthly income for the loan payment. The back-end ratio is generally 36%, which means that no more than 36% of the gross monthly income can be used for loan and monthly credit payments. Special situations and local customs could result in the use of different ratios, particularly in areas of high housing costs.

Character. Character deals with borrowers' credit history—which looks at how they have paid obligations in the past.

FICO credit score.   A FICO score is used to evaluate borrowers. The score is intended to predict a borrower's future credit performance. This credit scoring system was developed by Fair Isaac Corporation. It is used by most lenders, as well as Freddie Mac and Fannie Mae. The higher the score, the more creditworthy the borrower. The score is based on a great many credit factors.

Capital.   This refers to liquid assets, such as bank accounts, retirement accounts, stocks and bonds, and other assets readily convertible to cash to support the transaction should other factors become weak.

Fannie Mae's homebuyer program.   Fannie Mae's Community Home Buyer's Program offers flexibility to the qualifying ratios for homebuyers who take a homebuyer educational course. Freddie Mac has a similar program, Affordable Gold, which reduces or eliminates down payment requirements and provides for easier qualifying.

Prequalification.   Prequalification for a loan is based on information given to the lender (usually verbally or online) as to income, assets, and debts. The lender determines the maximum loan the applicant qualifies for based on verification of information and appraisal of the property. This process can be accomplished within minutes.

Preapproval.   Preapproval for a loan is the lenders' indication that they are willing and able to make the loan to the applicant when a suitable property has been secured by a real estate contract. The lender verifies the credit information and credit history and FICO score before preapproval.

Subprime lenders.   Subprime lenders will make loans to borrowers who fail to qualify for loans with conventional lenders. The no-qualifying loans will be made with higher interest and/or loan origination fees to offset the greater risk.

Affordability index.   The National Association of REALTORS® established an affordability index that indicates the percentage of families having the median family income that can qualify for an 80% loan for the median priced home. Affordability is influenced by area housing costs, interest rates, and income.

SETTLEMENT (CLOSING)

A real estate settlement is the closing of a transaction where a deed conveying the title is exchanged for cash and/or a security instrument and all costs are paid and/or prorated.

Before closing, the buyer will ascertain that the title is marketable through either title insurance or an attorney's title opinion based on the abstract of title. The buyer will also want to ascertain before closing that the property is in the condition agreed on and that any special contractual conditions have been met. A final walk-through inspection is often arranged by the agreement of the parties.

Sometimes, a real estate settlement is the responsibility of the listing broker; however, in most areas, settlements are handled by escrow or title companies (closing agents) or attorneys. Presettlement includes the following activities:

■ Ordering the preliminary title report for title insurance or an update of the abstract and a title opinion

- Obtaining statements from lenders as to loan balances being assumed or paid off, as well as assumption costs and/or prepayment penalties

- Prorating taxes, insurance, rents, and the like as applicable (In most states, the seller is responsible for costs and is entitled to income up to and including the date of closing, but in a few states, the closing day is the buyer's responsibility.)

- Arranging for the transfer of insurance policies being assumed (The seller bears the risk of loss before closing. However, if the buyer is given possession before closing, the risk of loss could be borne by the buyer.)

- Obtaining leases and arranging for their assignment

- Preparing bills of sale for personal property

- Obtaining a certificate of occupancy (This may be required for new structures.)

- Drafting all deeds, notes, mortgages, and so forth (In a real estate settlement, the person giving an instrument normally pays to draft it and pays notarization fees. The party receiving the instrument customarily pays for its recording.)

- Drafting settlement statements

- Obtaining certificates required by state law, such as smoke detector certificates and municipal lien certificates

- Complying with state and federal disclosure and reporting requirements

At the settlement, all signatures are obtained and funds disbursed. The closing agent generally arranges for the recording of all documents (loan documents and any deed transferring title).

In a face-to-face closing, both the buyers and the sellers have an opportunity to examine the closing statement before the exchange of title and consideration. Lenders customarily attend face-to-face closings to make certain that existing loans are properly paid off and that new loans are properly signed. Lenders generally require that evidence of property casualty insurance be provided before closing. Lenders also may require that they be protected by a lenders' policy of extended-coverage title insurance.

The closing agent generally provides separate closing statements for the buyer and the seller, showing all debits and credits and the amount to be paid or received. Credits are pluses (amounts a party is entitled to), and debits are minuses (amounts to be paid or subtracted from amounts due).

Credit and debits are different for buyer and seller. For example, whereas the seller is entitled to the sales price (credit), the buyer is responsible for this amount (debit).

When a buyer assumes a loan or gives the seller a new second mortgage, it reduces the amount needed for a purchase. Therefore, the transaction is a credit against the sales price for the buyer and a debit to the seller against funds to which the seller is entitled.

While loans against the property may be paid off by the seller before closing, generally the closing agent writes checks to pay off existing loans that are not being assumed. The payoff of existing loans is a debit to the seller because it reduces the amount the seller is entitled to.

Closing generally involves the proration of some items, such as taxes, rents, insurance, service fees, etc. Prorations vary by state with some using actual days and others using a 30-day month. In some areas, the seller is responsible for the day of closing, while in other areas, it is the responsibility of the buyer.

Figure 6.6 indicates common debits and credits of closing. Chapter 8 includes settlement math problems.

FIGURE 6.6

Common Debits and Credits

SELLER'S CLOSING STATEMENT	
Debit Seller	**Credit Seller**
Title insurance or abstract costs*	Purchase price
Survey fee (if required)	Balance in loan impound accounts
Payoff of existing loan	Prepaid insurance (if policy is assumed)
Prepayment penalty	
Loan being assumed	
Seller financing	
Earnest money received from buyer	
Commission to be paid broker	
Taxes (could be credit or debit)	Taxes (could be credit or debit)
Documentary transfer stamps (transfer tax)	
Cost to notarize deed	
Cost to draft deed	
Recording costs of new mortgage (if seller financing). Note: The party who gives an instrument generally pays to prepare and acknowledge it. The party receiving it pays to record it.	
Termite inspection fee	
Termite correction work required	
Recording satisfaction of mortgage being paid off	
Prepaid rents	
Rental security deposits	
Attorney's fees	
Unpaid utility bills	
New loan points (as agreed by the parties or required by law)	
Cash to be received at closing	

FIGURE 6.6 (CONT.)	BUYER'S CLOSING STATEMENT	
Common Debits and Credits	**Debit Buyer**	**Credit Buyer**
	Sales price	Loans being assumed
	Recording deeds received	Money paid to seller or deposited with agent
	Drafting new mortgages	
	Notarizing new mortgages	New mortgage to be given to seller
	Balance in impound accounts of loans being assumed	Interest on loans being assumed (if paid in arrears)
	Insurance policies being assumed	
	Attorney's fees	Prepaid rent
	Interest paid in advance	Rental security deposits
	Advance taxes and insurance for impound account	Unpaid utility bills
	Appraisal fee for new loan	
	New loan costs	
	Taxes (could be credit or debit)	Taxes (could be credit or debit)
	New survey (could be paid by seller)	
	Fuel oil in tank	Balance paid at closing

*In some areas, the buyer pays the title insurance.

Transfer tax.   Most states and local communities have a real property transfer tax. The seller generally pays this tax, although local custom varies. The tax is usually based on the seller's equity being transferred, although in some areas, it is based on sales price. If the tax were based on equity, when loans are assumed, the tax would be charged on the difference between sales price and the loans being assumed, but if the property were to be refinanced, it would be based on the full purchase price.

Foreign Investment in Real Property Tax Act (FIRPTA).   FIRPTA requires that a buyer withhold estimated taxes equal to 10% of the sales price when the seller is a foreign national. The purpose of the act is to prevent evasion of tax on gains. Exempt from withholding are purchases of personal residences where the purchase price is less than $300,000. Many states have enacted similar withholding requirements.

IRS reporting.   Settlement agents (brokers, attorneys, and escrows) must report the closing price (gross sales price) on IRS Form 1099-S. This applies to one-to-four residential unit buildings.

Personal property.   Personal property included in a real estate transaction is transferred by a written **bill of sale** that describes the property being transferred, indicates it is being conveyed, names the vendee (buyer), and is dated. The vendor (seller) signs the bill of sale.

IRS Form 8300.   Cash transactions of more than $10,000 must be reported to the IRS on Form 8300. This applies to total cash in related transactions. This prevents money laundering of untaxed dollars.

YOUR PERTINENT STATE INFORMATION

1. What are the regulations and disclosures applicable to mortgage loan brokers?

2. Identify your state's special loan programs.

3. What are your state's usury rates?

4. What happens when a usurious rate of interest is paid?

5. What are the allowable late charges?

6. What are the allowable prepayment penalties?

7. Is a lock-in provision enforceable? If so, when?

8. What are your state's restrictions on balloon payments?

9. Do impound accounts bear interest?

10. What theory is followed as to mortgages?

11. What are your state's trust deed procedures?

12. What are your state's trust deed foreclosure notices and reinstatement rights?

13. What is your state's common reference for "land contract"?

14. What are the land contract foreclosure procedures?

15. What is the notice requirement for mortgage foreclosure?

16. What are the mortgage foreclosure sale procedure and the effect?

17. What are the mortgage reinstatement and redemption rights?

18. What are your rights to deficiency judgment?

19. Is a strict foreclosure possible?

20. May mortgages be foreclosed through nonjudicial foreclosure?

21. What are your nonjudicial foreclosure procedures?

22. Describe any state loan disclosure requirements.

23. Does your state regulate prepayment penalties?

24. Does your state limit late charges and set grace periods?

25. Does your state allow lock-in loans?

26. Does your state have an antipredatory lending law?

27. Are balloon payments subject to limitations in your state?

28. Who handles closings in your state?

29. Who is responsible for the day of closing?

30. What are the disclosures or certificate requirements for closing?

31. Does your state require buyer withholding of part of the sales price when the seller is a foreign national?

CHAPTER 6 QUIZ

1. The effective rate of interest describes
   A. APR.
   B. the nominal rate of interest.
   C. compound interest.
   D. the usury rate.

2. The financing instrument that describes all the terms of the borrowers promise to pay is the
   A. mortgage.
   B. bill of sale.
   C. note.
   D. trust deed.

3. What is the benefit of having FHA insurance?
   A. It pays off the loan if the buyer dies or becomes disabled.
   B. It pays for any needed corrective measures not revealed by FHA appraisal.
   C. It protects the lender against foreclosure losses should the buyer default.
   D. It is a comprehensive homeowners policy.

4. A veteran wishes to buy a home with a VA loan. The owner will not lower the price below $175,000, but the CRV is for $173,000. The veteran
   A. cannot buy the home.
   B. could have the seller carry a $2,000 second mortgagee.
   C. could borrow $2,000 from another lender.
   D. could pay $2,000 as a down payment.

5. A buyer defaulted on a loan and the lender foreclosed. Why would this foreclosure adversely affect the seller's credit rating?
   A. The buyer took "subject to" the seller's loan.
   B. The buyer used the seller as a personal reference with the lender.
   C. There was a novation on the loan.
   D. The buyer's loan was an adjustable loan.

6. A borrower was offered an adjustable-rate mortgage that provided for a margin of 2.25 points. It was to be based on an index that was at 4.75%. The lender was offering an introductory rate 1.75% less than would otherwise be payable. What is the introductory rate being offered?
   A. 3%
   B. 5.25%
   C. 7%
   D. 8.75%

7. The financing instrument giving the lender the right to initiate a judicial foreclosure in the event of the borrower's default is called a
   A. note.
   B. mortgage.
   C. land contract.
   D. trust deed.

8. A mortgage insurance premium (MIP) is associated with what type of loan?
   A. VA
   B. FHA
   C. Conventional
   D. Freddie Mac

9. A builder purchased a lot with seller financing. The seller's loan would allow for a later construction loan to be the priority loan. The loan obtained contained a
   A. release clause.
   B. defeasance clause.
   C. subordination clause.
   D. due-on-sale clause.

10. IRS Form 1099-S is used to
    A. report real property exchanges.
    B. compute tax on capital gains.
    C. report sales prices.
    D. report cash transactions.

11. Which of the following is regarded as personal property?
    A. Mortgage
    B. Vacant lot
    C. Fixture
    D. Air rights

12. Who is responsible for the government's monetary policy?
    A. U.S. Treasury
    B. Federal Reserve
    C. HUD
    D. FDIC

13. A note given with a mortgage is the
    A. security for the loan.
    B. primary evidence of the debt.
    C. hypothecation agreement.
    D. guarantee of payment.

14. Which of the following is an expansionary policy of the Federal Reserve?
    A. Lowering taxes
    B. Raising the discount rate
    C. Raising the reserve requirements
    D. Buying federal securities

15. A seasoned loan is a
    A. priority loan.
    B. long-term loan.
    C. loan that includes incentives for early payment.
    D. loan with a payment history.

16. An owner was in default on a mortgage payment. The lender could call the entire loan balance due if the loan contained
    A. a due-on-sale clause.
    B. an "or more" clause.
    C. a defeasance clause.
    D. an acceleration clause.

17. On a real estate closing transaction involving an exclusive-right-to-sell listing, the commission is a debit to the
    A. buyer and a credit to the seller.
    B. seller and a credit to the buyer.
    C. seller.
    D. buyer.

18. On a buyer's closing statement, the buyer is debited for
    A. loans being assumed.
    B. a down payment given to the agent.
    C. a new loan being given to the seller.
    D. the sales price.

19. Which of the following lenders uses its own funds to fund loans that will be sold in the secondary mortgage market?
    A. Mortgage broker
    B. Department of Veterans Affairs
    C. Fannie Mae
    D. Mortgage banker

20. A buyer would have to seek new financing if the seller's existing loan
    A. contained an alienation clause.
    B. was seller carryback financing.
    C. had a prepayment penalty.
    D. was a nonconforming loan.

21. A tenant in a foreclosed property was on a month-to-month tenancy. If the new owner wants the tenant to vacate, how long a notice should be given?
    A. 30 days
    B. 60 days
    C. 90 days
    D. 120 days

22. The three parties to a trust deed are
    A. mortgage, mortgagee, and trustee.
    B. vendor, vendee, and borrower.
    C. trustor, mortgagor, and mortgagee.
    D. trustor, trustee, and beneficiary.

23. What kind of loan provides that a borrower's loan eligibility benefits are restored when the loan is paid off?
    A. Construction loan
    B. Conventional loan
    C. VA loan
    D. Growing equity mortgage

24. An example of negative amortization is a loan
    A. where the amount applied to interest declines each month.
    B. that is only partially amortized.
    C. where the payments are insufficient to cover the loan interest.
    D. where monthly payments are "plus interest" rather than "including interest."

25. Which of the following is *NOT* a characteristic of a qualified mortgage?
    A. A 20-year amortized loan
    B. A loan where points and fees amounted to 2.5%
    C. A loan that could be sold to Fannie Mae
    D. An option ARM

26. Seller financing where the seller takes back a loan written for the amount of existing loans plus part or all of the seller's equity is called
    A. compensating balance.
    B. a wraparound mortgage.
    C. an open mortgage.
    D. a blanket mortgage.

27. MERS refers to
    A. short sale regulations.
    B. a private mortgage database.
    C. judicial foreclosure.
    D. a mortgage assistance provider.

28. First notice of foreclosure cannot be issued until the homeowner is delinquent for
    A. 30 days.
    B. 90 days.
    C. 120 days.
    D. 180 days.

29. Which of the following is the fund source for loans made by commercial banks?
    A. HUD
    B. FHA
    C. FDIC
    D. Deposits

30. A lender charged an illegal rate of interest. This is called
    A. a buydown.
    B. usury.
    C. subordination.
    D. impound interest.

31. An elderly couple has difficulty paying their expenses although they own their home free and clear. A solution to their problem, without requiring them to move, is
    A. a participation mortgage.
    B. a growing equity mortgage.
    C. a reverse-annuity mortgage.
    D. an adjustable-rate mortgage.

32. Which of the following lenders may consider making a loan to a person who had a poor credit and job history?
    A. HUD
    B. FHA
    C. An insurance company
    D. A subprime lender

33. The activities of Fannie Mae include
    A. insuring mortgages.
    B. guaranteeing mortgages.
    C. raising and lowering the federal discount rate.
    D. purchasing mortgages originated by others.

34. Equal monthly payments on an amortized loan
    A. reduce the loan principal in equal monthly amounts.
    B. compound the interest.
    C. apply decreasing amounts to the interest.
    D. apply decreasing amounts to the principal.

35. A tenant is protected in a foreclosure situation if the lease contains
    A. a subordination clause.
    B. an alienation clause.
    C. a nondisturbance clause.
    D. an assignment.

36. A deed of trust moves title and a limited power of sale from the
    A. mortgagor to the mortgagee.
    B. trustor to the trustee.
    C. trustor to the beneficiary.
    D. beneficiary to the trustor.

37. An impound account is the property of the
    A. mortgagor.
    B. mortgagee.
    C. beneficiary.
    D. trustee.

38. A type of loan that provides for increases in loan payments when interest rates rise is
    A. a graduated payment mortgage.
    B. a growing equity mortgage.
    C. an adjustable-rate mortgage.
    D. a shared appreciation mortgage.

39. One hundred percent financing for a home purchase most likely involves
    A. a conventional loan.
    B. an adjustable rate loan.
    C. a VA loan.
    D. a piggyback loan.

40. A deed of reconveyance is signed by the
    A. trustor.
    B. trustee.
    C. beneficiary.
    D. vendor.

41. A foreclosed owner's rights after a foreclosure sale relate to
    A. redemption.
    B. a deficiency judgment.
    C. hypothecation.
    D. defeasance.

42. What advantage might a land contract have to a buyer, compared with a conventional mortgage?
    A. Lower down payment
    B. Amortization
    C. Longer term
    D. More protection from foreclosure

43. A home sold for $142,000. The lender demanded that the buyer pay 1.75 points for an 80% loan. What amount did the buyer pay in loan points?
    A. $1,750
    B. $1,902
    C. $1,988
    D. $2,485

44. A lender had a claim against the borrower after the property securing the loan was sold at a foreclosure sale. The lender had a
    A. subordination agreement.
    B. deficiency judgment.
    C. wraparound loan.
    D. right of redemption.

45. A lender is able to decide if a loan to be made is eligible for FHA insurance. This ability of the lender is called
    A. direct endorsement.
    B. prequalification.
    C. MIP.
    D. funding.

46. A defeasance clause in a mortgage provides for
    A. the lien to be increased by later advances.
    B. the lien to be released by payment of the note.
    C. the assumption of the mortgage with the permission of the mortgagee.
    D. a private foreclosure sale.

47. A buyer was denied a loan because he had been late in paying obligations that resulted in a low
    A. front-end ratio.
    B. back-end ratio.
    C. loan-to-value ratio.
    D. FICO score.

48. Which of the following is an open market transaction of the Federal Reserve?
    A. Lowering the discount rate
    B. Selling government securities
    C. Raising bank reserve requirements
    D. Increasing government spending

49. Increasing the points asked for a loan in the absence of any economic change should have what effect on the loan?
    A. Increase the risk
    B. Reduce the interest
    C. Increase the payments
    D. Shorten the loan term

50. How is the front-end qualifying ratio for a loan determined?
    A. PITI (monthly payment) ÷ gross monthly income
    B. Net monthly income ÷ monthly PITI payment
    C. (PITI + monthly debt) ÷ gross monthly income
    D. Gross monthly income – loan guarantee

51. A buyer needed a new loan to purchase a property. The lender insisted on a lender's extended-coverage title policy. On the closing statement, the policy is a
    A. credit to the seller.
    B. debit to the seller.
    C. debit to the buyer.
    D. debit to the lender.

52. Which of the following loans is expected to have the highest initial interest rate?
    A. An adjustable-rate mortgage
    B. A 30-year fixed-rate mortgage
    C. A 15-year fixed-rate mortgage
    D. A 5-year fixed-rate rollover mortgage

53. The front-end qualifying ratio is
    A. the down payment divided by the purchase price.
    B. total monthly housing costs divided by gross monthly income.
    C. the ratio of down payment to monthly payment.
    D. the ratio of interest cost to total monthly payment.

54. A motel buyer obtained a purchase mortgage that covered the real estate, as well as furnishings. This is
    A. an open-end mortgage.
    B. a packaged mortgage.
    C. a participation mortgage.
    D. an 80-20 loan.

55. The back-end qualifying ratio is the
    A. ratio of net income to PITI.
    B. total housing expenses plus monthly credit obligations divided by gross monthly income.
    C. ratio of current rental costs to estimated ownership costs.
    D. monthly gross divided by amount to be financed.

56. A FICO score is important in that it determines
    A. whether a buyer has sufficient income.
    B. whether the property meets construction minimum standards.
    C. whether a buyer is worthy of credit.
    D. the size of the loan the buyer can qualify for.

57. An alienation clause is incompatible with
    A. a due-on-sale clause.
    B. an "or more" clause.
    C. an assumable loan.
    D. a subordination clause.

58. A subordination clause in a mortgage that the seller is carrying benefits the
    A. lender.
    B. seller.
    C. trustee.
    D. mortgagor.

59. A wraparound loan offers which benefit to the seller?
    A. Leverage
    B. Amortization
    C. Arbitrage
    D. Points

60. A reservist who was called to active military duty is unable to make his mortgage payments. He is protected against foreclosure by the
    A. Homestead Act.
    B. Service Members Civil Relief Act.
    C. Real Estate Settlement Procedures Act.
    D. FHA Act.

61. The advantage of a straight note over an amortized note for the borrower is
    A. taxes and insurance included in payments.
    B. shorter loan.
    C. lower total interest costs.
    D. lower monthly payments.

62. When borrowing money secured by personal property, the borrower signs a
    A. trust deed.
    B. land contract.
    C. security agreement.
    D. bill of sale.

63. The ratio between loan and value is called the
    A. ARM.
    B. PITI.
    C. PMI.
    D. LTV.

64. Which of the following is inverse to the loan-to-value ratio?
    A. Loan costs
    B. Buyer equity
    C. Interest rate
    D. Capitalization rate

65. Loans that meet the underwriting standards of Fannie Mae or Freddie Mac are called
   A. institutional loans.
   B. conforming loans.
   C. portfolio loans.
   D. open-end loans.

66. A loan that offers a buyer what amounts to a line of credit is
   A. an open-end loan.
   B. a participation loan.
   C. an ARM.
   D. a VA loan.

67. A convertible ARM is a loan that
   A. can be prepaid without penalty.
   B. may be converted to a fixed-rate loan.
   C. has a cap that may be lowered.
   D. has an adjustable margin.

68. Which of the following is exempt from Foreign Investment in Real Property Tax Act withholding?
   A. Undeveloped property
   B. Sales where the capital gain was less than $300,000
   C. Personal residences under $300,000
   D. Nonresidential property

69. The percentage of American families that can afford to buy the average home is measured by the
   A. FICO score.
   B. front-end ratio.
   C. affordability index.
   D. collateral.

70. A middleperson who locates borrowers and lenders is a
   A. mortgage broker.
   B. mortgage banker.
   C. credit union.
   D. savings bank.

71. Which of the following lenders makes loans to borrowers with poor work and credit history?
   A. FHA
   B. A commercial bank
   C. A subprime lender
   D. HUD

72. A lienholder refused to take a deed in lieu of foreclosure because of the
   A. expense as compared to foreclosure.
   B. time delay as compared to foreclosure.
   C. possibility of other liens taking a priority position.
   D. costs associated with title insurance.

73. A satisfaction indicates a mortgage has been paid off. What is given when a deed of trust has been paid off?
   A. Deed of reconveyance
   B. Beneficiary statement
   C. Trustee's deed
   D. Mortgage note

74. Bare legal title refers to the interest of a
   A. vendee under a land contract.
   B. trustor under a trust deed.
   C. beneficiary under a trust deed.
   D. trustee under a trust deed.

75. A borrower pays 2% above an index rate. This additional amount is called the
   A. cap.
   B. margin.
   C. ceiling.
   D. LTV.

76. A house is purchased, and part of the transaction involves a new deed of trust. A search of the county records would show a deed of trust from
   A. grantor to grantee.
   B. lender to trustee.
   C. trustee to trustor.
   D. trustor to trustee.

77. Typical loan-qualifying ratios are
   A. 5/10.
   B. 20/30.
   C. 28/36.
   D. 75/80.

78. Which of the following mortgages is seller financing, where the existing seller loan is to be retained by the seller?
   A. Blanket
   B. Package
   C. Reverse
   D. Wraparound

79. By paying two extra points to the lender, a buyer was able to reduce the rate of interest by 0.25%. This is considered
    A. usury.
    B. a buydown.
    C. subrogation.
    D. a RESPA violation.

80. Which of the following lenders receives compensation for placing a loan but does not continue to service the loan?
    A. Mortgage broker
    B. Mortgage banker
    C. Fannie Mae
    D. Pension fund

CHAPTER 6 QUIZ ANSWERS

1. **(A)** The annual percentage rate (APR) is the true rate of interest, adjusting the nominal rate stated in the note for loan costs. (143)

2. **(C)** The note evidences the debt. The mortgage is the lien. (161)

3. **(C)** FHA insurance protects the lender up to insurance limits. (176)

4. **(D)** While secondary financing is not allowed at the time of a VA loan, and VA loans greater than the CRV are not permitted, the veteran may still purchase the home by paying the difference in cash. (175, 177)

5. **(A)** The seller remained liable on the loan. (171)

6. **(B)** The margin 2.25% plus the index of 4.75% equals 7%. The introductory rate is 1.75% less. (168)

7. **(B)** Judicial foreclosure for a mortgage. Not for land contract or trust deed. (164)

8. **(B)** The MIP is unique to FHA insurance. (175, 176)

9. **(C)** This makes the purchase money loan secondary to a construction loan. (172)

10. **(C)** The settlement agent must report the sale to the IRS. (183)

11. **(A)** It is a chattels real. (161)

12. **(B)** The Fed controls our monetary policy, but not fiscal policy. (166)

13. **(B)** The note is the promise to pay; the mortgage is the security for the note. (161)

14. **(D)** Increases money in circulation. Answers (B) and (C) are contractionary policies and (A) is not a Federal Reserve–controlled action. (166–167)

15. **(D)** Because of the reduced likelihood of default, a seasoned loan could sell at a premium over a new loan on the secondary mortgage market. (170)

16. **(D)** Payments all become due upon a default. (172)

17. **(C)** The commission is a seller's obligation (debit) and is never a credit. (182)

18. **(D)** The other answer options are credits that reduce the amount the buyer needs to close. (183)

19. **(D)** Mortgage brokers seldom use their own funds. The VA only guarantees loans. (174)

20. **(A)** An alienation clause is a due-on-sale clause that prohibits loan assumption. (172)

21. **(C)** If tenant was on a lease, then tenancy continues until the lease expires unless the owner wants to occupy the unit. (166)

22. **(D)** Trustor is borrower and trustee holds title to protect beneficiary. (162)

23. **(C)** The veteran is then eligible for a new VA loan. (178)

24. **(C)** The loan balance increases each month. (167)

25. **(D)** An option ARM is not amortized, which is a requirement. (169, 175)

26. **(B)** The seller benefits by an interest higher than that provided by the existing low-interest loans. (169)

27. **(B)** A private firm that maintains a central mortgage database and holds mortgage notes. (165)

28. **(C)** Part of Dodd-Frank Act. (164)

29. **(D)** The "source" is the bank deposits. (174)

30. **(B)** A rate that exceeds a statutory limit. (170)

31. **(C)** They could receive payments, as with an annuity. (168)

32. **(D)** Charges high cost for funds to offset greater risk. (174)

33. **(D)** It is active in the secondary mortgage market. (178)

34. **(C)** They also result in increasing amounts applied to the principal. (167)

35. **(C)** Lender agreed to honor lease. (172)

36. **(B)** The trustee holds naked legal title in trust until the trustor pays the beneficiary or default causes a sale. (162)

37. **(A)** The borrower actually owns the prepaid insurance and taxes that are paid to the lender, which holds them in trust. (173)

38. **(C)** Up to the increase allowed by the cap because the index would rise. (168)

39. **(C)** No-down-payment VA loans are possible. Others require down payments. (175 , 177)

40. **(B)** It returns legal title from the trustee to the trustor when the trust deed has been paid off. (162–163)

41. **(A)** Statutory right to redeem property (some states). (164–165)

42. **(A)** Sellers often sell with lower down payments on land contracts because of easy foreclosure in many states. (163)

43. **(C)** Eighty percent of $142,000 is $113,600; $113,600 × 0.0175 = $1,988. (170–171)

44. **(B)** A judgment for the difference between amounts realized at the foreclosure sale and the amount due on the note. (165)

45. **(A)** Direct endorsement shortens the loan processing time because FHA approval is not required. (177)

46. **(B)** The mortgage is canceled when the note is paid. (171)

47. **(D)** Score predicts borrower's future credit performance. (180)

48. **(B)** The Fed buys and sells government securities on the open market to regulate the money supply. (167)

49. **(B)** Points are really prepaid interest. (170–171)

50. **(A)** Answer (C) describes the back-end ratio. (179)

51. **(C)** Borrower must pay for title policy protecting lender. (181–182)

52. **(B)** Adjustable-rate mortgages usually have a low initial rate of interest. Short-term loans have less risk so are lower rates than long-term loans. (168)

53. **(B)** Total housing cost is principal, interest, taxes, and insurance (PITI). (179)

54. **(B)** Packaged mortgage loan covers real and personal property, which is enumerated. (169)

55. **(B)** PITI plus monthly credit obligations divided by gross monthly income (179)

56. **(C)** The qualifying ratios show amount of loan possible, but the FICO score is based on credit history and other factors. (180)

57. **(C)** Alienation clause makes loan due and payable when property is alienated (sold) so it cannot be assumed. (172)

58. **(D)** Because the buyer (the mortgagor) could use the seller's equity to borrow on the property. A new loan would take priority over the loan with the subordination clause. (173)

59. **(C)** Can make money on interest differential between the existing loan and the wraparound loan. (169)

60. **(B)** If the reason for the problem is a military call to active duty, the serviceperson can delay foreclosure and obtain a reduced interest rate, and is protected from family eviction. (166)

61. **(D)** Because straight note is interest only. (Also called a term note.) (167)

62. **(C)** Financing statement is recorded to place lien on personal property. (170)

63. **(D)** Loan-to-value ratio (179)

64. **(B)** The higher the LTV, the lower the buyer's equity. (179)

65. **(B)** Fannie Mae or Freddie Mac will purchase them. They are qualified mortgages. (179)

66. **(A)** The borrower may increase the loan up to a determined limit. This is common for home equity loans. (169)

67. **(B)** At the lender's prevailing interest rate plus a stated amount. Period for conversion is specified. (169)

68. **(C)** Withholding is the buyer's responsibility. The closing agent may have the seller complete certificate of nonforeign status. (183)

69. **(C)** Index was established by the National Association of REALTORS®. (180)

70. **(A)** Brings borrowers and lenders together. (174)

71. **(C)** At a high rate of interest to offset risk. (174)

72. **(C)** While foreclosure would wipe out junior liens, a deed could transfer title with junior liens intact. (165)

73. **(A)** The title is returned to the trustor. (162–163)

74. **(D)** The trustee has legal title, but the trustor has possession and equitable title. (162)

75. **(B)** Interest on an ARM is figured at the index plus the margin. (168)

76. **(D)** Trustor signs deed of trust, which is given to trustee to hold as security. Records would also show the deed from a seller to the trustor. (162)

77. **(C)** Front-end and back-end ratios. (pages 179)

78. **(D)** New loan written for existing encumbrances, as well as seller's equity. (page 169)

79. **(B)** Points and interest are related. Points are really prepaid interest by the borrower. (page 171)

80. **(A)** Loan origination fees are loan broker's profit, and they seldom service loans they arrange. (pages 174)

7

Leases, Rents, and Property Management

LEASES

Leasehold Estates

A lease is an agreement that transfers from a lessor (owner) to a lessee (tenant) the exclusive use and possession of property for a designated period of time.

While fee simple and life estates are considered freehold estates, leasehold interests are nonfreehold estates. Leasehold estates are personal property (chattels real).

There are four types of estates possible for lessees.

1. *Estate for years.* A lease interest for a definite period of time is called an *estate for years.* Such a lease does not automatically renew itself. Because an estate for years ends at the end of its specific term, no notice is required for termination. State laws provide for the maximum term of a leasehold interest, which is often 99 years.

2. *Periodic tenancies.* These leases are from period to period, such as month to month or year to year, and automatically renew themselves unless either party gives notice. Generally, notices to end the tenancy must be delivered or posted on the property within a specified number of days, often 30, before termination.

3. *Tenancy at will.* Tenancy at will describes a lease for an unspecified period where permissive possession was given without an agreement as to tenancy. An example of a tenancy at will is a seller who gives a buyer occupancy before a closing and without any rental agreement or a lessor who gives a prospective tenant possession before finalizing a lease. Statutory notice, typically 15 or 30 days, is required to terminate such a tenancy.

    Tenant-at-will interests may not be assigned and cease on sale of the property or the death of tenant or landlord. Other leases generally bind the estates of the parties.

4. *Tenancy at sufferance.* If a tenant properly comes into possession of real property, but wrongfully holds over or continues occupancy after expiration of the lease, a tenancy at sufferance arises. An example is a tenant who fails to leave at the end of a fixed-term lease or one who gives notice but fails to leave. Occupancy by a former owner after a completed foreclosure or after condemnation under eminent domain also results in a tenancy at sufferance.

A tenant at sufferance may be removed by an *ejectment action* without formal notice or by a formal eviction procedure. If an owner accepts rent from a tenant at sufferance, however, the tenant becomes a periodic tenant. If a periodic tenancy is established, a proper notice must be given before an action for eviction.

Types of Leases

Under a lease, the **lessor** (owner) subordinates the right of possession to a **lessee** (tenant). The legal term **demise** refers to the conveyance of a leasehold interest. There are several basic types of leases.

Gross lease. A **gross lease** (or flat lease) is a fixed-rate rental where the tenant pays an agreed flat amount and the owner pays the taxes and insurance, as well as agreed-on maintenance and repairs. Although a long-term gross lease ensures having a tenant, there is a danger of being tied to a low rental during an inflationary period. Most residential leases are gross leases.

Index lease. A long-term gross lease is disadvantageous to an owner during an inflationary period where the tenant is paying a below-market rent. This risk can be offset by use of an index lease, with rent increases tied to an index, such as the Consumer Price Index (CPI).

Graduated lease. A lease that has a fixed rent but has agreed-upon rent increases at specified times is a **graduated lease** (or step-up lease).

Net lease. The **net lease**, a long-term commercial lease, provides that the owner will receive a fixed, or net, amount as rent. The tenant pays the maintenance and operating expenses. To protect the purchasing power of the rent received, the net rent could be adjusted with the CPI. A **triple net lease** describes a net lease where the lessee also pays taxes and insurance, as well as all maintenance and operational expenses.

Percentage lease. The **percentage lease**, commonly used in shopping centers, gives the owner a percentage of the tenant's gross receipts. Generally, businesses with higher markups pay higher percentages. A percentage lease might include a minimum rent, a covenant to remain in business, advertising requirements, and hours of operation. As an incentive for greater volume, percentage leases often provide for reductions in the percentage paid as rent as the volume increases. To obtain a desirable **anchor tenant**, a major store that generates high traffic, a shopping center might offer extremely desirable terms. Having the anchor tenant would allow increased base rent for other tenants and increase their volume.

Sale-leaseback. Under this arrangement, a commercial property is sold to an investor and the former owner becomes a tenant. Generally, a long-term net lease is used, with provisions for inflation-adjusted increases. The seller benefits because the sale frees capital for operational use, the rent is fully deductible as a business expense, and the balance sheet of the business will no longer show a long-term mortgage debt.

Oil and gas lease.   Such a lease, sometimes called a vertical lease, gives the lessee the right to drill and extract gas and oil, paying an initial lease fee plus a royalty fee based on what is taken. Oil and gas leases differ from mineral, oil, and gas rights, which are ownership rights separate from the property for which no fees or royalties are paid. While mineral, oil, and gas rights are regarded as real property, oil and gas leases, like all other leases, are considered to be chattels real, which are personal property interests.

Ground lease.   A **ground lease** is the lease of the land alone. The tenant owns or separately leases the structures that have been legally separated from the land. One purpose in leasing rather than purchasing the land is that leasing reduces the initial investment. At the end of the ground lease, the improvements become the property of the lessor. **Ground rent** is not the same as ground lease. Ground rent is usually regarded as that portion of a lease amount that is attributable to the land.

Lease Provisions

Description of premises.   The lease must contain an unambiguous description of the premises leased.

Term.   Unless a longer term is clearly stated, the lease generally is considered a periodic tenancy for the length of the rent-paying period. State laws govern the maximum length of a lease, which is frequently 99 years. Leases for agricultural purposes and oil and gas leases might have different maximum terms.

Quiet enjoyment.   The tenant is entitled to **quiet enjoyment** of the premises without interference from the lessor, and the lessor will defend the lessee's right of possession against claims of third parties. Quiet enjoyment is usually considered an implied covenant of the lease.

Habitability.   Residential leases carry an implied, if not a written, **covenant of habitability**. State law specifies requirements, which usually include a weather-tight structure; operational heat, plumbing, and electrical systems; and pest-free premises at the time of rental.

Use of premises.   Leases often contain clauses specifying the particular use that the tenants may have for the premises. If there is no limitation, the tenant can use the premises for any legal purpose.

Amount of rent.   The rent, or a formula to determine rent, must be set forth in the lease. A property manager must make certain that rents don't violate restrictions imposed by local rent control ordinances. Violations of rent ordinances could subject both the owner and the property manager to penalties.

Repairs.   Leases generally provide for who is responsible for what repairs. In residential property, the lessor is responsible for the roof, the walls, and the windows; the heating and cooling system; and any appliances included.

Renewal options.   Leases for fixed periods often provide for **renewal options** at specific rents or formulas to determine the rents for additional periods of time.

Option to purchase.   A lease might provide that the lessee has the right to purchase the leased premises at a designated price during a stated period. An option may provide that a portion of the rent be applied to the purchase price.

Right of first refusal.   A right of first refusal can be given to a lessee for rental or purchase. The lessee has the right to rent or purchase the property at the price and terms that the owner is willing to rent or sell the property to another party. Because the owner is not obligated to sell or rent beyond the term of the lease, the lessee has no rights unless the owner wishes to sell or rent to another party.

Automatic renewal.   Some leases provide that they automatically renew for a like period unless notice to terminate is given. States generally require that such provisions in residential leases be in boldface type. It is not allowed in all states.

Subletting.   A lease can prohibit the lessee from subletting the premises. Under a sublease, the lessee becomes a sublessor and leases all or part of the premises to a third party. Unless the lease prohibits subletting, generally the lessee can sublet.

Assignment.   A lease can prohibit an assignment whereby the entire lease is transferred to a third-party assignee. A lease might provide for assignment with permission of the lessor.

Forfeiture.   A lease may provide that a material breach of a provision of the lease can end the tenant's rights; nonpayment of rent is not generally considered to be such a breach. If a landlord collects rent after the tenant has breached a provision allowing forfeiture, the landlord may have waived the right to declare forfeiture.

Holdover clause.   A **holdover clause** provides for a significant rent increase should a tenant fail to give up possession at the end of the lease. It serves to discourage a tenancy at sufferance by forcing the tenant to vacate or negotiate a new lease.

Nondisturbance clause.   Mortgagees agree not to terminate tenancy in the event the prior mortgage is foreclosed.

Escalator clause.   An **escalator clause** provides for rent to fluctuate. It may be based on the Consumer Price Index, or increases in owner costs relating to taxes, insurance, maintenance, and/or operational costs.

Exculpatory clause.   This is a hold-harmless clause by which the tenant agrees that the landlord is not liable for any loss or injury because of the condition of the premises. The tenant agrees to refrain from holding the landlord accountable for any losses suffered. In many states, an **exculpatory clause** is unenforceable in a residential lease.

Recapture clause.   A **recapture clause** in a percentage lease gives the lessor the right to terminate the lease if the lessee does not achieve a specified volume of sales.

Security deposit. This deposit is paid by the lessee and held by the lessor to ensure that the property is returned to the lessor in good repair at the end of the lease, with the exception of normal wear and tear. The lessor can use the money to repair damage or for rent owed but must return the balance, if any. A **security deposit** is taxed to the lessor as income only if the lessee forfeits it. The last month's rent paid in advance is taxed when it is received.

Most states regulate the amount of the security deposit that can be collected for residential rentals, and several states require that the lessor pay interest on these funds. Nonrefundable cleaning or security deposits are not allowed in many states.

Fixtures. The lease may provide for the removal of improvements, or it may provide that improvements shall be considered fixtures and stay with the realty.

Insurance. A commercial lease might require that the lessee carry insurance that protects the lessor against injuries to others.

Signature. In many states, one party can be held bound to a written lease he did not sign if rent was paid or accepted after receipt of a copy of the lease signed by the other party.

Acknowledgment. In most states, recording a lease requires that it be acknowledged before a notary. In some states, leases beyond a statutory period must be recorded to give the lessees rights against subsequent purchasers.

Estoppel certificate. In this certificate, also called a certificate of no defense, the tenant acknowledges lease obligations and that the tenant has no claims against the landlord that would offset the obligations. While not in the lease, it is obtained by the owner and given to the buyer for the buyer's protection.

Uniform Residential Landlord and Tenant Act

A number of states have adopted all or part of the **Uniform Residential Landlord and Tenant Act**, which is designed to provide uniformity as to the rights and duties of residential landlords and tenants. The act contains the following provisions:

- If no period for the rental is set, it is a periodic tenancy on a month-to-month basis, unless rent is collected weekly (in which case it is a week-to-week rental).

- If no rental amount is specified, the amount is fair rent (which could be determined by a court).

- If either party signs a lease and the other party, after receiving the lease, pays or collects the rent without objection; the other party is bound to the lease.

- The tenant need not agree to limit the landlord's liability (except as to common areas), and the lease may not require the tenant to give up rights under the act, agree to confess judgment on any claim arising under the lease, or pay the lessor's attorney's fees.

- Within five days of possession, the parties must make a joint inventory as to the condition of the premises and furnishings with a signed copy to be given to each party.

- The maximum security deposit is one month's rent for unfurnished units (one and one-half month's rent for furnished units) plus half a month's rent for tenants having pets. The lessor must promptly return the deposit at the end of the lease less damages (an itemized list must be provided). If lessor fails to do so, the lessee will be entitled to the return of the amount wrongfully withheld plus damages of one and a half times that amount (many states have modified the security deposit limitations and set time periods for return of security deposits).

- The landlord may establish reasonable rules applicable to all tenants, but the landlord must give notice of the rules at the time of rental.

Landlord and Tenant Rights and Responsibilities

The Uniform Residential Landlord and Tenant Act sets forth rights and obligations of residential landlords and tenants. The act only applies to residential tenancies. Most states have adopted the act in total or in part. Therefore, all provisions of the act may not apply to your state.

The act requires that the landlord and tenant act in good faith.

Tenant's rights.   The following are the tenant's rights under the act:

- Tenants cannot agree to waive or forgo legal rights or remedies.

- Tenants are entitled to a habitable dwelling clean and free of vermin at the beginning of the tenancy.

- Tenants have the right to be present at inspection for security deposit at end of lease.

- Tenants must be given the address of the agent or landlord.

- Tenants must be provided garbage receptacles (applies to four-or-more-unit dwellings).

- If the property is destroyed by fire or other casualty, tenants can immediately terminate the lease and recover prepaid rent and security deposits.

- If a landlord unlawfully excludes or removes tenant from premises or diminishes services, the tenant can recover possession or terminate tenancy.

- If a landlord collects rents after knowing of a tenant breach of a lease provision, the landlord will have waived the right to terminate based on the breach.

Tenant's responsibilities.   The act provides the following tenant responsibilities:

- The tenant may not unreasonably withhold permission for the landlord to enter the premises.

- The tenant cannot apply the security deposit to the last month's rent.

- The tenant must comply with reasonable rules related at the time of rental.

- Use will be solely as a dwelling unless otherwise specified.

- The tenant will abide by housing and health codes, keeping the premises clean, and properly disposing of garbage. The tenant must take reasonable care in using the premises.

- The tenant may not intentionally damage the premises or allow others to do so.

- The tenant may not use the premises in a manner that unreasonably interferes with neighbors' quiet enjoyment of the premises.

Landlord's rights.   The following are the landlord's rights under the act:

- Landlords are entitled to a return of the premises at the end of the tenancy.

- Landlords have right of access in case of emergency, without notice and with reasonable notice to inspect, and repair, as well as to show premises to prospective tenants in the final 30 days of tenancy (the landlord may not abuse access to harass tenants).

- Landlords have the right to enforce lease provisions and reasonable tenant rules agreed to by the tenant.

- If a tenant's breach concerns failure to repair or replace damaged items, landlords, after reasonable notice, can enter the premises and make necessary repairs and replacements and charge the reasonable cost of the work to the tenant.

Landlord's responsibilities.   The act provides for these landlord responsibilities:

- The landlord will give reasonable notice before entry and will not enter without permission except in cases of extreme emergency.

- The landlord will inform the tenant as to the name and address of the person responsible for managing the property and the person who will receive legal notices.

- The landlord will place security deposits in an account for that purpose.

- The landlord will make repairs necessary to keep the premises fit for habitation, as well as maintain common areas.

- The landlord is responsible for garbage receptacles (four or more units). Running water, hot water, and heat are to be provided unless the lease makes these tenant responsibilities or the tenant has exclusive control over the water and/or heat installations.

- If the landlord fails to arrange for required services within a reasonable period of time, the tenant can arrange for the services and sue for damages.

- The landlord may not increase the rent, decrease services, or evict a tenant who complains to a landlord or government agency or joins a tenant organization (**retaliatory eviction**).

- If the landlord breaches the rental agreement, the tenant can sue for damages and a court order to correct the breach. The tenant may also terminate the rental agreement, based on a material breach by the landlord, by giving the landlord a 30-day notice of contract breach. The landlord can remedy the breach within the 30-day period and stop termination.

- If a landlord's breach is such that it significantly affects the tenant's use and quiet enjoyment of the premises (constructive eviction), the tenant can terminate the tenancy and sue for damages.

Lease Termination

End of period.   A lease for a definite period of time (estate for years) ends with the expiration of the lease period.

Merger.   A lease is terminated if the lessor and the lessee become the same person. If a tenant under a long-term lease purchases the property and later sells it, the tenant is without a lease. It would have been lost by **merger** because the former tenant couldn't own the property in fee simple and also be her own tenant with a lesser leasehold interest.

Breach.   A lease may be terminated by either lessor or lessee for a material breach of lease provisions. The tenant may be evicted after statutory notice by an unlawful detainer action.

Eviction procedure varies from state to state, but generally there is notice, often three days, to quit, quit or cure, or quit or pay rent. If the tenant fails to comply, an **unlawful detainer action** is commenced, which is the court eviction procedure. The court then issues an order for the tenant to vacate. This order is called a writ of possession or restitution.

If a tenant breaches a lease by abandoning the premises, the landlord should notify the tenant that he is liable on the remainder of the lease. Generally, the lessor can only sue for rent that has become due. The lessor has a reasonable duty to mitigate (reduce) damages by attempting to rerent the premises.

Constructive eviction.   A breach by the landlord of a material lease provision or the implied right of quiet enjoyment, disturbing the tenant's reasonable use, could be treated by the tenant as an act of *constructive eviction*, and the tenant could vacate without further lease liability.

Notice.   State law provides for a notice period (as well as the form of notice) to terminate or modify a periodic tenancy (such as month to month). Notice periods vary by states, but under the Uniform Residential Landlord and Tenants Act, the notice period is 10 days for a week-to-week tenancy and 30 days for a month-to-month tenancy.

Destruction of premises.   In the absence of an agreement to the contrary, destruction of the premises would terminate the tenancy.

Eminent domain.   The taking of the premises under the power of **eminent domain** would terminate the lease; however, the tenant might be entitled to compensation for the value of the leasehold.

Condemnation.   Condemnation for health or safety reasons also would serve to terminate the lessee's responsibility.

Commercial frustration.   Unforeseen events not contemplated at the time of the lease could be grounds to terminate a commercial lease. For example, if a lease specified the sale of a particular product only and that product became unavailable or illegal, the lessee might terminate for commercial frustration.

Bankruptcy.   Bankruptcy of the tenant could terminate lease obligations.

Surrender.   The landlord's acceptance of the return of possession before expiration of the lease would terminate all obligations under the lease.

Foreclosure.   The foreclosure of a mortgage recorded before a commercial lease agreement could terminate the lease unless the lender has agreed that the lease will have priority (nondisturbance clause).

Unconscionable agreement.   A court may refuse to enforce any agreement that is so unfair to one party that it offends the conscience of the court.

Dangerous tenant.   If the tenant commits a violent act on the premises or threatens other tenants or their property, creates hazardous conditions or otherwise affects health, safety of life, or property, then the tenant can be evicted.

Abandonment.   The Uniform Residential Landlord and Tenant's Rights Act provides that a tenant's unexplained or extended absence from the premises for 30 days or more without payment of rent will be prima facie evidence of abandonment as would a tenant's voluntary termination of utilities or removal of possessions. If the landlord believes the tenant has abandoned premises, the landlord should post and mail a notice to the tenant that the landlord intends to reenter the premises within 10 days. The landlord may remove the tenant's possessions and store them for 30 days. After this period, the possessions may be sold and the proceeds applied to rent, damages, attorney fees, and costs.

Protecting Tenants at Foreclosure Act of 2009

Before May 20, 2009, foreclosure of a prior lien would wipe out a residential tenant's lease. The Protecting Tenants at Foreclosure Act of 2009 provides that the lease survives foreclosure and allows tenants to remain until the lease terms expires. However, if a buyer at foreclosure intends to occupy the property, the lease may be terminated with 90 days' notice.

In case of month-to-month tenancies, the tenant is entitled to 90 days' notice to vacate.

State laws that give tenants greater rights, as well as local rent control ordinances requiring just cause for eviction, are not preempted by the federal act.

Assignment and Sublease

Generally, the lease can prohibit assignments and subleases. If the tenant wrongfully assigns or sublets, the lessor can consider the action a breach and evict or waive the breach and accept the assignment or sublease. If the lease provides for assignments or subleases with the approval of the lessor, most courts have held that approval cannot be unreasonably withheld.

Unless a lease specifically prohibits assignments or subleases, the lessee can assign or sublease.

Assignment.   In an **assignment**, the lessee transfers all interests to another. The assignee becomes the tenant of the lessor and pays the rent to the lessor in accordance with the original lease. Although the original lessee remains secondarily liable under the lease, the assignee is primarily liable.

Sublease.   Also called a sandwich lease, the **sublease** makes the lessee, under the master lease, a lessor who takes on his own tenant. The lessor, under a sublease, can lease all or a portion of the premises.

The sublessee pays the rent under the sublease to the sublessor, and the sublessor, the original lessee, pays to the lessor. The original lessee remains primarily liable for fulfillment of the lease terms. An advantage to a lessee of a sublease rather than an assignment is that the sublease could require more rent than the original lease. See Figure 7.1 for a comparison of assignment and subletting.

FIGURE 7.1

Assignment

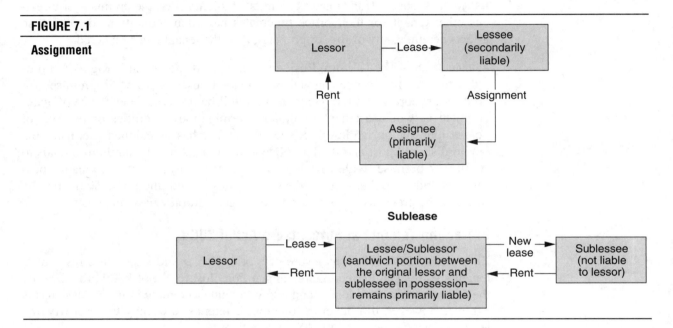

Rental-related Discriminatory Laws

Our civil rights laws apply to rentals as well as sales.

Civil Rights Act of 1866.   This law pertains only to race and prohibits any racial discrimination in the sale or leasing of real estate.

Civil Rights Act of 1968.   This is our fair housing act and, as amended, prohibits discrimination based on national origin, color, religion, and sex. It prohibits broker discrimination in rentals.

The Fair Housing Amendments Act of 1988.   This law extended protection to familial status and handicapped.

Americans with Disabilities Act (ADA).   The act requires handicapped accessibility to places of public accommodations. If a broker has 15 or more employees, the ADA provisions for accessibility apply to the broker's office.

State laws may also apply to discrimination. Discriminatory practices are covered in greater detail in Chapter 5.

PROPERTY MANAGEMENT

A broker has the same legal duties to an owner in **property management** as to a client in listing a property for sale. The property manager generally handles these responsibilities:

- Renting units and collecting rents
- Arranging for maintenance and repairs
- Hiring and firing onsite personnel
- Providing a complete accounting to the owner

While obligated to be fair and reasonable to tenants and live up to lease obligations, the property manager is the agent of the owner and must act in the owners' best interests. The broad authority given to a property manager means that this person is usually regarded as a general agent of the owner as to management. The property management contract should require that the agent account for all income and expenses paid, provide statements to the owner, keep tenant deposits and other owner funds in a trust account, use diligence in carrying out the provision of the agreement, and obey all laws and regulations.

The owner should agree to provide the manager with applicable records, carry adequate liability insurance and workers' compensation to protect owner and broker, indemnify the broker for any costs or expenses relating to the management, and pay all fees as agreed by contract.

Managers customarily receive a percentage of the gross income based on the type of property and management duties. A minimum management fee and a leasing commission also might be included as compensation. A minimum management fee is important when property is vacant. A separate leasing commission is customarily a percentage of the rent for the entire lease. On long-term leases, the percentage tends to be lower for later years than for the first year.

The manager also might be entitled to compensation for evictions, supervising improvements, and fire damage rehabilitation, as well as representing the owner before public agencies. Kickbacks from suppliers would constitute a secret profit and would breach the agent's fiduciary duty.

While residential property is the most common property under management, because there is so much of it, a property manager could manage commercial, industrial and office space, as well as storage facilities, mobile home parks, condominium associations, and even boat docking facilities. The government employs many property managers for government housing projects, as well as within state and federal general services administrations.

Property Management Obligations and Duties

The property manager's obligations and duties include the following:

- Establishing a rental schedule that will bring the highest yield consistent with good economics
- Merchandize the space and collect the rents

- Create and supervise maintenance schedules and repairs
- Supervise all purchasing
- Develop a policy for tenant-resident relations
- Develop employee policies and supervise employee operations
- Maintain proper records and make regular reports to the owner
- Qualify and investigate prospective tenants' credit
- Prepare and execute leases
- Prepare decorating specifications and secure estimates
- Hire, instruct, and maintain satisfactory personnel to staff the building(s)
- Audit and pay bills
- Advertise and publicize vacancies through selected media and broker lists
- Plan alterations and modernization programs
- Inspect space frequently
- Keep abreast of economic and competitive market conditions
- Pay insurance premiums and taxes and recommend tax appeals when warranted
- Protect the property as well as it is reasonably possible

Licensing of Property Manager

Licensing for property managers is regulated by state real estate laws. Generally, a broker's license is required to operate a property management business and a salesperson's license is required to obtain management contracts and to lease for compensation. Licensing usually is not required for resident managers who show properties, rent, and collect rents when they are not paid on a commission basis.

Professional Designations

These are a number of professional designations for property managers. The Institute of Real Estate Management (IREM) of the National Association of REALTORS® gives the designation Certified Property Manager (CPM) to individuals who have met stringent requirements. IREM also has the Accredited Resident Manager (ARM) designation. The Accredited Management Organization (AMO) designation is given to a company.

Property Management Contracts

Property management agreements customarily include the following:

- The period of the contract. The agreement may include an automatic renewal provision unless notice to terminate is given. Provisions for termination may be set forth.
- The owner turning over any security deposits to the manager
- The owner agreement to turn all keys and entry codes over to the broker

- Provision for the owner to provide the agent with a cash reserve and to maintain the reserve with a minimum balance. The cash reserve is used to pay obligations incurred by the broker or due the broker in meeting obligations regarding the property

- The brokerage fee for management, renting, and other services rendered by the broker

- Trust account provisions requiring security deposits and cash reserves, as well as rents and other funds received, to be placed in a trust account

- Owner indication of ownership interest, lenders' loan payment to be made, and service providers

- Listing of owner's insurance agent

- The broker's rights listed, including right to place rental signs, to hire and discharge employees, as well as service providers, and to cooperate with other brokers

- A disclosure that the broker may represent other owners (as well as tenants) involving comparable property and the possible conflict of interest

- On termination of the management agreement, unexpended trust money to be turned over to the owner

- The period for accounting to the owner, including all receipts and expenditures, as well as a remittance to the owner of funds in excess of security deposits and minimum reserves

- Broker withdrawal of the compensation due for the accounting period from the trust account

- The statement of accounts to include
  - security deposits received or returned,
  - rent receipts itemized by unit,
  - itemized list of expenditures, and
  - end-of-period balances

- Provision for the broker to pay employee Social Security contributions and withheld taxes from the trust account, as well as property taxes, workers' compensation coverage, special assessments, property and liability insurance, loan payments and other payments required to be made

- If needed, provision that advertising costs to fill vacancies be paid either by the owner or the broker

- If needed, provision for termination if the property is sold

- Agreement that agent will be reimburses as to any legal action arising out of proper due diligence in managing the property

- Agreement that in the event of a dispute, parties will attempt to mediate the problem with a neutral mediator

- In the event of a legal action, the entitlement of the prevailing party to attorney fees

- Broker agreement to use diligence in performance of the agreement. Specific duties may be enumerated.

Rent Schedules and Financial Terms

Rent schedules are established to maximize the net income for a property considering rents, rent concessions and the vacancy factor. Scheduled rents are based on 100% occupancy at the stated rent. Effective rent may be less because of rental concessions granted. In setting rents, property managers realize that they are not competing with units that are currently renting but with comparable rentals in the marketplace.

Net operating income (NOI) is the balance left from gross income after deducting all fixed and operating expenses and considering an allowance for uncollected rents. In determining net operating income, mortgage payments (debt relief) or depreciation are not deducted.

Cash flow (also called net spendable) is the actual cash on hand after deducting all cash expenses.

Security

Security, for both tenant and property, is an important aspect of property management. Some items that property managers should consider include the following:

- Emergency evacuation plans
- Properly marked exits
- Exterior and interior lighting in common areas.
- Appropriate landscaping to avoid hidden and/or dark areas around entrances
- Fire extinguishers, alarms, and fire suppression systems
- Entry-resistant doors and windows (quality of locks, solid-core doors, and window locks)

A property manager should not advertise that a building is safe or secure because this could be regarded as a warranty.

Occupational Safety and Health Act (OSHA)

OSHA developed standards for safety and health. Any employer who has seven or more employees must keep records and file reports with OSHA.

OSHA covers such things as types of ladders and their condition, use of safety goggles, and protective clothing. It is important to property managers in the realm of maintenance and repairs. Employers must protect employees' health and safety. OSHA concentrates on mechanical and chemical hazards, and there are reporting requirements as to work-related incidents and records of chemicals used in workplace.

OSHA requires mandatory posting of labor law posters in employee work areas. The fine for a violation is up to $7,000, but if the violation is willful, the fine can be up to $70,000.

Besides federal law, many states have their own occupational safety and health laws.

Foreign Investment in Real Property Tax Act (FIRPTA)

Property managers who remit rent payments to a foreign owner must withhold 30% of the gross rent unless exempt by tax treaty. Property managers who fail to comply can be held liable for 30% of gross rent plus penalties and interest.

IRS Reporting

Any person who receives rental income must provide IRS Form 1099-S for all service providers of $600 or more.

OWNER'S OBLIGATIONS, DUTIES, AND LIABILITIES

Owners have the following responsibilities:

- Provide manager with all keys, openers and codes
- Provide payment books, loan information, and copies of maintenance contracts
- Indemnify the broker for costs resulting from legal action where broker was performing properly in accordance with the management agreement
- Provide or turn over to the broker an insurance policy covering property damage, liability, and workers' compensation
- Provide names of owner's insurance agent
- Owner's internet and cell phone contact information
- Owner must make up any projected shortage in the property account and keep the reserves at agreed amount

Liability of Owners

Owners can be held liable for injuries caused by the condition of their property in accordance with state law. This liability applies to guests, invitees. and in some cases even trespassers. Under the **attractive nuisance doctrine**, in some states, owners have a special duty to children if the property is likely to attract young children, even if they are trespassers. Many state statutes provide that owners are not liable for injuries to recreational user trespassers (recreational use immunity).

Owners may also be liable for acts of the property manager based on vicarious liability for acts of an agent.

Owners have been held liable for acts of a tenant when the landlord knew of dangerous propensity of a tenant but failed to take action against it.

In some states, landlords have been held liable for moral and drug-related offenses on the property where the landlord knew of the problem and failed to act.

YOUR PERTINENT STATE INFORMATION

1. What is the maximum period for leases?

2. Are there special provisions regarding inclusion of automatic renewal provisions in residential leases?

3. Is an exculpatory clause enforceable for residential leases?

4. Has your state adopted the Uniform Residential Landlord and Tenant Act?

5. Describe the eviction process in your state.

6. What are the security deposit limitations in your state?

7. How long does a landlord have after the end of tenancy to return the security deposit?

8. What are the notice requirements for periodic tenancy?

9. Are landlords liable for injuries to recreational user trespassers?

10. How long does a broker have after receipt of trust monies to deposit the funds in a trust account?

11. May trust accounts be interest-bearing? If so, how is interest handled?

12. How much, if any, broker funds may be kept in the trust account?

CHAPTER 7 QUIZ

1. An estate for years is created by
   A. express agreement.
   B. adverse possession.
   C. operation of the law.
   D. holding over.

2. The tenant who remains in possession after the lease expires
   A. is on a periodic tenancy.
   B. has a freehold interest.
   C. is a tenant at sufferance.
   D. has a servient tenement.

3. The effect of a lease assignment is that the
   A. entire lease interest is transferred.
   B. assignee makes rent payments to the assignor.
   C. assignee is a tenant of the assignor.
   D. assignor remains primarily liable on the lease.

4. In accordance with the Uniform Residential Landlord and Tenant Act, a lessor may properly require that the tenant
   A. pay a security deposit equal to two months' rent.
   B. agree to a limitation on the owner's liability.
   C. pay any lessor attorney fees arising from a dispute.
   D. restrict use of the premises to residential purposes.

5. A lease prohibited assignment or subletting without the owner's prior approval. The lessee assigned without asking the lessor. The assignment is
   A. void.
   B. voidable.
   C. unenforceable.
   D. illegal.

6. The Uniform Residential Landlord and Tenant Act provides that the tenant
   A. can agree to hold the landlord harmless for actions of the landlord.
   B. may apply the security deposit to the last month's rent.
   C. may not unreasonably withhold permission for the landlord to enter the premises.
   D. will make the repairs necessary to keep the premises fit for habitation.

7. A property manager's contract calls for 4.5% of the rental with a monthly minimum of $200. The gross income for March was $11,000, but operations expenses were $9,450 and fixed expenses totaled $3,840. The property manager's fee for March was
   A. $0.
   B. $94.50.
   C. $200.
   D. $495.

8. Because the value of a property has dramatically increased, it is in the economic *BEST* interest of a tenant on a long-term lease who no longer needs the space to
   A. assign the lease.
   B. surrender the premises.
   C. sublet.
   D. abandon the premises.

9. A lessee has a right that will exist only if the lessor is willing to make a deal. What is this right?
   A. An option
   B. A right of first refusal
   C. A nondisturbance agreement
   D. An estopped certificate

10. A lessee is relieved of all obligations under the lease when the
    A. lessee is evicted for rent arrearage.
    B. property is sold.
    C. lessee is constructively evicted.
    D. lessee can no longer afford to pay the rent.

11. A lease in which the lessee's total monthly rent costs remain unchanged for the term of the lease is what type of lease?
    A. Gross
    B. Net
    C. Percentage
    D. Graduated

12. Broker L, who manages property for M, approaches tenant N for back rent a day after M dies. N refuses to pay. The broker should
    A. give N statutory notice to quit or pay rent.
    B. start an unlawful detainer action.
    C. turn the matter over to a collection attorney.
    D. take no further action.

13. J leased to K, who subleased to L. The lease between K and L could be regarded as
    A. a sandwich lease.
    B. an assignment.
    C. a master lease.
    D. a flat lease.

14. Partial lease interests were transferred by a lessee. This is
    A. a step-lease.
    B. a gross lease.
    C. an assignment.
    D. a sublease.

15. Under the Uniform Residential Landlord and Tenants Act, landlords must provide garbage receptacles
    A. for all residential renters.
    B. if there are four or more units.
    C. if there are one to four units.
    D. for all furnished rentals.

16. What type of long-term lease is *BEST* for a commercial tenant during an inflationary period?
    A. Gross
    B. Percentage
    C. Index
    D. Net

17. A property manager is in trouble because of compensation received. This compensation was a
    A. percentage of the gross.
    B. fee for leasing.
    C. fee for supervising repairs.
    D. kickback from a supplier.

18. A landlord collects rent after knowing the tenant breached a material provision of the lease. The landlord
    A. has waived the breach.
    B. can proceed with eviction based on the breach.
    C. can insist on compliance with the breached provision.
    D. has created an estate at will.

19. What are a tenant's rights under a lease when a prior lien forecloses and the buyer at foreclosure wishes to occupy the unit?
    A. The lease ended with the foreclosure, and the tenant is entitled to a 30-day notice.
    B. The lease continues until expiration.
    C. The tenant is entitled to a 90-day notice to vacate.
    D. The tenant is entitled to the value of the unexpired lease term.

20. G leased a commercial building to S for 10 years. After six months, S moved out without notice. G advertised for a tenant. G's actions relate to
    A. liquidated damages.
    B. mitigation of damages.
    C. punitive damages.
    D. severance damages.

21. A child was injured when he fell through the floor in an abandoned house. If the owner was held liable for the injury, the house was probably considered
    A. an encroachment.
    B. an attractive nuisance.
    C. a hazardous substance.
    D. an implied easement.

22. One reason a company would sell and then lease back its real property is
    A. the deductibility of interest.
    B. to reduce monthly expenses.
    C. liquidity.
    D. the tax benefits of depreciation.

23. A tenant abandoned the premises with three years remaining on the lease. The landlord cannot
    A. occupy the unit.
    B. advertise the property for rent.
    C. sue for all rent due to the end of the lease.
    D. lease for a lesser or greater amount than the tenant was paying.

24. An owner expects to rent each of 10 units for $1,000 per month, amounting to $10,000 in gross income. The $10,000 is called
    A. scheduled rent.
    B. effective rent.
    C. net operating income.
    D. cash flow.

25. A CPM designation applies to
    A. appraisal.
    B. property inspection.
    C. mortgage bankers.
    D. property management.

26. A lessor believes the desirability and sales volume of a large retail store will increase dramatically in the next few years. In negotiating a long-term lease for the premises, the lessor will ask for what type of lease?
    A. Flat
    B. Triple net
    C. Percentage
    D. Gross

27. A woman rented a summer cottage for the first two weeks in July. What type of tenancy does she have?
    A. Estate for years
    B. Estate at will
    C. Periodic tenancy
    D. Tenancy at sufferance

28. An example of constructive eviction is a
    A. tenant who refuses to pay rent.
    B. tenant being given a notice to quit or pay rent.
    C. landlord cutting off the tenant's heat and water.
    D. tenant who remains in possession after termination of the lease.

29. A valid lease must include
    A. an exculpatory provision.
    B. the specified use of the premises.
    C. a definite termination date.
    D. a description of the premises.

30. A lessee would have the greatest protection with
    A. an estate for years.
    B. an estate at will.
    C. a tenancy at sufferance.
    D. a periodic tenancy.

31. Most properties under property management are
    A. industrial.
    B. commercial.
    C. undeveloped.
    D. residential.

32. A tenancy based on permissive occupancy without any tenancy agreement is a
    A. month-to-month lease.
    B. freehold interest.
    C. tenancy at sufferance.
    D. tenancy at will.

33. An owner died, which immediately ended a tenant's rights. What kind of tenancy was it?
    A. Tenancy at will
    B. Tenancy at sufferance
    C. Periodic tenancy
    D. Estate for years

34. Constructive eviction by a residential landlord includes all of the following *EXCEPT*
    A. raising the rent.
    B. unannounced entries.
    C. allowing a vermin problem to continue unabated.
    D. failure to provide heat.

35. A residential lease has an implied covenant of
    A. acknowledgment.
    B. exculpation.
    C. merger.
    D. habitability.

36. The fine for a non-willful single OSHA violation may be
    A. $5,000.
    B. $10,000.
    C. $25,000.
    D. $100,000.

37. A tenant on a long-term lease purchased the building from his landlord and resold it to investors at a profit, making no mention of lease rights. The lease was terminated by
    A. commercial frustration.
    B. merger.
    C. surrender.
    D. recordation.

38. In the absence of a notice to terminate, a lease that automatically renews itself is a
    A. periodic tenancy.
    B. tenancy for years.
    C. gross lease.
    D. ground lease.

39. OSHA deals with property
    A. security.
    B. appraisals.
    C. safety.
    D. financing.

40. A tenant has the right to meet the terms offered by any prospective new tenant when the current lease expires. What is this right called?
    A. Holdover provision
    B. Option
    C. Right of first refusal
    D. Extension agreement

41. The Uniform Residential Landlord and Tenant Act provides that
    A. a one-year lease is created when no rental period is agreed to.
    B. if no rental amount is specified, then no rent can be collected.
    C. the tenant must sign an exculpatory clause if requested to do so.
    D. the maximum security deposit for unfurnished units is one month's rent.

42. A lease where a lessee becomes a lessor is
    A. a sale-leaseback.
    B. a sublease.
    C. an assignment.
    D. an option lease.

43. A landlord served a tenant with an unlawful detainer action because the tenant called a building inspector regarding a code violation. The landlord's action was
    A. constructive eviction.
    B. retaliatory eviction.
    C. preemptory eviction.
    D. proper.

44. The amount left over from rentals after deducting all cash expenses is called
    A. gross rent.
    B. net operating income.
    C. cash flow.
    D. scheduled rent.

45. A property manager was penalized because the manager remitted rent received to an owner. The reason for the penalty was a violation of
    A. OSHA.
    B. FIRPTA.
    C. RESPA.
    D. the Dodd-Frank Act.

46. The initial action in an eviction for nonpayment of rent is
    A. an unlawful detainer action.
    B. a writ of possession.
    C. a seizure notice.
    D. a notice to quit or pay rent.

47. A lessor wants a tenant to protect the lessor from claims of others based on problems concerning the premises. What type of insurance does the lessor want the lessee to carry?
    A. Public liability
    B. Errors and omissions
    C. Homeowners
    D. Fire and extended coverage

48. A residential tenant on a long-term lease learned that a prior mortgagee foreclosed on the property. While the new owner does not intend to occupy the leased premises, the tenant should understand that
    A. the tenancy is now month to month.
    B. a 90-day notice to vacate will end the tenancy.
    C. there is a tenancy at will.
    D. the lease remains valid.

49. IRS Form 1099 must be given by the property manager for service providers paid
    A. $500 or more.
    B. $600 or more.
    C. $1,000 or more.
    D. $10,000 or more.

50. An owner wants to structure the lease to provide income benefits like an annuity but also wants inflation protection. To a long-term net lease, she added a provision relating to
    A. the Consumer Price Index.
    B. EMF.
    C. a right of first refusal.
    D. quiet enjoyment.

51. FIRPTA withholding for foreign owners of rental property is
    A. 10% of net income.
    B. 10% of gross income.
    C. 30% of net income.
    D. 30% of gross income.

52. A lessor allowed a residential rental to become uninhabitable. Which of the following is *FALSE*?
    A. There is now an estate at sufferance.
    B. The tenant can terminate the lease.
    C. The landlord cannot collect rent.
    D. The tenant may be entitled to damages.

53. A lessee defense against eviction for non-payment of rent is that the
    A. tenant is on welfare.
    B. tenant is an unmarried mother.
    C. rent charged is higher than for other similar units.
    D. premises are not habitable.

54. A nondisturbance clause provides that the
    A. landlord will not disturb the tenant.
    B. tenant will not disturb the landlord.
    C. lease will be honored by the lender.
    D. tenant will not sue the landlord for any breach.

55. A property manager's real estate license was revoked because the agent
    A. received a percentage of contractor fees as part of the agent compensation.
    B. collected a fee as a percentage of rents received.
    C. received kickback checks from suppliers and contractors.
    D. charged leasing fees, as well as percentage fees.

56. An agreement whereby the lessee gives premises to the lessor before the expiration of the lease, thus ending lease obligations, is
    A. an eviction.
    B. an unlawful detainer.
    C. a foreclosure.
    D. a surrender.

57. The term *unlawful detainer* is used in connection with a
    A. trustee.
    B. lender.
    C. tenant.
    D. agency.

58. A landlord may enter leased premises without tenant notification
    A. when the tenant is behind in rent payments.
    B. anytime during daylight hours.
    C. only in an emergency.
    D. if the landlord believes premises are being used for an illegal purpose.

59. An option differs from a right of first refusal in that
    A. the optionor must exercise the option.
    B. the optionee must exercise the option.
    C. the optionor has no discretion if the optionee exercises the option.
    D. either the optionor or the optionee can exercise the option.

60. At the end of a 30-year ground lease, the building erected by the lessee
    A. will become the property of the lessor.
    B. must be removed by the lessee.
    C. is considered a trade fixture.
    D. remains the property of the lessee, who is entitled to pay market rents for the ground lease.

61. Before a lease agreement, the owner let the prospective tenant take possession. Based on these facts, the tenant has a
    A. tenancy at sufferance.
    B. tenancy at will.
    C. gross lease.
    D. periodic tenancy.

62. A sale-leaseback offers the buyer/lessor the advantage of
    A. making operational capital available.
    B. removing obligations from the balance sheet.
    C. the tax deductibility of rents.
    D. long-term income.

63. Parties to a dispute ask for mediation. The parties
    A. are bound to the mediator's decision.
    B. have given up their rights to use the courts.
    C. need not reach an agreement.
    D. must also agree to arbitrate.

64. A property manager was fined because an employee did not wear a protective breathing apparatus when spraying for insects. The fine is related to
    A. property habitability.
    B. OSHA
    C. FIRPTA.
    D. IREM.

65. Effective rent is less than scheduled rent because of
    A. taxes and insurance.
    B. debt payments.
    C. income tax on profit.
    D. vacancies and rental concessions.

66. Which of the following is personal property?
    A. Oil and gas leases
    B. Oil and gas rights
    C. Single-family owner-occupied dwelling
    D. Air rights

67. *IREM* is an acronym that deals with
    A. foreign investment.
    B. a type of lease.
    C. property management.
    D. tenant rights.

68. A characteristic of a tenancy at will is that it is
    A. for an indefinite period.
    B. without permission.
    C. automatically renewed.
    D. assignable.

69. An estate for years is created by
    A. a devise.
    B. express contract.
    C. implied contract.
    D. escheat.

70. An exculpatory clause in a lease means that
    A. all repairs will be made by the tenant.
    B. the lease cannot be assigned.
    C. the tenant will not hold the landlord liable for damage or injury.
    D. the tenant is entitled to quiet enjoyment.

71. A landlord can charge a tenant extra if the tenant
    A. is disabled.
    B. receives rent from public assistance.
    C. has a pet.
    D. has a child.

72. A tenant's commercial lease was not terminated when the lessor's interests were lost by foreclosure. The lease contained
    A. a nondisturbance clause.
    B. an antimerger clause.
    C. a subordination clause.
    D. a holdover provision.

73. A buyer is protected against a tenant's claim of setoffs against rent because the tenant signed
    A. an estoppel certificate.
    B. a nondisturbance clause.
    C. an antimerger clause.
    D. a subordination clause.

74. An invitee is injured when a stair rail breaks. The insurance coverage that would protect the owner is
    A. workers' compensation.
    B. liability.
    C. casualty.
    D. fire.

75. Which of the following describes a sublease?
    A. The sublessee becomes the tenant of the lessor.
    B. The entire leasehold is transferred.
    C. The sublessee is a tenant of the lessee.
    D. The sublessee becomes primarily liable on the lease.

76. A broker does not want to modify his office to accommodate an employee with a disability. Legally, the broker is *NOT* obligated to do so if there are
    A. 10 employees.
    B. 20 employees.
    C. 100 employees.
    D. 150 employees.

77. A property manager would *LEAST* likely accept as compensation
    A. a set monthly fee.
    B. a percentage of the gross.
    C. a percentage of the net.
    D. rental fees.

78. A property manager, in remitting rent to an owner, only sent 70% of the gross rent due the owner. The reason for withholding rent from the owner was *MOST* likely that the
    A. owner was a foreign national.
    B. property had deferred maintenance.
    C. tenant ordered the withholding.
    D. tenant was a foreign national.

79. A tenant informed a new owner of an agreement with the former owner to be allowed six months' free rent based on the tenant's repairs to the property. The new owner does *NOT* have to honor the agreement because
    A. it was made by another.
    B. the tenant had signed an estoppel certificate.
    C. the lease was not recorded.
    D. of the exculpatory clause.

80. A tenant vacated premises with two years remaining on the lease. The landlord could *NOT*
    A. treat the abandonment as a surrender.
    B. attempt to rerent to mitigate damages.
    C. sue for rent as it becomes due.
    D. sue for the entire two years' rent based on the lease.

CHAPTER 7 QUIZ ANSWERS

1. **(A)** Because it is a lease for a specified period of time, there must be specific agreement. (195)

2. **(C)** In many areas, the holdover tenant can be treated like a trespasser. (196)

3. **(A)** The assignee makes rent payments to the original lessor. (203–204)

4. **(D)** Unless the lease authorizes other use. (200)

5. **(B)** The owner can consider it a material breach and terminate the lease or accept the assignment. (203)

6. **(C)** Entry must be for a reasonable purpose with reasonable notice. (200)

7. **(D)** Fee is based on gross receipts not net. (205)

8. **(C)** Could sublet for a greater rent than currently charged (204)

9. **(B)** A right to buy or lease at a price and terms that the owner is willing to accept from another. (198)

10. **(C)** Lessor breached lease, so lessee, who vacates, is relieved of all further lease obligations. (202)

11. **(A)** It is also called a flat lease. (196)

12. **(D)** The agency agreement terminated with the death of the principal. (205)

13. **(A)** Subleases are called sandwich leases. (204)

14. **(D)** While an assignment transfers all interests, a sublease can transfer a partial interest. (204)

15. **(B)** Otherwise the tenant supplies garbage receptacles. (200)

16. **(A)** The rent would not increase; therefore, it would not be good for the landlord. (196)

17. **(D)** The property manager cannot make a secret profit. (205)

18. **(A)** And cannot evict for the breached condition. (203)

19. **(C)** If the buyer did not wish to occupy the unit, the lease survives. (203)

20. **(B)** The lessor has a duty to keep tenant damages as low as reasonably possible. (202)

21. **(B)** There is a special duty of owners when property is likely to attract children. (209)

22. **(C)** To obtain cash from an illiquid asset. (196–197)

23. **(C)** Can only sue for rent due. (202)

24. **(A)** Rent with no concessions and full occupancy. (208)

25. **(D)** Certified property manager. (206)

26. **(C)** This would mean greater rent as retail volume increases. (196)

27. **(A)** A lease for a definite period of time. (195)

28. **(C)** Constructive eviction is wrongful conduct by a landlord that interferes with the tenant's quiet enjoyment, allowing the tenant to vacate and end all lease obligations. (202)

29. **(D)** Must specify what is leased. (197)

30. **(A)** A lessee who is not in default is assured possession for a set period. (195)

31. **(D)** Most common property type. (205)

32. **(D)** It is personal and cannot be assigned. (195)

33. **(A)** Ceases on death of tenant or landlord. (195)

34. **(A)** The others interfere with the tenant's quiet enjoyment. (202)

35. **(D)** Also implied covenant of quiet enjoyment. (197)

36. **(A)** A fine may be up to $7,000. (208)

37. **(B)** When the tenant purchased the building, there was no longer a tenancy because the lesser interest (leasehold) was merged into the ownership. (202)

38. **(A)** Such as a month-to-month lease. (195)

39. **(C)** Occupational Safety and Health Act. (208)

40. **(C)** Right of first refusal can be for leasing as well as purchase. (198)

41. **(D)** And 1.5 months for furnished units (many states have modified these amounts). (200)

42. **(B)** Tenants get their own tenant. (203)

43. **(B)** This is a defense against unlawful detainer. (201)

44. **(C)** Net spendable all-cash payments include mortgage payments. (208)

45. **(B)** Failure to withhold 30% when owner is a foreign national. (209)

46. **(D)** Usually a three-day notice followed by the unlawful detainer action. (202)

47. **(A)** With the landlord as a named insured. (199)

48. **(D)** According to the Protecting Tenants at Foreclosure Act of 2009. (203)

49. **(B)** IRS reporting. (209)

50. **(A)** The Consumer Price Index is commonly used in leases, so rent reflects the actual purchasing power. (198)

51. **(D)** A 10% figure applies to sale proceeds. (215)

52. **(A)** An estate of sufferance is a holdover estate. (196, 202)

53. **(D)** The landlord breached the duty to keep the premises habitable and cannot force rent collection. (197, 201)

54. **(C)** The mortgagee agrees not to terminate the lease in the event of a foreclosure. (198)

55. **(C)** Kickbacks violate the agent's fiduciary duty. (205)

56. **(D)** If a landlord accepts premises as a surrender, all obligations end. An abandonment is not a surrender. (203)

57. **(C)** It is a formal eviction procedure. (202)

58. **(C)** Otherwise, reasonable notice is required. (201)

59. **(C)** If the optionee exercises the option, the optionor must comply. (198)

60. **(A)** The lessee gives up real property improvements. (197)

61. **(B)** Possession given without agreement. (195)

62. **(D)** Others are advantages to seller/lessee. (196–197)

63. **(C)** Mediation is only an attempt to seek resolution by bringing in a third party. (207)

64. **(B)** Occupational safety. (208)

65. **(D)** The amount of gross rent received is less than maximum scheduled rent. (208)

66. **(A)** Chattels real. Royalties rather than rent are paid. (197)

67. **(C)** Institute of Real Estate Management. (206)

68. **(A)** Tenancy with permission, and unassignable. (195)

69. **(B)** Because it has a definite term, it had to be expressly created. (195)

70. **(C)** Hold-harmless clause. (198)

71. **(C)** An extra charge is allowed. (204)

72. **(A)** Otherwise a prior mortgage foreclosure could wipe out the tenant's rights. (198)

73. **(A)** Tenant acknowledges lease obligations and that he has no claims to offset amount due. (199)

74. **(B)** Claims for injury to people or property of others. (199)

75. **(C)** The original lessee is liable on the lease, and the sublessee is only liable to his lessor (original lessee). (204)

76. **(A)** If there are 15 or more employees, the employer must modify the premises to the extent reasonably possible for employee access. (204)

77. **(C)** There may be no net. (205)

78. **(A)** Foreign Investment in Real Property Tax Act (FIRPTA) requirement. (209)

79. **(B)** The tenant acknowledged lease obligations and that the tenant had no claims against the landlord to offset the obligations. (199)

80. **(D)** Can only sue for rent due, not future rent. (202)

Brokerage Operations and Ethical and Legal Business Practices

TRUST ACCOUNTS

In the normal course of business, real estate brokers receive monies that belong to other parties, such as earnest money deposits received with an offer or rent received from tenants where the broker is a property manager. The money must be safeguarded and accounted for according to state law. These monies are considered trust funds and must be available for proper distribution or returned when required. Recordkeeping practices for trust funds are established by state statute.

A trust account must be in a financial institution. In most states, it must be a federally insured account.

Every broker who receives money for others must have a trust account. If trust money was placed in a broker's personal account, even if it were used solely for trust money, the funds are not protected. Personal creditors of the broker or the brokerage office could freeze the funds that were to be held in trust.

Many states allow the title or escrow company that is closing the transaction to hold the trust funds. In such cases, the brokerage may choose not to have a brokerage trust account.

A broker may hold a buyer's deposit check uncashed before acceptance of an offer at the direction of the buyer. This is common because buyers are reluctant to place a large amount of money in checking accounts until they know they have a purchase contract. The seller should be informed that the buyer's deposit will not be placed in trust until the offer is accepted. After acceptance of the offer, the check must be deposited in the trust account unless directed by the seller to be held uncashed. State law dictates how long a broker can hold checks received in trust before the funds are deposited in the trust account.

If a deposit is in any form other than cash or check, such as a personal note, the broker must inform the seller as to the form of the deposit. The same holds true for postdated checks that cannot be deposited.

In most states, trust accounts must be demand deposits (checking accounts) in federally insured institutions. A buyer might specify that a deposit be kept in an interest-bearing account as a condition of an offer. The interest accruing before closing is credited to the party depositing the funds.

Some states allow trust funds for purchase contracts and/or lease security deposits to be in interest-bearing accounts and several states allow the broker, by agreement, to share in the designated portion of the interest earned. When an interest-bearing account is used, an accounting must be made of interest received.

State law may require that any individuals other than the broker be bonded if they have authority to disburse trust funds. A **fidelity bond** covers the wrongful appropriation of funds. Because the broker is responsible for loss of trust funds, a fidelity bond should be considered.

State law generally allows a broker to keep some personal funds in the trust account (such as $100) to cover bank charges, as well as to keep the account open should there be no trust funds in deposit. State law also provides a time period during which the broker should remove earned commissions from the trust account.

Should a transaction fail to close after an offer was accepted, the broker should not turn the deposit over to either buyer or seller without the approval of both parties. When both parties make claims on trust account funds, the broker should commence an **interpleader action** in which the funds are turned over to the court and the court will decide on the disposition of the funds.

The broker cannot retain any trust account funds because of a separate claim the broker may have against the party entitled to the funds (**offset**).

A deposit should not be turned over to the seller before closing without the buyer's written concurrence. The funds must be protected.

Earnest money.   The deposit received with an offer to buy or lease is called earnest money. The purpose of a deposit is to show that the buyer is acting in good faith and intends to complete the transaction if the offer is accepted.

There is no statutory requirement that an offer include earnest money, but sellers may be reluctant to accept an offer with no or a very small earnest money deposit. Offers usually provide that sellers can keep the earnest money deposit should the buyers breach the agreement. With a very small deposit and a lengthy closing period, buyers might use their purchase agreement as an option to buy and tie up the property at low cost. They would complete the purchase if they were able to find another buyer at a profit or forfeit their earnest money if they were unable to do so.

Investors have found that a larger-than-usual earnest money deposit can lower the chance that sellers will reject the offer.

If a deposit is received with an offer and the offer is rejected, the broker must return the deposit to the person making it. The broker should never return a deposit until the deposit check has cleared because there would be a shortage in the trust account if the deposit check failed to clear after the deposit was returned.

Commingling.   Commingling is combining client funds with the broker's personal funds. If found guilty of commingling, the broker's license can be restricted, suspended, or revoked by the state licensing agency.

Commingling occurs when

- trust money is held by the broker, beyond a state-mandated time period, and not deposited in a trust account;

- personal or company funds are deposited in the trust account (beyond a maximum of broker funds allowed by the state);

- trust funds are deposited in a broker's account, other than the trust account; or

- earned commissions are left in the trust account beyond a period allowed by the state.

A common violation occurs when a broker deposits earnest money and/or rental deposits from her own property into her trust account. These are broker funds, not funds held for clients.

Conversion.   Conversion is appropriating another's property. It is theft and subjects the perpetrator to criminal penalties. In addition, state licensing agencies can suspend or revoke the perpetrator's real estate license.

Brokers who remove commissions from the trust account before they are earned (sale has closed) are guilty of conversion because they are not entitled to the money. This will result in a shortage in the trust account.

Property managers who have trust accounts covering more than one owner's property and pay bills for one owner out of funds held for another owner are also guilty of conversion.

Trust fund accounting.   Brokers have a duty to safeguard client funds, and accounting for trust funds is also an important fiduciary responsibility. Records should be kept that will enable the broker to accurately account for all monies to clients and to know the amount of money held for the beneficiary at all times. The records should also be able to prove whether the trust account is in balance.

Unless a state mandates a specific form of recordkeeping, records should be in accordance with generally acceptable accounting practice and can be in ledger books or computer records.

Trust fund records should include

- a journal, recording in chronological order the sequence of trust fund deposits and disbursements;
- a beneficiary ledger, showing status of each beneficiary in chronological sequence as well as account balance; and
- a cash ledger, showing a bank balance as affected by recorded transactions (the ledger should be in the form of debits and credits).

There are many software options that simplify trust account recordkeeping.

INDEPENDENT CONTRACTOR VERSUS EMPLOYEE

The employment contract between real estate broker and salesperson specifies either an employee or independent contractor relationship. Employees customarily operate under the control and direction of employers, whereas independent contractors are hired for specific jobs and generally are not under direction as to how the jobs are to be accomplished. Many states consider real estate salespeople to be employees, despite agreements that specify otherwise. The reasoning is that because a broker has a duty of supervision, the salesperson must be an employee. In a number of states, a broker may delegate the authority to supervise salespersons and licensed, as well as unlicensed, assistants to a licensed salesperson.

Because real estate salespeople are paid by commission, they are not entitled to unemployment compensation benefits. However, state law may require that brokers carry workers' compensation insurance to cover on-the-job injuries to salespersons.

The Internal Revenue Service (IRS) will treat real estate salespeople as **independent contractors** and thus exempt the broker from deducting withholding tax or making employer Social Security contributions, if

1. they are licensed as salespeople or broker associates;
2. pay is related to sales success, not to hours worked; and
3. a written contract states that, for tax purposes, the salesperson will be treated as an independent contractor.

Despite the IRS classification of a real estate salesperson as an independent contractor, state law holds the employing broker responsible for the salesperson's wrongful actions, as though the salesperson were an employee. The broker would not, however, be liable for criminal acts of the salesperson that were not directed by the broker.

An **associate broker** is a broker who works for the broker-in-charge. The status of an associate broker as to being an employee or independent contractor is not clear. If supervision is involved, the associate broker could be an employee as to liability of the employing broker. Without supervision, the associate broker could be considered an independent contractor.

Salespeople may receive payment for acts requiring a real estate license only from their own broker. It is a violation of state law for a salesperson to be paid by another broker or directly by an owner for an act requiring a real estate license.

Because salespeople act for their own broker, they must identify their broker when dealing with others. While a salesperson's name might be shown in an advertisement, the employing broker's name must also be included.

Office Operations

Many real estate offices have an office procedures manual that covers duties, responsibilities, and procedures. These might cover floor time, office meetings, training sessions, caravans, handling new listings, and other office activities.

Simply having a procedure manual is not enough. The broker has a duty of supervision and must insure that proper and legal procedures are followed. Even if supervision is delegated, the broker may still be responsible for wrongful acts of salespeople in the course of their real estate activities.

Salesperson Insurance

Because of possible liability, brokers should make certain that salespeople are covered with high-limit-liability automobile coverage, as well as errors and omissions (E&O) coverage.

Commission Arrangements

While some income is generated from property management, leasing fees, or additional services, most of the average broker's income is derived from buyers' and/or sellers' commission relating to real estate sales. There are different types of broker sales operations:

- *100% commission office.* In a 100% office, the salespeople pay the broker a desk fee and keep all the commissions generated by their individual activities. The broker's gross is relatively assured based on the number of salespeople. A variation is a transaction fee where a salesperson pays an agreed fee for every transaction and keeps the balance.

  All 100% commission offices are not alike. They differ as to services provided by the broker and fees charged. The broker remains responsible for the operation of the salespeople and retains duty of supervision.

- *Discount brokerage.* Some brokers charge lower percentage fees than most other brokers. Often lower fees are combined with lesser services offered. In order to encourage cooperation of other brokers on sales, discount brokers, when splitting, often absorb some commissions or all of the difference in commissions because of lower fees.

  Some discount brokers agree to give back a portion of the commission received to their clients.

- *Fixed-fee brokers.* Some brokers now offer a fixed fee for sales transactions rather than a commission based on sales price.

■ *A la carte pricing*. Some brokers charge separate fees for services rendered, regardless of the property being sold.

There might be separate fees for placing the property on the internet, preparing ads, and preparing a property flyer, as well as a fee for handling a sale.

Commission splits.   Commission splits vary between brokers and might also vary between salespeople. A salesperson who generated most of his leads and requires less supervision might negotiate a higher commission than a salesperson who requires greater supervision and support. Similarly an office that spends a great deal generating leads might pay a lower commission split than a similar office with a more modest advertising budget.

Team concept.   Real estate salespersons often organize as teams within a real estate office. Some are relatively informal and others have team leaders, with duties delegated to team members. An advantage to team members is a steadier income because of sharing. Delegation also tends to increase total team revenue.

Salesperson Training

It is in brokers' best interests that salespeople be as productive as possible. It is also of utmost importance that they act in a professional, legal, and ethical manner. A great deal of brokerage business is the result of referrals from satisfied buyers and sellers. The reputation of a firm has value. In addition, the broker could be held responsible for wrongful acts of salespeople (**vicarious liability**).

Professional designations.   Working for professional designations requires formal course work and training. A number of professional organizations offer designations in both general and specialized areas. Members of the National Association of REALTORS® (NAR) who can use the designation *REALTOR®* can achieve a number of professional designations. The following are just a few of these designations:

■ Graduate REALTOR® Institute (GRI)

■ Member Appraisal Institute (MAI)

■ Certified Property Manager (CPM)

To understand and meet the needs of various groups in the changing demographics of the real estate marketplace, NAR offers training and an At Home with Diversity certification.

The National Association of Real Estate Brokers (NAREB) was formed by African American real estate brokers at a time when African Americans could not become members of other broker organizations. The organization also offers training programs and professional designations. Members use the designation *Realtist*.

Office Recordkeeping

Office records should meet a broker's needs and will likely include the following:

- Transaction records (A record should be kept of every transaction, including copies of all signed contracts, inspection reports, disclosures, and settlement documents. State law sets the period for which records must be kept. Records should also be kept of transactions that fail to close.)

- Trust account records

- Cash receipt and cash disbursement journal

- General ledger (summarize financial transactions)

- Payroll and commission records

In addition, records of work orders should be kept, and expenditures should be broken down as to category, such as rent, utilities, telephone and internet, advertising, supplies, professional dues and fees, and insurance.

Broker financial management.   The successful broker strives to allocate expenditures to achieve the greatest net benefits. The broker's budget is based on geographic marketplace and the intended scope of the brokerage operation.

Some financial terms of importance to a broker are the following:

- *Gross income* is the total commission earned by an office before any commission splits.

- *Company dollar* is the amount left for the broker after deducting commission splits. The company dollar is the *adjusted gross income* of a broker.

- The *operating expense* includes all overhead of rent, utilities, salaries, insurance, advertising, et cetera. Some expenses are *fixed expenses* (such as license fees), but others are *variable expenses* (such as advertising), which can be adjusted as conditions change.

- The *cash flow* is net spendable income. It is what is left after all expenses are paid.

- The *desk cost* per salesperson is computed by dividing all office expenses by the number of salespeople. For example, if total operating expenses are $150,000 and there are six salespeople in an office, then the desk cost to the broker for each salesperson is $25,000. If a salesperson is unable to generate at least $25,000 in company dollars, that salesperson is a financial drain on the broker.

- By showing assets and liabilities, the *balance sheet* indicates the net worth of a firm

- By showing income and expenses, the *profit and loss statement* shows the profit or loss for a time period.

- *Net operating income (NOI)* is income after all operational expenses, not including debt service.

Allocation of expenses in budgeting planning is more of an art than a science and is related to each broker's special needs as well as the economy and must be reviewed and adjusted as conditions change.

Licensing.   Generally, a real estate broker's license is required to perform any act involving real estate for another and for compensation.

Parties who are acting as principals buying and selling real estate for themselves need not be licensed because they are not acting as agents.

Besides principals to a transaction, most state laws exempt the following from licensing, even though they handle real estate transactions for others:

- A party acting under the order of a court
- Executors and administrators of estates
- Persons operating under a power of attorney
- Government employees
- Attorneys handling real estate transactions incidental to their practice of law
- Salaried employees of lending institutions
- Resident apartment managers
- Clerical workers in real estate offices

Unlicensed assistants.   Assistants work for licensees and are employees of their employing broker or salesperson. The broker must make certain that unlicensed assistants do not perform activities requiring a real estate license. They may perform acts not requiring a license, such as webpage updates, setting appointments, handing out preprinted material, preparing comparative market analyses, and placing signs. They cannot negotiate for listings or sales.

Advertising.   The largest single expense for most real estate offices is advertising. Until recent years, newspaper advertising was the principal media used by most real estate offices.

The internet is now the most productive media for real estate firms using webpages, blogs, social media sites, multiple listing services, and real estate property sites. Most property buyers use the internet as a primary search tool.

Advertising regulations.   Advertising must be honest. It cannot be deceptive or unfair; advertisers must be able to justify their claims. The Federal Trade Commission enforces truth-in-advertising laws.

The Truth in Lending Act (TILA) makes bait-and-switch advertising a crime. Bait and switch involves advertising a product or service that is not available or won't be sold in order to generate traffic, which is then diverted to other products or services. An example is advertising a house in a highly desirable area at a low price, when such a property is not available, in order to make contact with buyers.

TILA also requires complete financial disclosure if trigger terms are use in the advertisement. Trigger terms include the

- amount or percentage of down payment,
- number of payments or period of repayment,
- amount of payments, and
- amount of finance charges.

If the advertisement includes any of these trigger terms, then the ad must include

- the amount or percentage of down payment,
- repayment terms, and
- the annual percentage rate (APR) (this rate considers loan costs and points and costs in addition to the nominal rate—the rate stated on the note).

Advertising the APR by itself does not trigger these disclosures.

Blind ads are ads that fail to indicate that the advertiser is an agent. The ad appears to be a seller's ad. Blind ads are prohibited by state law and can result in disciplinary action by state regulatory agencies.

ETHICAL AND LEGAL BUSINESS PRACTICES

Ethics

The law sets minimum standards of conduct that our society allows. Ethics goes beyond what is allowed. Ethics is doing what is right. The best rule of ethics is the golden rule: "Do unto others as you would have them do unto you."

It is unethical to make statements of fact that you do not personally know to be true. It is also unethical to fail to correct a material misconception of a buyer or a seller. Both of these clearly do not pass the test of the golden rule.

A licensee should cooperate fully with any agency investigation concerning real estate activities. Licensees should seek to eliminate dishonest behavior and should report known violations of law or regulations to the appropriate government agency or regulatory body.

Misrepresentation.   Misrepresentation is a false statement or the concealment of a material fact with the intent of inducing another party to act. Another example is a promise made with no intention of keeping it. Misrepresentation can result in agreements being voided, civil damages, and license suspension or revocation.

Duty of good faith.   Acting in good faith means that the action is honestly done. In real estate, there is the implied duty of agents to act in good faith in all brokerage operations. Fair dealing must be the standard for dealing with clients and customers.

Due diligence.   Due diligence means the party will act in good faith using proper care and effort to meet an obligation. When an agent takes an exclusive sale listing, the agent agrees to use due diligence to consummate a sale.

Unauthorized practice of law.   Only lawyers may legally practice law. While real estate professionals deal with the law, they should not attempt to practice it.

Agents should not make suggestions as to how a buyer should take title because this could be construed as the unauthorized practice of law. Brokers and salespersons should never try to discourage a party from seeking legal advice or indicate that it is unnecessary.

While the use of a standard contract form is not the practice of law, drafting a contract may be considered the unauthorized practice of law, as could preparing a complex lease by cutting and pasting clauses from multiple lease forms.

Forms of Business Ownership

The real estate brokerage business includes a number of business ownership options. The form chosen can affect ease and cost of formation, taxation, and personal liability. Choices include the following:

1. *Sole proprietorship.* Sole proprietorship is the easiest business entity to form. All that is required is a business license from the city or the county where the firm will be located. If the business will operate under a name other than the legal name of the sole proprietor, then the state fictitious name ("doing business as") statute must be complied with. Fictitious names must meet filing and advertising requirements that let others know that the owners are operating under a name other than their legal names.

    In writing a contract, it may be necessary to sign the personal name followed by "dba (doing business as) _____." Failure to comply with the fictitious-name requirements means that the business does not legally exist. Therefore, the business might be unable to bring legal action in the name of the business for claims the business has against others.

    A sole owner is responsible for all decisions and management. The sole owner is entitled to all profits of the business and pays personal income tax on the profits even if they are left in the business.

    The sole proprietor who is entitled to all profits is similarly personally liable for all losses. This personal liability can be a significant disadvantage of a sole proprietorship because personal assets could be subject to the business claims of creditors.

    Besides liability, another disadvantage of sole proprietorship is the access to capital. The capital for a sole proprietorship comes from the owner's personal assets and borrowing power. Many sole proprietorships fail because they are undercapitalized.

    Sole proprietorships lack continuity. If the owner dies or becomes incapacitated, the business cannot continue.

2. *General partnership.* A general partnership consists of two or more part-
    ners, each of whom has personal liability for acts of the partnership. Each
    partner plays an active role in the management of the partnership. Partner-
    ship interests do not have to be equal, though they are equal unless agreed
    otherwise.

    In some states, partners in real estate partnerships must all be licensed
    as brokers, but other states allow a broker to be a partner with a licensed
    salesperson. Where a salesperson is a partner, the broker-in-charge is liable
    to the state for the actions of all partners.

    Only a business license fee and fictitious name filing, if applicable, is
    required to form a general partnership. A partnership name is fictitious if it
    does not contain the surnames of all partners.

    No written agreement is required to form a partnership, though it is
    strongly suggested that there be one. An agreement to share in the profits of
    a business may be considered by the courts to be an agreement to share in
    the losses, making the agreement a partnership.

    The partners share assets and liabilities with unlimited personal liability.
    Each partner is liable for the partnership acts of the other partners, who can
    obligate the partnership.

    A partnership can be formed unintentionally if the words or actions of the
    parties cause another party to act to their detriment because of the belief a
    partnership existed. The parties are estopped from denying the partnership.

    While partnerships must file tax returns, they do not pay income tax. The
    partners are personally taxed for their individual share of the profits. Simi-
    larly, the partners can deduct their own personal share of losses from other
    income on their income tax return.

    An advantage of a partnership is that the assets of two or more partners
    combine to provide more capital for the business. Another advantage is
    having someone else to rely on in management.

    Upon the death or incapacity of a partner, the partnership ceases unless
    there is an agreement otherwise. The heirs of the deceased are not entitled
    to become partners (because a partnership requires consent), but they are
    entitled to that partner's share of the partnership assets. If the business is to
    continue, a new partnership or business must be formed.

3. *Limited partnership.* A limited partnership consists of at least one general
    partner, who has the same unlimited liability as in a general partnership
    and conducts the business, and one or more limited partners. Limited
    partners have limited liability for debts of the partnership. Their liability is
    generally limited to losing their investment.

    Limited partners are precluded from participating in the management of
    the business. Limited partners who are found to be actively engaged in
    managing partnership activities could lose their limited liability and have
    unlimited liability as a general partner. Limited partners must not appear
    to be general partners, so the partnership name cannot include the name of
    limited partners.

A certificate of limited partnership or similar document generally must be filed with the state before the partnership business can begin. A business license and compliance with the fictitious name statute are also required.

Limited partnerships are a way to raise capital without giving up control of a business. For the investor, it allows an investment without risk beyond the original investment, and it allows the investor to share in profits.

Unlike with general partners, limited partners' interests can be sold and inherited.

While the general partners of a real estate brokerage partnership must have real estate licenses, the limited partners need not be licensed.

4. *Limited liability company (LLC).* A limited liability company (LLC) is a hybrid that combines the limited liability of a corporation with the tax advantages of a partnership. No one is personally liable for obligations of the LLC, and the profit or loss is passed on to the investor. Although the LLC must file a tax return, it can elect to be taxed as a sole proprietor or as a partnership. Profit is taxed to the principal; it is not subject to double taxation. Many real estate brokerage firms have elected to do business as LLCs.

The name chosen for an LLC must be different than the name of any other LLC in that state, and the name must indicate it is an LLC or limited company. There may be additional state name restrictions.

An LLC requires less paperwork and reporting than an S corporation or C corporation. In some states, a single party can form an LLC, but other states require two or more principals.

LLCs are more costly than partnerships because of filing fees and renewal fees or special taxation.

To form an LLC, articles of organization must be filed, usually with the secretary of state's office. The articles include basic information about the business, principals, and place of business. Some states require publication of a statement of the business being operated as an LLC and its location.

While an operating statement is not generally required, it can set forth the structure of the LLC and provide rules and regulations. If a member dies or leaves, in some states the LLC ends unless covered by an operating statement. In many states, transfer of LLC interest is restricted by required approval of other members.

5. *Corporations (chapter C corporations).* A corporation is an association of people who pay separate taxes. A C corporation is a legal entity—a legal person—and has a life separate from its owners. Theoretically, a corporation can live forever. Corporations have the same rights and responsibilities of individuals and can contract, hire, own property, pay taxes, and bring lawsuits in the name of the corporation. Because the corporation is a separate entity from the owners, the individuals who own stock in the corporation are not personally liable for debts or acts of the corporation.

If a principal in a corporation commingles personal and corporate funds or uses corporate funds for personal use, the courts could "pierce the corporate veil" and hold that party personally liable for the corporation's debts and actions.

A corporation is owned by its shareholders, who elect a board of directors. The directors appoint officers, who run the corporation.

To form a corporation, articles of incorporation are filed with the state. The articles set forth the nature of the corporation, establish the amount of stock, and identify its officers. After the articles of incorporation are approved, the directors prepare the corporate bylaws that cover how the corporation will operate.

C corporations pay taxes on profits. Profits that are distributed to stockholders are also taxed, so corporations are subject to double taxation.

State law governs C corporations, which must provide for meetings, recordkeeping, and ongoing fees.

In addition to limited liability, a significant benefit of C corporations is access to capital by the sale of stock or corporate bonds. Another benefit is fringe benefits, such as health and insurance benefits, which are considered corporate expenses—the recipient doesn't have to pay taxes on the benefits received. Other fringe benefits are education expenses, transportation costs, moving and housing costs, meals, fitness club membership, et cetera.

The corporate benefits and liability protection can be obtained with a an S corporation, which avoids double taxation.

6.   *S corporation.* An S corporation is a corporation that elects to be treated for tax purposes as a tax-through entity. While the corporation pays no income tax, the income is taxed to the stockholders. Besides liability protection, the stock is freely transferable. The life of an S corporation is independent of the life of any person and theoretically could be forever.

The requirements of a chapter S corporation include

- only one class of stock,

- no more than 100 stockholders,

- no nonresident alien stockholders, and

- the agreement of every stockholder.

To form an S corporation, the business must file a business charter in the appropriate state to become a corporation. Then all shareholders must sign IRS Form 2553.

A disadvantage is that some states charge fees and/or taxes for S corporations. Other disadvantages include the time and cost of formation, requirements for shareholder meetings with minutes, adoption of bylaws, and stock transfer and records maintenance.

Many real estate professionals prefer LLCs to chapter S corporations.

YOUR PERTINENT STATE INFORMATION

1.   How long does a broker have after receipt of trust monies to deposit the funds in a trust account?

2.   May trust accounts bear interest? If so, how is interest handled?

3. How much, if any, broker fund money may be kept in a trust account?

4. How long can earned commissions be left in a trust account?

5. Are there state-mandated recordkeeping requirements for trust accounts?

6. Can a salesperson be a partner with a broker in your state?

7. Can all trust monies be held in a single trust account?

8. Must there be written contracts between broker and salespersons?

9. Must a broker have worker's compensation coverage for salespersons?

CHAPTER 8 QUIZ

1. A salesperson may be compensated for real estate service by
   A. the owner.
   B. another broker.
   C. another salesperson.
   D. the salesperson's employing broker.

2. A buyer's earnest money deposit was placed in the broker's escrow account when a purchase offer was received. The owner gave a counteroffer, but the buyer refused it and has requested return of her deposit. The seller has requested that the deposit not be returned to the buyer. The broker should
   A. give the deposit to the broker's principal.
   B. return the deposit to the buyer.
   C. keep the deposit in the escrow account.
   D. file an interpleader action.

3. One of the requirements for a real estate salesperson to be considered an independent contractor by the IRS is that the
   A. salesperson be paid a salary.
   B. salesperson not be responsible to a broker.
   C. broker-salesperson contract states that the salesperson be treated as an independent contractor for tax purposes.
   D. salesperson not be supervised by a broker.

4. An agent received a cash deposit, which he placed in his personal bank account and then wrote a personal check to the trust account. This action is
   A. commingling.
   B. conversion.
   C. embezzlement.
   D. proper conduct.

5. An unlicensed party can receive compensation for handling a sale when the party
   A. is an attorney who has a valid sale listing.
   B. charges a fixed fee not a percentage commission.
   C. is an employee of a licensee.
   D. is acting under court order.

6. In 2014, a broker has $306,000 in gross income. He paid his salespersons $180,000 in commissions and has office operations expenses of $92,000. The broker's cash flow was
   A. $34,000.
   B. $126,000.
   C. $214,000.
   D. $306,000.

7. As to question 6, what is the broker's company dollar?
   A. $34,000
   B. $126,000
   C. $214,000
   D. $306,000

8. As to question 6, if the broker has three salespersons, what is the desk cost?
   A. $11,666
   B. $30,666
   C. $71,333
   D. $102,000

9. A balance sheet shows
   A. expenses.
   B. profit or loss.
   C. cash receipts.
   D. net worth.

10. The reason that some states allow brokers to keep some broker funds in trust accounts is to
    A. protect broker funds from broker creditors.
    B. cover bank fees.
    C. simplify trust accounting.
    D. avoid bank charges.

11. A broker withdrew her commission from the trust account before a sale closing. This is
    A. conversion.
    B. commingling.
    C. a novation.
    D. proper if all funds have been deposited in the account.

12. A salesperson kept all commissions earned on her transactions but paid her broker $2,150 each month. This is an example of a
    A. discount broker.
    B. a la carte pricing.
    C. 100% commission agreement.
    D. a fixed fee agency.

13. A broker can properly
    A. charge discount fees for services.
    B. pay salespersons a draw against commissions from trust monies.
    C. pay commissions to salespersons of other brokers.
    D. keep cash received in an office safe until closing.

14. A sale failed to close and each party blamed the other party. The buyer and the seller have each demanded the earnest money deposit. The broker should
    A. give the funds to the party depositing the funds.
    B. give the funds to the broker's principal.
    C. give the funds to the state licensing authority.
    D. commence an interpleader action.

15. An ad for a property did not include the broker's name but indicated "agent." The ad is
    A. a blind ad.
    B. a violation of the Truth in Lending Act.
    C. proper as-is.
    D. grounds for license revocation.

16. Which of the following statements regarding ethics and the law is *TRUE*?
    A. If it is legal, it is ethical.
    B. If it is illegal, it is unethical.
    C. Legality and ethics are synonymous.
    D. A legal act could be unethical.

17. L failed to pay $5,000 to broker M as an agreed commission payment should L's tenant N renew a lease. L later gave broker M a deposit of $10,000 with a purchase offer. The seller refused the offer. Which action of broker M is proper?
    A. Hold the $10,000 in trust until M's claim is adjudicated.
    B. Give L $5,000 and use the other $5,000 to offset the commission claim.
    C. Turn the funds over to the court to decide who is entitled to the deposit.
    D. Return the $10,000 to L.

18. Why do some states consider real estate salespersons to be employees?
    A. Licensing
    B. IRS determinations
    C. Supervision
    D. Compensation by commission

19. Who is the trustee of a real estate trust account?
    A. Closing agent
    B. Broker
    C. Buyer
    D. Seller

20. A real estate salesperson used her name in an advertisement. This was proper if she
    A. also included her license number.
    B. also included the name of her broker.
    C. indicated she was a real estate salesperson.
    D. included a physical address.

21. In the absence of any agreement, interest earned on trust monies belongs to
    A. the party depositing the funds.
    B. the broker.
    C. the party to whom the funds are eventually to be disbursed.
    D. both the broker and the owner of the funds.

22. Brokers are protected from conversion of trust funds by their salespersons with
    A. bonding.
    B. the state surety fund.
    C. errors and omissions (E&O) insurance.
    D. the state licensing law.

23. A broker received a purchase offer without
    earnest money. The broker should
    A. return the offer to the offeror.
    B. hold the offer until earnest money is
       provided.
    C. present the offer to the owner.
    D. inform the owner of an illegal offer.

24. A sale results in an $8,200 commission.
    The salesperson kept the entire commission
    because the salesperson worked for a
    A. fixed fee broker.
    B. discount broker.
    C. broker with a la carte pricing
    D. 100% office.

25. A new LLC made an offer to purchase with
    a token earnest money deposit and requested
    three months for closing. The buyer's actions
    indicate that it
    A. is seeking a tax advantage.
    B. is a serious buyer.
    C. is treating the purchase as an option.
    D. intends to use the property as a new
       office.

26. Who can use the designation REALTOR®?
    A. Any state-licensed salesperson
    B. Any state-licensed broker
    C. Only brokers with the GRI designation
    D. Members of the National Association of
       REALTORS®

27. A seller's agent filed to correct an erroneous
    assumption made by a buyer. This failure
    breached the broker's
    A. duty of due diligence.
    B. duty of good faith.
    C. fiduciary duty.
    D. mandated disclosures.

28. A $9,200 commission was split 50/50
    between the listing office and the seller's
    office. If the listing salesperson was to get
    60% of the office share, how much did the
    listing salesperson receive?
    A. $1,840
    B. $2,760
    C. $2,840
    D. $4,600

29. A broker placed a deposit check in a safe
    and presented an offer. The owner accepted
    the offer with closing in 20 days. Five days
    before closing, the broker deposited the
    check, which was not honored by the bank.
    The owner did not know of the uncashed
    check. The broker's action is
    A. conversion.
    B. commingling.
    C. fraud.
    D. misrepresentation.

30. A broker took earned commissions out of
    a trust account and deposited them in a
    business account. Business account checks
    were then issued to cooperating brokers and
    salespersons. This action
    A. violated the real estate law.
    B. was conversion.
    C. was commingling.
    D. was proper.

31. An office manager was paid a weekly salary
    plus a monthly bonus based on total office
    sales. According to the IRS, the manager's
    status was that of
    A. employee.
    B. independent contractor.
    C. co-broker.
    D. designated broker.

32. The accounting record that shows net worth
    but not profitability is the
    A. balance sheet.
    B. profit and loss statement.
    C. net operating income.
    D. desk cost.

33. Debt service is *NOT* considered in
    determining
    A. the profit and loss statement.
    B. cash flow.
    C. net operating income.
    D. operating expense.

34. An office has 12 salespeople and total
    operating expenses averaging $18,000 per
    month. What is the monthly desk cost per
    salesperson?
    A. $1,250
    B. $1,500
    C. $3,000
    D. $3,250

35. What a broker receives after all cash expenses are paid is called
    A. net operating income.
    B. company dollars.
    C. gross income.
    D. cash flow.

36. Income is *NOT* considered when preparing
    A. a balance sheet.
    B. a profit and loss statement.
    C. cash flow.
    D. NOI calculations.

37. A real estate license is *NOT* required for
    A. a salaried real estate salesperson.
    B. a nonresidential real estate salesperson.
    C. a clerical worker who only sells real estate occasionally.
    D. an attorney while practicing law.

38. An unlicensed assistant may *NOT*
    A. schedule appointments.
    B. make listing presentations.
    C. hand out preprinted brochures.
    D. arrange showings.

39. Today, the *MOST* effective media for a real estate firm are
    A. classified ads.
    B. display ads.
    C. internet advertising.
    D. business cards.

40. A broker explained to a buyer the advantage of taking title as joint tenants. This action
    A. violated the brokers ethical duties.
    B. is required if the broker is a buyer's agent.
    C. was the unauthorized practice of law.
    D. was proper if broker did not tell the buyer how to take title.

41. A false statement made by a party who didn't know whether it was true and that influences parties to act to their detriment is considered
    A. criminal fraud.
    B. misrepresentation.
    C. puffing.
    D. nonactionable fraud.

42. A real estate broker took an exclusive sale listing and made no effort to sell the property. The broker breached the duty of
    A. accounting.
    B. due diligence.
    C. loyalty.
    D. disclosure.

43. A broker prepared a lease by cutting and pasting clauses from other leases and drafting paragraphs for other matters. The broker
    A. must have the CPM designation.
    B. has failed to exercise due diligence.
    C. must have the GRI designation.
    D. is guilty of the unauthorized practice of law.

44. A broker designated charges for placing signs, preparing internet listings, placing properties on different websites, preparing virtual tours, preparing offers, and handling closings. This is considered
    A. discount brokerage.
    B. a la carte pricing.
    C. fixed-fee brokerage.
    D. a 100% commission office.

45. In the course of a sale, a buyer stated, "This is what I want—a home on a full acre so I can keep a horse." The agent knew the parcel was only half an acre but failed to correct the buyer. If the buyer purchases the property based on this misconception, the broker's action constitutes
    A. puffing.
    B. misrepresentation.
    C. bait and switch.
    D. no violation of law.

46. Bait-and-switch advertising is described as
    A. advertising one property when you have many similar properties.
    B. advertising an unavailable property in order to sell other properties.
    C. offering a premium to buy a property when the premium will not be provided.
    D. advertising a low-cost property in hopes of selling higher-priced properties.

47. An advertiser does not have to make complete financial disclosure when the only finance reference in the ad was
    A. period for repayment.
    B. amount of down payment.
    C. APR.
    D. amount of payments.

48. A broker received an offer on a property that was not listed for sale and was owned by the broker. The earnest money deposit was placed in the broker's trust account. This action
    A. was commingling.
    B. was conversion.
    C. violated implied duty of good faith.
    D. was proper.

49. A broker gave a salesperson an advance on commissions earned by writing a check from the trust account. This is an example of
    A. commingling.
    B. fraud.
    C. conversion.
    D. a RESPA violation.

50. An associate broker is
    A. a buyer's agent.
    B. a broker who works for a broker.
    C. any licensed salesperson.
    D. the same as a REALTOR-ASSOCIATE®.

51. Which of the following people would seek the professional designation MAI?
    A. A property manager
    B. An industrial broker
    C. An appraiser
    D. A home inspector

52. Vicarious liability refers to
    A. liability of owners as to crimes of tenants.
    B. state liability for actions of licensees.
    C. liability of employers for acts of employees.
    D. liability of wrongdoers for their actions.

53. A broker's records should cover all
    A. lease transactions.
    B. sale transactions.
    C. sales that fail to close.
    D. of these.

54. In an ad, which of the following is a trigger term mandating further disclosure?
    A. Low down payment
    B. Payments like rent
    C. 36 easy payments
    D. 4.5% APR

55. John Jones goes into business as Hilltop Realty. Which of the following is *FALSE*?
    A. He must have a broker's license.
    B. He must obtain a business permit.
    C. He must file articles of incorporation.
    D. The business must comply with the fictitious-name statute.

56. The easiest form of business ownership to start a business is
    A. sole proprietorship.
    B. general partnership.
    C. limited partnership.
    D. limited liability company.

57. The acronym *DBA* refers to
    A. agency responsibility.
    B. fictitious business names.
    C. chapter S corporations.
    D. vicarious liability.

58. Which of the following business types is limited to 100 or fewer participants?
    A. Chapter S corporation
    B. Limited partnership
    C. Limited liability corporation
    D. General partnership

59. A partner in a partnership with a general partner has no liability beyond the investment. This is
    A. a chapter S corporation.
    B. a limited partnership.
    C. an LLC.
    D. a general partnership.

60. An advantage of a chapter S corporation over an LLC is
    A. ease of formation.
    B. limited liability.
    C. continuity of operation.
    D. avoidance of double taxation.

61. Having a life separate from its owners describes a
   A. general partnership.
   B. limited partnership.
   C. limited liability company.
   D. corporation.

62. A business entity that pays income taxes is a
   A. C corporation.
   B. chapter S corporation.
   C. general partnership.
   D. limited liability corporation.

63. All participants must agree to change to which of the following types of ownership?
   A. Chapter S corporation
   B. LLC
   C. Limited liability partnership
   D. Corporation

64. A member of the National Association of Real Estate Brokers can use the designation
   A. REALTOR®.
   B. Realtist.
   C. MAI.
   D. CPM.

65. A licensed real estate broker working under the management of another broker is
   A. an associate broker.
   B. a REALTOR®.
   C. an assistant broker.
   D. a general partner.

66. If only one person is responsible for the debt of the organization, the organization may be
   A. an LLC.
   B. a limited partnership.
   C. a chapter S corporation.
   D. a chapter C corporation.

67. A business in which two or more individuals share in profits and losses describes a
   A. sole proprietorship.
   B. general partnership.
   C. limited liability company.
   D. chapter S corporation.

68. A written document is not required to form a
   A. general partnership.
   B. limited liability company.
   C. chapter S corporation.
   D. chapter C corporation.

69. A person with an ownership interest in a real estate brokerage firm is not licensed. This is proper because
   A. it is a sole proprietorship.
   B. the person is a general partner.
   C. the person works under the supervision of a licensee.
   D. the person is a limited partner.

70. Which of the following is *TRUE* as to a chapter S corporation?
   A. There can be no more than two classes of stock.
   B. A majority of stockholders must agree to formation.
   C. Nonresident aliens can be stockholders.
   D. There can be no more than 100 stockholders.

71. A woman handled the sales of 23 properties in one year, resulting in a substantial income. She did *NOT* require a real estate license because she
   A. acted as a sole proprietor.
   B. acted as a principal.
   C. was a principal in an LLC.
   D. was married to a licensed broker.

72. An earnest money check was held uncashed by a broker after acceptance of an offer. This was proper because
   A. the buyer directed it.
   B. the seller directed it.
   C. the amount was nominal.
   D. it as a short sale.

73. A broker would *MOST* likely be responsible for a salesperson's
   A. federal income tax withholding.
   B. health insurance.
   C. Social Security withholding and contributions.
   D. workers' compensation insurance.

74. A broker failed to have a trust account but was not in violation of the law because
    A. deposits were all made out to an escrow company.
    B. the broker was a consultant and did not receive trust money.
    C. the broker operated as an LLC.
    D. either deposits were all made out to an escrow company or the broker was a consultant and did not receive trust money.

75. The phrase *pierce the corporate veil* refers to
    A. making records public.
    B. holding parties personally liable.
    C. the criminal liability of wrongdoers.
    D. suing a corporation as if it were an individual.

76. A demand deposit is a deposit in
    A. an escrow account.
    B. a checking account.
    C. a money market account.
    D. any of these.

77. A real estate broker must
    A. have salespeople.
    B. be licensed by the state.
    C. have a trust account.
    D. post a fidelity bond.

78. An interpleader action refers to a legal action to
    A. compel other parties to litigate a dispute.
    B. break up a general partnership.
    C. dissolve a corporation.
    D. form an LLC.

79. The acronym *GRI* refers to
    A. an appraisal.
    B. an NAR designation.
    C. a form of business organization.
    D. the Truth in Lending Act.

80. A broker received a personal note as an earnest money deposit with an offer. The broker should
    A. present the offer.
    B. hold the offer until the note is honored.
    C. deposit the note in the trust account.
    D. do none of these.

CHAPTER 8 QUIZ ANSWERS

1. **(D)** The only person who can pay salespeople for an act requiring a real estate license is their broker. (225)

2. **(B)** Because the offer was rejected by the counteroffer, the deposit must be returned. The seller never had a claim to the funds. (223)

3. **(C)** The other two requirements are that they be licensed and that pay be related to sales, not hours worked. (224)

4. **(A)** The agent mixed personal and trust funds monies in a personal account. (223)

5. **(D)** Such as a trustee or an administrator. The attorney is acting as a broker, not an attorney. (228)

6. **(A)** Cash flow is net spendable after deducting commissions paid and operating expense from the gross income. (227)

7. **(B)** Company dollar is gross income less commission splits. (227)

8. **(B)** Desk cost is office expense of $92,000 divided by number of salespersons . (227)

9. **(D)** Shows assets and liabilities. Others are in profit and loss statement. (227)

10. **(B)** Otherwise a disbursement check could be returned "NSF" because of bank charges. (222)

11. **(A)** It is theft because the broker is not entitled to any portion of the trust monies until closing or deposit is forfeited. (223)

12. **(C)** Salesperson keeps 100% of commissions earned but pays broker a fee. (225)

13. **(A)** There is no problem in cutting fees, but answer (B) is conversion and (D) is commingling. Only the salesperson's broker can compensate the salesperson. (225)

14. **(D)** Force the parties to adjudicate their claims. (222)

15. **(C)** The word *agent* or *broker* identifies the advertiser as an agent. (229)

16. **(D)** What is unethical may be legal today but become illegal in the future. (229)

17. **(D)** Trust monies cannot be held by the broker to offset any claims the broker may have against the party depositing the funds. (222)

18. **(C)** Broker has duty to supervise salespeople. (224)

19. **(B)** The broker is the trustee of the trust account. (221)

20. **(B)** The salesperson cannot appear to act as a broker. The broker's name must appear in the ad, even if it is paid for by the salesperson. (225)

21. **(A)** Until closing, the interest belongs to the person depositing the funds. (222)

22. **(A)** Fidelity bonds would indemnify the broker. A surety bond protects a party from the other party's failure to perform. Errors and omissions insurance covers negligence, not theft. (222)

23. **(C)** Earnest money is not required. (222)

24. **(D)** But paid the broker a fee. (225)

25. **(C)** They can go ahead with the purchase or walk away without personal liability. (222)

26. **(D)** It is a registered name only for broker members of NAR. (226)

27. **(B)** Duty of honest dealings. Could also be misrepresentation. (229)

28. **(B)** 60% of $4,600. (226)

29. **(B)** Holding check uncashed without authority of owner after acceptance. (223)

30. **(D)** Earned commission is broker funds. (223)

31. **(A)** IRS requires that pay be related to sales success, not hours worked. (224)

32. **(A)** Shows assets and liabilities. (227)

33. **(C)** But other office operating costs are deducted from gross. (227)

34. **(B)** Divide $18,000 by 12. (227)

35. **(D)** All expenses, including debt service, deducted from gross. (227)

36. **(A)** Does not show income and expenses. Only shows assets and liabilities. (227)

37. **(D)** Exempt from licensure. (228)

38. **(B)** Engaging in real estate activities requiring a license. (228)

39. **(C)** Most buyers use the internet. (228)

40. **(C)** Explaining the law. (230)

41. **(B)** It was false and caused another party to rely on it. (229)

42. **(B)** Must exercise reasonable and diligent effort and care. (230)

43. **(D)** Drafting a legal document. (230)

44. **(B)** Charging for each service selected by client. (226)

45. **(B)** Misrepresentation can be a negative act in failing to correct misconception. (229)

46. **(B)** Bait property is unavailable or won't be sold at price advertised. (228)

47. **(C)** "Annual percentage rate (APR)" is not a trigger term. (229)

48. **(A)** Personal funds are being mixed with trust funds. (223)

49. **(C)** Personal taking of trust monies. (223)

50. **(B)** Usually as a salesperson. (224)

51. **(C)** The NAR designation Member Appraisal Institute. (226)

52. **(C)** As well as principal for acts of agent. (224)

53. **(D)** All transactions and trust monies. (224, 227)

54. **(C)** Number of payments is a trigger term. (229)

55. **(C)** Could do so in other than a corporate form. (230–233)

56. **(A)** It requires only a business permit and perhaps fictitious name compliance. (230)

57. **(B)** "Doing business as" fictitious name. (230)

58. **(A)** Taxed as a partnership. (233)

59. **(B)** Limited partner liability limited to investment. (231)

60. **(C)** Death of a party has no effect on business entity. (233)

61. **(D)** Life of a corporation can theoretically be eternal. (232)

62. **(A)** Pays taxes and dividends also taxed (double taxation). (232–233)

63. **(A)** They change from a C corporation. (233)

64. **(B)** A registered trade name. (226)

65. **(A)** An associate broker chooses not to have his own office. (224)

66. **(B)** With one general partner. (231)

67. **(B)** Unlimited liability. (231)

68. **(A)** Can be verbal or even implied. (231)

69. **(D)** Inactive in management. (228, 231–232)

70. **(D)** Limitation on size. (233)

71. **(B)** Selling her own property. (228)

72. **(B)** Before acceptance, the buyer can direct it. (221)

73. **(D)** Required in most states. (224)

74. **(D)** No trust monies were kept by the broker. (221)

75. **(B)** For example, when corporate and personal assets mix, the business is not acting as corporation, so the people are personally liable. (232)

76. **(B)** Checking accounts are demand deposits. (222)

77. **(B)** Trust account is necessary only if there is trust money received. (228)

78. **(A)** Such as two parties claiming entitlement to trust funds. (222)

79. **(B)** Graduate Realtor Institute. (226)

80. **(A)** But inform the seller of the form of the deposit. (222)

C H A P T E R 9

Mathematics of Real Estate

Approximately 10% of the questions on the general portion of your real estate examination will include some mathematics.

The mathematics on your state license examination require an understanding of simple addition, subtraction, multiplication, division, some basic formulas, percentages, and decimals. If you understand this material and are able to work the problems at the end of this chapter, you should have no difficulty with mathematics on your examination.

DECIMALS AND PERCENTAGES

A fraction such as ½ can be converted to a decimal by dividing the numerator (top number) by the denominator (bottom number):

$$1 \text{ (numerator)} \div 2 \text{ (denominator)} = 0.5$$

Further examples:

$$¾ = 3 \div 4 = 0.75$$

$$⅝ = 5 \div 8 = 0.625$$

To convert a decimal to a percentage, move the decimal point two places to the right and add a percentage sign. For example, 0.6 becomes 60%.

To convert a percent to a decimal, move the decimal point two places to the left and drop the percentage sign. For example, 60% equals 0.6.

Percentage Problems

There are three components to a percentage problem:

1. The percentage rate

2. The whole number

3. The part of the whole number

If you know any two of the above numbers or one of the numbers and the rate, you can find the third component using these three formulas:

$$\text{part} \div \text{whole} = \text{rate}$$

$$\text{part} \div \text{rate} = \text{whole}$$

$$\text{rate} \times \text{whole} = \text{part}$$

Finding the Rate

To find the rate, use the following formula:

$$\text{part} \div \text{whole} = \text{rate}$$

If the part is 20 and the whole is 50, then $20 \div 50 = 0.40$, or 40%.

Problem. $12,000 was paid as commission on a $200,000 sale. What percent commission was paid?

$$\text{part} \div \text{whole} = \text{rate}$$

$$\$12,000 \div \$200,000 = 0.06$$

Rate of commission = 0.06, or 6%

Problem. An investor earned $1,200 interest on a $20,000 investment for one year. What was the interest rate earned?

$$\text{part} \div \text{whole} = \text{rate}$$

$$\$1,200 \div \$20,000 = 0.06$$

Interest rate = 0.06, or 6%

In real estate, percentage returns are based on net income, which is part of the whole:

$$\text{net} \div \text{whole} = \text{rate}$$

Divide into the Net

Percentage returns (rates) could be based on total price paid, down payments, or an owner's equity:

$$\text{net} \div \text{total price} = \text{rate}$$

$$\text{net} \div \text{down payment} = \text{rate}$$

$$\text{net} \div \text{owner's equity} = \text{rate}$$

Problem. An investor earned $24,150 on a $350,000 investment for one year. What was his percentage return?

$$\text{part} \div \text{whole} = \text{rate}$$

$$\$24,150 \div \$350,000 = 0.069$$

Percentage rate = 0.069, or 6.9%

Problem.   An owner has an $80,000 mortgage against a property worth $120,000. If the property nets $4,000 per year, what is the owner's percentage return on equity?

$$\text{value} - \text{mortgage} = \text{equity}$$

$$\$120,000 - \$80,000 = \$40,000$$

$$\$4,000 \div \$40,000 = 0.1$$

Percentage return on the owner's equity is 0.1, or 10%.

Finding the Whole Number

The formula to find the whole is

$$\text{part} \div \text{rate} = \text{whole}.$$

If the part is 20 and the rate is 40%, (40% as a decimal is 0.40), then

$$20 \div 0.40 = 50 \text{ (whole)}.$$

Problem.   Six percent commission was paid on a sale. The commission totaled $12,000. What was the selling price?

$$\text{part} \div \text{rate} = \text{whole (selling price)}$$

$$\$12,000 \div 0.06 = \$200,000$$

Selling price is $200,000.

Problem.   An investor received $1,200 in interest for one year on a 6% investment. How much was invested?

$$\text{part} \div \text{rate} = \text{principal (whole)}$$

$$\$1,200 \div 0.06 = \$20,000$$

$20,000 was invested.

Problem.   Assume a seller wanted to net $23,500 from the sale of a lot after she had paid a 6% commission:

$$\$23,500 = 94\% \text{ of sales price}$$
(because it is sales price after 6% commission is paid);
94% as a decimal is 0.94.

$$\text{part} \div \text{rate} = \text{whole}$$

$$\$23,500 \div 0.94 = \text{whole}$$

The whole is $25,000; and after the 6% commission ($1,500) is paid, the seller will have $23,500 left.

Problem.   The property sold for $80,000, which is 40% more than it cost the seller. What did the seller originally pay?

$80,000 is 40% more than cost, or 140% of cost (1.4 as a decimal).

$$part \div rate = whole$$

$$\$80,000 \div 1.4 = \$57,142.86$$

Original cost is $57,142.86.

Finding the Part

To find the part of the whole number, multiply the percentage rate as a decimal by the whole number. If the rate is 40% (0.40 as a decimal) and the whole number is 50, then 0.40 × 50 = 20.

Commission is a percentage of the selling price (part of the whole) and is determined by multiplying percentage rate × selling price (the whole number):

$$rate \times whole = whole$$

If the rate was 5% (0.05) and the selling price (whole) was $200,000, then the commission is $10,000:

$$0.05 \times \$200,000 = \$10,000$$

Problem.   Assume a home sold for $165,000, which was 12% less than its list price. If it had sold at its list price, how much would the broker be entitled to if there were a 6% commission agreement?

Step 1:   Find the list price.

The home sold for 88% of list price (12% less than list price):

$$part \div percentage = whole$$

$$\$165,000 \div 0.88 = \$187,500$$

Whole (list price) = $187,500

Step 2:   Find the part of the whole (commission).

$$percentage \times list\ price = commission$$

$$0.06 \times \$187,500 = \$11,250$$

This is what the commission would have been if the property had sold at list price.

INTEREST

Interest is the percentage return received or paid for the use of money. It is normally given as an annual rate.

Finding the Interest

To determine the amount of interest earned, take the amount of the loan (principal) times the rate of interest times the time (period) of the loan:

$$principal \times rate \times time = interest$$

The interest earned on $20,000 at 6% for one year is

$$\$20,000 \times 0.06 \times 1 = \$1,200.$$

Interest earned over six months is

$$\$20,000 \times 0.06 \times 0.5 = \$600.$$

Finding the Principal

The principal is computed using this formula:

$$part \div rate = whole$$

If $6 were earned in interest over a one-year period and the interest rate was 6%, then

$$part \div rate = whole;$$

$$\$6 \div 0.06 = \$100.$$

The whole (principal) is $100.

Finding the Interest Rate

Interest rate is found using this formula:

$$part \div whole = rate$$

If $6 were earned in interest over a one-year period on an investment of $100, then

$$part \div whole = rate;$$

$$\$6 \div \$100 = 0.06.$$

The percentage of interest is 0.06, or 6%.

Finding the Time

If rate of interest, amount of interest earned, and principal amount are known, the period of investment can be found by dividing interest earned by the amount of the principal times the rate of interest:

$$interest\ earned \div (principal \times rate) = time$$

Earnings of $1,200 on a $20,000 investment at 6% means the investment must have been for one year:

$$interest\ earned \div (principal \times rate) = time$$

$$\$1,200 \div (\$20,000 \times 0.06) = time$$

$$\$1,200 \div \$1,200 = 1$$

Note that if you are still uncertain of the correct formula, test the formula by inserting known figures. For example, you know that $100 (principal) at 6% (rate of interest) for one year (time) will earn $6 (interest earned). If a given formula works properly when these test numbers are inserted, the formula likely is correct.

Plus Interest

A payment of $100 per month plus interest at 12% on a $10,000 loan would mean a first-month payment of $200.

$$\$10,000 \times 0.12 = \$1,200 \text{ annual interest}$$

$$\$1,200 \div 12 \text{ months} = \$100 \text{ monthly interest}$$

$$\$100 + \$100 \text{ principal} = \$200 \text{ first-month payment}$$

The second month's payment on the same loan ($9,900 balance) is $199.

$$\$9,900 \times 0.12 = \$1,188 \text{ annual interest}$$

$$\$1,188 \div 12 \text{ months} = \$99 \text{ monthly interest}$$

$$\$99 + \$100 \text{ principal} = \$199 \text{ second-month payment}$$

The third month's payment on the loan ($9,800 balance) is $198.01.

$$\$9,800 \times 0.12 = \$1,176 \text{ annual interest}$$

$$\$1,176 \div 12 \text{ months} = \$98 \text{ monthly interest}$$

$$\$98 + \$100 \text{ principal} = \$198 \text{ third-month payment}$$

With plus interest loans, the principal decreases by the same amount each month while the amount of interest paid decreases each month, as do the total payments.

Including Interest

For a $10,000 12% loan, equal monthly payments of $110.11 would amortize (liquidate) the loan over 20 years. The payments are constant and include principal and interest. The first month's payment is applied as follows:

$$\$10,000 \times 0.12 = \$1,200 \text{ per year}$$

$$\$1,200 \div 12 = \$100 \text{ per month}$$

$10.11 is paid on principal (balance of $110.11 payment).

The second month's payment is applied as follows:

$$\$99.90 \text{ interest}$$

$$\$9,989.89 \times 0.12 = \$1,198.79 \text{ per year}$$

$$\$1,198.79 \div 12 \text{ months} = \$99.89 \text{ per month}$$

$10.22 is paid on principal (balance of $110.11 payment)

Thus, an amortized equal-payment loan will result in the amount applied to principal increasing each month and the amount applied to interest decreasing by a like amount.

TAXES

As stated in Chapter 2, taxes on real property are ad valorem, taxed according to value. A tax rate normally is expressed per dollar of evaluation, or it could be per $100 or $1,000 of evaluation. Tax evaluation is set by a tax assessor and need not be the same as market value.

Assume a property was assessed at 50% of its market value of $80,000. If the tax rate is 0.03794 per dollar of evaluation, multiply the rate by the evaluation to determine the taxes.

If the rate above were expressed per $100 of evaluation, it is 3.794 per $100, or $3.79 and 4 mills per $100. To determine the property tax, simply move the decimal point two places to the left to find the rate per dollar of evaluation and multiply the rate by the evaluation. A **mill** is ⅒ of a cent or ⅟₁,₀₀₀ of a dollar. It is expressed as a decimal as $0.001.

An **equalization factor** is used in some parts of the country to make the assessed value more realistic. The assessed value is multiplied by the equalization factor to determine the value for tax purposes.

If property is assessed at $125,000 and the equalization factor is 1.34, then the value to which the tax rate would apply is $167,500 ($125,000 × 1.34).

PRORATIONS

Prorating problems are more likely to be on broker examinations than on salesperson examinations.

To prorate means to divide proportionally. In real estate, we divide income and expenses between buyer and seller at closing.

Items to be prorated at closing may include prepaid rent, taxes, insurance (when the policy is assumed), prepaid service policies, interest, and so on. For proration purposes, use 365 days for the calendar year and the actual days in the month unless an exam question states otherwise. Your examination question will also indicate who is responsible for the date of closing.

Note that, in some areas, prorations do not use calendar days but instead use the banker's method, which is based on every month having 30 days and using a 360-day year.

Example.   Assume a contract for a home alarm system was paid in advance for one year at a cost of $485.45.

$$\$485.45 \div 365 = \$1.33 \text{ daily cost}$$

Assume that the seller paid the contract in advance, starting July 1, 2014; and the contract was assumed by the buyer, with the buyer responsible for the September 10, 2014, closing date. The seller is responsible for July, August, and nine days in September.

31 days (July) + 31 days (August) + 9 days (September) = 71 days

71 × $1.33 = $94.43

The buyer is responsible for the balance of the contract.

$485.45 – $94.43 = $391.02

The buyer is debited with $391.02 (prorated unused portion of the contract), and the seller is credited this amount at settlement.

Interest Proration

Interest on loans is, in most states, paid in arrears, which means that a loan payment due August 1 would cover the July interest. In the case of a loan assumption during the month of July, the buyer is paying the entire July payment with the August payment. Therefore, the seller would owe the buyer for that portion of the month that the seller was responsible for.

Assume closing is July 15. If the seller is responsible for the day of closing, then the seller is responsible for 15 days' interest. If the buyer were responsible for the day of closing, the seller would only be responsible for 14 days' interest. To determine seller responsibility, divide the interest for the month of July by 31 to find the daily rate and then multiply by the number of days of seller responsibility. The seller is debited this amount and the buyer credited this amount in the closing statement.

AREA AND VOLUME

Square Footage

To find the square footage of a square or rectangle, multiply the length (in feet) by the width (in feet).

For example, a 40' × 140' lot contains 5,600 square feet.

A right triangle is half a rectangle. Therefore, the square footage of a right triangle is one-half the length times the width. The square footage of the 50' × 60' rectangle shown in Figure 9.1 is 3,000. Half of that number—1,500 square feet—is the area of the triangle.

FIGURE 9.1

Square Triangle

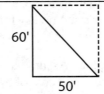

When determining square feet of a building, we ordinarily use exterior measurements excluding garages and porches. *Floor space*, however, uses interior dimensions.

Price Per Square Foot

To find the price per square foot, divide price by square feet.

For example, assume a rectangular lot is 200 feet wide and 300 feet deep.

$$200 \times 300 = 60,000 \text{ sq. ft.}$$

If the lot is priced at $150,000, then the price per square foot is as follows:

$$\$150,000 \div 60,000 \text{ sq. ft.} = \$2.50 \text{ per sq. ft.}$$

Square Yards

A yard is three linear feet, so a square yard is 3 feet by 3 feet. There are 9 square feet in 1 square yard (see Figure 9.2).

FIGURE 9.2

Square Yard

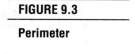

Be sure to convert square feet to square yards, or vice versa, to match the problem or answers.

Perimeter

The perimeter is the outer boundary of an area. To find the perimeter of an area, first determine all the dimensions. For example, find the perimeter of the parcel in Figure 9.3.

FIGURE 9.3

Perimeter

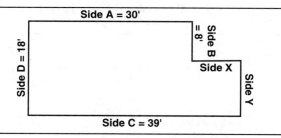

Side X is 9 feet because side A (30 feet) plus X equals 39 feet. Side Y is 10 feet because side B (8 feet) plus Y equals 18 feet. Therefore, 30 feet (A) plus 8 feet (B) plus 9 feet (X) plus 10 feet (Y) plus 39 feet (C) plus 18 feet (D) equals 114 linear feet.

Assume a 3-foot walk was to be built around the perimeter of the area and you needed to know the number of square feet for the walk. You would start by drawing the parcel and walk (see Figure 9.4).

FIGURE 9.4

Perimeter with 3-Foot Walk

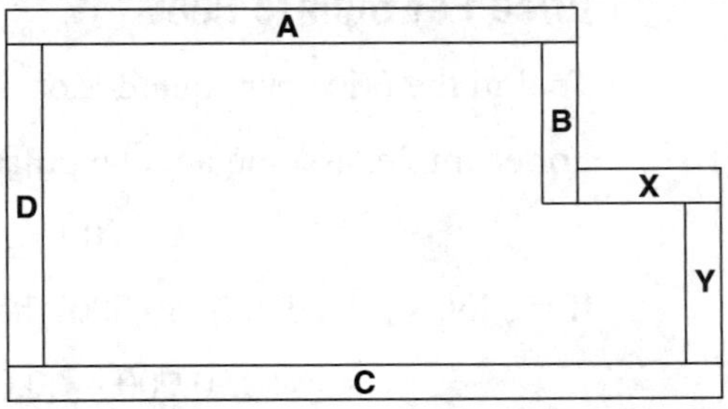

The walk on side A is	36' × 3', or	108 sq. ft
The walk on side B is	8' × 3', or	24 sq. ft.
The walk on side X is	9' × 3', or	27 sq. ft.
The walk on side Y is	10' × 3', or	30 sq. ft.
The walk on side C is	45' × 3', or	135 sq. ft.
The walk on side D is	18' × 3', or	54 sq. ft.
Total sq. ft. of walk	=	378 sq. ft.

To find the number of square yards, divide by 9:

$$378 \div 9 = 42 \text{ square yards}$$

Volume

In some areas of the country, appraisers use a cubic-foot method. To find the volume (cubic measure), multiply length by width by height. For example, a cubic yard contains 27 cubic feet (3' × 3' × 3') (see Figure 9.5). Therefore, a room 10' × 9' × 8' contains 720 cubic feet.

FIGURE 9.5

Cubic Yard

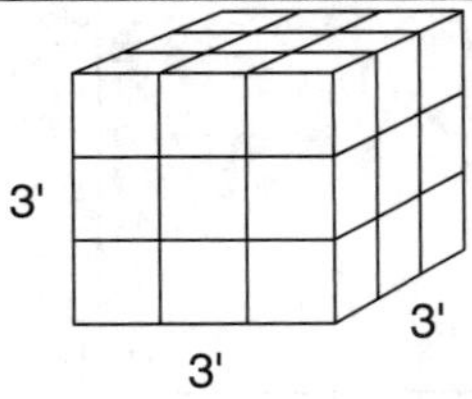

To change cubic feet to cubic yards, divide by 27.

A board foot (used to price lumber) is 144 cubic inches. A board 1 ft × 1 ft × 1 inch = 1 board foot.

FINDING ONE DIMENSION OF A RECTANGLE

To find one dimension of a rectangular-shaped parcel when one dimension and the total square area are known, divide the known dimension into the area.

area ÷ known dimension = unknown dimension

The diagram below shows a rectangular parcel having a width of 100 feet and a total area of one acre (1 acre = 43,560 square feet).

1 acre

100'

Therefore the depth of the rectangle is as follows:

$$1 \text{ acre} \div 100 \text{ ft} = \text{depth}$$

$$43,560 \text{ ft} \div 100 \text{ ft} = 435.6 \text{ ft}$$

AMORTIZATION

Problem.   Using the amortization table in Figure 9.6, assume C borrowed $130,000 at 7% interest for 30 years and D borrowed $130,000 at 8% interest for 15 years. D's total interest payments are what percentage of C's total interest payments?

FIGURE 9.6	No. of Years	6%	7%	8%	9%
Monthly Amortization	5	19.33	19.80	20.28	20.76
Table for a $1,000	10	11.10	11.61	12.13	12.67
Loan	15	8.44	8.99	9.56	10.15
	20	7.16	7.75	8.36	9.00
	25	6.44	7.07	7.72	8.40
	30	6.00	6.65	7.34	8.05

Because payments are monthly, C makes 360 payments (12 × 30). Payments are $6.65 per $1,000, or $864.50 per month (130 × 6.65).

$$864.50 \times 360 = \$311,220 \text{ total payments for 30 years}$$

$$\$311,220 - \$130,000 \text{ principal} = \$181,220 \text{ interest paid}$$

D would make 180 monthly payments on a 15-year loan (12 × 15). Monthly payments are $9.56 per $1,000, or $1,242.80 per month ($9.56 × 130).

$$\$1,242.80 \times 180 = \$223,704 \text{ total payments for 15 years}$$

$$\$223,704 - \$130,000 \text{ principal} = \$93,703 \text{ interest paid}$$

C paid $181,220 interest, and D paid $93,704 interest.

Find the rate (percentage) that D's interest payments are to C's interest payments.

$$\text{part} \div \text{whole} = \text{rate}$$

$$\$93,704 \text{ (D's interest)} \div \$181,220 \text{ (C's interest)} = 0.517, \text{ or } 51.7\%$$

If the question had asked, "C's total interest is what percent of D's total interest?" then C's interest is the part and D's interest is the whole.

$181,220 (C's interest) ÷ $93,704 (D's interest) = 1.93, or 193%

If the question had asked, "How much more did C pay in interest than D paid?" then

$181,220 (C's interest) − $93,704 (D's interest) = $87,516
(amount that C paid in excess of the interest paid by D).

CHAPTER 9 QUIZ

1. An office manager was paid $1,000 per month plus 0.0025% of all office sales. In November, she received $2,780. This amount was based on monthly sales of
   A. $556,000.
   B. $712,000.
   C. $912,000.
   D. $1,112,000.

2. What investment is necessary for a yield of $500 per month at 6% interest?
   A. $8,333.33
   B. $60,000
   C. $100,000
   D. $120,000

3. A 30-acre rectangular parcel has 660 feet on the street side. What is the depth of the parcel in feet?
   A. 738.42
   B. 963.7
   C. 1,240
   D. 1,980

4. A list price was set to leave the owner with $90,000 after a 6% commission was deducted from the sales price. What was the list price?
   A. $95,400
   B. $95,745
   C. $95,905
   D. $96,000

5. Which is the correct formula to determine the interest rate?
   A. Interest earned ÷ principal = interest rate
   B. Interest earned × principal × time = interest rate
   C. Interest earned ÷ time = interest rate
   D. Interest earned × time = interest rate

6. The next monthly interest payment on a loan balance of $17,835 is $132.28. The interest rate on the loan is
   A. 6.78%.
   B. 7.4%.
   C. 8.9%.
   D. 13.48%.

7. On a 70-foot-by-70-foot rectangular lot, the side yard building setbacks are 10 feet. The front yard setback is 25 feet, and the rear setback is 20 feet. What is the maximum square footage possible for a one-story structure?
   A. 1,000
   B. 1,200
   C. 1,250
   D. 4,900

8. A woman purchased four lots at $12,000 each and divided them into six lots that were sold for $9,600 each. What was the woman's percentage of profit based on her cost?
   A. 6%
   B. 12%
   C. 20%
   D. 24%

9. A man purchased a property for $175,000. The man wishes to sell the property. If the total selling costs will equal 11% of the sales price, how much will the property have to appreciate in value for the man to break even?
   A. $19,612
   B. $20,311
   C. $21,629
   D. $23,730

10. A mill is expressed as
    A. $0.001.
    B. $0.01.
    C. $0.1.
    D. $1.0.

11. A house purchased four years ago for $50,000 has increased in value by 10% each year since purchase. The house is now worth
    A. $66,550.
    B. $70,000.
    C. $73,205.
    D. $90,000.

12. A builder received a bridge loan for $72,500 at 12% interest. If his total interest costs were $5,075, how many months did it take the builder to pay off the loan?
    A. 4.5 months
    B. 6 months
    C. 7 months
    D. 8 months

13. A property with a gross annual income of $20,000 has a value of $120,000. The only expense is the 11% interest payment on a $100,000 straight mortgage. What is the owner's percentage return on equity?
    A. 16.6%
    B. 20%
    C. 22.2%
    D. 45%

14. A one-acre site has a 40-by-100-foot rectangular building. The building occupies what percentage of the site?
    A. 0.025%
    B. 2.5%
    C. 9.2%
    D. 11.1%

15. A man sold a note to a woman at a 32% discount. The man received $5,304. What was the amount due on the note?
    A. $1,697
    B. $6,800
    C. $7,420
    D. $7,800

16. A 50-acre rectangular industrial site fronting on a highway is 1,000 feet deep. Assuming a sales price of $3,000 per acre, what is the price per front foot?
    A. $68.87
    B. $74.93
    C. $150.00
    D. $3,443.52

17. A fully rented 10-unit apartment building has rents of $500 per unit per month. A 10% rent increase brings a 10% vacancy factor. The gross income
    A. remains the same.
    B. increases 1%.
    C. increases 9%.
    D. decreases 1%.

18. A driveway was one-half mile long and was two acres in total area. How wide was the driveway?
    A. 11 feet
    B. 21 feet
    C. 33 feet
    D. 37 feet

19. A 6-foot-wide sidewalk is to be constructed inside the perimeter (on the lot line) of two adjacent sides of a 60-by-100-foot rectangular corner lot. The sidewalk will contain how many square feet?
    A. 900
    B. 924
    C. 960
    D. 1,600

20. A 6-foot-wide sidewalk is to be constructed outside the perimeter of two adjacent sides of the lot described in question 19. The sidewalk will contain how many square feet?
    A. 960
    B. 996
    C. 1,032
    D. 1,660

21. How many cubic yards of concrete, 18 feet wide and 4 inches thick, are needed in a 30-foot driveway?
    A. 7
    B. 20
    C. 180
    D. 540

22. The last monthly interest payment on a mortgage was $825.77. If the interest rate is 7.2%, what is the balance due on the principal?
    A. $118,764
    B. $131,741
    C. $137,628
    D. $158,730

23. A seller and a buyer have agreed to split all closing costs, with the seller paying 60% and the buyer paying 40%. The costs are as follows: title insurance, $420; fees for drafting and recording documents, $222; miscellaneous costs, $248. How much more will the seller pay than the buyer?
    A. $178
    B. $184
    C. $196
    D. $204

24. A man purchased a lot for $9,000, and he listed the lot for sale at 40% more than he paid. Unable to find a buyer, he reduced his price by 30%. He found a buyer at the reduced price. After paying a 7% commission, what was the profit or loss?
    A. Profit of $207
    B. Profit of $270
    C. Loss of $180
    D. Loss of $797.40

25. A buyer has agreed to buy a house for $140,000 with a $20,000 down payment. The balance is to be paid under a contract for deed having interest payments only. Interest is to be at 9.5%, with the total principal amount due in five years. How much interest will the buyer pay under the life of the contract?
    A. $46,812
    B. $47,500
    C. $57,000
    D. $64,000

26. How many acres is 348,480 square yards?
    A. 2.66
    B. 8
    C. 24
    D. 72

27. Builders' blueprints frequently use the scale of 0.25 inches equals 1 foot. If a plan indicated a family room 10.5 inches by 3.5 inches, what would floor tile cost at $7.60 per square yard?
    A. $496.50
    B. $622.32
    C. $1,489.60
    D. $4,468.80

28. A salesperson was to receive 30% of the office share of the commission for obtaining a listing. The salesperson listed a house for $185,000, and it was sold for $170,000 by another office, with the selling office receiving one-half of the 6% commission. The salesperson's listing commission was
    A. $1,530.
    B. $3,060.
    C. $3,330.
    D. $10,200.

29. A 90-by-60-foot building needs floor covering. Sixty percent of the building will be carpeted at a cost of $16 per square yard, and the remainder will be tiled at a cost of $8 per square yard. The cost of the floor covering will be
    A. $2,560.
    B. $5,760.
    C. $7,680.
    D. $23,040.

30. A rectangular lot with 80 feet of frontage has adjoining rectangular lots of equal 160-foot depth on each side. One of these side lots contains 12,800 square feet, and the other has 9,600 square feet. The combined front footage of the three lots equals how many feet?
    A. 140
    B. 200
    C. 220
    D. 250

31. A man willed his estate as follows: 54% to his wife, 18% to his daughter, and 16% to his son, and the remainder to his church. The church received $79,000. The daughter received
    A. $105,333.
    B. $118,500.
    C. $355,500.
    D. $658,333.

32. A woman divided three sections of land into parcels of 20 acres each and then sold 16 of the parcels for $4,000 each. The remainder sold for $5,000 each. What was the total sales price?
   A. $64,000
   B. $84,000
   C. $264,000
   D. $464,000

33. A 100-acre parcel is to be subdivided. Seventeen percent of the land will be used for streets. How many 80-by-120-foot lots are possible?
   A. 349
   B. 376
   C. 411
   D. 437

34. An income property sold for $400,000 to an investor who planned on a 9% return on investment. An investor who wanted a 12% return would have paid how much for the property?
   A. $300,000
   B. $330,000
   C. $360,000
   D. $400,000

35. A broker listed a lot for $23,000 with a 7% commission agreement. The broker brought in an offer of $20,000. The owner agreed to accept the offer if the broker paid the delinquent property taxes of $240. The broker agreed. What percentage commission did the broker actually earn on this sale?
   A. 5.8%
   B. 6.2%
   C. 6.4%
   D. 6.7%

36. An investor owes $90,000 on a building worth $120,000. The net income is $6,000, which would give the investor a percentage return on equity of
   A. 10%.
   B. 20%.
   C. 30%.
   D. 40%.

37. Five condominiums were sold at $165,000, $195,200, $225,000, $265,600, and $296,000. Together the units have annual property maintenance expenses of $15,400, which the owners share on a pro rata basis, based on the cost of their units. The lowest-priced unit had a monthly assessment of
   A. $57.56.
   B. $156.56.
   C. $184.65.
   D. $221.52.

38. Of the following transactions, which will result in the greatest net proceeds to the seller?

Sales Price	Commission	Closing Costs
A. $110,000	7%	$1,280
B. $108,000	6%	$1,308
C. $106,000	4%	$820
D. $105,000	3%	$980

39. The monthly amortized payments on a 7%, 30-year, $100,000 amortized loan are $665.31. How much will be paid for interest over the amortization period?
   A. $96,851
   B. $139,511
   C. $159,674
   D. $239,511

40. The last month's interest on a 12% amortized loan was $923.18. What was the balance due?
   A. $1,178.16
   B. $7,693.00
   C. $92,318.00
   D. $110,781.00

41. A rectangular property sold for $6,400, or $0.40 per square foot. The parcel had a depth of 200 feet. What price did the buyer pay per front foot?
   A. $16
   B. $32
   C. $40
   D. $80

42. A fire insurance policy has a one-year premium of $430.70. What is the policy's daily
proration?
    A. $1.14
    B. $1.18
    C. $1.20
    D. $1.26

43. A property that offers a 7.5% return on the
listing price has a monthly net of $810. The
property is listed at
    A. $9,720.
    B. $10,800.
    C. $129,600.
    D. $138,400.

44. A woman sold a lot for 30% more than she
paid for it. She invested the entire sales price
at 14% interest. The interest on this investment gave her $820 per year. What did the
woman originally pay for the lot?
    A. $4,505
    B. $5,123
    C. $5,857
    D. $9,837

45. An apartment has an annual gross income
of $64,000. The net income is 30% of the
gross. An investor who wants an 11% return
on the purchase price would pay no more
than
    A. $174,545.
    B. $192,000.
    C. $581,818.
    D. $831,168.

46. A 120-by-80-foot rectangular warehouse
with a 15-foot-high ceiling is listed for sale
at $55 per cubic yard. What is the list price
per square foot?
    A. $20.37
    B. $27
    C. $30.55
    D. $53.33

47. A man took out a $30,000, 15-year home
equity loan at 9% interest with monthly payments of $304.28. How much of his second
payment would apply to interest?
    A. $224
    B. $228
    C. $247
    D. $293

48. A woman purchased six acres of land for
$1,800 per acre and divided them into 14
lots, which she sold for $1,150 each. What
percentage is her return on the purchase
price?
    A. 18%
    B. 21%
    C. 25%
    D. 49%

49. What are the taxes for a home if it is taxed
at 120% of its appraised value of $382,000
and the tax rate is 21.6 mills per dollar of
evaluation?
    A. $4,584
    B. $8,251
    C. $8,404
    D. $9,901

50. A business had sales of $1,500,000 and a
markup of 90% of cost. What was the cost of
merchandise sold?
    A. $789,474
    B. $812,622
    C. $971,600
    D. $1,120,333

51. A listing office gives 50% of the gross commission to the selling office and splits the
remainder, 40% to the broker and 60% to the
listing salesperson. A salesperson's listing
was sold by another office for $189,500.
Assuming a 6% commission, the salesperson's share is
    A. $2,842.
    B. $3,411.
    C. $5,685.
    D. $11,370.

52. In order to earn $1,000 per month on a $200,000 investment, the investment would have to yield a return of
   A. 4.5%.
   B. 5%.
   C. 6%.
   D. 10%.

53. The amount of $2,610 was equal to three months' interest on an $87,000 investment. What was the rate of return?
   A. 11.5%
   B. 12%
   C. 12.1%
   D. 12.3%

54. The equation I = PRT is used regarding
   A. loans.
   B. trust accounts.
   C. discount points.
   D. construction advances.

55. A 2-by-8-inch board that is 9 feet long contains
   A. 8 board feet.
   B. 9 board feet.
   C. 12 board feet.
   D. 15 board feet.

56. A triangular lot has 1,000 feet on one side of a 90° angle and 400 feet on the other side of the angle. How large is the property?
   A. 0.5 acres
   B. 400,000 square feet
   C. 200,000 square feet
   D. 14.3 acres

57. If one pound of wire is 66 feet long, how many pounds of wire would it take to run a triple strand wire fence around a section?
   A. 640
   B. 960
   C. 2,620
   D. 3,840

58. The first quarterly interest payment on a $55,000 loan at 6% interest is
   A. $550.
   B. $600.
   C. $660.
   D. $825.

59. The sales price of a home was $250,000. The seller paid a 6% prepayment penalty on an existing $180,000 loan, total closing costs of $3,850, and a 6% commission. How much did the seller receive?
   A. $38,600
   B. $40,350
   C. $70,000
   D. $220,350

60. A listing provided for a 6% commission. The contract of sale provided that in the event of buyer default, after expenses one-half of the forfeited deposit would go to the broker and one-half to the owner. After making a $30,000 deposit on an $800,000 purchase, the buyer defaults. Escrow expenses were $1,450. The broker will receive
   A. $13,550.
   B. $14,275.
   C. $15,000.
   D. $15,725.

61. A wooden beam 12 inches by 20 inches by 24 feet in length contains how many board feet?
   A. 240
   B. 360
   C. 480
   D. 640

62. A property worth $1,000,000 is assessed at 25% of its value. The tax rate is 2% of the assessed value. Taxes are
   A. $2,500.
   B. $5,000.
   C. $10,000.
   D. $20,000.

63. Last month, the interest on a 6% amortized loan was $194.61. What was the loan balance?
   A. $36,874
   B. $37,614
   C. $38,922
   D. $39,141

64. A man wishes to come out even on a home he purchased for $372,000. If he will pay a 6% commission and closing costs of $4,200, what must he sell the home for to meet his objective?
   A. $400,000
   B. $400,213
   C. $401,500
   D. $398,500

65. Interest paid on a $280,000 loan at 5.5% is $3,850. What is the period of the loan?
   A. 3 months
   B. 4 months
   C. 5 months
   D. 6 months

66. A man paid an annual pest control bill of $386 for one year starting September 1. On December 10, the man sold the property to a woman who agreed to prorate the cost, with the woman being responsible for the date of closing. Assuming prorating on a 365-day year, how would this be shown on a closing statement?
   A. Credit seller $206.81
   B. Credit buyer $206.81
   C. Debit seller $279.19
   D. Debit buyer $279.19

67. What is the interest for one month on a $300,000 loan at 6.375%?
   A. $1,426.21
   B. $1,593.75
   C. $3,811.17
   D. $19,125

68. A woman sold a house for cash and received $148,752 from escrow. Her only expense was a 6% commission and $1,648 in closing costs. What was the selling price?
   A. $150,750
   B. $153,816
   C. $160,000
   D. $161,200

69. Which parcel of land is largest?
   A. 10% of a township
   B. Two sections
   C. A parcel 5,280 feet by 10,560 feet
   D. The NW¼ of SE¼ of SW¼ of NW¼

70. A property valued for taxes at $200,000 has a tax of $4,000. The tax rate per dollar is
   A. 2 mills.
   B. 2.5 mills.
   C. 20 mills.
   D. 200 mills.

71. A $100,000 loan can be amortized with monthly payments of $844 over 15 years or $717 on a 20-year basis. The 20-year loan results in total payments of what percentage of the 15-year total payments?
   A. 85%
   B. 113%
   C. 118%
   D. 124.6%

72. A woman gets $1,100 each month from an investment at 10% interest. She invested
   A. $11,000.
   B. $110,000.
   C. $132,000.
   D. $142,000.

73. A purchaser was required to give a lender a deposit equal to three months' taxes and insurance. If the tax rate was 15 mills per dollar of assessed value, the property was assessed at $280,000, and insurance cost for one year was $540, what was the amount of the deposit?
   A. $1,026
   B. $1,185
   C. $2,370
   D. $4,740

74. A home sold for $4,000,000, but the seller took a 20% loss on his purchase price. What did he originally pay?
   A. $4,200,000
   B. $4,800,000
   C. $5,000,000
   D. $5,200,000

75. Which of the following transactions will result in the greatest net to the seller?

Sales Price	Commission	Closing Costs
A. $365,000	6%	$3,855
B. $370,000	7%	$4,420
C. $362,500	4%	$2,480
D. $359,000	4%	$0

76. A man sold a lot for 30% more than the purchase price. He invested the money and made a 14% profit on it. This profit was $8,200. What did the man originally pay for the lot?
   A. $45,055
   B. $52,230
   C. $58,570
   D. $98,370

77. A woman borrowed $360,000 on a 6% straight loan. Her total interest cost was $10,800. The loan was for how long?
   A. 15 days
   B. 4 months
   C. 5 months
   D. 6 months

78. An amount of $2,610 was earned in three months on an investment yielding 12%. What was the principal?
   A. $85,000
   B. $85,900
   C. $86,200
   D. $87,000

79. If the interest payment was $2,007.40 last month on a mortgage balance of $385,420, what was the interest rate of the mortgage?
   A. 6.25%
   B. 6.375%
   C. 7.5%
   D. 12%

80. The last monthly mortgage payment included interest of $2,049.78. The interest rate on the mortgage was 6.5%. What was the principal balance at the time of the payment?
   A. $24,597.36
   B. $294,768.00
   C. $369,841.00
   D. $378,421.00

CHAPTER 9 QUIZ ANSWERS

1. **(B)** $2,780 – $1,000 (salary) = $1,780 attributable to sales. (247)

   $1,780 ÷ 0.0025 = $712,000 total office sales

2. **(C)** $500 per month = $6,000 per year. (247)

   $6,000 ÷ 0.06 = $100,000 = $100,000 investment yielding $6,000 per year at 6%

3. **(D)** Known dimension = 660'. Total area 30 acres, or 30 × 43,560 = 1,306,800 square feet. To find one dimension of a rectangle when total area and other dimensions are known, divide the known dimension into the total area. (254–255)

   1,306,800 ÷ 660 = 1,980

4. **(B)** $90,000 is left after 6% of the sale is taken out, so 94% of list price is $90,000. (247)

   $90,000 ÷ 0.94 = $95,744.68, rounded off to $95,745 list price

5. **(A)** The rate is the part divided by the whole. (248–249)

   part ÷ whole = rate

6. **(C)** Monthly interest of $132.28 × 12 = yearly interest of $1,587.36. (248–249)

   interest earned (part) ÷ principal (whole) = rate

   $1,587.36 ÷ $17,835 = 0.089, or 8.9%

7. **(C)** Building maximum width is 50 feet because there are 10-foot setbacks on each side. Maximum depth is 25 feet because front yard and rear yard setbacks total 45 feet (70' – 45'). Multiply width (50') by depth (25') to find square footage. (252–254)

8. **(C)** 4 lots at $12,000 each = $48,000 cost

   6 lots at $9,600 each = $57,600 selling price

   $57,600 – $48,000 = $9,600 profit (246–247)

   To find percentage, divide the net by the cost:

   $9,600 (net) ÷ $48,000 (cost) = 0.2, or 20%

9. **(C)** To break even, the sales price must be $175,000 plus 11% of the sales price, so $175,000 = 89% of the sales price.

   $175,000 (part) ÷ 0.89 (rate) = $196,629

   Sales price is $196,629. But the question asks for appreciation, so $196,629 – $175,000 = $21,629. (247)

10. **(A)** A mill is $1/10$ of a cent, and a cent is 0.01. (251)

11. **(C)** The house has appreciated in value by 10% each year. (250)

    $50,000 + 10% = $55,000 value at end of 1st year

    $55,000 + 10% = $60,500 value at end of 2nd year

    $60,500 + 10% = $66,550 value at end of 3rd year

    $66,550 + 10% = $73,205 value at end of 4th year

12. **(C)** To find the time, you can use the following formula. (249)

    interest earned ÷ (principal × rate) = time

    $5,075 ÷ ($72,500 × 0.12) = time

    $5,075 ÷ $8,700 = 0.5833 of a year

    1 month ÷ 12 months in a year = 0.0833

    Divide 0.5833 by 0.0833 to find time in months or, as an alternative:

    $72,500 × 0.12 = $8,700 interest

    $8,700 ÷ 12 = $725 interest cost per month

    $5,075 ÷ $725 = 7 months

13. **(D)** Gross = $20,000

Expenses = 11% of $100,000 or $11,000. Net is $20,000 − $11,000 = $9,000.

Equity is the difference between value ($120,000) and the mortgage ($100,000), or $20,000. (246–247)

$9,000 net ÷ $20,000 equity = 0.45, or 45% return

14. **(C)** 40' × 100' = 4,000 sq. ft., 1 acre = 43,560 sq. ft. (248, 254–255)

4,000 ÷ 43,560 = 0.092, or 9.2%

15. **(D)** Note sold at 32% discount, so it sold at 68% of amount due. (247)

$5,304 ÷ 0.68 = $7,800

16. **(A)** 50 acres = 43,560 × 50 = 2,178,000 sq. ft. (254–255)

To find one dimension of a rectangle, divide the total area by the known dimension.

2,178,000 ÷ 1,000 = 2,178 feet frontage

Sales price was 50 × $3,000 or $150,000. To find price per front foot divide cost ($150,000) by front footage (2,178):

$150,000 ÷ 2,178 = $68.87 per front foot

17. **(D)** 10 × $500 = $5,000 per month

9 (10% vacancy) × $550 = $4,950, or $50 less in rent, which is 1% of $5,000. (246)

18. **(C)** Divide total area (87,120 sq. ft. because it is 2 acres) by known dimension (2,640' because it is one-half mile). (254–255)

19. **(B)** (100' × 6') + (54' × 6') = 924 sq. ft. (don't count the corner area twice). (252–259)

20. **(B)** (100' × 6') + (60' × 6') + (6' × 6') = 996 sq. ft. (don't miss the corner). (252)

21. **(A)** 18' × 30' = 540 square feet. Four inches thick is one-third of a foot, so the cubic footage of the driveway would take one-third of 540 square feet. (254)

540 ÷ 3 = 180 cubic feet

Because there are 27 cubic feet in a cubic yard, 180 ÷ 27 = 6.67 yards (7 yards).

22. **(C)** $825.77 is interest for 1 month, so for a year it is $825.77 × 12, or $9,909.24. (247)

$9,909.24 ÷ 0.072 = $137,628

23. **(A)** $420 + $222 + $248 = $890 total costs (251–252)

$890 × 0.6 = $534

$890 × 0.4 = $356

$534 − $356 = $178

24. **(D)** $9,000 paid × 1.40 (listed at 40% more than paid) = $12,600 (list price); $12,600 × 0.30 = $3,780 (reduction). (248)

$12,600 − $3,780 = $8,820 sales price

$8,820 × 0.07 = $617.40 commission

$8,820 − $617.40 = $8,202.60

$9,000 − $8202.60 = $797.40 loss

25. **(C)** $140,000 − $20,000 = $120,000 balance

$120,000 × 0.095 × 5 = $57,000 (246)

26. **(D)** 348,480 sq. yd. × 9 (number of square feet in a square yard) = 3,136,320 sq. ft. Divide by the number of square feet in an acre. (252–254)

3,136,320 ÷ 43,560 = 72 acres

27. **(A)** Each inch would equal 4 feet, so 10.5" = 42' and 3.5" equals 14'. (252–254)

42 × 14 = 588. sq. ft.

There are 9 square feet in a square yard, so:

588 ÷ 9 = 65.33 yards

65.33 × $7.60 = $496.50 cost of floor tile

28. **(A)** $170,000 × 0.06 = $10,200. The office share was one-half, or $5,100.

$$0.30 × $5,100 = $1,530 \text{ commission}$$
(248)

29. **(C)** (248, 252–254)

$$90' × 60 = 5,400 \text{ sq. ft.}$$
$$5,400' ÷ 9 = 600 \text{ sq. yards}$$
$$60\% \text{ of } 600 = 360$$
$$360 × $16 = $5,760$$
$$40\% \text{ of } 600 = 240$$
$$240 × $8 = $1,920$$
$$$5,760 + $1,920 = $7,680 \text{ cost of floor covering}$$

30. **(C)** The two side lots have 12,800 and 9,600 square feet, or a total of 22,400 square feet. (254–255)

The depth is 160 feet. Frontage is 22,400 divided by 160, or 140 feet. With the 80 feet of the central lot, the combined total is 220 feet.

31. **(B)** The church received 12% of his estate: (248)

$$12\% \text{ of estate was } $79,000$$
$$$79,000 ÷ 0.12 = $658,333.33$$

Total estate was $658,333.33. The daughter received 18%, or $658,333.33 × 0.18.

32. **(D)** There are 640 acres in a section, so three sections equal 1,920 acres. (254)

$$1,920 ÷ 20 = 96 \text{ 20-acre parcels}$$
$$16 \text{ sold at } $4,000 \text{ each} = $64,000$$
$$80 \text{ sold at } $5,000 \text{ each} = $400,000$$
$$$64,000 + $400,000 = $464,000 \text{ sales price}$$

33. **(B)** $100 × 43,560 = 4,356,000$ square feet (248, 252–254)

$$17\% \text{ or } 740,520 \text{ sq. ft. for streets}$$
$$4,356,000 − 740,520 = 3,615,480 \text{ net}$$
$$80 × 120 = 9,600 \text{ square feet}$$
$$3,615,480 ÷ 9,600 = 376.6$$

34. **(A)** Whole × rate = part

$$$400,000 × 0.09 = $36,000, \text{ which is return}$$

For 12% return:
$$$36,000 ÷ 0.12 = $300,000 \text{ (247, 248)}$$

35. **(A)** 7% of $20,000 = $1,400 − 240 = $1,160 net

To find percentage return, divide net by sales price. (248)

$$$1,160 ÷ $20,000 = 0.058, \text{ or } 5.8\%$$

36. **(B)** (246–247)

$$\text{net} ÷ \text{equity} = \text{percentage return}$$
$$$6,000 ÷ $30,000 = 0.2$$

37. **(C)** The total cost of all units (whole) = $1,146,800 (246, 248)

$$$165,000 \text{ lowest-priced unit} ÷ $1,146,800 = 0.14388, \text{ or } 14.388\% \text{ of total costs}$$

Rate for unit is 0.14388, or 14.388% of total costs.

$$$15,400 × 0.14388 = $2,215.75 \text{ per year}$$
$$$2,215.75 ÷ 12 = $184.65 \text{ per month}$$

38. **(C)** $110,000 − $7,700 − $1,280 = $101,020 (248)

39. **(B)** $665.31 × 12 (months) × 30 (years) = $239,511 in total payments. Deduct the principal ($100,000) to determine the interest paid. (255, 256)

40. **(C)** 12% per annum is 1% per month. So $923.18 is 1% of $92,318 (247).

$$\text{interest earned} ÷ \text{rate of interest} = \text{principal}$$
$$($923.18 × 12 \text{ months}) ÷ 0.12 = \text{principal}$$
$$$11,078.16 ÷ 0.12 = $92,318$$

41. **(D)** (252–254)

$$$6,400 ÷ $0.40 = 16,000 \text{ sq. ft.}$$
$$16,000 ÷ 200 = 80' \text{ wide}$$
$$$6,400 ÷ 80 = $80 \text{ per front ft}$$

42. **(B)** Use 365 days unless question indicates otherwise. (251–252)

$$\$430.70 \div 365 = \$1.18$$

43. **(C)** Monthly net is $810, so $810 × 12 = $9,720 per year. (247)

$$\$9,720 \div 0.075 = \$129,600$$

44. **(A)** (247)

$$\$820 \div 0.14 = \$5,857 \text{ sales price}$$

45. **(A)** Net is 30% of $64,000, or $19,200. (246–247)

$$19,200 \div 0.11 = \$174,545$$

46. **(C)** 120' × 80' × 15' = 144,000 cubic feet. (252–254)

$$\$144,000 \div 27 = 5,333.33 \text{ cubic yards}$$
$$5,333.33 \times \$55 = \$293,333.33 \text{ list price}$$
$$120 \times 80 = 9,600 \text{ sq. ft.}$$
$$\$293,333.33 \div 9,600 = \$30.55 \text{ per sq. ft.}$$

47. **(A)** (255–256)

$$0.09 \times \$30,000 = \$2,700$$
$$\$2,700 \div 12 = \$225 \text{ first month's payment}$$
$$\$304.28 - \$225 = \$79.28, \text{ applied to principal}$$
$$\$30,000 - \$79.28 = \$29,920.72, \text{ balance after first payment}$$
$$0.09 \times \$29,920.72 = \$2,692.86$$
$$\$2,692.86 \div 12 = \$224 \text{ interest}$$

48. **(D)** (246)

$$\$1,150 \times 14 = \$16,100 \text{ sales price}$$
$$\$1,800 \times 6 = \$10,800 \text{ purchase price}$$
$$\$16,100 - \$10,800 = \$5,300 \text{ profit}$$

To find the percentage return on the purchase price, divide the purchase price into the net.

$$\$5,300 \div \$10,800 = 0.49, \text{ or } 49\%$$

49. **(D)** Apply the equalization factor 1.2 and multiply by a tax rate of 21.6 mills (0.0216). (251)

$$\$382,000 \times 1.2 = \$458,400 \times 0.0216 = 9,901$$

50. **(A)** Cost was marked up 90%, so merchandise sold at 190% of cost. (248)

$$1,500,000 \div 1.9 = \$789,474$$

51. **(B)** $11,370 total commission; $5,685 to selling office. J gets 60% of the $5,685 remaining. (248)

52. **(C)** Rate = part ÷ whole. Part desired $1,000 per month, or $12,000 per year. The whole is $200,000. 12,000 divided by 200,000 = 0.06, or 6%. (246)

53. **(B)** Rate = part ÷ whole. $2,610 for 3 months; so $10,440 is one year's return. (246)

$$\$10,440 \div \$87,000 = 12\%$$

54. **(A)** Interest = principal × rate × time. (246)

55. **(C)** (254)

$$2 \times 8 \times (9 \times 12) = 1,728 \text{ cubic inches}$$
$$1,728 \div 144 = 12 \text{ board feet}$$

56. **(C)** Right triangle contains ½ area of rectangle. 1,000' × 400'. (254)

57. **(B)** A section is 5,280 feet per side, or 21,120 feet around. Three strands = 63,360'. (253)

$$63,360 \div 66 = 960 \text{ pounds}$$

58. **(D)** Interest = principal × rate × time. Principal is $55,000, rate is 6%, and time is 0.25 (quarter of year). (249)

59. **(B)** Sales price $250,000 (248)

$250,000 sales price – $180,000 loan – $10,800 prepayment penalty – $15,000 commission – $3,850 closing cost = $40,350 to seller

60. **(B)** $30,000 − $1,450 = $28,550. ½ of
    $28,550 = $14,275. (248)

61. **(C)** (254)

$$24 \times 12 = 288$$

$$12 \times 20 \times 288 = 69,120 \text{ cubic inches}$$

$$69,120 \div 144 = 480 \text{ board feet}$$

62. **(B)** 25% of $1,000,000 = $250,000 assess-
    ment. 2% × $250,000 = $5,000. (251)

63. **(C)** 194.61 was one month's interest (247)

$$194.61 \times 12 = \$2,335.32 \text{ annual interest}$$

$$2,335.32 \div 0.06 = \$38,922 \text{ loan balance}$$

64. **(B)** $372,000 + $4,200 = $376,200.
    $376,200 will be 94% of sales price
    (6% commission). (247)

$$\$376,200 \div 0.94 = \$400,213$$

65. **(A)** (247)

$$\$3,850 \div (\$280,000 \times 0.055) = \text{time}$$

$$\$3,850 \div \$15,400 = 0.25 \text{ (one quarter of a year, or 3 months)}$$

66. **(D)** $386 ÷ 365 = 1.0575 per day cost

    September 30 days, October 31 days,
    November 30 days + 10 days in Decem-
    ber = 101 days seller was responsible
    for. 101 × 1.0575 = $106.81 responsi-
    bility of seller; buyer is responsible for
    $386 − $106.81, or $279.19. Seller's
    closing statement would show a credit
    of this amount, and buyer's statement
    would show it as a debit. (251–252)

67. **(B)** Rate × whole = part. 6.375 as a deci-
    mal is 0.06375. 0.06375 × $300,000 =
    $19,125. This is for one year, so divide
    by 12 to find one month's interest.
    (248)

68. **(C)** $148,752 + $1,648 = $150,400 (94% of
    the sale price)

$$\$150,400 \div 0.94 = \$160,000 \text{ (247)}$$

69. **(A)** (A) is 3.6 sections or 640 × 3.6 = 2,304
    acres (252–254)

    (B) is 2 sections or 2 × 640 = 1,280 acres

    (C) is 1 miles × 2 miles or 2 sections =
    1,280 acres

    (D) is 2.5 acres

70. **(C)** 4,000 ÷ 200,000 = 0.02, or 2 cents per
    dollar, which is 20 mills. (246)

71. **(B)** $844 × 12 (1 year) × 15 = $151,920
    (251–252)

$$\$717 \times 12 \text{ (1 year)} \times 20 = \$172,080$$

$$\$172,080 \div \$151,920 = 1.13, \text{ or } 113\%$$

72. **(C)** $1,100 × 12 = $13,200 per year. (247)

$$\$13,200 \div 0.10 = \$132,000$$

73. **(B)** A mill is ¹⁄₁₀ of a cent. 15 mills is
    0.015 × assessed value of $280,000
    = $4,200/year. Insurance is $540 per
    year so $4,200 + $540 = $4,740 taxes +
    insurance for one year. 3 months is one
    quarter of a year, so $4,740 × 0.25 =
    $1,185. (251–252)

74. **(C)** $4,000,000 = 80% of whole seller paid.

$$\$4,000,000 \div 0.80 = \$5,000,000. \text{ (247)}$$

75. **(C)** For (A) $365,000 − $21,900 (6%) −
    $3855 = $339,245 net. (248)

    For (B) $370,000 − $25,900 (7%) −
    $4,420 = $339,680 net.

    For (C) $362,500 − $14,500 (4%) −
    $2480 = $345,520 net.

    For (D) $359,000 − $14,360 = $344,640

76. **(A)** $8,200 was 14% profit. (247)

$$\$8,200 \div 0.14 = \$58,571$$

    $58,571 was 30% more than the lots
    purchase price or 130% of price paid.

$$\$58,571 \div 1.3 = \$45,055$$

77. **(D)** (249)

interest earned ÷ (principal × rate) = time

$10,800 ÷ ($360,000 × 0.06) = time

$10,800 ÷ $21,600 = 0.5

0.5 years = 6 months

78. **(D)** (247)

part ÷ rate = whole

Because $2,610 was earned in three months, return is $10,440 for one year.

$10,440 ÷ 0.12 = $87,000

79. **(A)** (246)

part ÷ whole = rate

Part is $2,007.40 for one month. For one year, $2,007.40 × 12 = $24,088.80, so

$24,088.80 ÷ $385.420 = 0.0625 interest.

80. **(D)** (247, 248)

part ÷ whole = rate

$2,049.78 is for one month, so $2,049.78 × 12 = $24,597.36 interest for one year.

$24,597.36 ÷ 0.065 = $378,421

REVIEW TESTS

The five review tests have been weighted to substantially reflect the emphasis given to the various areas on the Pearson VUE Salespersons examination.

We have attempted to arrange these five examinations in an ascending order of difficulty. For example, if you take the Level I exam first, your score should be higher than your score would be if you took the Level V examination first.

Some of the questions we have included are more likely to be covered on a broker's examination than on a salesperson's examination, particularly questions in Levels IV and V.

DIFFICULTY LEVEL I

1. Which broker action is an example of blockbusting?
   A. Refusing to sell or rent to prospects because of race
   B. Refusing to rent to families with children
   C. Soliciting listings based on a fear of racial change in an area
   D. Directing people to an area based on race

2. The phrase *definite duration* refers to
   A. a life estate.
   B. an estate for years.
   C. an estate at will.
   D. a periodic tenancy.

3. A lease that automatically renews itself, in the absence of notice, is
   A. an estate for years.
   B. a net lease.
   C. a periodic tenancy.
   D. a percentage lease.

4. A man just sold a condominium for $80,000. This gave him a 20% profit on what he paid. What did the man pay?
   A. $64,000
   B. $66,666
   C. $120,000
   D. $662,800

5. A property has a variety of liens against it. Which of the following deeds would give the grantee the greatest protection against the existing liens?
   A. Gift deed
   B. Quitclaim deed
   C. Warranty deed
   D. Tax deed

6. A business wishes to increase its liquidity while reducing its long-term debt. This is possible with a
   A. piggyback loan.
   B. sale-leaseback.
   C. wraparound loan.
   D. nonconforming loan.

7. In real estate, the term *steering* refers to
   A. directing buyers to properties that best meet their needs.
   B. engaging in the qualification process for buyers.
   C. directing people to or away from areas based on race, religion, or national origin.
   D. dividing apartment buildings into adult-only and family areas.

8. In a buyer's closing statement, the selling price is
   A. a debit to the buyer.
   B. a credit to the buyer.
   C. assumed by the seller.
   D. less the amount to be paid for commission.

9. What household deduction from income does a homeowner have for tax purposes?
   A. Home interest
   B. Insurance cost
   C. Depreciation
   D. Maintenance expense

10. The requirement that the booklet *Protect Your Family from Lead in Your Home* be given to buyers and lessees applies to
    A. single-family homes only.
    B. one-to-four residential unit building only.
    C. all property built before 1968.
    D. residential property built before 1978.

11. A requirement of a valid deed is that the deed be
    A. dated.
    B. acknowledged.
    C. recorded.
    D. signed by the grantor.

12. Which of the following is both a lien and an encumbrance?
    A. A restrictive covenant
    B. An easement
    C. A lease
    D. A mortgage

13. To locate buyers for other properties, a broker advertised a property that was not available but which would generate great interest. The broker's action violated
    A. RESPA.
    B. the Truth in Lending Act.
    C. the Americans with Disabilities Act.
    D. the Sherman Antitrust Act.

14. There is an inherent conflict of interest between the owner and the broker when there is
    A. an exclusive agency listing.
    B. an exclusive-right-to-sell listing.
    C. a net listing.
    D. an open listing.

15. The first step in the appraisal process is to
    A. determine the highest and best use.
    B. do a reconciliation.
    C. define the problem.
    D. determine land value.

16. A property manager may properly refuse to rent a second-floor apartment to
    A. an unmarried pregnant woman.
    B. a blind person with a guide dog.
    C. a person who is ill with AIDS.
    D. a person addicted to drugs.

17. Market value is defined as
    A. assessed value less depreciation.
    B. the probable price a willing, informed buyer would pay to a willing, informed seller.
    C. subjective value.
    D. utility value of the property to the owner.

18. An owner sold a property without any help of an agent; however, he was obligated to pay a commission to the agent. What type of listing did the agent have?
    A. Exclusive agency listing
    B. Exclusive right-to-locate property listing
    C. Exclusive-right-to-sell listing
    D. Open listing

19. A lessee has the right to have a portion of the rent apply to a purchase. The lessee has
    A. an option to purchase.
    B. an exculpatory clause.
    C. a recapture clause.
    D. a condemnation right.

20. A federally mandated disclosure deals with
    A. asbestos.
    B. lead paint.
    C. radon.
    D. toxic mold.

21. If no period is set for a residential tenancy but rent is to be paid monthly, the lease is a
    A. periodic tenancy.
    B. lease for one month only.
    C. lease for one year.
    D. week-to-week rental.

22. When there is FHA financing, a borrower must receive a notice dealing with
    A. the importance of a home inspection.
    B. government munitions storage.
    C. the existence of brownfields.
    D. toxic mold.

23. An apartment complex of 420 units has 21 vacancies. What is the vacancy rate?
    A. 4%
    B. 5%
    C. 6%
    D. 7%

24. A minor cannot list property the minor owns with a broker because
    A. a minor cannot appoint an agent.
    B. of the statute of frauds.
    C. of the statute of limitations.
    D. of laches.

25. Which of the following is *TRUE* of a blind ad?
    A. It fails to include the owner's name.
    B. It omits the property address.
    C. It does not include a price.
    D. It fails to indicate the advertiser is an agent.

26. A builder wanted the listing to reflect $85 per square foot for a 2,500-square-foot home plus $75,000 for the lot after the 6% commission was paid. What should the home be listed at to meet the builder's wishes?
   A. $212,500
   B. $287,500
   C. $304,750
   D. $305,851

27. A buyer of property did not know the property had previously been used as a chemical disposal site. The buyer was held liable for cleanup costs under
   A. the doctrine of vicarious liability.
   B. CERCLA.
   C. RESPA.
   D. FIRPTA.

28. Salesperson J's contract with his broker K calls for a 50/50 split of all listing and sales commissions received by the office. J sells a home listed by broker L for $180,000. L's listing provides for a 6% commission. If L splits the sales commission 40/60, with 60% going to the selling office, what will J earn on the sale?
   A. $3,240
   B. $5,400
   C. $6,480
   D. $10,800

29. In an exclusive listing, the broker's promise to use diligence makes the listing
   A. a unilateral contract.
   B. a bilateral contract.
   C. voidable.
   D. an illusory contract.

30. The four tests of a fixture do *NOT* include
   A. intent.
   B. cost.
   C. attachment.
   D. adaptability.

31. How many acres are contained in the legal description: NW¼ of the SW¼ of the NE¼ of the SE¼ of Section 18, T4N, R2E, San Bernardino Base Line and Meridian?
   A. 2.5
   B. 5
   C. 7.5
   D. 10

32. A borrower has a right to see the Uniform Settlement Statement
   A. within three days of loan application.
   B. within seven days of loan application.
   C. seven days before closing.
   D. on the business day before closing.

33. Which of the following is an example of involuntary alienation?
   A. Dedication
   B. Will
   C. Deed
   D. Sheriff's sale

34. The right of survivorship exists in
   A. joint tenancy.
   B. both tenancy in common and community property.
   C. tenancy by the entirety.
   D. both joint tenancy and tenancy by the entirety.

35. A father and son could hold title together
   A. in severalty.
   B. in tenancy by the entirety.
   C. as joint tenants.
   D. as community property.

36. When using the income approach, an appraiser is interested in
   A. accrued depreciation.
   B. the capitalization rate.
   C. reproduction cost.
   D. comparable sales.

37. A man breached a contract to sell a property to a woman. This resulted in a loss to the woman of $40,000, which a court awarded to her. What type of damages was awarded?
   A. Liquidated
   B. Compensatory
   C. Punitive
   D. Nominal

38. What is the function of a real estate appraisal?
   A. Set market value
   B. Determine market value
   C. Estimate market value
   D. Establish the cost

39. A home was sold for $270,000 with an 80% loan. The buyer paid $5400 in points. How many points did the buyer pay?
    A. 0.2
    B. 2.2
    C. 2.5
    D. 2.8

40. Court-determined breach-of-contract damages that exceed the actual loss suffered are
    A. liquidated damages.
    B. punitive damages.
    C. compensatory damages.
    D. specific performance.

41. In depreciating a residential income property for tax purposes, you would base the depreciation life on
    A. age-life tables.
    B. the observed condition of the property.
    C. 27.5 years.
    D. 39 years.

42. The act of signing a deed is the
    A. execution.
    B. ratification.
    C. verification.
    D. notarization.

43. Broker B is the sole agent of owner O. Buyer Y submits an offer on O's property through broker B. Y knows that broker B is not his agent, but Y tells B he will raise the offer by $20,000 if O does not accept. What should B do?
    A. Submit the offer and tell O that Y will pay more
    B. Submit the offer but consider O's statement confidential
    C. Refuse to submit the offer
    D. Terminate the agency with O and submit offer as agent of Y

44. To alienate property means to
    A. borrow against it.
    B. transfer it.
    C. improve it.
    D. appraise it.

45. When would a vendee buying under a land contract receive a deed?
    A. On closing
    B. After the statutory period
    C. On default
    D. When the contract is paid in full

46. A lender under a deed of trust is called the
    A. trustor.
    B. mortgagor.
    C. trustee.
    D. beneficiary.

47. Which of the following is an attorney-in-fact?
    A. Person acting under a court order
    B. Attorney at law acting in a legal capacity
    C. Agent appointed by a power of attorney
    D. Attorney acting in a state where he is not legally licensed to practice

48. The real estate seller's agent must disclose to a buyer that a
    A. prior owner had died of AIDS.
    B. home has latent defects known to the agent.
    C. owner must sell or property will be foreclosed.
    D. price asked is above a recent appraised value.

49. In renting an apartment, a property manager may properly
    A. refuse to rent to persons suspected of having AIDS.
    B. check with prior landlords as to any previous problems.
    C. charge rent in excess of rent control maximum with the consent of the tenant.
    D. charge a higher security deposit to tenants having seeing eye dogs.

50. Liquidation of a loan with equal payments is called
    A. acceleration.
    B. compounding.
    C. amortization.
    D. ballooning.

51. Taking title by adverse possession requires
    A. permission of the owner.
    B. use that is not known by the owner.
    C. use that is nonexclusive.
    D. hostile use.

52. A requirement of every valid contract is that the
    A. contract be in writing.
    B. signatures be notarized.
    C. parties be at least 21 years old.
    D. offer be accepted.

53. A transfer of equitable title coupled with a retention of legal title describes a
    A. mortgage.
    B. land contract.
    C. trust deed.
    D. bill of sale.

54. A deed restriction is *BEST* described as
    A. a general lien.
    B. a specific lien.
    C. a constructive lien.
    D. an encumbrance.

55. A facilitator or intermediary is a
    A. buyer's agent.
    B. seller's agent.
    C. dual agent.
    D. neutral mediator.

56. A broker's duty to keep a principal fully informed demonstrates
    A. ethical conduct.
    B. continuing responsibility.
    C. fiduciary obligation.
    D. informed consent.

57. A minor discrepancy concerning a title is
    A. the color of title.
    B. a cloud on the title.
    C. the chain of title.
    D. a broken title.

58. The premium for a homebuyer's title insurance is paid
    A. monthly with the mortgage payment.
    B. annually.
    C. on issuance of the title policy.
    D. by the original subdivider for all subsequent holders.

59. An example of liquidated damages in a real property purchase contract is
    A. damages paid to induce a party to contract.
    B. the forfeiture of a deposit.
    C. damages for willful action in excess of compensatory damages.
    D. damages for a loss suffered because an owner diverted the flow of surface water.

60. The annual percentage rate is
    A. the nominal rate.
    B. interest charges only.
    C. greater than the nominal rate.
    D. the nominal rate reduced by financing charges.

61. Collateral for a real estate loan is the
    A. property.
    B. borrower.
    C. note.
    D. mortgage insurance.

62. A clause in a mortgage that provides for the assignment of rents benefits the
    A. tenant.
    B. mortgagor.
    C. mortgagee.
    D. property manager.

63. The secondary mortgage market refers to
    A. secondary financing.
    B. loans made by noninstitutional lenders.
    C. high-risk loans.
    D. the resale mortgage marketplace.

64. Fannie Mae activities include
    A. insuring mortgages originated by financial institutions.
    B. guaranteeing mortgages originated by financial institutions.
    C. raising and lowering the discount rate to control the economy.
    D. purchasing mortgages originated by financial institutions.

65. A straight 9% loan at 75% of a property's appraised value earned first-year interest of $19,680. What was the property's valuation?
    A. $182,000.
    B. $218,666.
    C. $249,700.
    D. $291,555.

66. A property manager is an agent. Which regard to agency, the property manager
    A. is the agent of the owner.
    B. is the agent of the tenant.
    C. serves in a dual agency capacity representing owner and tenant.
    D. is a transaction broker.

67. Which of the following is a lien?
    A. An easement.
    B. A restrictive covenant.
    C. Delinquent taxes.
    D. A use in violation of zoning.

68. A lease with a fixed rent that also has agreed-on rent increases at specified times is
    A. a net lease.
    B. a step-up lease.
    C. an index lease.
    D. a variable annuity lease.

69. The term *earnest money* refers to
    A. commissions.
    B. deposits given with purchase offers.
    C. funds in addition to the purchase price.
    D. the last month's rent given in advance by a tenant under a lease.

70. The brokers in a community agreed that they would not cooperate with a large broker who offered lower rates of commissions and who wished to expand to their area. This agreement is
    A. market allocation.
    B. price-fixing.
    C. a group boycott.
    D. redlining.

71. Three brokers, who all had open listings on the same property, had contact with a party who purchased directly from the owner. The broker who is entitled to a commission is the
    A. first broker who had contact with the buyer.
    B. last broker to talk to the buyer before purchase.
    C. broker who had the most extensive contact with the buyer.
    D. broker who started an uninterrupted chain of events leading to the sale.

72. A joint tenancy between two single persons will become a tenancy in common if one person
    A. dies without a will.
    B. sells his interest to the other.
    C. dies leaving the interest to another.
    D. sells his interest to a third party.

73. A lender using an LTV of 80% on a triplex appraised at $420,000 would make a maximum loan on the property of
    A. $160,000.
    B. $336,000.
    C. $380,000.
    D. $420,000.

74. A requirement for an enforceable earnest money contract for the sale of real estate is that it be
    A. acknowledged before a notary public.
    B. properly recorded.
    C. in writing.
    D. accompanied by cash, a money order, or a cashier's certified check.

75. The Real Estate Settlement Procedures Act applies to federally related purchase loans
    A. for all real estate transactions.
    B. only if there is secondary financing.
    C. of one to four residential units.
    D. for all types of residential property.

76. A property manager may properly obey the principal's request to
    A. rent only to working families that can show an adequate income from their job.
    B. adopt tenant rules that will discourage families with children from renting.
    C. leave a unit vacant.
    D. put families with children in one building and adults only in another building.

77. An owner didn't want to sell or develop an undeveloped commercial lot but wanted additional income. This could be accomplished by a
    A. sale-leaseback.
    B. piggyback loan.
    C. ground lease.
    D. wraparound loan.

78. A man leased land to a woman one week before the man took title to the land. The man now claims that the lease is not valid because he had no right to lease it at the time of the lease. Which of the following statements is *TRUE*?
    A. The woman has a valid lease because of novation.
    B. The man is estopped from denying the validity of the lease.
    C. The lease is void because the lessor lacked the right to lease.
    D. The statute of frauds entitles the woman to compensatory damages.

79. An example of a void contract is a contract
    A. entered into because of misrepresentation by the seller.
    B. for an illegal purpose.
    C. entered into because of undue influence.
    D. with inadequate consideration.

80. One salesperson in a broker's office had single agency with a buyer, while another salesperson in the same office had single agency with the seller on the same transaction. This situation describes
    A. unilateral agency.
    B. dual agency.
    C. designated agency.
    D. transaction broker.

DIFFICULTY LEVEL I ANSWERS

1. **(C)** Inducing panic selling due to fear of entry of people of different race, color, religion, or national origin. (138)

2. **(B)** An estate for years is a lease for a definite period. (195)

3. **(C)** A periodic tenancy that renews unless notice given by lessor or lessee to terminate—generally 30 days. (195)

4. **(B)** The whole = the part ÷ rate; the part is $80,000 and the rate is 120%, or 1.2 as a decimal. (247)

5. **(D)** Tax liens are priority liens, so tax sales generally wipe out all junior liens. (48)

6. **(B)** Generates purchase price plus removes mortgage from balance sheet. (196–197)

7. **(C)** Prohibited by Civil Rights Act of 1968. (138)

8. **(A)** The buyer must come up with this amount. It is a credit to the seller. (183)

9. **(A)** With some limitations, interest is deductible, as well as property taxes. (80)

10. **(D)** Federal requirement. (129)

11. **(D)** It is presumed dated as of delivery. While it needs to be acknowledged to be recorded, it is valid between the parties without recordation. (46–47)

12. **(D)** It is a money charge (lien), as well as a charge or burden against the property. (30, 35)

13. **(B)** Bait-and-switch advertising is a violation of the Truth in Lending Act. (144)

14. **(C)** The broker wants a sale at the highest price possible, while the owner wants a quick sale that will meet her net. (112)

15. **(C)** The appraiser must determine the interest to be appraised in what property and for what purpose. (76)

16. **(D)** Drug addicts are not a protected group. (139)

17. **(B)** With reasonable time to sell. The marketplace determines market value; appraisers only estimate it. (65)

18. **(C)** The agent gets paid no matter who makes the sale. (112)

19. **(A)** While not a requirement of purchase option agreements, it is a common provision. (198)

20. **(B)** The *Protect Your Family From Lead in Your Home* booklet must be given to buyers and tenants. (129)

21. **(A)** Tenancy would customarily be the length of rent-paying period. (195)

22. **(A)** Also required when dwelling is HUD owned. (133)

23. **(B)** Rate = part ÷ whole, or 21 ÷ 420. (246)

24. **(A)** Minors lack contractual authority, so they can't appoint agents to do what they cannot do themselves. (98)

25. **(D)** It is grounds for disciplinary action. (229)

26. **(D)** 2,500 × $85 = $212,500 (building) + $75,000 for lot = $287,500. This equals sale price after 6% is taken out, or 94% of sale price. Whole = 287,500 (whole) ÷ 0.94 (percentage rate). (247)

27. **(B)** Buyer can escape liability if appropriate inquiry was made as to prior use and possible problems. (130)

28. **(A)** 6% of $180,000 = $10,800 commission. 60% of $10,800 = $6,480 (0.60 × 10,800): J gets 50% or $3,240. (251–252)

29. **(B)** It is a promise for a promise. The owner's promise is to pay a commission. (112)

30. **(B)** The fourth test is agreement. (2)

31. **(A)** Because a section contains 640 acres, one quarter of a section is 160 acres, one quarter of 160 equals 40, one quarter of 40 equals 10, and one quarter of 10 equals 2.5. (6)

32. **(D)** But the good-faith estimate is given within three business days of loan application (RESPA). (146)

33. **(D)** A forced or involuntary conveyance. (42, 43)

34. **(D)** Joint tenancy has survivorship rights and tenancy by the entirety is a form of joint tenancy. Other forms of ownership, including community property, do not have survivorship rights. (11)

35. **(C)** Answer (A) is one person alone; (B) and (D) are only for married couples. (11)

36. **(B)** Answers (A) and (C) are for cost approach, and (D) is for sales comparison. (72)

37. **(B)** It compensates the woman for the amount of damages suffered. (103)

38. **(C)** It is only an estimate as of the date of the appraisal. (65)

39. **(C)** 80% of $270,000 = $216,000. Rate (points) = $5,400 (part) ÷ $216,000 (whole). (246)

40. **(B)** They are damages awarded to punish or make an example of a person for outrageous conduct. (103)

41. **(C)** The IRS dictates the depreciated life for tax purposes. (83)

42. **(A)** To execute a document is to sign it. (46)

43. **(A)** B is agent of O and so has duties to O of relaying all pertinent information. (109)

44. **(B)** An alienation is a transfer. (42)

45. **(D)** Unless the contract calls for the contract to become a mortgage, the deed is not given until contract has been paid in full. (163)

46. **(D)** The beneficiary is the recipient of the payments, and the deed of trust is given for the beneficiary's benefit. (162)

47. **(C)** Can be specific or general. Need not be an attorney-at-law. (108)

48. **(B)** Must disclose known property defects. Cannot disclose the presence of AIDS and others violate fiduciary duty. (109)

49. **(B)** Credit, employer, and prior-landlord checks are proper. Others are prohibited. (204)

50. **(C)** A partially amortized loan would have a balloon payment before it is paid in full. (167)

51. **(D)** Use must be exclusive, open, notorious, and hostile (without right). (43)

52. **(D)** Mutual consent is a necessary requirement of a contract. Only specified contracts need be in writing. (98)

53. **(B)** Vendor keeps legal title and gives vendee possession and equitable title. (163)

54. **(D)** It burdens the property but is not a monetary charge against the property (lien). (32)

55. **(D)** Allowed in some states. (107)

56. **(C)** A fiduciary duty is one of trust. Disclosure is a specific fiduciary duty. (109)

57. **(B)** Anything that casts doubt on the title. (48)

58. **(C)** It is a one-time charge that protects only the insured and her heirs. (51)

59. **(B)** Purchase contracts usually provide for forfeiture of deposit as seller's sole remedy in event of buyer breach. (103)

60. **(C)** It is adjusted upward based on loan costs from the rate in the note (nominal rate). (143)

61. **(A)** It is the security for the note that is the evidence of the debt. (179)

62. **(C)** The lender (mortgagee) has the right to collect the rents if the mortgagor is in default. (172)

63. **(D)** Fannie Mae, Freddie Mac, and Ginnie Mae are active in the secondary mortgage market. (173)

64. **(D)** It provides a secondary mortgage market so lenders can get cash, if desired, by selling conforming loans. (178)

65. **(D)** Whole = part ÷ percentage; whole loan = $19,680 (part) ÷ 9% (rate) = $218,666 (loan). The loan is 75% of valuation, so use the same formula again. Whole (value) = $218,666 (part) ÷ 75% or 0.75 (rate). (247)

66. **(A)** In rare cases, tenants could have property managers who negotiate and oversee their leased property. (205)

67. **(C)** A lien is a money charge against a property. (35)

68. **(B)** The increases are set forth in the lease. (196)

69. **(B)** Earnest money deposits may also be given with lease applications. (114)

70. **(C)** A violation of the Sherman Antitrust Act. (142–143)

71. **(D)** This would determine who the procuring cause is. (112)

72. **(D)** Answers (A) and (B) would result in a tenancy in severalty, and the interest cannot be passed by will. (11)

73. **(B)** LTV is loan to-value-ratio. 80% (0.80) × $420,000. (173)

74. **(C)** Statute of frauds requires that every real estate sales contract be in writing. Earnest money is not essential to the contract, and between the parties, recording is not necessary. (99)

75. **(C)** FHA and VA loans or a federally insured lender or resale to a federally related buyer would make the loan federally related. (146)

76. **(C)** Other answers discriminate against families or violate the Equal Credit Opportunity Act. (204)

77. **(C)** The owner keeps title, gets rent, and, at the end of the lease, gets the improvements. (197)

78. **(B)** Doctrine of estoppel. Cannot now deny right claimed in order to influence lessee. (99–100)

79. **(B)** The others may be voidable. (99)

80. **(C)** Two agents in same office with separate single agency obligations to the parties. (107)

DIFFICULTY LEVEL II

1. A standard policy of title insurance protects the purchaser from title problems relating to
    A. forgery in the chain of title.
    B. zoning changes.
    C. matters not of public record.
    D. rights of parties in possession.

2. A purchaser paid $138,000 for an investment property. He spent $24,000 on improvements, took $32,000 in depreciation, and sold the property for $138,000. What is the taxable gain?
    A. $0
    B. $8,000
    C. $24,000
    D. $32,000

3. Which of the following tenancies is a freehold interest?
    A. Life estate
    B. Estate for years
    C. Estate at will
    D. Periodic tenancy

4. What is the last action against a debtor?
    A. Lis pendens
    B. Attachment
    C. Execution
    D. Judgment

5. A lender's extended policy of title insurance goes beyond standard coverage by including
    A. forgery.
    B. undisclosed spousal interests.
    C. failure of delivery of prior deeds.
    D. defects discovered by property inspection.

6. FHA loans are made by
    A. HUD.
    B. the FHA.
    C. qualified lenders.
    D. the Federal Reserve.

7. A person who is responsible to another only as to results is
    A. an agent.
    B. a servant.
    C. an employee.
    D. an independent contractor.

8. What type of contract is an exclusive listing in a broker's inventory before sale?
    A. Executed bilateral contract
    B. Executory bilateral contract
    C. Executed unilateral contract
    D. Executory unilateral contract

9. An oil and gas lease is classified as
    A. personal property.
    B. an emblement.
    C. a remainder interest.
    D. a reversionary interest.

10. Lenders will often offer an introductory rate on an ARM less than the index plus the margin to
    A. allow for negative amortization.
    B. provide a cap rate.
    C. induce a borrower to agree to an ARM.
    D. provide for depreciation.

11. A borrower keeps control of the loan collateral but gives the lender a lien. This is called
    A. a pledge.
    B. hypothecation.
    C. reconciliation.
    D. a collaterally secured loan.

12. In renting apartments, a property manager may require that
    A. unmarried mothers have lease cosigners.
    B. the security deposit be $200 per person for each unit.
    C. all lessees provide three character references.
    D. families without children receive a $100 discount from scheduled rent.

13. A landlord would have proper cause to evict a single person who
    A. joined a tenant organization.
    B. became pregnant.
    C. complained to health authorities about the condition of the rental.
    D. refused to pay the last month's rent when the security deposit was greater than the rent due.

14. Homeowners insurance includes
    A. mortgage life coverage.
    B. flood insurance.
    C. earthquake damage.
    D. liability protection.

15. A property is purchased based on fraudulent income statements prepared by the listing broker. Therefore, the sale contract is
    A. void.
    B. voidable.
    C. valid.
    D. illegal.

16. A real estate license is required by
    A. a developer selling more than 10 homes.
    B. an attorney-in-fact selling property for a principal.
    C. a trustee selling under court order.
    D. an attorney at law taking a listing.

17. A broker listed a widow's property for an 8% commission. After the sale, the widow discovered that the broker had been listing similar property at a 6% commission. Based on these facts, the
    A. broker has done nothing wrong.
    B. broker can lose her license.
    C. widow can recover from the state recovery fund.
    D. widow is entitled to a refund.

18. A woman leased property to a man for 20 years. One year later, the woman died intestate, leaving no heirs. The effect of the woman's death is that the
    A. lease ended with her death.
    B. the man owns the property.
    C. state will acquire the property without the lease.
    D. state will acquire the property subject to the lease rights of the man.

19. An owner advertised a home for $300,000. A buyer sent the owner a letter stating, "I hereby accept your offer to sell the home advertised at a price of $300,000." In this situation, the buyer
    A. has a unilateral contract.
    B. can obtain specific performance if N refuses to convey.
    C. has the right to void the contract.
    D. is an offeror.

20. The act that requires accessibility to places of public accommodation is
    A. RESPA.
    B. the Americans with Disabilities Act.
    C. the 1988 Fair Housing Amendments Act.
    D. the Civil Rights Act of 1968.

21. A broker closed a sale and received a commission from the buyer and the seller. The double payment of commission was proper if
    A. the listing did not prohibit it.
    B. both parties agreed to it.
    C. the listing was nonexclusive.
    D. separate services were performed for both parties.

22. A property manager has a chance for a management contract for a large commercial building that has been vacant for three years. The manager should insist on a
    A. holdover clause.
    B. minimum fee.
    C. percentage fee for repairs.
    D. fee based on net income.

23. When a new mall opened, rental income for the old mall was reduced by $4,600 per month. Assuming a 12.5% capitalization rate, what was the loss in value for the old mall?
    A. $36,800
    B. $55,200
    C. $441,600
    D. $538,996

24. A man agreed to buy a woman's farm, but the deed given by the woman had the wrong legal description, describing land that the woman did not own. The man, who wants the land bargained for, would ask the court for the remedy of
    A. rescission.
    B. accord and satisfaction.
    C. novation.
    D. reformation.

25. A tenant's five-year lease expired on June 1. On June 2, the tenant's continued occupancy is a
    A. tenancy in common.
    B. periodic tenancy.
    C. tenancy at sufferance.
    D. license.

26. With an assessed value of $149,500, an equalization factor of 118%, and a tax rate of 0.018, the taxes are
    A. $2,691.
    B. $2,791.
    C. $3,175.
    D. $3,764.

27. Rental security deposits are handled on a closing statement as
    A. credits to the buyer.
    B. credits to the seller.
    C. debits to the buyer.
    D. prorated items.

28. A lender agrees to make an 80% loan on a $248,000 home purchase. The lender wants 1.5 points to make the loan. The point charges will amount to
    A. $1,984.
    B. $2,976.
    C. $3,000.
    D. $3,720.

29. The use of verbal evidence to show that a contract means something other than it states is prohibited by the
    A. statute of frauds.
    B. parol evidence rule.
    C. statute of limitations.
    D. rule against perpetuities.

30. A seller agreed to a substitution of buyers in a purchase contract. This is a
    A. reformation.
    B. novation.
    C. satisfaction.
    D. rescission.

31. The term *quiet enjoyment* refers to
    A. the neighborhood.
    B. the tenant's right of possession.
    C. the tenant's right to use without interference from owner or others claiming an interest.
    D. habitability.

32. High humidity can lead to hazardous conditions relating to
    A. radon gas.
    B. perchlorate.
    C. toxic mold.
    D. PCBs.

33. A broker who has a property listing receives two purchase offers on the same property from two different offices. How should the broker proceed with the presentation of the offers?
    A. Only the highest-priced offer need be submitted.
    B. Both offers must be presented at the same time.
    C. The second offer should be presented only if the first offer is rejected.
    D. The broker must return the second offer received to the offering broker and present a single offer to the owner.

34. The zoning of a parcel was changed from agricultural use to manufacturing. This is an example of
    A. downzoning.
    B. upzoning.
    C. conservation zoning.
    D. bulk zoning.

35. In a sale transaction, a broker worked directly with a buyer and a seller but represented neither party. The broker
    A. made a controlled business arrangement.
    B. served as a facilitator.
    C. was a designated agent.
    D. was involved in split agency.

36. The Federal Emergency Management Agency is responsible for
    A. enforcement of CERCLA.
    B. waste disposal site approval.
    C. flood hazard area maps.
    D. EMF regulations.

37. The seller is required to disclose to the buyer
    A. the status of existing loans.
    B. known defects in the property.
    C. the chain of title.
    D. all latent defects.

38. Ingress and egress refer to
    A. assumability.
    B. leases.
    C. easements.
    D. transferability.

39. A man's business activities consist of bringing prospective borrowers and lenders together for loans secured by the borrower's property. These activities are those of a
    A. mortgage banker.
    B. mortgage broker.
    C. mortgagee.
    D. mortgagor.

40. With a capitalization rate of 5%, an appraiser would say that each additional dollar of expenses affects the value of income property by
    A. raising it $20.
    B. lowering it $5.
    C. lowering it $10.
    D. lowering it $20.

41. A lender might prefer to make an FHA or VA loan rather than a conventional loan because of the
    A. lower risk.
    B. higher interest.
    C. longer investment period.
    D. federal tax benefits.

42. Loan-to-value ratio refers to the ratio of the loan to
    A. appraised value.
    B. assessed value.
    C. book value.
    D. utility value.

43. Fidelity bonds protect a broker against
    A. employee turnover.
    B. employee theft.
    C. liability for injury.
    D. damage to property.

44. What is an attorney-in-fact?
    A. A properly licensed lawyer
    B. An agent operating under a power of attorney
    C. A court-appointed guardian
    D. An agent authorized to act for both buyer and seller

45. What do owners under both joint tenancy and tenancy in common have in common?
    A. Equal right of possession
    B. Survivorship
    C. Interests acquired at the same time
    D. Equal interests

46. A valid deed requires
    A. recording.
    B. witnesses.
    C. acceptance.
    D. acknowledgment.

47. A duplex that rents for $550 per unit is located in the same area as a slightly smaller duplex in similar condition that rents for $480 per unit and just sold for $134,400. Based on these data only, the larger duplex has a value of
    A. $134,400.
    B. $140,000.
    C. $154,000.
    D. $155,000.

48. If a woman's interest in land entitles her to impose restrictions on its future use, her interest is
    A. a life estate.
    B. a nonfreehold interest.
    C. a fee simple estate.
    D. an estate for years.

49. In which clause in a deed would the phrase *to have and to hold* appear?
    A. Safety clause
    B. Habendum clause
    C. Execution clause
    D. Description clause

50. RESPA disclosures include
    A. a statement of material defects.
    B. good-faith estimate of settlement costs.
    C. environmental hazards.
    D. predatory lending.

51. You are allowed to make a solicitation call to a person on the National Do Not Call Registry if
    A. you have not called them before.
    B. you call on a for-sale-by-owner ad to obtain a listing.
    C. you know the party.
    D. your call is to a business telephone.

52. Purchasing subject to a loan means that the purchaser has what liability?
    A. Primary
    B. Secondary
    C. Deficiency
    D. No liability

53. The loan that would command the highest loan-to-value ratio is for
    A. a single-family residence.
    B. agricultural land.
    C. a residential lot.
    D. commercial property.

54. Federal regulations on using the internet for marketing purposes are set forth in
    A. RESPA.
    B. do-not-call regulations.
    C. the CAN-SPAM Act.
    D. the Federal Telephone Consumer Protection Act.

55. To determine monthly interest on a loan, the lender multiplied 0.006 by the loan principal owed. What was the interest rate of the loan?
    A. 0.6%
    B. 6.0%
    C. 7.2%
    D. 8.4%

56. In the absence of a specified closing date, a real estate transaction must close
    A. immediately.
    B. within 3 days.
    C. within 30 days.
    D. within a reasonable period of time.

57. The name of a firm ends with LLC, which indicates that the firm is
    A. licensed to conduct real estate activities.
    B. an S corporation.
    C. owned in severalty.
    D. taxed as a partnership.

58. A property manager determined that the lessee on a commercial lease had been declared incompetent before entering into the lease. The lease is
    A. void.
    B. voidable at the option of the lessee.
    C. voidable at the option of the lessor.
    D. voidable at the pleasure of the court.

59. It is a legal business practice to
    A. cut fees below what competitors are charging.
    B. agree with your competitors as to a uniform fee schedule.
    C. agree with your competitors not to advertise in a paper that is unfriendly to your profession.
    D. divide the local market geographically among your competitors so that buyers and sellers can be better served.

60. Exceptional landscaping and a hot spa that enhance the value of a residential property are classified as
    A. personal property.
    B. chattels real.
    C. amenities.
    D. beneficial encumbrances.

61. The seller agreed to pay 60% of the total closing-related charges, with the buyer paying 40%. Title insurance cost $438; miscellaneous fees and costs totaled $378.50. To the nearest dollar, how much more did the seller pay than the buyer?
    A. $163
    B. $327
    C. $490
    D. $817

62. SAFE licensing applies to
    A. home inspectors.
    B. mortgage loan originators.
    C. OSHA.
    D. risk management.

63. Which is the first and which is the second mortgage can be determined by
   A. title of the instrument.
   B. date of the mortgages.
   C. time and date of recording.
   D. amount of the liens.

64. An exculpatory clause in a lease
   A. provides for payment of needed repairs and maintenance.
   B. provides for forfeiture of lease rights should the tenant breach the lease.
   C. carries a warranty of habitability.
   D. holds the landlord harmless for loss or injury due to the condition of the premises.

65. A partially amortized loan has a
   A. prepayment penalty.
   B. balloon payment.
   C. due-on-sale clause.
   D. subordination clause.

66. It is proper to include in an ad that a property
   A. has a 55-year age restriction.
   B. is across the street from a Catholic church.
   C. owner prefers married couples.
   D. is in the most desirable Chinese neighborhood.

67. Freddie Mac mortgage activities are primarily involved in
   A. RESPA enforcement.
   B. the secondary mortgage market.
   C. enforcement of the Foreign Investment in Real Property Tax Act.
   D. direct loans for low-income homebuyers.

68. An unmarried couple purchased their residence together for $382,000. Three years later, they sold their residence for $750,000. They would have a tax liability on a gain of
   A. $0.
   B. $23,600.
   C. $73,600.
   D. $150,000.

69. A person died intestate. The court will appoint
   A. an executor.
   B. an administrator.
   C. a devise.
   D. a testator.

70. A tenant vacated premises with nine months remaining on the lease. To mitigate damages, the owner should
   A. improve the premises and advertise at a higher rent.
   B. bring legal action as each month's rent becomes due.
   C. keep the premises vacant until the lease expires.
   D. immediately advertise the premises for rent.

71. An example of voluntary alienation is
   A. a deed.
   B. escheat.
   C. eminent domain.
   D. police power.

72. A policy of insurance a broker would consider that is similar to medical malpractice coverage is
   A. a fidelity bond.
   B. errors and omissions coverage.
   C. a liability policy.
   D. a homeowner policy.

73. A broker realizes he has taken a listing from an owner who is demanding, argumentative, and unreasonable to the point where she wishes to cancel the listing. In this situation, she
   A. may transfer the listing to another broker.
   B. may unilaterally cancel the listing.
   C. may cancel upon giving statutory notice.
   D. must continue using best efforts until listing expires.

74. By increasing the amortization period of a loan, the
   A. monthly payment will decrease.
   B. interest rate will decrease.
   C. total loan costs will decrease.
   D. lender risk will decrease.

75. A deed transfers title when
    A. it is acknowledged.
    B. it is recorded.
    C. it is delivered.
    D. possession is given.

76. What does the term *procuring cause* relate to?
    A. Entitlement to commission
    B. Depreciation
    C. Exercise of options
    D. Mortgage insurance

77. An expansionary policy of the Federal Reserve is to
    A. raise taxes.
    B. raise discount points.
    C. lower reserve requirements.
    D. sell government securities.

78. The buyer on a fixed-rate FHA loan was informed that monthly payments were to increase. The reason for the increase is
    A. an increase in an index.
    B. increased taxes.
    C. an acceleration of the loan.
    D. adjustment to the margin.

79. What is the nominal rate of interest?
    A. The rate stated in the note
    B. The true rate expressed as the APR
    C. The minimum interest allowed by law
    D. The usury rate

80. An irrevocable listing is a sale listing
    A. for one-to-four residential unit buildings.
    B. where an advance fee was paid.
    C. coupled with an interest.
    D. for one year or less.

DIFFICULTY LEVEL II ANSWERS

1. **(A)** (C) and (D) are covered by extended-coverage policies. (51, 52)

2. **(B)** $138,000 cost + $24,000 improvements = $162,000 – $32,000 depreciation = $130,000 cost basis. A sale at $138,000 means a taxable gain of $8,000. (81–82)

3. **(A)** Life estates and fee simple are freehold estates. Leasehold interests are nonfreehold estates. (7)

4. **(C)** Sheriff's seizure and sale of assets after judgment. (36)

5. **(D)** The others are covered by the standard policy. (51–52)

6. **(C)** Institutional lenders approved by FHA. They may be able to have direct endorsement where the lender decides if the loan can receive FHA insurance. (177)

7. **(D)** Differs from an employee who is subject to supervision and control. (224–225)

8. **(B)** Executory because broker has not yet found a buyer and bilateral because there were mutual promises. (197)

9. **(A)** Lease interests are personal property (chattels real), but oil and gas rights are real property. (195)

10. **(C)** Also to qualify borrowers who could not qualify for a fixed rate loan. (168)

11. **(B)** As in a mortgage or deed of trust. (161)

12. **(C)** Reasonable and nondiscriminatory—others discriminate as to familial status. (140)

13. **(D)** This is prohibited by Uniform Residential Landlord and Tenant Act. (A) and (C) are a retaliatory eviction, and (B) is prohibited by Fair Housing Law. (201)

14. **(D)** Others require separate policies. (134)

15. **(B)** At the option of the purchaser. (100)

16. **(D)** The attorney isn't acting as an attorney but as a real estate broker. (228)

17. **(A)** Commissions are subject to negotiation. (113)

18. **(D)** Death of lessor does not terminate lease rights. (202–203)

19. **(D)** A newspaper ad is considered an invitation to negotiate and not an offer. The buyer's acceptance was merely an offer that required acceptance to form a binding agreement. (101)

20. **(B)** Must be accessible if readily achievable. (140–141)

21. **(B)** Both parties must agree to both dual agency and receiving any commission from another party. Otherwise it could be a breach of fiduciary duty. (106–109)

22. **(B)** Because handling a vacant property is costly in both time and effort. (205)

23. **(C)** $4,600 per month × 12 = $55,200 annual reduction. To find value of this amount, divide by the cap rate of 0.125. (72)

24. **(D)** To have the deed read as the parties intended it to read. (103)

25. **(C)** A holdover tenant has a tenancy at sufferance. (196)

26. **(C)** $149,500 assessed value × 1.18 equalization factor = $176,410, which the tax rate applies to; $176,410 × 0.018 = $3,175 taxes. (41)

27. **(A)** They must be turned over to the buyer. They are debits to the seller. (183)

28. **(B)** 0.80 (80%) × $248,000 = $198,400 loan. 1.5 points is 1.5% or 0.015; 0.015 × $198,400 = $2,976. (245–246)

29. **(B)** A contract that appears complete on its face cannot be altered by verbal testimony. (100)

30. **(B)** Substitution of parties. (104)

31. **(C)** It is an implied covenant in a lease. (197)

32. **(C)** Mold thrives in wet and damp conditions. (130)

33. **(B)** Otherwise it is a breach of broker's fiduciary duty. (109)

34. **(B)** It is the opposite of downzoning. It is a change to a higher or more productive use. (31)

35. **(B)** The broker was not an agent, so he had the duty of fair dealing but not agency duties. (107)

36. **(C)** They prepare maps and are concerned with disasters. (132)

37. **(B)** In a property report, only known defects need be disclosed. (132)

38. **(C)** Entering and exiting. (37)

39. **(B)** The man doesn't make loans but charges a fee to the borrower for arranging the loan. (174)

40. **(D)** Divide $1 by capitalization rate of 0.05 (as a decimal). (72)

41. **(A)** Because of FHA insurance or VA guarantee. (174–175)

42. **(A)** Lenders loan based on their appraisal. (173)

43. **(B)** Protection to broker and principal. (136)

44. **(B)** Not necessarily legally trained. (108)

45. **(A)** This is the only one of the four unities of joint tenancy also present in tenancy in common. (12)

46. **(C)** Although in some cases acceptance can be presumed. Between the parties recording is not required. (46)

47. **(C)** Unit that sold rented at $480 per unit or $960 per month. It sold for $134,400; $134,400 ÷ 960 = 140, which is the gross monthly rent multiplier; apply the multiplier of 140 to the other duplex renting for $550 per unit or $1,100 per month; 1100 × 140 = $154,000. (73)

48. **(C)** Because fee simple ownership has no time limitation, the owner can impose restrictions as to future use. (7)

49. **(B)** Defines extent of estate conveyed. (46)

50. **(B)** Must be provided within three business days of loan application. (146)

51. **(D)** Applies only to residential telephones. (148)

52. **(D)** But will be foreclosed if the payments are not made. (171)

53. **(A)** For some loans it can be 100% and seldom less than 80%. (175)

54. **(C)** The act requires identity of subject matter and sender. (145)

55. **(C)** 0.006 (one month) × 12 = 0.072 or 7.2% per year. (248–249)

56. **(D)** A court would decide what is reasonable if conflict arises. (115)

57. **(D)** A limited liability company (LLC) is taxed as a partnership. (232)

58. **(A)** A person declared incompetent cannot contract. (98, 100)

59. **(A)** The others are violations of the Sherman AntitrustAct. (142, 143)

60. **(C)** These are features that make a property more desirable and are considered when using the sales comparison approach as to the comparables. (69)

61. **(A)** Costs are $438 and $378.50, or a total of $816.50. Because seller pays 20% more than buyer, $816.50 × 20% = $163.30, rounded to $163. (245–246)

62. **(B)** The Federal Secure and Fair Mortgage Licensing Act of 2008 (SAFE). (149)

63. **(C)** Called the race of the diligent. Who records first gets first interest. (164)

64. **(D)** Not enforceable in residential leases. (198)

65. **(B)** Payments are based on an amortization schedule, but the balloon payment comes before loan can be paid off. (167)

66. **(A)** Exception under the 1988 Fair Housing Amendments Act. (140)

67. **(B)** Freddie Mac buys mortgages and sells securities (participation certificates) backed by a pool of mortgages. (178)

68. **(A)** Because each has $250,000 (universal) exclusion. (79–80)

69. **(B)** Appointed by the court to act as a representative of the deceased. An executor is named in a will by the decedent. (44–45)

70. **(D)** Duty to keep damages low. (202)

71. **(A)** The others are involuntary transfers. (46)

72. **(B)** This covers negligence of agent but not willful act. (135)

73. **(B)** Because an agency is a consensual relationship, either party can cancel but that party could be liable for compensatory damages. (110)

74. **(A)** But the total interest paid for the term of the loan would increase. (255–256)

75. **(C)** Title is transferred on delivery. (46)

76. **(A)** It determines entitlement to a commission on an open listing or exclusive agency listing. Must have started an uninterrupted chain of events that led to sale. (112)

77. **(C)** Lowering reserve requirements of banks frees money for lending. (B) and (C) are contractionary policies, and (A) is not a function of the Fed. (167)

78. **(B)** FHA loans have an impound account for taxes. (176)

79. **(A)** Which, because of loan fees, is less than the APR. (143)

80. **(C)** The owner cannot revoke a listing coupled with an agent's interest in the property. (110)

DIFFICULTY LEVEL III

1. An executory contract met the four requirements of a valid contract, but the contract could not be legally enforced. The reason was
   A. the statute of frauds.
   B. the statute of limitations.
   C. the parole evidence rule.
   D. it was unilateral.

2. On a real estate closing statement, prepaid rent is always a
   A. debit to the buyer.
   B. debit to the seller.
   C. credit to the seller.
   D. balance factor.

3. Meridians are of concern to
   A. an appraiser.
   B. a mortgage broker.
   C. a surveyor.
   D. a property manager.

4. To be eligible for a homeowner's capital gains exclusion,
   A. the home must be the principal or secondary residence.
   B. the homeowner must not have previously taken the exclusion.
   C. five-year ownership is required.
   D. two-year occupancy is required.

5. A grantor is a lessee in the case of a
   A. sandwich lease.
   B. sale-leaseback.
   C. gross lease.
   D. percentage lease.

6. Subleasing can be described as being
   A. an assignment.
   B. greater than an assignment.
   C. a hypothecation.
   D. less than an assignment.

7. Death of a party to an agreement voids the agreement when the agreement is
   A. a purchase contract.
   B. a land contract.
   C. an option to purchase.
   D. an exclusive-right-to-sell listing.

8. L took title to property under the name ML. When L sold the property, L signed the deed as KL, grantor. The buyer has
   A. a cloud on the title.
   B. color of title only.
   C. an exception on the deed.
   D. clean title.

9. An $1,800 loan is repaid with $600 payments every six months plus 9% annual interest. What is the total interest paid?
   A. $81
   B. $162
   C. $216
   D. $243

10. To what loan type would obligatory advances apply?
    A. Shared appreciation mortgage
    B. Construction loan
    C. Growing equity mortgage
    D. Participation mortgage

11. On October 1, a buyer mailed a purchase offer to a seller. On October 2, the man mailed a revocation of the offer to the seller. On October 3, the seller received the offer, and on October 4 mailed the acceptance to the buyer. On October 5, the seller received the buyer's revocation of the offer. What are the rights of the parties?
    A. The seller's acceptance was not effective because it was mailed after the revocation, so the offer was revoked.
    B. If the buyer received the seller's acceptance before the seller received the revocation, then a legal contract was formed.
    C. The buyer is obligated because the buyer's offer must remain open for a reasonable period of time.
    D. Because acceptance takes place upon mailing and revocation is not effective until received, a valid contract was formed.

12. A woman received a property by descent.
    Therefore, she received the property by
    A. escheat.
    B. dedication.
    C. inheritance.
    D. adverse use.

13. When parties own property as tenants in
    common, each owner
    A. must be mentioned in the same instru-
       ment (deed or will).
    B. owns an individual divided share of the
       property.
    C. must have acquired rights simultane-
       ously with the other owner(s).
    D. has ownership of no specific part of the
       property.

14. What effect do rising interest rates have on
    the value of a commercial property that is on
    a long-term lease at a fixed rent?
    A. They would result in the use of a lower
       capitalization rate.
    B. They would increase the gross
       multiplier.
    C. They would lower the property's value.
    D. They would require that the property
       be appraised using the cost approach to
       value.

15. The Real Estate Settlement Procedures Act
    applies to
    A. home equity loans.
    B. purchase loans on one-to-four residential
       unit buildings.
    C. loans for one-to-six residential unit
       buildings.
    D. residential, commercial, and industrial
       financing.

16. A parcel of land sold for $328,000, which was
    82% of its list price. What was it listed at?
    A. $268,960
    B. $387,040
    C. $400,000
    D. $437,000

17. A broker listed a property at $92,500 with
    $30,000 down and the balance at 7% inter-
    est. The broker brought in a full-price cash
    offer that the owner rejected. The broker is
    entitled to
    A. the full commission.
    B. half the commission.
    C. the commission split agreed on.
    D. nothing.

18. A residential lease provided that the landlord
    supply the water. The water to the building
    was cut off because the landlord had not
    paid the water bill. The tenant can leave the
    premises with no further lease obligations
    based on
    A. condemnation.
    B. surrender.
    C. constructive eviction.
    D. sufferance.

19. Under RESPA, a lender is required to pro-
    vide the purchaser with a
    A. good-faith estimate of closing costs.
    B. home protection warranty.
    C. mortgage insurance policy.
    D. certified appraisal.

20. A legal process used to clear a title is
    A. a quitclaim deed.
    B. an action to quiet title.
    C. an action in personam.
    D. a writ of mandamus.

21. A $7,000 investment in a straight mortgage
    earns $210 in three months. What is the
    annual percentage return on the investment?
    A. 9%
    B. 11%
    C. 12%
    D. 14%

22. The term *menace* is associated with
    A. restrictive covenants.
    B. contracts.
    C. easements.
    D. financing.

23. A contractor agreed to reduce the contract amount by $100 for every day completion of a home was delayed beyond a stated due date. This is an example of
    A. liquidated damages.
    B. compensatory damages.
    C. punitive damages.
    D. an illegal agreement.

24. Because a woman mistakenly measured from the wrong surveyor's stake, she built a fishing cabin on a neighbor's land. What are the rights of the parties?
    A. The neighbor would take title to the cabin by accession.
    B. The woman has the right to buy the land at its tax-appraised value.
    C. The woman is allowed to remove the improvements, provided any damage to the property is repaired.
    D. The neighbor retains title to the land, but the woman is allowed to use the cabin.

25. A one acre parcel sold for $58,900. The price per square foot was approximately
    A. $0.73.
    B. $0.94.
    C. $1.22.
    D. $1.35.

26. Which of the following does the CAN-SPAM Act of 2003 *NOT* require?
    A. Inclusion of an "opt-out" mechanism
    B. A subject line indicating that the email is an advertisement
    C. Written permission to send the message
    D. The sender's physical location

27. The broker's authority under a listing includes
    A. everything necessary to conclude a sale.
    B. any act performed in the owner's best interest.
    C. the customary authority of a general agent.
    D. only the authority granted or implied.

28. What law allows personal information about a neighbor to be available to a prospective purchaser?
    A. Americans with Disabilities Act
    B. Megan's Law
    C. 1988 Fair Housing Amendments Act
    D. Civil Rights Act of 1968

29. When using the income approach, an appraiser would consider
    A. accrued depreciation.
    B. original cost to build.
    C. market changes since comparable sales.
    D. capitalization rate.

30. An example of functional obsolescence is
    A. a building that, because of wear and tear, is no longer suitable for its intended purpose.
    B. a large commercial structure with inadequate onsite parking.
    C. an encroaching use.
    D. a political change that has reduced value.

31. The requirement that buyers be made aware of the importance of a home inspection applies to
    A. all loans by federally insured lenders.
    B. transactions subject to PMI.
    C. transactions involving FHA financing.
    D. all loans subject to RESPA.

32. The maximum civil penalty for the first discriminatory act in violation of the Americans with Disabilities Act is
    A. $5,000.
    B. $25,000.
    C. $45,000.
    D. $55,000.

33. All of the rights of ownership, including the rights to use, encumber, transfer, and exclude, are called
    A. emblements of title.
    B. the bundle of rights.
    C. chattels real.
    D. fructus naturales.

34. Because a property manager expects residential rental demand to exceed the rental supply within a short period of time, the manager wants new leases to
    A. reflect the CPI.
    B. be based on a percentage of the gross.
    C. be for relatively short terms.
    D. obligate the tenant to a long-term commitment.

35. By calling in a loan, the lender
    A. gives a new loan.
    B. accelerates loan payments.
    C. shortens the loan term.
    D. changes the interest rate.

36. A right of first refusal differs from an option in that the
    A. holder of the option right must exercise it.
    B. right of first refusal sets the exact price and terms.
    C. right of first refusal can be exercised only if the owner decides to sell or lease.
    D. right of first refusal is for leasing only, while the option is for purchase.

37. A woman agreed in writing to make a gift of her home to her friend. The agreement could be described as what type of contract?
    A. Valid
    B. Void
    C. Voidable
    D. Implied

38. As part of a purchase agreement, the seller agreed to complete a roof repair before closing. The seller now refuses to complete the repair. What rights does the buyer have?
    A. Reformation
    B. Accord and satisfaction
    C. Rescission
    D. Novation

39. In the acceptance of an offer, the offeree stated, "I accept the $1,950,000 purchase price, except I decline to remove the wallpaper in the entry as required in the offer. You are likely unaware that the paper is a one-of-a-kind design by Andy Warhol, so I am certain you won't want it removed." As to this acceptance,
    A. it is valid as it is substantially in accordance with the offer.
    B. the acceptance was really a counteroffer.
    C. if the owner sent a withdrawal of the exception, there is a binding contract.
    D. the acceptance was actually a novation.

40. A listing stated "14 acres MOL." What does *MOL* stand for?
    A. Measurement of land
    B. Measurement owner's liability
    C. More or less
    D. Measured on legal

41. A man owes $14,000 on a credit card bearing interest at 18%. The man is called to active duty in the U.S. Army Reserve. He has the right to
    A. disregard credit payments until active service ends.
    B. have the interest rate reduced to 6%.
    C. have the loan expunged.
    D. receive credit on principal for all interest paid.

42. An option does *NOT* become a binding contract on both parties until the
    A. consideration is paid.
    B. option is signed by both parties.
    C. option period expires.
    D. option is exercised.

43. The Uniform Residential Landlord and Tenant Act requires that the landlord inform the tenant about
    A. the basis of any rent increase.
    B. any encumbrances against the property.
    C. the name and addresses where notices should be sent.
    D. any pending sale of the premises.

44. Which of the following acts of a listing agent is proper conduct?
    A. Remaining silent about a plumbing problem when directed by the seller to not disclose the information to the buyer
    B. Telling a prospective buyer about a recent violent death on the premises
    C. Informing a prospective buyer to lower an offer because the seller would accept less
    D. Volunteering information to prospective buyers about the racial composition of the area

45. The activities of Fannie Mae in the secondary mortgage market serve to
    A. create a market for existing home loans.
    B. encourage lenders to make commercial loans.
    C. insure or guarantee home loans.
    D. make construction standards uniform.

46. A salesperson, working for a broker, was able to complete a complex transaction that benefited both the buyer and the seller. The parties wanted to show their appreciation by giving the salesperson additional compensation. The salesperson can receive this compensation from the
    A. seller.
    B. buyer.
    C. buyer and seller equally.
    D. broker.

47. What type of mortgage has compound interest?
    A. Straight
    B. Bimonthly
    C. Reverse annuity
    D. Amortized

48. A prospective office manager is offered a salary of $2,000 per month plus 5% of gross commissions paid to the firm. If the manager wants a minimum of $60,000 per year, average monthly gross office commissions must be
    A. $60,000.
    B. $64,000.
    C. $100,000.
    D. $120,000.

49. When title is conveyed to two persons not married to each other and no mention is made of how they are to take title, ownership is presumed to be as
    A. community property.
    B. tenants in common.
    C. joint tenants.
    D. tenants in the entirety.

50. One month after receiving a three-month option to purchase, the optionee notified the optionor that the option was being revoked. Which of the following is TRUE?
    A. The option is revoked, and the optionee is not entitled to any refund of consideration.
    B. The optionee is entitled to full refund of consideration paid.
    C. The optionee is entitled to two-thirds of the consideration paid.
    D. The option remains in effect.

51. An offer is terminated by
    A. rejection by the offeror.
    B. rejection by the offeree.
    C. revocation by the offeree.
    D. request for an extension by the offeree.

52. A woman is in the National Guard and is on duty overseas. She receives notice that her home mortgage will be foreclosed. The woman's rights include
    A. the right to appeal any foreclosure.
    B. staying the foreclosure until 90 days after the end of active service.
    C. the right to have interest forgiven.
    D. a one-year period of redemption after foreclosure.

53. The process of warehousing refers to
    A. loans being used as collateral for other loans.
    B. servicing mortgages for other owners.
    C. the process of assemblage.
    D. nonconforming loans.

54. On a closing statement, seller financing is shown
    A. as a prorated factor.
    B. as a credit to the buyer and a debit to the seller.
    C. as a debit to the buyer and a credit to the seller.
    D. not at all.

55. Which of the following statements regarding agency is *TRUE*?
    A. Death of the agent terminates the agency.
    B. Any agency can be terminated by repudiation by principal or agent.
    C. Termination of an agency relieves the agent of confidentiality duties.
    D. An agent can assign all interest in the agency to another agent.

56. A permanent loan that replaces a construction loan is a
    A. takeout loan.
    B. purchase money loan.
    C. packaged loan.
    D. participation loan.

57. A property owner paid $112,000 for a lot and spent $720,000 building an apartment building. He has since fully depreciated the improvements. The property owner has an adjusted cost basis of
    A. $112,000.
    B. $318,000.
    C. $430,500.
    D. $1,050,500.

58. Instruments that could contain subordination clauses are
    A. deeds.
    B. mortgages.
    C. leases.
    D. options.

59. Property of an owner was seized before a judgment was rendered. The seizure is
    A. an execution of the judgment.
    B. a sheriff's sale.
    C. an attachment.
    D. a lis pendens.

60. A, B, C, and D receive a farm from their parents in joint tenancy. D deeds her share to E, and B dies. How is title now held?
    A. A and C as joint tenants, and B's heirs and E as tenants in common
    B. A, C, and E as tenants in common
    C. A and C as joint tenants, with E as tenant in common
    D. A, C, B's heirs, and E as tenants in common

61. Lowering interest rates is expected to result in
    A. lower sale prices.
    B. more buyers entering the market.
    C. a reduction in sales activity.
    D. higher capitalization rates.

62. A monthly amortized loan payment differs from the prior month's payment in that the prior month's payment
    A. was a greater amount.
    B. was a lesser amount.
    C. applied more money to principal.
    D. applied more money to interest.

63. A new runway at an airport put a subdivision under the aircraft-landing pattern, which resulted in a lowering of values. This is considered
    A. functional obsolescence.
    B. external obsolescence.
    C. physical deterioration.
    D. inverse condemnation.

64. A property manager leased a store for three years. The first year's rent was $1,000 per month and was to increase 10% each year thereafter. The broker received 7% commission for the first year, 5% for the second year, and 3% for the balance of the lease. The total commission earned was
    A. $840.00.
    B. $1,613.00.
    C. $1,936.00.
    D. $2,784.70.

65. A loan that provides for future advances is
    A. an open-end loan.
    B. a shared appreciation loan.
    C. a growing equity mortgage.
    D. a blanket mortgage.

66. A broker made one of the salespeople the sole agent for an owner. That salesperson is considered
    A. a facilitator.
    B. a dual agent.
    C. the designated agent.
    D. a cooperating agent.

67. Disclosure must be made to a purchaser of
    A. the true reason the property is being sold.
    B. any serious health problem of prior occupants.
    C. any known neighborhood nuisance problem.
    D. actual annual utility costs.

68. A conveyance from J to K for life and then to L if L is still alive gives L a
    A. reversionary interest.
    B. fee simple
    C. contingent remainder interest.
    D. vested remainder interest.

69. Which of the following hazardous substances is associated with electrical equipment?
    A. Asbestos
    B. Radon
    C. PCBs
    D. Lead

70. What is a characteristic of both FHA and VA loans?
    A. Absence of prepayment penalties
    B. Absence of loan points
    C. Requirement of mortgage insurance
    D. Requirement of a certificate of reasonable value

71. Which of the following statements regarding the CAN-SPAM Act of 2003 is *TRUE*?
    I.   Solicitation emails must contain an opt-out mechanism.
    II. Solicitation emails must include a functioning return email address.
    III. Written permission is required to send a solicitation email.
    IV. Solicitation emails may only be sent within three months of an inquiry.
    A. I only
    B. I and II only
    C. I, II, and III only
    D. I, II, III, and IV

72. An owner may be required to make readily achievable modifications to premises because of
    A. RESPA.
    B. the Americans with Disabilities Act.
    C. the 1988 Fair Housing Amendments Act.
    D. the Civil Rights Act of 1968.

73. An income property is valued at $800,000 by an appraiser who used a capitalization rate of 8%. If the appraiser had used a capitalization rate of 6.5%, what is the appraiser's estimate of property value?
    A. $443,000
    B. $470,000
    C. $650,000
    D. $984,615

74. An example of a stigmatized property is a house
    A. condemned by the city as unfit for habitation.
    B. in an undesirable neighborhood.
    C. with numerous physical defects.
    D. regarded by the community as being unlucky.

75. The terms *good*, *valuable*, and *legal* refer to
    A. income.
    B. consideration.
    C. commission.
    D. capacity.

76. A 6-foot fence is to be built around all four sides of an 80-by-120-foot rectangular lot. The cost for the fence will be $2.50 per linear foot for labor plus $0.42 per square foot for material. What is the total cost of the fence?
    A. $1,008
    B. $1,168
    C. $2,008
    D. $2,168

77. A buyer paid one discount point to obtain a home loan. The point paid by the buyer
    A. is tax deductible by the buyer as interest.
    B. is added to the buyer's cost basis.
    C. is taxable as income to the buyer.
    D. may be depreciated by the buyer.

78. At closing, which of the following is customarily a debit to the seller?
    A. Loan points
    B. Listing broker commission
    C. Lender's extended coverage policy of title insurance
    D. Prepaid property taxes

79. Before the expiration of an exclusive listing, the owner terminated the listing without cause. Based on the owner's action, the broker
    A. is entitled to specific performance.
    B. is entitled to damages.
    C. can still earn a commission if a buyer can be located before the expiration date on the listing.
    D. has no recourse against the owner because listings can be terminated at will.

80. The American Taxpayer Relief Act increased the capital gains tax for high-income taxpayers to
    A. 15%.
    B. 20%.
    C. 25%.
    D. 28%.

DIFFICULTY LEVEL III ANSWERS

1. **(B)** While the contract was valid, it was unenforceable because of time lapse. (104)

2. **(B)** The seller has to turn over the unearned rent to the buyer. (182)

3. **(C)** Government north/south survey lines. (4)

4. **(D)** And it can be taken every two years. (79–80)

5. **(B)** The grantor sells and becomes a tenant of the grantee. (196–197)

6. **(D)** The original lease remains with the sublessor. (203–204)

7. **(D)** Death of principal or agent terminates an agency. (111)

8. **(A)** It is an apparent discrepancy causing doubt as to title. Is ML the same person as KL? (48)

9. **(B)** 9% (0.09) × $1,800 = $162 per year, or $81 for 6 months. (248–249)

    9% (0.09) × $1,200 = $108 per year, or $54 for 6 months.

    9% (0.09) × $600 = $54 per year, or $27 for 6 months.

    $81 + $54 + $27 = $162.

10. **(B)** They are the advances the lender is obligated to make as work meets agreed-upon stages of construction. (169)

11. **(D)** Acceptance was effective as soon as it was placed in the mail. (101)

12. **(C)** Acquiring property by inheritance. (45)

13. **(D)** An undivided interest in the whole. (12)

14. **(C)** Rising interest rates would result in the investor's using higher capitalization rates that would result in lower value. (72)

15. **(B)** That are federally related. (146)

16. **(C)** $328,000 part ÷ 0.82 percentage = whole. (247)

17. **(D)** The offer was not in accordance with terms specified in the listing. (112)

18. **(C)** Conduct that disturbs the tenant, forcing the tenant to vacate. (202)

19. **(A)** Within three business days of loan application. (146)

20. **(B)** Court makes determination of title. (A) is not a legal process. (43)

21. **(C)** 210 × 4 = $840 per year. Part ÷ whole = rate, so $840 ÷ $7,000 = 0.12, or 12%. (246)

22. **(B)** Menace makes a contract voidable by the injured party. (100)

23. **(A)** Agreeing to reasonably estimated damages before a breach. (103)

24. **(C)** The woman is an innocent improver, so she can remove the improvement. (40)

25. **(D)** Divide price paid ($58,900) by square feet in an acre ($43,560). (10)

26. **(C)** Required for fax, not email. (145)

27. **(D)** It is a special agency. (108)

28. **(B)** Buyer may be informed as to availability of data about sex offenders in the area. (133)

29. **(D)** Answers (A) and (B) relate to cost approach and (C) to sales comparison approach. For the income approach, the net income is divided by the capitalization rate. (72)

30. **(B)** Built-in obsolescence. (75)

31. **(C)** As well as HUD-owned property. (133)

32. **(D)** $110,000 for subsequent violations. (141)

33. **(B)** All beneficial rights of ownership. (1)

34. **(C)** So new leases can reflect the economic condition when leases expire. (196)

35. **(B)** Under an acceleration clause. (172)

36. **(C)** It is a chance to meet purchase or lease terms of another that the owner is willing to accept. (102)

37. **(B)** Because it lacks valuable consideration, love and affection cannot support a promise. (98, 100)

38. **(C)** Or the buyer could waive the seller's breach and insist on closing. (103)

39. **(B)** The counteroffer killed the original offer, which can no longer be accepted; however, the original offeror can accept the counteroffer. (102)

40. **(C)** Used when exact acreage is difficult to ascertain, as with a metes-and-bounds description. (3)

41. **(B)** Service Members Civil Relief Act. (166)

42. **(D)** When exercised, the optionee agrees to be bound. (102)

43. **(C)** A tenant contact person must be named. (200)

44. **(B)** Although state law might not require disclosure. (109–110)

45. **(A)** By buying FHA, VA, and conventional loans made by direct lenders. (178)

46. **(D)** The only party that can compensate a salesperson is the salesperson's own broker. (225)

47. **(C)** Because the interest accruing each month accrues on previously charged interest. (168)

48. **(A)** (247)

$$60,000 \div 12 = 5,000 \text{ per month}$$
$$5,000 - 2,000 \text{ (salary)} = 3,000 \text{ in needed commissions}$$
$$3,000 \div 0.05 = 60,000$$

49. **(B)** Joint tenancy must be stated or, in some states, be conveyed to the husband and wife. Answers (A) and (D) require marriage. (12)

50. **(D)** It is an irrevocable offer of optionor which the optionee need not accept but is not entitled to return of compensation if not exercised. (102)

51. **(B)** The offeror can revoke, but the offeree rejects. (102)

52. **(B)** Service Members Civil Relief Act. (166)

53. **(A)** Mortgage bankers borrow on inventory of loans. A short-term line of credit to make additional loans. (170)

54. **(B)** It is credited to the buyers as part of what they have to pay and deducted (debited) from what the sellers will receive at closing. (183)

55. **(A)** An agency coupled with an interest may not be terminated, confidentiality of an agency remains and an agency is a personal contract that cannot be assigned. (111)

56. **(A)** The take-out loan replaces (takes out) the construction loan. (170)

57. **(A)** Cost basis is cost less depreciation. Because only the $720,000 was depreciated, the cost basis is the cost of the land. (81)

58. **(B)** It makes a loan secondary in priority to a later recorded loan. (172)

59. **(C)** Attachment is a prejudgment lien to make certain there will be something to go against after a judgment. (36)

60. **C.** A and C owned an undivided three-quarters interest and E an undivided one-quarter interest. (11–12)

61. **(B)** Because more buyers could qualify for loans. (66–67)

62. **(D)** With an amortized loan, each month's payment applies less to interest and more to principal than the prior month's payment. (167)

63. **(B)** Forces outside the property and usually incurable. (75)

64. **(C)** (248)

    $0.07\ (7\%) \times \$12{,}000 = \$840$

    $0.05\ (5\%) \times \$13{,}200 = \$660$

    $0.03\ (3\%) \times \$14{,}520 = \$436$

    $\$840 + \$660 + \$436 = \$1{,}936$

65. **(A)** Up to an agreed-upon limit. Home equity loan approvals and home equity credit cards do the same thing. (169)

66. **(C)** Another salesperson could be the buyer's agent. Designated agency avoids the problems of dual agency. (107)

67. **(C)** Known detrimental information must be revealed. (109)

68. **(C)** Because title goes to a third party, it is a remainder interest contingent on L's living longer than K. (8)

69. **(C)** A carcinogen used in electrical transformers. (131)

70. **(A)** Neither penalizes prepayment. (175)

71. **(B)** Choices (III) and (IV) relate to telephone calls. (145)

72. **(B)** When required to make premises accessible to persons with a disability. (140)

73. **(D)** To find the interest earned (part): 0.08 interest rate × $800,000 = $64,000 net income. If we used 6.5%, we would capitalize the $64,000 income: $64,000 ÷ 0.065 = $984,615. (72)

74. **(D)** Nonphysical perception of the property. (110)

75. **(B)** Love and affection are "good" consideration but not "valuable." (99)

76. **(C)** 80' × 120' lot has 400' perimeter; 400' × 2.50 = $1,000; 6' × 400' = 2,400 square feet; 2,400 × 0.42 = $1,008 + $1,000 = $2,008. (252–254)

77. **(A)** In the year paid. Seller paid points increase cost basis. (80)

78. **(B)** The others are buyer debits. (182)

79. **(B)** While an owner can always terminate since agency requires consent, breach of agreement could expose party to damages if wrongful. (110)

80. **(B)** There is also a Medicare surcharge. (82)

DIFFICULTY LEVEL IV

1. If $1,925 is paid over a five-month period on a $30,000 straight mortgage, the interest rate is more than
   A. 8% but less than 10%.
   B. 10% but less than 12%.
   C. 12% but less than 14%.
   D. 14% but less than 16%.

2. Liens to be assumed by the buyer are shown in a settlement statement as
   A. buyer debits.
   B. seller debits.
   C. seller credits.
   D. balance factors.

3. A nonconforming loan is a loan that
   A. is delinquent in payments.
   B. is secured by personal property rather than real estate.
   C. does not meet the purchase requirements of Fannie Mae.
   D. lacks government guarantee or insurance.

4. The buyer under a sale-leaseback expects
   A. to free capital.
   B. an annuity type benefit.
   C. to trade on equity.
   D. to fully deduct rent payments.

5. As a result of eminent domain, the back 20% of a lot was taken for public use. What affect will the loss have on the lot's value?
   A. The value will decrease 20%.
   B. The value per square foot will increase.
   C. The value per square foot will remain constant.
   D. The lot value will be unchanged.

6. A veteran has made the last payment on a VA loan. The veteran is now entitled to
   A. the return of funding fees.
   B. restoration of loan benefits.
   C. proration of loan points.
   D. a policy of title insurance.

7. A function of the Federal Emergency Management Agency is to
   A. provide flood insurance.
   B. enforce CERCLA.
   C. designate flood hazard areas.
   D. set standards for home inspection.

8. A buyer's agent located a property that the buyer wishes to purchase. It is not listed for sale, and the seller refuses to pay the broker a commission. The broker should
   A. find another property for the buyer.
   B. submit the buyer's offer to owner.
   C. sue the seller for the commission.
   D. submit the claim to arbitration.

9. The person on a trust deed who is in the same position that a mortgagor is in on a mortgage is called a
   A. trustee.
   B. vendee.
   C. beneficiary.
   D. trustor.

10. The state wants to condemn a diagonal strip of land that bisects a farm. The farm value will decrease far more than the per-acre value offered for the land taken. The farm's owner should ask for
    A. severance damages.
    B. exemplary damages.
    C. nominal damages.
    D. an injunction.

11. The chain of title for a property is revealed in the
    A. preliminary title report.
    B. abstract.
    C. attorney's title opinion.
    D. standard policy of title insurance.

12. A fee simple subject to a condition subsequent will
    A. automatically revert to the grantor on breach of the condition.
    B. require that the grantor exercise the right of reentry.
    C. not be lost by failure to exercise rights.
    D. have its duration spelled out in the deed.

13. Debits on a seller's closing statement include
    A. seller financing.
    B. purchase price.
    C. fuel in tank.
    D. prepaid insurance.

14. A prior mortgage was foreclosed. The purchaser of the foreclosure wished to get rid of tenants with a three-year lease who were paying below-market rent. The owner must
    A. give a 30-day notice to vacate.
    B. give a 90-day notice to vacate.
    C. give a 120-day notice to vacate.
    D. honor the lease.

15. A woman gave a deed to a man for valuable consideration. The man did not take possession or record the deed. Which of the following statements of the man's rights is *TRUE*?
    A. The man would have greater rights than a subsequent purchase for value from the woman who records the deed.
    B. A recipient of a later gift deed from the woman who records would have greater rights than the man.
    C. The man's deed is void for lack of recording.
    D. Between the man and the woman, the man has title.

16. A real estate salesperson found that he received better responses to his newspaper ads when he did not indicate that the ad was placed by an agent. These ads
    A. breach the agent's fiduciary duty.
    B. are blind ads and subject the agent to disciplinary action.
    C. are proper if they include the equal housing opportunity logo.
    D. are proper if the newspaper is made aware that the ads were placed in an agency capacity.

17. A purchaser checks the county records and determines that the seller was the grantee on a deed of the property involved, but that there were no further recordings involving the grantee. The purchaser could reasonably assume that
    A. the seller has marketable title.
    B. there are no encumbrances against the property.
    C. taxes are current.
    D. the seller has not mortgaged the property.

18. How much can a lender charge for preparing the disclosure of loan costs that is required by the Real Estate Settlement Procedures Act?
    A. $50
    B. $100
    C. The actual preparation cost
    D. None of these

19. A feature of a VA loan is the
    A. use of pass-through certificates.
    B. application of the tandem plan.
    C. use of mortgage-backed certification.
    D. requirement of a funding fee.

20. In preparing a settlement statement, a broker should understand that
    A. the party who receives a deed pays to draft it.
    B. the party giving a deed pays to record it.
    C. unless agreed otherwise, buyer loan costs are split between buyer and seller.
    D. title insurance costs would never be a credit on a closing statement.

21. A topographical map has contour lines that are very close together in one area. It indicates
    A. a very high elevation.
    B. that the land is relatively flat.
    C. a low elevation.
    D. a steep slope.

22. A buyer believed the land he purchased from a seller had valuable minerals that the seller was not aware of. The buyer discovered he was mistaken. This is an example of
   A. unilateral mistake of fact.
   B. a voidable contract.
   C. misrepresentation.
   D. a void contract.

23. At closing, the lender requests $1,680, which will be kept in a special fund. This money is
   A. a security deposit.
   B. for taxes and insurance.
   C. to ensure against default.
   D. to cover points.

24. In the absence of permission to disclose, a listing broker may tell a prospective purchaser
   A. that the seller must conclude a sale.
   B. why the property is not desirable.
   C. what the owner actually will accept.
   D. what the owner originally paid.

25. Under RESPA, what are the maximum advance tax reserves that a lender can require at the time of the loan?
   A. Two months
   B. Three months
   C. Six months
   D. One year

26. A buyer is responsible for the cost of
   A. loan payoffs.
   B. drafting a new deed.
   C. prepaid rents.
   D. an appraisal fee.

27. Strict liability for cleanup of hazardous substances found on a property is provided for by which federal law?
   A. FIRREA
   B. FICO
   C. FIRPTA
   D. CERCLA

28. A man and a woman owned property together in joint tenancy. The man owed numerous creditors and several of them obtained judgments. The man died before the creditors were able to seize and partition the joint tenancy property. What are the creditors' rights?
   A. The judgment creditors become tenants in common with the woman.
   B. All the creditors are equal in status and have the right to one-half of the property.
   C. The probate court would take title to one-half of the property.
   D. The creditors have no right to the property.

29. A broker allowed a secretary to handle trust funds. The broker should be *MOST* concerned about having
   A. general liability insurance protection.
   B. errors and omissions coverage.
   C. a fidelity bond.
   D. coinsurance.

30. How many acres are in the S½ of the NW¼ of the SE¼ of the SW¼ of the NE¼ of a section?
   A. 1.25
   B. 2.5
   C. 5
   D. 10

31. A buyer knows the owner is considering an offer. The buyer asks the listing broker the amount of the offer so the buyer can exceed it. The broker should
   A. disclose because it is in the owner's best interests.
   B. disclose because a broker must reveal to a buyer everything the broker knows about a property.
   C. notify the owner of the request.
   D. tell the prospective buyer that no other offers can be considered while an offer is pending.

32. A piece of property is priced at $300,000, using a 6% capitalization rate. If the prospective investor wants an 8% return, the value of the property to the investor will be
    A. $210,000.
    B. $225,000.
    C. $270,000.
    D. $290,000.

33. A large shopping center may offer an anchor tenant a below-market-rate percentage lease
    A. because it hopes the volume will make up for the low percentage.
    B. because of the effect on other tenants' leases and volume.
    C. because of economics of scale.
    D. to reduce operational costs.

34. A property has a net operating income of $27,600 per year, and 8.5% is an appropriate capitalization rate. If the value of the land is $135,000, how much of the value is attributable to the building?
    A. $179,600
    B. $185,000
    C. $189,706
    D. $716,800

35. Which of the following restrictive covenants is enforceable?
    A. A property cannot be used for any commercial purpose that competes with the use of a neighboring parcel.
    B. The parcel cannot be occupied by non-Christians.
    C. The property must be kept in agricultural use.
    D. The property can only be sold to blood relatives of the original grantor.

36. The booklet *Shopping for Your Home Loan* is required to be given to borrowers. This requirement is set forth in
    A. RESPA.
    B. the Truth in Lending Act.
    C. the Equal Credit Opportunity Act.
    D. the Predatory Lending Act.

37. Before closing, the seller and the buyer agree to a rescission of their sales agreement, with the buyer asking the listing broker for the return of his deposit. The broker should
    A. return the deposit in full.
    B. deduct the commission due and return the balance.
    C. keep half of the commission due and return everything else.
    D. hold all monies for a court determination of the broker's rights.

38. A disadvantage of ownership in a cooperative versus condominium ownership is the
    A. restriction on profit on resale.
    B. danger that other owners might be unable to pay their shares toward the mortgage and taxes.
    C. personal liability of owners should they default on their payments.
    D. higher tax assessment.

39. A tenant on a long-term commercial lease wants to go out of business. Because the rent is worth much more than the tenant is paying, the tenant should consider
    A. assigning the lease.
    B. subletting the property.
    C. a novation.
    D. surrendering the premises.

40. A loan impound account belongs to the
    A. lender.
    B. broker.
    C. borrower.
    D. closing agent.

41. A lease uses the terms *minimum rent* and *gross income*. The lease is a
    A. gross lease.
    B. net lease.
    C. percentage lease.
    D. periodic tenancy.

42. A home inspector noticed that a home had a high humidity level. The inspector is especially concerned about the presence of
    A. toxic mold.
    B. PCBs.
    C. radon.
    D. EMFs.

43. A newspaper advertisement by a broker is considered
    A. an irrevocable offer.
    B. a revocable offer.
    C. an invitation to negotiate.
    D. a firm offer.

44. A man sold his residence of eight years for $400,000. He had paid $80,000 for the home and invested $30,000 in improvements. He remarried a year before the sale, and his new wife was living in the house at the time of sale. Assuming the man is in the 25% tax bracket, how much will he be taxed on the sale?
    A. Nothing
    B. $6,000
    C. $56,000
    D. $60,000

45. A broker violated the Sherman Antitrust Act when she
    A. refused to accept less than 6% as a listing commission.
    B. agreed with another broker to respect each other's designated territory.
    C. agreed with a group of brokers to cooperate on listings.
    D. agreed to abide by minimum ethical standards of a broker organization.

46. A landlord was found to be guilty of retaliatory eviction because the landlord
    A. refused to renew a one-year residential lease after the tenant complained to health authorities about a rodent problem.
    B. made unnecessary and loud repairs to harass a tenant.
    C. used threats and profanity toward the tenant.
    D. refused to clean common areas.

47. After street parking was made illegal, the rents of a small office building declined $1,000 per month. Assuming a capitalization rate of 9%, the building suffered a loss in value of
    A. $9,000.
    B. $81,000.
    C. $120,000.
    D. $133,333.

48. With the seller's knowledge, the buyer under an executory verbal purchase agreement made extensive improvements to a property. The seller later refused to honor the sale agreement. The buyer will likely assert
    A. the parole evidence rule.
    B. the statute of frauds.
    C. laches.
    D. the doctrine of estoppel.

49. A broker gave a salesman an advance on a commission for a sale not yet closed. This action
    A. violated the real estate law.
    B. is proper if paid from the broker's trust account.
    C. is proper if paid from broker's own funds.
    D. is considered conversion.

50. A unilateral contract that becomes bilateral upon being exercised is
    A. an exclusive listing.
    B. an option.
    C. a purchase contract.
    D. a mortgage.

51. An agency will continue even though
    A. the principal has repudiated the agency.
    B. the purpose of the agency has become impossible.
    C. all the officers and directors of the principal corporation have died.
    D. the agent has become mentally incapacitated.

52. A broker's fiduciary duty includes
    A. care and obedience.
    B. care, obedience, and accounting.
    C. obedience, loyalty, and disclosure.
    D. care, obedience, accounting, loyalty, and disclosure.

53. A loan provided that for a designated period, the borrower could choose to make a minimum payment less than the interest accruing. What type of loan did the borrower have?
    A. Zero-interest loan
    B. Package mortgage
    C. Option arm
    D. Wraparound loan

54. When a lender agrees to forgive a loan balance, the borrower should be concerned with
    A. imputed interest.
    B. possible tax liability.
    C. deficiency judgments.
    D. MERS.

55. When the IRS treats a real estate salesperson as an independent contractor,
    A. the broker must deduct Social Security and tax payments from the salesperson's compensation.
    B. the broker cannot supervise the salesperson's activities.
    C. the salesperson must be paid on a salary basis.
    D. there is a written contract indicating that the salesperson will be treated as an independent contractor.

56. A buyer offered to buy a seller's home for $150,000. The seller accepted the written offer with the notation, "Seller may remove the rosebushes by the patio." The seller received no further reply from the buyer, so the seller sent the buyer a signed memo: "I will leave the rosebushes." What are the buyer's obligations as to the purchase?
    A. The buyer is bound to her offer because the seller's memo removed the condition.
    B. The buyer's offer was never accepted, so the buyer is not obligated.
    C. Because the rosebushes are minor items, the buyer's acceptance formed an agreement binding the buyer.
    D. The contract is voidable at the option of either the buyer or the seller.

57. An ejectment action can be used against
    A. a tenant who has failed to pay the rent.
    B. an owner who has committed waste.
    C. a tenant at sufferance.
    D. a trustor who is in default.

58. A broker wants to advertise a property located in an African American neighborhood in a newspaper aimed at an African American readership. To do so, the broker needs to
    A. indicate compliance with the fair housing laws.
    B. also advertise properties in white neighborhoods in the same paper.
    C. include the Equal Housing Opportunity logo in the ad.
    D. identify the exact location in the ad.

59. Responsibility for disclosure under RESPA rests with the
    A. seller.
    B. broker.
    C. lender.
    D. title company.

60. A seller lied to a buyer about the zoning to induce the buyer to buy a 10-acre parcel. Before completion of the sale, the buyer learns of the deception. What are the contractual rights of the two parties?
    A. The sale is void as to both parties.
    B. The seller can be held to the sales agreement by the buyer.
    C. Either party can void the agreement.
    D. The agreement is binding on both parties, although the buyer may be entitled to damages after the closing.

61. A lender requires PMI. The lender is requiring
    A. a cosigner.
    B. mortgage insurance.
    C. a property inspection.
    D. home warranty protection.

62. A man gave a deed to a woman with an oral agreement that the deed was not to be recorded until after he died. The deed is
    A. valid.
    B. void.
    C. voidable.
    D. illegal.

63. A tenant with a disability intends to make extensive modifications to the interior of an apartment to meet particular needs relating to the disability. The tenant should realize that the landlord
    A. can condition approval to the modification on an agreement to restore the premises at the end of the tenancy.
    B. can insist on an additional security deposit to guarantee restoration.
    C. is obligated to pay reasonable modification costs.
    D. can refuse to allow the modification.

64. The lender under a construction loan will provide the builder with the final payment on
    A. receipt of the deed.
    B. receipt of the occupancy permit.
    C. notice of completion.
    D. expiration of the mechanic's lien period.

65. A man owns a lot free and clear valued at $30,000, on which he plans to construct a commercial building and lease it at an annual rent of $65,000. Total expenses are estimated at $11,000 per year. If an 8% net return is expected on the total investment, what will be the cost of the improvements?
    A. $435,750
    B. $595,000
    C. $645,000
    D. $675,000

66. Before closing, a buyer's property inspection revealed the presence of lead paint, which the seller refused to correct. In this situation, the buyer may
    A. deduct cost of remedy from purchase price.
    B. go through with the purchase and then demand compensatory damages.
    C. rescind the contract but will forfeit any earnest money deposit.
    D. rescind the contract and is entitled to return of earnest money deposit.

67. A lease clause provides that if the lease is not extended or renewed, the rents will increase 50% should the tenant fail to vacate. What type of clause is it?
    A. Defeasance
    B. Alienation
    C. Holdover
    D. Subordination

68. Losing a right due to the failure to assert it in a timely manner is called
    A. laches.
    B. dereliction.
    C. satisfaction.
    D. surrender.

69. A rectangular lot has an apartment structure on it worth $193,600. This value is the equivalent of $4.40 per square foot for the lot. If one lot dimension is 200 feet, what is the other dimension?
    A. 110 feet
    B. 220 feet
    C. 400 feet
    D. 880 feet

70. A seller was allowed to remain in possession for one week after close of escrow. Two days after closing, the property was destroyed by a tornado. Under the Uniform Vendor and Purchaser Risk Act, who bears the risk of loss?
    A. The seller, because sale is voidable before receiving possession
    B. The buyer and the seller equally, because loss is without fault
    C. The seller, because the seller had possession
    D. The buyer, because title had passed and the seller was not the cause of the loss

71. Monthly rent on a warehouse is set at $1 per cubic yard. Assuming the warehouse was 36-by-200 feet and 12 feet high, what is the annual rent?
    A. $3,200
    B. $28,800
    C. $38,400
    D. $86,400

72. A home was recently appraised at $210,000. Based on the appraisal, it has depreciated 30% in the three years since it was purchased. What was the original cost?
    A. $161,538
    B. $273,000
    C. $279,300
    D. $300,000

73. A standard policy of title insurance provides an owner protection against
    A. problems that are discovered by survey.
    B. unrecorded interests of a party in possession.
    C. unrecorded liens not known to the policyholder.
    D. defects apparent from public records.

74. A broker had agency duties to a buyer but none to the seller. This is considered a
    A. designated agency.
    B. single agency.
    C. split agency.
    D. limited agency.

75. A seller's agent lied to the buyer to induce the buyer to purchase a property. Who could be held liable if the buyer suffers a loss because of the agent's fraud?
    A. Agent only
    B. Agent and owner
    C. Owner only
    D. No one, based on caveat emptor

76. A listing contract for an open listing stated "6¢ of the sale price" for commission. The owner sold the property without an agent but offered the listing agent $0.06. The listing agent is entitled to
    A. $0.06.
    B. 6% of the sale price.
    C. a reasonable compensation.
    D. nothing.

77. Both FHA loans and VA loans may be obtained to purchase
    A. rental and owner-occupied housing.
    B. business and home loans.
    C. farm and business loans.
    D. a four-family apartment.

78. Under a sale-leaseback, the
    A. lessee is the seller.
    B. lessee retains the tax benefits of ownership.
    C. lessor has the tax deduction of rent.
    D. seller is the lessor.

79. A purchase agreement for a condominium unit in a resort community required the purchaser to allow a developer to handle rental and management of the unit. This is regarded as a
    A. corporation.
    B. limited liability corporation.
    C. security.
    D. partnership.

80. An attorney-in-fact violated fiduciary duty in
    A. purchasing the principal's property.
    B. leasing the principal's property to a third party.
    C. selling the principal's property.
    D. placing a lien on the principal's property.

DIFFICULTY LEVEL IV ANSWERS

1. **(D)** $1,925 ÷ 5 = $385 (1 month's interest). $385 × 12 = $4,620 (1 year's interest). $4,620 ÷ $30,000 = 0.154, or 15.4%. (246)

2. **(B)** They were owed by the seller, so the seller debits and the buyer credits. (182)

3. **(C)** Such as a jumbo loan above limits for purchase. (179)

4. **(B)** The seller would free capital and be able to deduct rent as an expense (business), but the buyer gains a steady income. (196–197)

5. **(B)** While the lot lost value, the rear portion has the lowest valuation (depth tables), so the square-foot value of the remaining portion would increase. (75)

6. **(B)** So another VA loan is possible. (178)

7. **(C)** FEMA provides maps of flood hazard zones. (132)

8. **(B)** And collect a commission from the buyer. (109, 113)

9. **(D)** Trustor and mortgagor are borrowers on a note who have possession of a property. (162)

10. **(A)** For the loss in value of the remaining land. (44)

11. **(B)** It shows all recorded documents from the original government conveyance (patent). (50–51)

12. **(B)** However, a fee simple determinable automatically ends the estate. (7)

13. **(A)** It is deducted from cash the seller is entitled to at closing. (182)

14. **(D)** Protecting Tenants at Foreclosure Act. (166, 203)

15. **(D)** Between-the-parties recording is not necessary, but it is to protect against later purchasers for value and liens. (49)

16. **(B)** The ad must indicate the advertiser is acting in an agency capacity. (229)

17. **(D)** Because a mortgage would have to be recorded to take priority over a purchaser. (164)

18. **(D)** No charge is allowed for RESPA disclosures. (146)

19. **(D)** Which varies, based on down payment. (175, 178)

20. **(D)** They are debited (paid) by one or both parties. (182, 183)

21. **(D)** When they are far apart, land is relatively flat. (7)

22. **(A)** The buyer's mistake does not allow the contract to be voided unless the seller had deceived the buyer into the belief. (98)

23. **(B)** This is an impound account. (173)

24. **(B)** Broker has duty to convey known negative information to the buyer. (109–110)

25. **(A)** Plus prorated amount to time of closing, to be placed in impound account. (146)

26. **(D)** Others are paid by or are debits of seller. Buyer pays appraisal for new loan. (183)

27. **(D)** The Comprehensive Environmental Response Compensation and Liability Act. (130)

28. **(D)** The woman owns property in severalty clear of creditor's rights. (12)

29. **(C)** Protection against employee misappropriation of funds. (222)

30. **(A)** Working backward, NE¼ (160 acres), SW¼ of it (40 acres), SE¼ of it (10 acres), NW¼ of it (2.5 acres), and S½ of it is 1.25 acres. (6)

31. **(C)** Fiduciary duty to disclose all pertinent information. (109)

32. **(B)** $0.06 \times \$300{,}000 = \$18{,}000$ net. $\$18{,}000 \div 0.08$ rate $= \$225{,}000$. (72)

33. **(B)** An anchor tenant (major store) will increase traffic and increase volume for other tenants. (196)

34. **(C)** Capitalize income: $\$27{,}600 \div 0.085 = \$324{,}706$. $\$324{,}706 - \$135{,}000$ land value $= \$189{,}706$ attributable to building. (72)

35. **(C)** If reasonable, it is enforceable. The others are restraint on trade, restraint on alienation, or fair housing violation. (30, 33)

36. **(A)** This is a RESPA requirement, as is the good-faith estimate of closing costs. (146)

37. **(A)** It is the buyer's money, and commission is owed by the seller. The broker may have a separate claim against the seller for commission. (222–223)

38. **(B)** Which could lead to foreclosure of entire property. (17)

39. **(B)** At a higher rent, thus keeping the difference. (204)

40. **(C)** It is kept by the lender to make certain funds will be available to pay taxes and insurance. (173)

41. **(C)** Percentage leases are based on gross income but usually have a minimum rent. (196)

42. **(A)** Moisture is conducive to mold. (130)

43. **(C)** It is not regarded as an offer that can be accepted. (101)

44. **(B)** $\$80{,}000$ cost + $\$30{,}000$ improvements = $\$110{,}000$ cost basis. A sale at $\$400{,}000$ means a gain of $\$290{,}000$. The man has $\$250{,}000$ exclusion, but his wife does not qualify for the exclusion (two-year occupancy). Therefore, $\$40{,}000$ is taxable at 15% capital gain rate. The man's income would not necessitate 20% rate or surcharge. (79–80)

45. **(B)** This is market allocation. (142–143)

46. **(A)** The others could constitute constructive eviction. (201)

47. **(D)** Capitalize annual loss of $\$12{,}000$ using the 9% rate. (72)

48. **(D)** The seller, by allowing the buyer to act to the buyer's detriment, is barred (estopped) from raising the defense of the statute of frauds. (99–100)

49. **(C)** If paid from the trust account, it is conversion. (221, 223)

50. **(B)** Before exercise of an option, the optionee is not bound. (102)

51. **(C)** A corporate life is separate from the lives of officers and directors. (111)

52. **(D)** All are included as fiduciary duties an agent has to the principal. (109)

53. **(C)** With minimum payments, there is negative amortization. When the option payment ends, there will be payment shock. (169)

54. **(B)** Debt relief is usually regarded as taxable income to debtor. (164)

55. **(D)** Treated as independent contractor for tax purposes. (224)

56. **(B)** The change was a counteroffer that rejected the buyer's offer. It cannot now be accepted. (102)

57. **(C)** Or a trespasser. Ejectment action is used against someone not legally in possession. (40)

58. **(B)** Otherwise it is steering. (138)

59. **(C)** It is a lender disclosure law. (146)

60. **(B)** Or the buyer can void the agreement, if desired. Voidable at the option of the injured party. (104)

61. **B.** Private mortgage insurance for low down payment conventional loans. (174)

62. **(A)** Between-the-parties recording is not necessary. The deed was delivered. If the man had kept possession of the deed, it would have been void (never delivered). (47, 49)

63. **(A)** 1988 Amendment to Civil Rights Act of 1968. (139)

64. **(D)** Alternatively, lien waivers are provided. (36)

65. **(C)** $65,000 gross income – $11,000 expenses = $54,000 net income. Capitalize the net using the 8% rate: $54,000 ÷ 0.08 = $675,000. Deducting the land value of $30,000 leaves $645,000 for the building. (72)

66. **(D)** While the seller is not obligated to correct the problem, the buyer can rescind. (115)

67. **(C)** The purpose is to induce the tenant to either agree to new lease or vacate the premises. (198)

68. **(A)** Undue delay that adversely affects the other party. (33)

69. **(B)** $193,600 ÷ $4.40 = 44,000 sq. ft. 44,000 total area ÷ 200' = 220' other dimension. (252–254, 254–255)

70. **(D)** But if title had not passed, the seller would bear risk of loss. (105)

71. **(C)** To find cubic feet, multiply length by width by height, or 36' × 200' × 12' = 86,400 cubic feet. Because a cubic yard has 27 cubic feet, 86,400 ÷ 27 = 3,200 cubic yards, or $3,200 per month. $3,200 × 12 = $38,400 annual rent. (254)

72. **(D)** $210,000 is 70% of original cost (depreciated 30%). $210,000 ÷ 0.70 = $300,000 original cost. (247)

73. **(D)** Others are covered by extended coverage policy. (51–52)

74. **(B)** Single agency where brokerage office represents only one party. (106)

75. **(B)** The principal is liable for the acts of the agent (vicarious liability), and the agent is liable for wrongful acts. (106)

76. **(D)** Since it is an open listing, the owner can sell without the agent and without commission. If it were an exclusive right to sell listing, the clerical error would be resolved in favor of the obviously intended 6%. (112)

77. **(D)** Both allow one-to-four residential unit buildings. VA loans require owner occupancy, and FHA loans are for housing only. (175)

78. **(A)** Who gives up ownership for a position as a tenant. (196–197)

79. **(C)** A security is a passive investment where the investor has no active role in management. (16)

80. **(A)** By acting as a principal and selling to herself, the agent would create a conflict of interest. This is a breach of fiduciary duty. (109)

DIFFICULTY LEVEL V

1. A broker's trust account ledger had the following entries:

Credits

Money in account	$8,000
Money due from other agents	6,000
	$14,000

Debits

Buyer deposits	$8,100
Rentals received and due owners	1,300
	$9,400

The account indicates a
A. surplus of $1,400.
B. surplus of $4,600.
C. shortage of $1,400.
D. shortage of $4,600.

2. What is the difference between origination points and discount points?
A. Discount points are for services.
B. Origination points raise the effective rate of interest.
C. There is no difference.
D. None of these.

3. A broker is instructed not to show a property while the owner, who is white, is away. While the owner is out of town, an African American couple requests to be shown the property. The broker should
A. show the property.
B. refuse to show the property.
C. ask HUD for an exception to the Fair Housing Act.
D. inform the prospects that the home is no longer available to buy.

4. A home was sold on September 30. Taxes are based on a fiscal year ending June 30. Taxes have not been paid for the current fiscal year. If the seller is responsible for the day of closing, which of the following statements is *TRUE* regarding the charges on the closing statement?
A. The buyer owes the seller for three months' taxes.
B. The buyer owes the seller for four months' taxes.
C. The seller owes the buyer for three months' taxes.
D. The seller owes the buyer for four months' taxes.

5. In determining the cost to build various structures on a vacant lot and the value the property would have with the improvements, an appraiser uses the
A. cost approach.
B. development method.
C. land residual method.
D. observed condition method.

6. State-licensed or certified appraisers are required by
A. FIRREA.
B. CERCLA.
C. FIRPTA.
D. Ginnie Mae.

7. Using a capitalization rate of 8%, what is the value of a property having a gross monthly scheduled income of $1,200, a 10% vacancy and collection loss factor, and monthly operating expenses of $280?
A. $10,000
B. $100,000
C. $120,000
D. $144,000

8. Which of the following is a requirement of a qualified mortgage?
A. They are for 40 years or less.
B. Points and fees must be less than 3% of the loan.
C. The down payment must be at least 20%.
D. FHA insurance is required.

9. L deeded property to M; however, the owner of the property was N. N later deeded the property to L. M would have a title problem if L's deed to M were a
   A. grant deed.
   B. quitclaim deed.
   C. special warranty deed.
   D. general warranty deed.

10. Which of the following acronyms relate to SAFE licensing?
    A. MLO
    B. MERS
    C. CERCLA
    D. FIRREA

11. RESPA provides that
    A. a disclosure be made of total finance charge for the term of the loan.
    B. the borrower be given a three-day right of rescission.
    C. predatory lending is prohibited.
    D. a Settlement Statement (HUD-1) be used.

12. A woman derives 90% of income from activities involving the sale of real estate. She is not a licensed real estate salesperson or broker, yet her activities are entirely proper if
    A. she is an employee of a licensed broker.
    B. her activities are restricted to nonresidential real property agency sales.
    C. she sells her own property.
    D. she is paid on a contract fee rather than a commission basis.

13. A home sale included a garden tractor. Ownership of the garden tractor is conveyed by a
    A. packaged deed.
    B. bill of sale.
    C. special warranty deed.
    D. financing statement.

14. A commercial building is leased for $3,200 per month. Assuming annual expenses of taxes at $4,700, utilities at $3,100, maintenance at $4,480, and management costs at $1,920, what is the value of the structure using a capitalization rate of 8%?
    A. $302,500
    B. $320,800
    C. $384,000
    D. $480,000

15. An offer is accepted one day after the offer period expires. The offeror can treat the late acceptance by the offeree as valid because of the principle of
    A. waiver.
    B. novation.
    C. accord and satisfaction.
    D. rescission.

16. The equator platform relates to
    A. government survey.
    B. short sales.
    C. appraisal.
    D. licensing.

17. An accountant has the greatest interest in
    A. book value.
    B. appraisal value.
    C. market value.
    D. assessed value.

18. A business will have to change its form because at least 25% of its income will be derived from passive investment. What is its current form?
    A. LLC
    B. General partnership
    C. S corporation
    D. REIT

19. You are negotiating a very complex sales agreement as the agent of a sophisticated seller. During the negotiation, it becomes obvious that the buyer, who is not represented by an agent and who is a first-time buyer, does not understand the legal and tax consequences of the agreement proposed by your principal. You should
   A. suggest the buyer seek professional advice.
   B. refuse to negotiate any further with the buyer.
   C. not concern yourself with the buyer's ignorance.
   D. analyze the buyer's situation and change your principal's proposal to help the buyer.

20. Which of the following contracts is void?
   A. A contract based on duress
   B. A contract based on fraud as to the subject matter
   C. A contract by a person judged incompetent
   D. A contract entered into because of undue influence

21. The agent innocently repeated false information to a buyer that the agent was given by the seller. Because of this false information, the buyer suffered a loss. The agent has some protection based on
   A. vicarious liability.
   B. the hold harmless clause.
   C. the safety clause.
   D. the arbitration clause.

22. P sells Greenacres to Q, who does not take possession or record. P then borrows against the property, giving a recorded mortgage to R. P later transfers title to S, without any consideration for the transfer, and S records the deed. What are the rights of the parties?
   A. P retains title because Q did not record and S did not pay consideration.
   B. Q has title subject to the mortgage to R.
   C. Q has title clear of the mortgage.
   D. S has title with a mortgage to R.

23. A property manager, in deciding about rents, would consider the
   A. capitalization approach.
   B. market comparison approach.
   C. cost approach.
   D. residual approach.

24. A seller's agent breached a fiduciary duty. The agent
   A. refused to follow illegal instructions of the principal.
   B. cannot remember what became of the $10,000 cash deposit the agent received.
   C. presented an offer to the owners for less than the list price, although the owners had indicated that they did not want to see such an offer.
   D. refused to tell a buyer why the seller was selling.

25. A homeowner cannot cancel private mortgage insurance until the
   A. principal balance is reduced to 75% of the purchase value.
   B. principal balance is reduced to 80% of the purchase value.
   C. principal balance is reduced to 90% of the purchase value.
   D. loan is paid in full.

26. L wishes to build a rectangular structure 30 feet wide, 160 feet deep, and 24 feet high with a flat roof. M offers to build the structure for $8.50 per square foot. P offers to build the structure for $0.375 per cubic foot. Whose offer is lower and by how much?
   A. M's by $2,400
   B. M's by $4.75 per square foot
   C. P's by $2,400
   D. P's by $1.62 per square foot

27. A broker is involved in a controlled business arrangement when the broker
   A. personally owns the building and rents space to his real estate firm.
   B. owns a mortgage company that rents space within the real estate sales office and works with the broker's buyers.
   C. acts as a dual agent.
   D. represents only one buyer.

28. As used by lenders, qualifying ratios refer to
    A. collateral.
    B. capacity.
    C. character.
    D. points.

29. A deed was signed with an *X*. The deed is
    A. voidable.
    B. void.
    C. unenforceable.
    D. valid if witnessed.

30. In a real estate transaction, who is the seller's agent when the listing office has a single agency?
    A. The salesperson that obtained the listing
    B. The broker of the salesperson who obtained the listing
    C. The cooperating broker who obtained the offer to purchase
    D. The MLS

31. A limited partner was held personally liable for the debts of the partnership because
    A. the partnership was not incorporated.
    B. the partner took an active role in management.
    C. there were fewer than 75 investors.
    D. the partnership had invested in mortgages.

32. A property manager of a mall is worried that a prospective tenant will not be able to generate the gross that the manager expects, even though the tenant has agreed to the percentage lease and minimum rent. To protect the owner in this situation, the property manager would include which clause in the lease?
    A. Exculpatory
    B. Holdover
    C. Recapture
    D. Right of first refusal

33. A buyer entered into a contract to purchase a home through a broker. Before closing, the buyer asked the broker whether he could enter the residence and paint, as well as make minor repairs. The broker should
    A. refuse the request.
    B. allow the buyer to enter if the buyer agrees to prorate settlement to date of possession.
    C. relay the request to the owner.
    D. allow buyer to enter only if a licensed contractor is used.

34. A lender's requirement for a loan that the borrower retain a minimum balance would result in a
    A. collaterally secured loan.
    B. compensating balance.
    C. discount loan.
    D. construction loan.

35. A written promise made for a written promise of another is
    A. a unilateral contract.
    B. a consideration.
    C. an accord and satisfaction.
    D. a novation.

36. Zoning that sets forth building height and setback limitations is
    A. incentive zoning.
    B. bulk zoning.
    C. spot zoning.
    D. conservation zoning.

37. A property manager would prefer shorter-term residential leases when
    A. there is a high vacancy factor.
    B. interest rates and inflation are increasing.
    C. the property is subject to rent control.
    D. overbuilding is likely.

38. A commercial lot was 200 feet deep before it lost 50 feet of its rear depth because of eminent domain. If the value of the lot before the taking was $600,000, using the 4-3-2-1 approach, what is the lot value after the taking?
    A. $450,000
    B. $500,000
    C. $540,000
    D. $560,000

39. The greatest liquidity in a real estate investment is with
    A. an LLC.
    B. a REIT.
    C. a close corporation.
    D. a general partnership.

40. A broker received a full price offer on one of her listings. She recommended acceptance, and the offer was accepted. After acceptance, she discovered that a huge mall was to be built on the adjacent parcel and zoning was to be changed from agriculture to commercial. What should the broker do?
    A. Recommend that the owners renounce the agreement
    B. Notify the owner of the facts
    C. Contact the buyer to renegotiate the price
    D. Remain silent as the agreement has been reached

41. A purchaser paid points to get a loan, resulting in
    A. the effective rate of interest exceeding the nominal rate.
    B. an increase in the nominal rate of interest.
    C. the nominal rate of interest exceeding the effective rate.
    D. an increase in monthly payments.

42. What type of agency could be created by inaction of the principal?
    A. Express agency
    B. Agency by estoppel
    C. Agency by ratification
    D. Designated agency

43. The variance in the VA funding fee is based on the
    A. down payment.
    B. amount of the loan.
    C. amount of the VA guarantee.
    D. veteran's credit rating.

44. In what type of business entity would every investor avoid personal liability?
    A. Limited partnership
    B. General partnership
    C. Joint venture
    D. LLC

45. A note was given with a mortgage. The purpose of the note was to
    A. be security for the mortgage.
    B. evidence the debt.
    C. provide a lien on the property.
    D. create a real property interest.

46. A fee-simple determinable differs from a fee simple on condition subsequent in that for a fee simple determinable,
    A. the duration may be determined from the deed.
    B. the grantor must physically retake the premises.
    C. failure to assert rights will result in the loss of the rights.
    D. it can only involve personal property.

47. An advantage of seller financing to the seller could be
    A. a government guarantee.
    B. that profit is taxed in the year received.
    C. the avoidance of capital gains tax.
    D. no tax on interest received.

48. After notice to neighboring owners, a public hearing is held before granting
    A. a building permit.
    B. a zoning variance.
    C. title insurance coverage.
    D. a tax shelter.

49. A broker was entitled to a commission when the owner sold the property without the agent after expiration of a listing. The reason for the broker's rights was the
    A. estoppel certificate.
    B. safety clause.
    C. nondisturbance clause.
    D. escalator clause.

50. A broker listed a home for $105,000 with an exclusive-right-to-sell listing that specified a 6% commission. While the listing was in effect, the broker received a verbal offer of $100,000. The broker relayed the offer to the owner, who signed a written acceptance. The broker transmitted the acceptance to the buyer but was informed that the buyer had found another property and would not complete this purchase. The broker is entitled to
   A. $6,000 commission from the buyer.
   B. $6,000 commission from the seller.
   C. specific performance from the buyer.
   D. nothing.

51. A lot has three possible uses. As a gas station, an investment of $342,000 would provide a net income of $27,832; as a fast-food location, an investment of $620,000 would yield a net income of $52,800; and leased as a parking lot, the site with improvements of $45,000 would yield $12,000 net income. Assuming a capitalization rate of 8% for all three investments, which use would result in the highest and best use of the land?
   A. Gas station
   B. Fast-food restaurant
   C. Parking lot
   D. Leaving property undeveloped

52. A lessor wished to end a tenancy. The lessee is *BEST* protected if the lessee had a
   A. tenancy at will.
   B. tenancy at sufferance.
   C. month-to-month tenancy.
   D. tenancy for years.

53. A man's activities consist of originating loans secured by real property using his own funds and then selling the loans to lending institutions and investors while retaining loan-servicing responsibilities. The man's activity is that of a
   A. mortgage broker.
   B. mortgage banker.
   C. mortgage loan correspondent.
   D. mortgagor.

54. A lender must inform the borrower that
   A. paying more than required reduces total interest costs.
   B. the loan and the servicing of the loan may be assigned.
   C. a longer loan term means more interest paid.
   D. a greater down-payment would mean lower monthly payments.

55. A 10-year loan has equal amounts applied to principal each month. The loan is for $100,000, and the interest rate is 6%. What is the amount of the first loan payment?
   A. $416.66
   B. $833.33
   C. $1,333.33
   D. $1,433.33

56. A tenant's five-year lease expired three years ago, but the tenant has remained on the premises paying rent each month. The tenancy is
   A. at will.
   B. at sufferance.
   C. periodic.
   D. for years.

57. Participation certificates refer to
   A. partnerships.
   B. securities.
   C. cooperatives.
   D. limited partnerships.

58. Four houses sold for a total of $386,000. The second house sold for $14,000 more than the first house, and the third house sold for $6,000 more than the second house. The fourth house sold for $9,000 more than the third house. What did the fourth house sell for?
   A. $80,750
   B. $94,750
   C. $100,750
   D. $109,750

59. What damages can an owner obtain from a trespasser when no actual damages occurred?
    A. Liquidated
    B. Injunction
    C. Nominal
    D. Compensatory

60. There are four units in a common interest development. The bylaws of the homeowners association provide for the apportionment of shared common area costs in proportion to the original purchase price of the units. The original sale prices were $87,500, $75,800, $62,900, and $58,500. If the common area annual costs come to $17,800, what is the share for the *MOST* expensive unit?
    A. $3,560
    B. $4,760
    C. $4,870
    D. $5,470

61. In accordance with the Americans with Disabilities Act, a place of public accommodation includes
    A. one to four residential units.
    B. all residential units.
    C. a retail store.
    D. only property built after 1988.

62. The Federal Reserve uses open-market transactions to
    A. discount loans.
    B. increase government spending.
    C. change bank reserve requirements.
    D. buy and sell government securities.

63. A lease clause in which a mortgagee agrees to honor a lease should the mortgagee foreclose is
    A. a nondisturbance clause.
    B. an attachment.
    C. a subrogation.
    D. a subordination.

64. The distance between section 12 in one township and section 7 in the adjacent township to the east is
    A. 5 miles.
    B. 6 miles.
    C. 10 miles.
    D. 11 miles.

65. A woman deeds property to a man. After the conveyance, the parties agree to rescind the transaction. How can they accomplish this?
    A. By writing "canceled" on the deed and both signing it
    B. By the man returning the deed to the woman
    C. By the man giving a new deed to the woman
    D. By destroying the deed

66. To accommodate a disability, a tenant had handrails installed in the public hallways leading to the tenant's apartment. As to the installation of the handrails, the
    A. landlord must reimburse the tenant's costs.
    B. tenant must remove them when the tenancy ends.
    C. tenant must post a bond for removal costs.
    D. tenant has acted within the law.

67. An example of statutory dedication is
    A. a deed containing a reservation.
    B. recording an approved subdivision map showing areas dedicated to public use.
    C. eminent domain.
    D. deeding property to a government entity.

68. RESPA requirements include
    A. a limitation on brokerage fees.
    B. a prohibition of a broker affiliation with a provider of services for a real estate closing.
    C. the prohibition of a broker's receiving a referral fee from a lender.
    D. maximum allowable interest.

69. Required seller disclosures include
    A. flood hazard areas and prior flood disaster assistance.
    B. the reason for the sale.
    C. the amount of commission the seller is required to pay.
    D. former residents who had AIDS.

70. The W½ of the NW¼ of the NW¼ of the SE¼ of the SW¼ of a section is to be paved for parking at a cost of $1.14 per square foot. The total paving cost will be
    A. $15,519.
    B. $31,035.
    C. $62,073.
    D. $124,146.

71. A broker received a $10,000 check as earnest money with an offer to purchase. The broker has kept the check uncashed in the office safe for over a week. The broker's actions are proper if the
    A. listing did not require earnest money.
    B. broker was insured for any loss.
    C. buyer requested it not be cashed until acceptance.
    D. check was made out personally to the broker.

72. An executed real estate purchase contract could be voided based on
    A. a unilateral mistake of fact.
    B. a mutual mistake of fact.
    C. lack of consideration.
    D. the fact that the agreement was verbal.

73. An earnest-money deposit is given with an offer to purchase to
    A. validate the contract for recording.
    B. compensate the broker if the offer is not accepted.
    C. indicate good faith of purchaser.
    D. cover settlement costs.

74. Without the owner's permission, a seller's agent told a buyer that the seller was desperate and would lose the property to foreclosure unless it could be quickly sold. Which fiduciary duty did the agent break?
    A. Care
    B. Loyalty
    C. Disclosure
    D. Obedience

75. A tenant verbally agrees to lease a landlord's store for six months starting next month. A week before she is to take occupancy, the tenant notifies the landlord that she is revoking the agreement because she has found a better location at a lower rent. What are the rights of the parties?
    A. The lease is valid, and the landlord can hold the tenant to the agreement.
    B. The tenant is liable for three weeks' rent because she failed to give a 30-day notice.
    C. The lease is void because it was verbal.
    D. The lease is voidable because it was verbal.

76. A mortgagee will benefit by a blanket mortgage because of
    A. shorter foreclosure time.
    B. personal liability.
    C. the guarantee.
    D. greater security.

77. The lender must provide the borrower with a booklet prepared by the Federal Reserve when financing involves
    A. more than one lender.
    B. balloon payments.
    C. an adjustable rate loan.
    D. other than federally related financing.

78. When listing a property for sale, a seller tells a broker that he will not sell to a particular buyer, whom the seller has had problems with. The broker receives an offer from that buyer for the seller's property. The broker must
    A. return the offer to the buyer with no explanation.
    B. return the offer to the buyer, giving the reason.
    C. accept but not present the offer from the buyer.
    D. present the offer to the seller.

79. Taxes are paid on a calendar year. The seller paid taxes of $1,788.50 for the year. The closing was on February 25, with the seller responsible for the date of closing. The closing statement will reflect a
    A. seller credit of $274.
    B. seller credit of $1,514.10.
    C. seller credit of $1,606.
    D. buyer debit of $274.50.

80. The absence of a "time is of the essence" clause in a purchase agreement means
    A. there is no time limitation for performance.
    B. performance must be by the dates specified.
    C. there shall be a 30-day leeway for all dates.
    D. performance must be within a reasonable period of time of dates specified.

DIFFICULTY LEVEL V ANSWERS

1. **(C)** There is only $8,000 in the account, and there should be $9,400. (180–183)

2. **(D)** It is the opposite of answers (A) and (B). (80, 170)

3. **(B)** This refusal is based on obeying the principal's instructions that were reasonable and did not discriminate. (109)

4. **(C)** Because the seller had possession during this period. The actual days the seller is responsible for is 92 (31 days for July, 31 days for August, and 30 days for September). (251–252)

5. **(B)** Determine the cost to build for each use and deduct the cost from the value the property would have if built, which gives the value of the land for that use. It would indicate the highest and best use. (74)

6. **(A)** Federal Financial Institutions Reform, Recovery and Enforcement Act. (76)

7. **(C)** $1,200 monthly gross – $120 (10 percent monthly vacancy and collection loss) – $280 monthly operating expenses = $800 monthly net. $800 × 12 = $9,600 annual net. $9,600 ÷ 0.08 cap rate = $120,000. (72)

8. **(B)** And 30 years or less plus ability to repay. (175)

9. **(B)** The other deeds would convey after-acquired title. A quitclaim deed only transfers grantor's interest at that time. (48)

10. **(A)** The Federal Secure and Fair Enforcement Mortgage Licensing Act (SAFE) requires mortgage loan originators (MLO) to meet minimum standards. (149)

11. **(D)** The others deal with the Truth in Lending Act. (146)

12. **(C)** A person need not be licensed to sell her own property. Not acting as an agent for others. (228)

13. **(B)** Used to transfer title to personal property. (46)

14. **(A)** $3,200 rent × 12 = $38,400 per year. (72)

    $4,700 taxes + $3,100 utilities + $4,480 maintenance + $1,920 management = $14,200

    $38,400 – $14,200 = $24,200 net

    $24,200 ÷ 0.08 = $302,500

15. **(A)** A person can waive any provision that is for his sole benefit. (104)

16. **(B)** An online short sale request and authorization site. (164)

17. **(A)** Other values are of little interest to an accountant. (65)

18. **(C)** An S corporation cannot have more than 20% passive income. (15)

19. **(A)** Duty of fair dealing with buyer. (109–110)

20. **(C)** The others are voidable. (98, 100)

21. **(B)** The hold-harmless clause entitles the agent to be compensated for the loss from the principal. (114)

22. **(B)** Because R had no notice, R has a prior lien. A person receiving title by gift does not take priority over an unrecorded deed for value. (49–50)

23. **(B)** Market rents are considered for comparable property. (69–70)

24. **(B)** This is a breach of the duty of care (obvious negligence). (109)

25. **(B)** And the mortgage is current on payments. (174)

26. **(A)** 30' × 24' × 160' = 115,200 cubic feet; 115,200 × \$0.375 = \$43,200. 30' × 160' = 4,800 sq. ft.; 4,800 × \$8.50 = \$40,800; \$43,200 − \$40,800 = \$2,400. (252–254)

27. **(B)** The broker controls the service provider. (147)

28. **(B)** To determine if buyer qualifies for a loan. (179)

29. **(D)** An illiterate grantor can convey title if the grantor has capacity to convey. (47)

30. **(B)** The broker, not the salesperson, is the agent (in a designated agency, the salesperson could be the agent). (106)

31. **(B)** Lost limited liability because of active roll. (14)

32. **(C)** If the tenant is a poor operator and is unable to reach required gross, the lease can be terminated. (198)

33. **(C)** This is not the agent's decision. The agent has a duty to relay request to the owner. (109)

34. **(B)** The result is to increase the effective rate of interest received by the lenders because the borrower receives a lower rate of interest on the deposit balance than is paid on the loan. (170)

35. **(B)** A promise is consideration for promise of another. It is a bilateral contract. (97, 98)

36. **(B)** Zoning for development density. (31)

37. **(B)** As renewals will likely be for higher rents. (196)

38. **(C)** The 4-3-2-1 approach to depth valuation is that 40% of the value is in the first 25% of the depth, 30% in the next 25% of depth, 20% of value in the next 25% of depth, and 10% of value in the rear 25% of depth. The lot lost the rear 25% of the lot, or 10% of its \$600,000 value. (75)

39. **(B)** REIT shares can be freely traded on stock exchanges. (15–16)

40. **(B)** The disclosure duty of material facts continues to closing the transaction. (109)

41. **(A)** The nominal rate is the rate named, but the effective rate is the APR, which considers points and costs. (143)

42. **(B)** The owner could be barred from denying an agency if the owner failed to notify a party the owner knew believed an agency existed. (108)

43. **(A)** The lower the down payment, the higher the funding fee. (178)

44. **(D)** All have limited liability. In a limited partnership, the general partner is liable. (15)

45. **(B)** A note is the primary evidence of the debt, and the lien (mortgage or trust deed) is given to secure the note. (161)

46. **(A)** The grantor must physically retake the premises, or the right will be lost, with a fee simple on condition subsequent. (7)

47. **(B)** Can spread capital gain over a number of years. (81–82)

48. **(B)** As well as conditional use permit and rezoning. (30)

49. **(B)** Provides for entitlement to commission if sold within stated period after expiration of listing to a party the agent had negotiated with. (114)

50. **(D)** A verbal offer for real estate, when accepted, does not result in a contract. (99–100)

51. **(C)** This is development method. Determine value of developed property and deduct development cost to find land value for the use. (74)

Gas station: $27,832 ÷ 0.08 = $347,900 value – $342,000 (development cost) = $5,900 attributable to land.

Fast food: $52,800 ÷ 0.08 = $660,000 – $620,00 = $40,000 attributable to land.

Parking lot: $12,000 ÷ 0.08 = $150,000 – $45,000 = $105,000 attributable to land.

52. **(D)** The tenant knows the fixed period of tenancy. (195)

53. **(B)** Unlike a mortgage broker, the mortgage banker or mortgage company uses its own funds to fund loans. (174)

54. **(B)** Required by RESPA. (147)

55. **(C)** This is a loan with equal principal payments plus interest. Since interest will decline each month, total payments will decrease. The principal is $100,000, and there are 120 payments in 10 years, so $100,000 ÷ 120 = $833.33 applied to principal every month. The loan is plus interest, so 0.06 × $100,000 = $6,000 per year, or $500 for the first month. $833.33 + $500 = $1,333.33 first month's payment. (248–249)

56. **(C)** It is a tenancy at sufferance until landlord accepts rent, and then it becomes a periodic tenancy. (195)

57. **(B)** Issued by Freddie Mac and backed by a pool of mortgages. (178)

58. **(D)** H + (H + $14,000) + (H + $20,000) + (H + $29,000) = $386,000.

4 houses + $63,000 = $386,000

$386,000 – $63,000 = $323,000

$323,000 + 4 = $80,750

1st house: $80,750

2nd house: $94,750 ($80,750 + $14,000)

3rd house: $100,750 ($94,750 + $6,000)

4th house: $109,750 ($100,750 + $9,000) (248)

59. **(C)** A token amount. While an injunction is possible, an injunction is not damages. (103)

60. **(D)** Total purchase price. $284,700. To find percentage, divide the part by the whole. $87,500 ÷ 284,700 = 0.3073, or 30.73%. $17,800 shared cost × 0.3073 = $5,470. (248)

61. **(C)** Nonresidential affecting commerce. (140)

62. **(D)** To increase or decrease the money supply. (167)

63. **(A)** Without the clause, the foreclosure of a prior mortgage or trust deed will terminate the lease. (198)

64. **(C)** Sections 7 through 11 (five sections) in the first section, plus sections 8 through 12 (five sections) in the adjoining section. (5)

65. **(C)** A deed is only used once. Since the deed to the man gave title to him, he must deed back to the woman. (46)

66. **(D)** And need not restore modifications to public areas. (139)

67. **(B)** The recording of a map is considered dedication. (42)

68. **(C)** Prohibits kickbacks. (146)

69. **(A)** Federal requirement. (132)

70. **(C)** Going backward the parcel will be found to contain 1.25 acres. 43,560 × 1.25 = 54,450 sq. ft. × $1.14 = $62,073. (6, 252–254)

71. **(C)** Before acceptance, broker can hold check uncashed at buyer's written direction. (221)

72. **(B)** Basis for rescission. Lack of consideration could void an executory contract. (98)

73. **(C)** Not required for a valid contract. (222)

74. **(B)** Had a duty to keep information confidential, and telling about the owner breaches owner loyalty. (109)

75. **(A)** The lease could be completed within one year, so it need not be in writing. (99–100)

76. **(D)** Blanket mortgage covers more than one property. (169)

77. **(C)** Entitled to a copy of *Consumer Handbook on Adjustable-Rate Mortgages*. (147)

78. **(D)** Every offer must be presented to the owner unless it is clearly frivolous. (109)

79. **(B)** The seller is responsible for 31 days in January and 25 days in February, a total of 56 days. Daily tax proration is $1,788.50 ÷ 365 = $4.90 per day. $4.90 × 56 = $274.40. The seller paid $1,788.50 and used $274.40 and so is entitled to a credit of $1,514.50. The buyer is debited this amount. (251–252)

80. **(D)** The dates are not firm as courts can allow reasonable delays. (115)

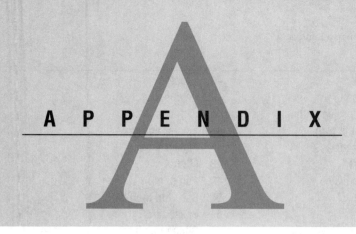

A P P E N D I X

While not included in the Pearson VUE content outline, construction-related questions are often included in the state portion of examinations. This appendix is an aid for the state portion of your real estate examination.

CONSTRUCTION DIAGRAM

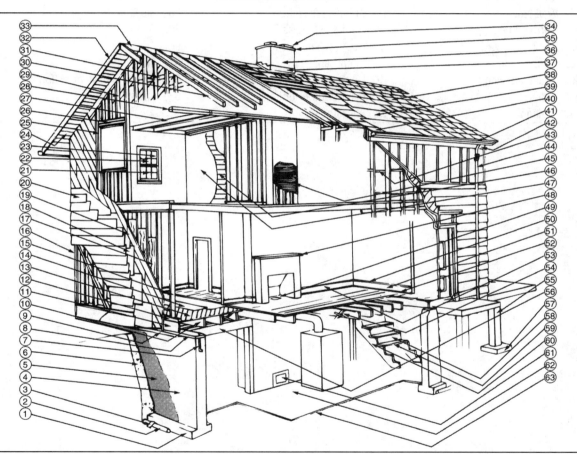

1. Footing	22. Muntin	43. Firestop
2. Foundation drain tile	23. Window sash	44. Downspout
3. Crushed washed stone	24. Eave (roof projection)	45. Laths
4. Foundation wall	25. Window jamb trim	46. Plaster board
5. Dampproofing or weatherproofing	26. Window header	47. Plaster finish
6. Backfill	27. Ceiling joist	48. Mantel
7. Anchor bolt	28. Top and tie plates	49. Ash dump
8. Sill plate	29. Gable stud	50. Base top moulding
9. Termite shield	30. Rafters	51. Baseboard
10. Floor joist	31. Collar ties	52. Shoe moulding
11. Band or box beam	32. Gable end of roof	53. Finish moulding
12. Sole plate	33. Ridge beam	54. Cross bridging
13. Subflooring	34. Chimney flues	55. Pier
14. Building paper	35. Chimney cap	56. Girder
15. Wall stud	36. Chimney	57. Footing
16. Corner studs	37. Chimney flashing	58. Riser
17. Insulation	38. Roofing shingles	59. Tread
18. House wrap	39. Roofing felt/ice and water membrane	60. Stringer
19. Wall sheathing	40. Roof sheathing	61. Cleanout door
20. Siding	41. Eve trough or gutter	62. Concrete basement floor
21. Mullion	42. Frieze board	63. Crushed washed stone

GLOSSARY

This glossary has been designed as a quick reference to help students understand the language of the real estate profession. A complete vocabulary review before your state examination also will serve to bring together the many different facets of real estate that you have been studying. Some of the terms included may not apply to your state because they may be regional in nature. Terms that you are less likely to encounter may not be in the text material but have been included in this glossary, both to aid your general understanding and to allow the glossary to serve as a resource tool.

As an aid, remember that words ending in "-or" are givers: *donor, grantor,* and *optionor.* Words ending in "-ee" are receivers: *donee, grantee,* and *optionee.*

100% location   The best retail location within a community.

100% office   Office where salespersons pay a regular fee to the broker but receive 100% of the commissions they earn.

abandonment   Voluntarily giving up possession of property or a claim or right.

abatement   A legal action to stop a nuisance. Also can be a reduction of a property tax assessment.

absorption rate   The rate at which new or vacant space (such as office space) will become occupied.

abstract of judgment   A condensation of a court judgment. When recorded, the judgment becomes a general lien on the property of the debtor within the county where recorded.

abstract   A history of every recorded document dealing with a property. It is examined to determine whether there is marketable title.

abstractive method   A means of obtaining land value by deducting the value of improvements from the total property value.

accelerated depreciation   Any method of depreciation for tax purposes that gives greater initial depreciation than the straight-line method. Accelerated depreciation is no longer allowed.

acceleration clause   A provision in a note making all payments due on the happening of a certain event (such as missing a payment or selling the property).

acceptance   An act or agreement that forms a contract.

accession   Obtaining title as a result of attaching or joining property to other property.

accommodation party   A third person (cosigner) who signs a negotiable instrument agreeing to be personally liable to the payee.

accord and satisfaction   The act of accepting a different consideration than agreed; for example, if there is a dispute as to performance and one party accepts less than what was bargained for originally.

Accredited Management Organization (AMO)   A professional designation awarded to a management company by the Institute of Real Estate Management.

Accredited Resident Manager (ARM)   A professional designation for resident property managers awarded by the Institute of Real Estate Management.

accretion   A gradual buildup of soil by action of water or wind.

accrued depreciation   Depreciation to date; measured by the difference between the replacement cost new and the present value.

acknowledgment   A declaration customarily made before a notary, certifying that the signing of an instrument is the signer's own free act.

acre   A measure of land equal to 43,560 square feet.

action in personam   A legal action against a person. When recorded, a judgment from such an action is a general lien against all of a debtor's property in the county where recorded.

action in rem   A legal action against property. When recorded, a judgment from such an action is a specific lien against the particular property involved in the action.

actual notice   Personal knowledge of an interest or instrument.

ad valorem   A tax according to value; real property taxes are considered to be ad valorem taxes.

ademption   Disposal of property by a testator before death. It defeats the rights of a specific beneficiary under the will. (The beneficiary is not entitled to the sale proceeds or value.)

adjustable-rate mortgage (ARM)   A mortgage bearing a rate of interest subject to change (based on a particular index) during the term of the loan. ARMs generally have caps on the interest that can be charged.

adjusted basis   Acquisition cost less depreciation plus cost of improvements. The adjusted basis is deducted from the sales price to determine gain or loss.

adjusted gross income   Gross income adjusted for a vacancy factor and collection loss.

adjusted market price   The adjustment of a comparable property's sales price to account for differences in features and amenities of a property under appraisal (using the market comparison approach).

administrator   A man appointed by a probate court to administer the estate of a deceased; a female appointee is an administratrix.

advance commitment   A lender agreement to provide permanent financing upon completion of a construction project.

advance fees   Fees paid in advance of services rendered.

adverse possession   A means of obtaining title from another by open, hostile, and continuous use for a statutory period of time. In some states, adverse possession also requires payment of taxes.

aesthetic zoning   Zoning for conformance appearance such as architectural style requirements.

affidavit   A statement sworn to under oath or by affirmation before a notary.

affirmation   A formal declaration as to the truthfulness of a statement; made by a person whose religious beliefs prohibit swearing under oath.

affirmative easement   An easement that allows the easement holder a right of use over the land of another.

affordability index   An index of the National Association of REALTORS® that measures the median family income ability to support a mortgage for the median price home. An index of 100 means that the median income is equal to the amount necessary to afford the median price home.

after-acquired interest   An interest acquired by a grantor after he or she has conveyed property. Under some deeds, after-acquired interest is said to pass to the grantee.

age-life tables   Appraisal tables that indicate the economic life for various types of structures.

agency by estoppel   An agency created when the principal's words or conduct lead another to believe in the agency and thereby act to the other's detriment.

agency by ratification   An agency created by a principal approving an unauthorized act of another.

agency coupled with an interest   An irrevocable agency under which the agent has an interest in the subject matter of the agency.

agency   A contractual relationship in which one person (an agent) represents another (a principal).

agent   A person representing and acting in behalf of another.

air lot   A described airspace over a property that is subject to being transferred.

air rights   The rights of property owners to the reasonable use of the airspace over their property. Air rights are considered to be real property and can be separately leased or conveyed.

alienation   A transfer of property or property rights.

alluvion   Soil added gradually to land by action of water or wind (accretion). The soil belongs to the land it is added to by this accretion process.

alteration   Modification of a contract or note by one party without the consent of the other. Alteration voids the contract.

amend escrow instructions   A change in the escrow instructions after they have been signed. The signatures of both buyer and seller are required to amend the instructions.

amenities   Features of a property that enhance the satisfaction and use of the property; for example, an extra bath, a flower garden, mature shade trees.

American Land Title Association (ALTA)   A type of title insurance policy providing extended coverage to the lender. The same extended coverage also may be available for the buyer.

American Taxpayer Relief Act of 2012   Increased capital gains for high-income taxpayers.

Americans with Disabilities Act (ADA)   Provides for handicapped accessibility for places of public accommodation.

amortized loan   A loan that is liquidated by equal payments.

anchor bolt   A bolt that ties the mudsill (the lowest board in a house) to the foundation.

anchor tenant   A major tenant, usually located at one end (or both ends) of a shopping center. Lesser shops benefit by being between or close to anchor tenants.

ancillary probate   A probate for real property located in a state other than the domicile of the deceased.

annexation   Adding to something, as when a city annexes outlying land. Personal property can become real property by being joined to it.

annual percentage rate (APR)   An interest rate expressed in simple interest considering all finance charges.

anticipation   Value changes based on anticipated future use and income.

anticipatory breach   An action or a statement of a party before the performance due date that indicates the party will breach the contract. The other party can bring suit upon anticipatory breach without waiting for an actual breach.

antimerger clause   A clause in a mortgage that prevents loss of lien priority should the lienholder receive a deed. Otherwise, a deed in lieu of foreclosure would convey title subject to later liens.

The Appraisal Foundation   Organization responsible for the *Uniform Standards of Professional Appraisal Practice (USPAP)*.

appraisal   An estimate of market value.

appurtenance   A right, benefit, or attachment that transfers with real property; for example, buildings, easement rights, and water rights.

arbitrage   Taking advantage of the interest rate differential by buying at one interest rate and selling at a higher interest rate by either land contract or the use of a wraparound loan.

arbitration   A nonjudicial process for resolution of disputes whereby the parties agree to abide by a decision made by a third person.

arm's-length transaction   A bargain freely entered into without duress, undue influence, or collusion (deceit).

articles of incorporation   Filed with the state, they set forth the activities a corporation may engage in.

artificial monument   A surveyor point for metes-and-bounds descriptions that is man-made, such as an iron stake, a fence, or a canal.

as is   A phrase intended to mean that the seller does not warrant a property's condition. Such a phrase, however, does not protect the seller in cases of concealment or fraud. Some courts hold that it applies only to readily observable defects, not to known but undisclosed latent defects.

asbestos   A mineral formerly used for insulation and in housing products. Asbestos dust is a hazardous material.

assemblage   The act of bringing adjacent parcels of land under one ownership; the opposite of subdividing. Assemblage usually results in an increase in value. *See also* plottage.

assessed value   Value placed by a tax assessor.

assessment   The process of valuing a property for taxation purposes.

assets   Property owned by or owed to a business or person.

assignee   One who receives an assignment.

assignment of rents   A mortgage clause that allows the mortgagee to collect rents during the foreclosure period. Could also be a transfer of rents to a third party.

assignment   The complete transfer of one person's rights to another. The assignee takes over the rights and duties of the assignor.

assignor   One who makes an assignment.

associate broker   Person who has met real estate broker requirements but works for a broker in a salesperson capacity.

assumption   The act of taking over the responsibilities for an obligation and agreeing to be liable personally for the obligation. A deficiency judgment might be possible against an assuming party.

attachment   The legal seizure of property under court order before a judgment when there is belief that the property will not be available after judgment.

attestation   The act of witnessing; to attest is to bear witness. Formal wills require witnesses.

attorney-in-fact   A person operating as an agent (not an attorney-at-law) under a power of attorney.

attornment   An agreement between owner and sublessee that the owner will recognize the sublease and the sublessee will pay the owner should the sublessor's interests be foreclosed.

attractive nuisance   A doctrine holding the owner of land liable for injury to children due to the unsafe condition of property where property is likely to attract children as trespassers.

avulsion   The sudden tearing away or loss of real property by action of water, such as a river's changing course.

axial growth   City growth along transportation routes from the city center (resembles the spokes of a wheel).

back-end ratio   The ratio of gross income to loan payments (PITI) plus long-term installment debt payments. Used to qualify buyers.

bailment   Giving possession of personal property to another but retaining title; for example, storing goods in a warehouse, renting a trailer, giving existing mortgages to a lender as security for a loan.

balance sheet   A financial statement showing assets and liabilities. The balance sheet shows net worth.

balloon payment   A final installment of an unamortized loan that exceeds the previous payments.

banker's interest   Interest based on a 30-day month and a 360-day year.

bankruptcy   A legal procedure to eliminate unsecured debts. To eliminate secured debts, the security must be surrendered.

bargain and sale deed   A deed for consideration that uses the terms *bargain* and *sale*. It contains no warranties other than an implied interest by the grantor.

base line   The principal east and west surveyor lines established by government survey.

baseboard   A molding placed against the wall on the floor around a room.

basis   Cost plus improvements less depreciation. Used to determine profit for tax purposes on sale.

batten   Wood strips used to cover joints; used in board-and-batten siding.

beam   A horizontal structural member giving support to a structure.

bearer paper   A negotiable instrument made out to cash or bearer that can be transferred without endorsement.

bearing wall   A wall with a footing under it that bears the load of the structure.

benchmark   A marker placed by a government surveyor showing elevation above sea level and used by surveyors as a reference point.

beneficiary   The person receiving payments under a deed of trust; similar to a mortgagee.

beneficiary deed   A deed that does not take effect until death of grantor (allowed in several states).

beneficiary statement   A statement of a lender of the balance due on a loan.

bequeath   To give personal property by will.

bequest   Personal property that is given by will.

betterment   An actual improvement (not a repair) to real estate.

bilateral contract   A mutual exchange of promises whereby each promise is consideration for the other promise.

bill of sale   A written agreement transferring title to personal property.

binder   Insurance coverage given by an agent before the issuance of a policy or payment of a premium.

blanket mortgage A mortgage covering more than one property.

blended mortgage rate A refinance rate that is less than the current market rate but more than the old rate.

blind advertising An advertisement that fails to indicate that the advertiser is a real estate agent.

blind pool A syndicate in which the property to be purchased will be selected after the money has been raised.

blockbusting The act of inducing panic selling for gain by exploiting the fear of loss in value because minority members are moving into an area. Blockbusting is illegal under the Civil Rights Act of 1968.

blue-sky laws Security registration requirements to protect consumers against investments in fraudulent schemes.

board foot A unit of lumber measurement equal to 144 cubic inches (1' × 1' × 1").

book value Cost plus improvements less depreciation taken; the value assigned an asset for bookkeeping purposes.

boot Money, personal property, or debt relief given to even off a trade. Boot is taxable to the person receiving it.

breach The breaking of a law or contract.

broker A licensed agent employed by a principal for real estate transactions. Only a broker can employ a salesperson.

broker's net income An income figure that does not consider a vacancy factor, collection costs, or management expenses.

brownfields Areas where soil has been contaminated by chemical discharges.

Btu (British thermal unit) The unit of heat needed to raise one pound of water one degree Fahrenheit. The Btu is used to rate the capacity of heating and air-conditioning units.

budget mortgage A loan by which the borrower pays one-twelfth of the estimated property tax and insurance payment with each monthly payment.

buffer zone An area separating different land uses, often a green area.

building line The setback from the lot line.

building permit Construction permit issued by local building inspector office.

bulk sales act A part of the Uniform Commercial Code; requires recording and publication of sales not in the course of normal business. It applies to the sale of stock in trade when a business is sold. If the act is not complied with, the sale is void as to the vendor's creditors, who can then treat the stock as if the vendor still owned it.

bulk zoning Zoning for density with height, setback, and open space requirements.

bundle of rights All rights incidental to ownership, such as rights to lease, use, encumber, sell, exclude, and so forth.

business opportunity A business including stock, fixtures, and goodwill.

buy down A financing technique in which a seller makes a purchase more attractive by paying a lender points to lower the effective interest rate on a mortgage.

buyer agency Agency where agent is the buyer's representative rather than the seller's agent.

buyer's agent An agent representing the buyer rather than the seller.

buyers' market A market condition characterized by more sellers than buyers, so buyers have a more commanding position.

bylaws The rules of how a corporation will be governed; sets forth the authority of its officers.

CAN-SPAM Act Protects consumers from unsolicited and misleading emails.

cap A limit, usually on the interest rate or rate increases, on an adjustable-rate mortgage (ARM).

capital asset A physical asset such as land, a building, and equipment, usually for a business or trade. Capital assets other than land may be depreciated.

capital gain Profit from the sale of a business or an investment property. Capital gains held over one year are treated favorably for income tax purposes.

capital loss Loss from the sale of a capital asset or other real property. For tax purposes, there is no deductible loss from the sale of a residence, although a gain is taxable.

capitalization method   An appraisal approach whereby the net income of an investment property is capitalized to determine its value (the net income is divided by a capitalization rate).

capitalization rate   A desired rate of return for an investment that is divided into the net income to determine a property's value.

cash flow   The net spendable cash remaining after all cash outlays are subtracted from the gross income.

caveat emptor   "Let the buyer beware."

certificate of eligibility   Obtained by the veteran to be eligible for a VA loan. The veteran must submit discharge information.

certificate of occupancy   Frequently required before a new structure can be occupied; usually provided by the building inspector.

certificate of reasonable value (CRV)   An appraisal required for VA loans.

certificate of title   Evidence of title issued by a registrar under the Torrens title system.

Certified Property Manager (CPM)   The highest designation awarded by the Institute of Real Estate Management.

cessation deed   A deed used to dedicate land to a public agency.

chain of title   The history of a property showing all conveyances from the original government conveyance (called the *patent*).

chain   A surveyor measurement of 66 feet.

chattels mortgage   A mortgage of personal property; generally has been replaced by financing statements under the Uniform Commercial Code.

chattel   An item of personal property.

chattels real   A personal property interest in real property, such as a lease, mortgage, trust deed, land contract, or share in a real estate syndicate.

check   A 24-mile-by-24-mile area formed by guide meridians and parallels under government survey that corrects for the curvature of the earth.

circuit breaker   Prevents fires by disconnecting electrical service when a circuit becomes overloaded (replaces fuse).

Civil Rights Act of 1866   Law that prohibits race discrimination in housing.

Civil Rights Act of 1964   Law that prohibits discrimination in government-related housing.

Civil Rights Act of 1968   Title VIII of this act is called the federal Fair Housing Act. It prohibits discrimination.

client   Principal that employs the agent.

close corporation   Corporation where stock is not actively traded and majority stockholders actively manage the corporation.

closing statement   The final accounting showing all debits and credits in the sale of real property or a business; also called a settlement statement.

cloud on title   A claim, document, or discrepancy that casts doubt on the marketability of a title.

cluster zoning   Zoning allowing units to be placed close together but with green areas so the density is maintained.

codicil   An amendment to a will that requires the same formalities as the will itself.

coinsurance   A requirement that a property carry a minimum coverage (usually 80% of replacement cost) in order to collect 100% of the loss. If a person carries a lesser percentage of the amount required, that person receives only that percentage of the loss suffered.

collateral   Property that secures a loan.

collaterally secured   Secured by other loans.

color of title   Because of a defect, having only the appearance of title instead of true title; for example, a title under a forged deed.

commercial acre   The amount left in an acre after deducting land for streets and walks; less than 43,560 square feet.

commingling   The act of mixing personal funds and a principal's funds; considered grounds for disciplinary action.

commission   An agent's fee or percentage for successfully completing a sale or lease.

common elements   Areas in a common interest subdivision owned in common with other owners and used by all of the owners.

common law   The unwritten law of England established by court precedent. English common law is the basis for U.S. statutory real estate law.

Community Apartment Project   A residential tenancy in common with each owner having exclusive right of occupancy of a unit.

community property   Property acquired during marriage that is considered equally owned by both spouses. Presently, community property states are Arizona, California, Idaho, Louisiana, Nevada, New Mexico, Texas, Washington, Wisconsin, and Hawaii.

Community Reinvestment Act   Requires federally regulated lenders to publicize lending availability to low-income borrowers.

compaction   The compressing of soil so that it will support a structure.

company dollar   The broker's share of the gross commission earned before expenses.

comparables   Properties used to estimate the value of a property using the sales comparison method.

comparative market analysis   An appraisal prepared by an agent adjusting recent comparable sales to indicate the likely sales price of a property.

comparative unit method   An appraisal method to determine replacement cost. In general, the method is based on current price per square foot or cubic foot of similar construction.

compensating balance   The requirement of a lender that a borrower keep a specified balance on deposit with the lender.

compensatory damages   Money damages awarded to indemnify the injured party for a loss because of another's wrongful act.

complete escrow   An escrow for which everything necessary to be done has been accomplished.

compound interest   Interest that compounds on interest as well as principal. Because interest is paid monthly on standard real estate loans, it is simple, not compound, interest.

Comprehensive Environmental Response, Compensation, and Liability Act (CERCLA)   Federal law that sets forth responsibility for environmental cleanup of hazardous sites.

computerized loan origination (CLO)   Requires disclosure of any fees and that fees can be saved by applying direct to lenders. Loan application through the internet.

concentric circle growth   City growth in rings from the city center.

concurrent estates   More than one estate in the same real property at the same time (one person could have a fee simple interest and another, a leasehold estate).

condemnation   (1) The legal action to take property for public use by eminent domain. (2) The process of declaring property unfit for use.

condition precedent   A condition that must happen before the vesting of title in another. Until the condition occurs, title remains with the grantor.

condition subsequent   A transfer of title with the requirement that a specified condition be met. If the condition is breached, the grantor must declare a forfeiture and retake the property within a reasonable period of time.

conditional loan commitment   A promise to make a loan on a property to a buyer yet unknown, so long as the buyer otherwise qualifies for the loan.

conditional sales contract   A security sales agreement for the sale of personal property where title remains with the vendor (the vendee has possession). Title is transferred only when goods are paid for (has generally been replaced by financing statements).

conditional use permit   Special permission for a use not otherwise allowable under the zoning but considered under special criteria in the zoning.

condominium   A vertical subdivision with common ownership of land and common areas and individual ownership of the units.

conforming loan   A loan that meets the purchase requirements of Fannie Mae or Freddie Mac.

conformity   A property will have its maximum value when it is located in an area of similar properties.

conservation easement   Negative easement requiring that land be kept in a natural or agricultural state.

conservator   A person appointed by the probate court to manage and protect the assets of one who is unable to handle his or her own affairs.

consideration   Something of value given or promised in exchange for a promise, an act, or property of another. A promise made without consideration is deemed void and unenforceable. Love and affection, although deemed good consideration, is not regarded as valuable consideration to support a promise or an act of another.

constructive eviction   An act of a property owner that interferes with a tenant's quiet possession, thus allowing the tenant to consider the lease at an end and be free from further obligations.

constructive notice   The notice given by occupancy or recording to subsequent purchasers or lienholders of a prior interest in the property.

Consumer Price Index (CPI)   An index that reflects by its changes the changes in the purchasing power of the dollar; widely used as a measurement of inflation.

contingent remainder   A remainder interest in property that will vest only if some specified contingency is met, such as the holder outliving a life tenant.

contour lines   Topographical lines on a map that follow elevations. Lines close together indicate a slope, and lines far apart indicate a relatively level area.

contract of adhesion   A one-sided take-it-or-leave-it contract.

contract   An agreement, enforceable by law, between two or more competent parties for consideration to perform or not to perform a legal act.

controlled business arrangement (CBA)   A company that offers a variety of services such as title insurance, property insurance, mortgage banking, home inspection, etc. (one-stop shopping), through firms where the broker has an ownership interest.

conventional loan   A loan made by a conventional lender without government guarantee or insurance.

conversion   Taking property entrusted to you and converting it to your own use; a form of larceny.

conveyance   The transfer of an interest or title to a property. Real estate is conveyed by a deed.

cooperating broker   A sales broker selling the listing of another.

cooperative   An apartment structure owned by a corporation wherein each shareholder occupies a specific unit under a proprietary lease.

corner influence   An increase in value of commercial property because of the additional traffic and exposure of being located on two streets.

corporation   A separate legal entity whose shareholders are not liable personally for corporate debts.

corporeal property   Tangible property (real or personal).

correction line   Surveyor corrections to compensate for curvature of the earth.

correlation   Interpreting value by combining two or more methods of appraisal; also called reconciliation.

cost approach   A method of appraisal whereby the cost to replace the structure is calculated. Accrued depreciation is determined and deducted from the replacement cost; the land value is then added to determine property value.

counteroffer   An offer from the offeree that rejects the original offer and makes the original offeree an offeror.

covenant   A promise that runs with the land.

crawlspace   The space between the ground and the floor on a house not built on a slab or with a basement.

credit   A plus factor on a buyer's or a seller's closing statement.

creditor   One to whom something is owed.

cripple   Vertical piece of 2-by-4-inch framing above or below an opening (window or door).

cubage   The number of cubic feet in a structure.

cul-de-sac   A dead-end street having a rounded end. It is desirable for housing because there is no through traffic.

cumulative zoning   Zoning that allows the designated category of use, as well as less restrictive uses.

curable depreciation   Depreciation that can be economically corrected.

curtail schedule   A payment schedule that indicates principal reduction of a loan for each payment.

curtesy   A common-law right of a husband in the estate of his deceased wife. Some states have made this a statutory right to a life estate in the wife's property, whereas other states grant undivided fee simple interest in a portion of the wife's estate.

customer   The buyer or the seller not represented by the agent.

datum plane   A surveyor's horizontal plane from which elevations and depths are measured.

dealer   A person who makes a regular part of his income by buying and selling property.

debit   A minus factor on a buyer's or a seller's closing statement.

debt capital   Money raised by a business by borrowing through bonds or other debentures.

debtor   One who owes money to a creditor.

decedent   A person who has died.

declaration of homestead   A formal procedure of recording a homestead declaration. It protects the homestead from unsecured creditors up to a statutory amount.

declaration of restrictions   A declaration of the restrictive covenants recorded by the subdivider. In each deed, the subdivider usually incorporates the restrictions by referencing the recording of the document.

dedication   The gift of real property to a governmental unit, usually by a subdivider, in order to gain approval. If the dedication is given for a particular purpose and that purpose is later abandoned, the land dedicated may revert to the grantor.

deed in lieu of foreclosure   A deed from owner to lienholder. Unlike foreclosure, it may not wipe out junior encumbrances.

deed of reconveyance   A deed given by the trustee to the trustor when the trustor has paid the beneficiary in full. It is used for trust deeds to remove the lien in the same manner as a satisfaction is used to remove a mortgage.

deed of trust   The transfer of title from the trustor (borrower) to a trustee (third party) as security for a note to a beneficiary (lender).

deed   A document that conveys title to real property from a grantor to a grantee.

default clause   A mortgage provision that allows a junior lienholder to cure any default of a prior lien (and then foreclose on his or her own lien).

default   The breach of a promise or an agreement.

defeasance clause   A mortgage provision that defeats (or cancels) the mortgage on the full payment as agreed.

defeasible estate   An estate that can be lost should a certain event take place.

deferred maintenance   Maintenance that has been postponed.

deficiency judgment   A judgment obtained when a foreclosure sale does not satisfy a debt. Deficiency judgments are difficult to obtain in many states because of restrictions on them. In some states, they are not allowed at all.

degree   A measurement for angles, used in metes-and-bounds descriptions. One degree (1°) is $1/360$ of a circle.

delivery   The actual transfer of an interest; requires the intent to make an irrevocable transfer.

demise   The transfer of a leasehold interest.

Department of Housing and Urban Development (HUD)   Federal department that establishes rules and regulations concerning housing and real property in the United States.

Department of Veterans Affairs (VA)   A federal governmental organization dedicated to serving U.S. veterans.

depreciation   A loss in property value from any cause.

depth table   An appraiser's table that determines additional value attributable to additional depth.

dereliction   Land that is created by the recession of water. It belongs to the adjacent landowners. Also called reliction.

descent   Hereditary succession by act of law when property does not pass by will.

designated agency   An agency where one salesperson in the listing broker's office is designated the agent of the owner. If the listing office sells the property, the selling salesperson is the agent of the buyer. Also called split agency.

designated broker   The licensed broker who has the direct responsibility for the real estate activities of a firm.

desk cost   The office overhead cost per desk. It is determined by dividing overhead by the number of salespeople in an office.

desktop underwriter   A computer program developed by Fannie Mae that allows loan applications to be processes in a few minutes.

determinable fee   An estate that would end on the happening of an event that may or may not happen.

development method   An appraisal method to determine land value where cost of development is deducted from estimated value after development.

devise   The passing of real property by will.

devisee   The person receiving real property by will.

devisor   The testator or testatrix who transfers real property by will upon his or her death.

diminishing returns   A point where additional improvements fail to increase value to cover the cost of improvements.

direct endorsement   A lender authorized to make FHA-insured loans without FHA prior approval.

discount point   Fee charged by mortgage provider to increase the effective rate of interest.

discount rate   Rate charged by the Federal Reserve to member banks for loans.

discounting a loan   Selling a loan for less than its face value (common with second mortgages or loans bearing low interest rates).

disintermediation   The sudden withdrawal of savings from lending institutions, resulting in a tight money market.

distribution   The apportionment and division of an estate in probate after debts and costs have been paid.

documentary transfer tax   Formerly a federal tax on real property conveyances that, when abandoned by the federal government, was adopted in many states. Also called revenue stamps.

Dodd-Frank Act   Protects consumers by regulating appraisers and lenders.

domiciliary probate   Probate in the deceased's state of residence.

dominant tenement   An estate using the land of another under an easement. The easement is an appurtenance to the dominant tenement.

donee   The person who receives a gift.

donor   The person who gives a gift.

double escrow   The use of one escrow to purchase and resell a property.

dower   A wife's common-law right in the estate of her husband should she survive him. In some states, it is a statutory right, such as one-third interest.

downzoning   A change in zoning resulting in a lower-density use or lesser use.

dragnet clause   A provision extending a mortgage to cover future obligations that may arise between the parties; used in an open-end mortgage.

drive-by appraisal report   Report based on exterior viewing, area and sales in area.

dual agency   An agency created when an agent acts for the buyer, as well as the seller in a transaction.

due diligence   The process of investigation and evaluation expected of a reasonably prudent person under the circumstances.

due-on-sale clause   A type of acceleration clause in a note that makes all future payments due when a property is sold. It prevents an assumption of the loan. Also called an alienation clause.

duress   The use of force or threat to make a person act; makes a contract voidable.

earnest money   A good-faith deposit made by an offeror with an offer.

easement appurtenant   A beneficial easement that transfers with the land.

easement by estoppel   An easement created when one person's words or actions lead another to believe in the existence of an easement, causing the second person to act to his own detriment. The person who made the assertion will be estopped by court action from denying the existence of the easement.

easement by necessity   An easement granted when there is no other possible access to a property.

easement by prescription   An easement created by open, notorious, and hostile use of property for a prescribed period of time.

easement in gross   A personal easement to use land of another where there is no dominant tenement being benefited.

easement   The right of a person to use another's land.

economic life   That period for which improvements give a return attributable to the improvements alone.

economic rent   The rental value of a property in the marketplace.

economics of scale   The savings possible by increasing production.

effective age   An age placed on property for appraisal purposes based on the condition of the property. The effective age may be more or less than the chronological age.

effective gross income   The gross income less the vacancy factor and an allowance for collection loss.

egress   A way to exit a property.

ejectment   A legal action to oust an encroacher or a trespasser.

elevation   (1) Views of a structure from various directions on a builder's plans. (2) Height above sea level.

emancipated minor   A minor who, under state law, may contract as an adult.

emblements   Cultivated annual crops; considered to be personal property.

eminent domain   The government right to take private property (title or easement) for public use. It is not under police power because the owner is paid for the property taken.

employee   A person who works under the direction and supervision of an employer.

enabling act   A legislative act that confers power on local governments that they would not have otherwise. Zoning and planning powers were given under enabling acts.

encapsulation   Sealing off hazardous substances, such as painting over lead paint.

encroachment   A trespass by placing an improvement on or over the land of another.

encumbrance   Anything that affects title or limits use, such as liens, easements, or restrictions.

Endangered Species Act   Species listed as endangered or threatened have federal habitat protection.

endorsement   The signature of a holder on the back of a negotiable instrument.

energy efficiency ratio (EER)   The efficiency evaluation of electrical systems and appliances.

entitlement   That portion of the loan the VA guarantees.

environmental impact report (EIR)   A report required for projects that may have a significant effect on the environment.

Environmental Protection Agency (EPA)   An agency that enforces federal environmental standards.

Equal Credit Opportunity Act (ECOA)   A federal act that prohibits credit discrimination based on age, sex, race, or marital status, or from public assistance.

equal dignities rule   If an act must be in writing, the agency agreement appointing someone to perform the act must also be in writing.

equalization factor   A factor to bring into line low assessed valuations in some areas. The assessed value is multiplied by the factor to determine the value that the tax rate will be applied to.

equator platform   A standardized short sale system used by many lenders that allows agents to apply for short sales online.

equilibrium point   The price that results in a number of buyers equal to the goods available.

equitable title   An interest in property before receipt of legal title. Examples are a trustor under a trust deed, or a buyer under a sales contract (land contract).

equity capital   Money raised by a business through selling shares in the business.

equity of redemption   The right of a mortgagor to redeem during and after foreclosure; governed by state statute.

equity   (1) The difference between the value of a property and the liens against it. (2) That which is right or just.

erosion   The wearing away of soil by acts of wind and/or water.

errors and omissions (E&O) insurance   Malpractice insurance carried by brokers and salespeople.

escalator clause   A contract or lease provision allowing for payments to rise or fall.

escape clause   Lets a party out of contract responsibilities in the event of stated situations.

escheat   The reversion of property to the state when a person dies intestate and without known heirs.

escrow   A neutral depository that handles real estate closings as agent for the buyer and the seller.

estate   An interest in property.

estate at will   A leasehold estate for an undetermined time period; may be terminated at any time by the lessor or lessee. Most states require a statutory notice period.

estate for life   A freehold interest whereby a person has property for her life or the life of another named person. The life tenant cannot encumber the property beyond her interest. At the end of the estate, the interest either reverts to the grantor or passes as a remainder interest to a third party.

estate for years   A lease for a definite period of time, the result of an express agreement.

estate of inheritance   An estate that can be inherited, such as a fee simple estate.

estate on a condition subsequent   An estate given based on a specific condition. Upon breach of the condition, the grantor can declare a breach and regain the property.

estoppel   A doctrine whereby a party is barred from raising a defense when that person's acts or words induced another party to act to his detriment.

estoppel certificate   Statement by borrowers as to amount owed and loan terms and that they have no defense or offsets against lender (obtained when loan is to be sold), or by tenants that they have no offset or defense against lease obligations.

estover   Necessity that the law allows, such as the right of a tenant to use timber for fuel and repair needs.

et al.   "And others."

et ux.   "And wife."

ethics   Doing what is right, measured by application of the golden rule.

eviction   A dispossession by process of law.

exception in a deed   An exclusion in a deed; deeding only part of a property.

excess land   Land that does not contribute economically to use and/or value.

exchange value   The value a property has as to other goods.

exclusionary zoning   Zoning that excludes a stated use.

exclusive agency listing   A listing whereby the broker is the exclusive agent of the owner and is entitled to a commission if the broker or any other agent sells the property. If the owner sells the property without an agent, the broker is not entitled to a commission.

exclusive-right-to-sell listing   A listing whereby the agent is entitled to a commission if the property is sold during the listing term by anyone, including the owner.

exculpatory clause   A contract provision excusing a party for injuries to another; frequently used by lessors in leases. Exculpatory clauses do not affect the rights of third parties who may be injured on the premises.

execute   To sign a document.

executed contract   A contract where all performance has been completed.

execution of judgment   The action of the sheriff in seizing and selling property of the debtor to satisfy a judgment.

executor   A man appointed by a will to administer the estate of a deceased; a woman is an *executrix*.

executor's deed   A deed during probate containing the warranty that the executor(trix) has not encumbered the property.

executory contract   A contract that has yet to be performed.

exemplary damages   Punitive damages awarded in excess of compensatory damages when an action was performed with willful intent.

express contract   A contract that is stated verbally or in writing, as opposed to an implied contract, which is understood but not stated.

extended coverage policy   Extends a basic fire policy (fire, lightning, and smoke) to cover additional perils, such as windstorm, hail, and riot.

extension of a lease   Continued occupancy under the terms of an existing lease. (A lease renewal is a new lease.)

facilitator   A person working as a liaison between buyer and seller but without agency duties. Also called an intermediary.

Fair Credit Reporting Act   Allows a person to know what is in her credit file and to have explanations inserted and information investigated and removed if wrong.

Fannie Mae   A private corporation, now under government conservatorship, that provides a secondary marketplace for mortgages.

feasibility study   A study of the economic practicality of an investment.

Federal Deposit Insurance Corporation (FDIC)   Insures bank and thrift deposits. The maximum federal insurance is $250,000 for an account.

Federal Housing Administration (FHA)   A federal agency that insures mortgage loans.

Federal Land Bank   A farm credit administrative agency that provides financing for farm purchases.

Federal Reserve System (the Fed)   A federal agency that regulates the money supply, interest rates, and reserve requirements of member banks.

fee   An estate of inheritance.

fee appraiser   An appraiser who works either as an independent contractor or for an independent appraisal firm.

fee simple determinable   A grant that automatically ends should a property no longer be used for a designated purpose.

fee simple   The highest ownership possible; has no time limit and can be transferred or inherited (the word *fee* means an inheritable estate). Also called fee simple absolute.

fee tail   An estate in which conveyance is limited to the descendants of the grantee.

FICO Score   Lender scoring system for loan worthiness.

fictitious name   A name that does not include the surname of every principal in a business. To use a fictitious name, the fictitious name publication and recording statutes must be complied with.

fidelity bond   Bond for employee covering employee honesty.

fiduciary   The duty of trust and honesty of an agent to the principal.

filtering down   The process in which housing passes down to lower economic groups.

Financial Institutions Reform, Recovery, and Enforcement Act (FIRREA)   Requires state licensing and certification of appraisers.

financing statement   An instrument filed by a lender on a personal property loan to give public notice that the goods are security for the loan (under the Uniform Commercial Code).

finder's fee   A fee paid to a nonlicensee for an introduction only; legal in some states.

fire block   A horizontal block between studs to prevent a fire from rising through a wall.

fire wall   A wall built of fireproof material to limit or contain a fire.

firm commitment   A loan commitment made for a particular borrower and property.

first right of refusal   *See* right of first refusal.

fixture   A former item of personal property that has become so connected to the realty that it has become part of the real property.

flat lease   A level-payment lease with no escalation clause; also called a gross lease.

floodplain   Level areas along waterways subject to inundation.

floodwater   The water overflowing a defined channel.

floor space   The interior square footage measured from the inside walls.

footing   The concrete poured in the ground on which the foundation rests. The footing distributes the building load to the soil.

foreclosure   The legal procedure whereby the lender forces the sale of property to pay indebtedness in the event of default.

Foreign Investment in Real Property Tax Act (FIRPTA)   Requires buyer withholding of taxes when the seller is a foreign national, except for exempt sales.

foundation   The masonry substructure on which the building rests. The foundation rests on the footing.

franchise   A right to distribute goods and services under a marketing plan established by a franchisor.

fraud   An intentional act or omission to deceive another to the detriment of that party.

Freddie Mac   A private entity under government conservatorship that serves as a secondary mortgage market and sells participation certificates.

freehold   A higher-interest category of estates (fee simple and life estates), as opposed to nonfreehold estates, which are leasehold interests.

front foot   A linear measurement of land based on the number of feet fronting on a road (could also refer to water frontage).

front-end ratio   The ratio of gross income to total loan payments (PITI); used to qualify buyers as to the amount of a loan.

functional obsolescence   Obsolescence that is built in by design or by construction.

funding fee   A fee paid by a veteran for a VA loan.

gable roof   A roof in which the two opposite planes slope down from a ridge line.

gambrel roof   A roof with a steep lower slope and a flatter upper slope; found on some barns and on Dutch colonials.

gap loan   A temporary loan, usually at a higher interest rate, where the borrower intends to obtain better financing; also called a bridge loan or swing loan.

general agent   An agent having all necessary authority to conduct a business or trade.

general lien   A lien against all property of a debtor (for example, judgment liens and federal tax liens).

general partner   A partner who is active in management and liable for the debts and actions of the partnership.

general power of attorney   A broad power given by a principal to an agent that enables the agent to act for the principal. A specific power of attorney allows the agent to act only in the manner and area specified.

general warranty deed   A deed where the grantor warrants title as to the claims of all others.

gift deed   A deed given for love and affection. Creditors of the donor can reach the property if it can be shown that the gift was made while the donor was insolvent in an effort to evade creditors. A recorded gift deed does not take precedence over a prior unrecorded deed by the grantor for value.

gift tax   A federal tax on gifts. Donor exemption of $14,000 annually per donee.

Ginnie Mae   A federal corporation that provides assistance for federally aided housing projects that are at below-market interest rates. Funds are raised through the sale of government-backed securities.

good consideration   Love and affection are considered good consideration for a completed gift transfer; however, they are not considered valuable consideration to enforce a promise to make a transfer.

good faith   Acting honestly without deception.

good funds   Closing funds where the checks have cleared; cashier's checks or certified checks.

government lot   A portion of land less than a quarter section because of physical features such as lakes that limit the size of the lot. Established by government survey.

government survey   The survey system used for most of the nation whereby land is measured from principal base lines and meridians and laid out in townships and sections.

grace period   A period allowed for late payments without penalty.

Graduate REALTORS® Institute (GRI)   A professional designation that requires seminar attendance and courses of study.

graduated lease   A step lease with payments that increase as of agreed-on dates.

graduated payment mortgage (GPM)   A loan where early payments are lower and increase during the term of the loan, making it easier for young people, whose incomes are likely to increase, to purchase property.

grandfather clause   A regulation that permits existing conditions or uses to continue despite new laws against them; applies to prior-use zoning.

granny flat   An extra apartment in a zoned single-family area. Sometimes allowed if used for relatives such as in-laws. Otherwise it would violate the zoning.

grant deed   A deed used in some states in conjunction with title insurance whereby the seller warrants that title has not been conveyed previously and that there is nothing against the property that the seller knows of that has not been disclosed to the buyer.

grant   A transfer of title.

grantee   The person who receives the grant from the grantor.

granting clause   A deed provision indicating that title is passing.

grantor   The person who makes the grant to the grantee.

grantor/grantee index   A recorder's index system by grantor/grantee name that makes it easy to research a title.

gridiron   The rectangular street system found in many cities usually based on government survey system.

gross income   The total income before any commission splits, other expenses or deductions.

gross profit   Gross sales less cost of the merchandise. To obtain net profit, all other expenses also must be deducted.

gross rent multiplier (GRM) method   An appraisal variation to get an approximate idea of value where gross income is multiplied by a gross rent multiplier. It does not take into account unusual expenses.

ground lease   A lease of land only; tenant puts in the improvements.

ground rent   The portion of the rent attributable to land rather than to improvements.

ground water   Underground nonflowing water.

group boycotting   An agreement to refuse cooperation with another business to reduce competition.

growing equity mortgage (GEM)   A mortgage with increasing payments, causing the principal to be rapidly decreased.

guardian   A person lawfully charged with managing the property of another who is legally incapable.

guide meridians   North-south survey lines running east and west of a principal meridians. They are 24 miles apart.

habendum   The "to have and to hold" clause in a deed indicating the extent of ownership being transferred (such as fee simple or life estate).

habitability   Reasonably fit for human habitation.

hard-money loan   A cash loan rather than seller financing.

head lease   A master lease under which the lessee subleases portions of the premises.

header   A beam over a window or door.

hereditament   Any item capable of being inherited.

highest and best use   That use which results in the greatest value for a property.

hip roof   A roof where all sides slope to the eaves.

historic structure   Structure listed on National Register of Historic Places or a state registry. There are tax incentives for restoration. as well as penalties for demolition and alteration.

holder in due course   A person who, in the course of commerce, takes a negotiable instrument good on its face for value before the due date, without notice of any defense of the maker.

hold-harmless clause   One party agrees to indemnify the other for any loss suffered because of the contract or lease.

holdover clause   A lease condition that provides for a very high rent should the tenant fail to vacate at the end of the lease, discouraging a holdover situation.

holdover tenant   A tenant retaining possession after expiration of the lease. *See* tenancy at sufferance.

holographic will   A handwritten, signed, and dated will. No witnesses are needed.

homeowners association (HOA)   A governing association for common interest developments established pursuant to the restrictive covenants of the development.

homeowners policy   A comprehensive insurance policy covering fire, vandalism, theft, liability, and other hazards.

homestead   A home on which a declaration of homestead has been filed to protect the home from unsecured creditors up to a statutory amount.

hypothecate   To give something as security without giving up possession.

illegal   In violation of an existing law.

illiquidity   An asset that is not readily convertible to cash. Real estate is considered to be illiquid.

illusory contract   An agreement that appears to be binding but in which one party actually is not bound; not enforceable.

implied agent   An agent not expressly appointed but implied by actions of the parties.

implied contract   An agreement not expressly stated but implied by actions of the parties.

implied easement   An easement implied when the grantor conveys property that is landlocked by other property of the grantor or where the grantor created the use, then sold the parcels separately.

impound account   A reserve for taxes and insurance kept by the lender to which the borrower pays, along with regular principal and interest payments; also called an escrow account.

improvement   An addition to property, such as a room or air-conditioning. Unlike repairs, improvements increase the cost basis of the property.

imputed interest   An interest rate that will be implied for tax purposes when a note shows a rate of interest less than a statutory minimum (a person will be taxed as if the minimum acceptable rate was received).

incentive zoning   Encourages particular improvements; for example, zoning that allows greater height if a public plaza is included.

inchoate right   A right not yet perfected, such as a mechanic's right to file a lien or a wife's dower rights that won't come into being until the death of her husband.

incompetent   A person who, because of age or mental capacity, lacks the legal ability to enter into valid contracts.

incorporeal property   Intangible property.

increment   Any increase in value.

incurable depreciation   Depreciation where the cost of correction is prohibitive.

indefeasible   Cannot be voided.

independent contractor   A contractor employed to complete a task who is not under the supervision or control of the employer.

index lease   A lease tied to an index such as the Consumer Price Index.

index method   A method of determining cost of replacement by taking the actual costs when built and applying the increases in the construction cost index since that date.

informal description   A description of property that is not a legal description, such as by street address or name of owner.

ingress   A means of entering.

injunction   A court action to cease and desist from a course of action.

interest only loan   Loan where interest only is paid. When due, loan must be paid off or recast.

interest rate   The percentage of a loan balance charged by the lender for the use of money.

interim loan   A short-term or gap loan.

intermediate theory (mortgage)   A security theory where title remains with the mortgagor but automatically transfers to the mortgagee in the event of default.

internal rate of return (IRR)   A method of measuring returns on investment that considers tax consequences.

interpleader action   An action requested by a party to determine rights when two or more people claim to have an interest in property, such as an action brought by a broker where the buyer and seller each claim rights to a deposit.

Interstate Land Sales Act (ILSA)   A federal disclosure act for projects of 25 or more unimproved lots to be sold in interstate commerce.

intestate   Dying without a will. Property passes to the heirs according to state statute governing intestate succession.

inverse condemnation   An action by an owner to force a government unit to take property when, by its action, the government has wrongfully restricted use.

involuntary lien   A lien imposed without consent of the landowner, such as a tax lien. A mortgage is a voluntary lien.

IRS Form 8300   Report to IRS on cash transactions over $10,000.

joint and several   The agreement to be liable together as well as separately.

joint liability   The agreement that each party will be equally liable for an obligation.

joint tenancy   An undivided interest with the right of survivorship. Owners must take title at the same time, by the same instrument, with equal interests, and with equal rights of possession.

joint venture   A partnership for a particular undertaking only. It differs from a standard partnership in that a sole joint venture partner cannot obligate the other joint venture partners.

joist   A horizontal board that supports a floor or ceiling.

judgment   The final order of a court as to money owed. When recorded, the judgment becomes a general lien on the property of the debtor.

junior lien   A subordinate lien as determined by the time of recording or the nature of the lien.

key lot   A lot having a number of other lots abutting a side line (undesirable for residential use).

key money   A payment made to the lessor to obtain a lease.

laches   The doctrine that upholds the loss of the right to enforce an agreement or a restriction because the delay in bringing action worked to the detriment of the other party.

land contract   A contract under which the seller keeps title while the buyer gets possession. Title passes when the property has been fully paid for. Also called a contract for sale.

land residual method   A means to determine land value by deducting the value of the income attributable to the improvements alone from the value of the income of the property.

landlocked   Property that has no access because of surrounding property and the absence of any easement.

late charge   A charge imposed by a lender for late payments. Late charges are regulated by state law.

latent defect   A defect not apparent from a reasonable visual inspection.

lateral support   The support a landowner has a duty to provide to the land of adjacent property owners.

latitude   Latitude is referenced by lines parallel to the equator and is measured in degrees (°), minutes (') and seconds (").

lease   A tenancy agreement between landlord (lessor) and tenant (lessee).

leasehold   A lease estate in realty; a nonfreehold or possessory interest only.

legacy   A bequest of money by will.

legal description   A description of real property by government survey; metes and bounds; or reference to a recorded lot, block, and tract.

lessee   A tenant under a lease.

lessor   A landlord who has given a lease.

leverage   The use of other people's money to make money. Purchasing real property with a minimum down payment is a use of leverage.

LIBOR rate London interbank offering rate used as index on adjustable-rate mortgages.

license A revocable privilege to use the land of another.

lien theory The theory in a majority of states that a mortgage is a lien and not a transfer of title. *See* title theory.

lien A monetary encumbrance that is secured by real estate.

life estate An estate in property for the life of a person that may not be inherited.

like-for-like An exchange of similar property that qualifies for a tax-deferred exchange; for example, real property for real property.

limited common elements Areas in a common-interest subdivision owned in common with other owners but designated for the exclusive use of particular owners, such as parking spaces or storage lockers.

limited liability company (LLC) A business entity with limited liability that is taxed like a partnership. It avoids the restrictions of S corporations or limited partnerships.

limited partnership A partnership in which one or more partners have liability limited only to the extent of their investments. Limited partners cannot be active in the business management.

link A surveyor's measure equal to 7.92 inches.

liquid Cash or assets readily convertible to cash.

liquidated damages Advance agreement as to the amount of damages for nonperformance when exact damages may be difficult to ascertain. If so unreasonable that the court considers them a penalty, they will not be enforced.

liquidity Ability to turn assets into cash.

lis pendens A recorded notice of a pending lawsuit concerning a property. Though not a lien, lis pendens provides constructive notice that an action is pending against the property.

listing An agency agreement between owner and broker wherein the owner authorizes the broker to attempt to find a buyer and agrees to pay a certain commission should the broker succeed.

littoral property Property located on the shore of a lake or an ocean.

littoral rights Rights of a property owner to reasonable use of lake, pond, or ocean water bordering the property. Also see riparian rights.

livable floor space The space measured by the interior of each room, excluding interior walls and closets.

loan-to-value ratio (LTV) The percentage of the value (or ratio) that a lender will lend against a property.

lock-in clause A provision that allows prepayment, provided full interest is paid as if the loan had gone to maturity; the borrower is "locked in" as to interest.

longitude Longitude is measured in terms of north-south meridians and is measured in degrees (°), minutes (') and seconds ('').

lot, block, and tract system Legal description based on reference to a recorded subdivision map.

maker The person who signs a negotiable instrument.

mansard roof A French-style roof with a steep lower slope and a very gentle upper slope.

margin of security The lender's security that is the difference between the mortgage amount and the value of the property.

margin The difference between the index rate and the rate of interest charged on an adjustable-rate mortgage.

market comparison approach An appraisal method wherein value is based on sales of comparable properties.

market price The price actually paid.

market value The price a willing, informed buyer would pay to a willing, informed seller, allowing a reasonable sale time.

marketable title A title that is clear of objectionable liens and encumbrances; a merchantable title.

markup The percentage added to cost to determine selling price.

master lease The original lease between lessor and lessee when the lessee later subleases.

master plan Comprehensive land use plan.

mechanic's lien A specific lien by a contractor, subcontractor, material man, or laborer for work performed or material supplied for a property but not paid for.

mediation A nonjudicial process to resolve disputes where a third party acts as a facilitator to aid the parties in reaching an agreement.

megalopolis An urban sprawl.

Member, Appraisal Institute (MAI) A professional membership designation of the Appraisal Institute.

menace A threat of force that makes a contract voidable.

merger The joining of a lesser right with a superior right so as to extinguish the lesser one; for example, a tenant having an estate for years buys the property in fee simple, in which case the lease is extinguished because the owner and tenant now are one and the same.

meridians Government surveyors' north-south lines that intersect base lines. Land is measured from the intersection of these lines.

metes and bounds Land description by measurements and boundaries.

mile A linear measure of 5,280 feet.

mill One-tenth of a cent, or $1/1,000$ of a dollar, written as $0.001. Property taxes often are expressed in mills.

mineral, oil, and gas lease Lease rights to extract minerals, oil, and gas for the lease period (a personal property interest).

mineral, oil, and gas rights The absolute right to extract minerals, oil, and gas (a real property interest).

minor Any person younger than contractual age.

misrepresentation A false statement to induce another to act. It makes a contract voidable at the option of the injured party. Unlike fraud, misrepresentation does not require intent to deceive.

mitigation of damages The duty of an injured party to use reasonable efforts to keep the damages as low as possible when the other party breaches a contract.

monetary policy Policy of Federal Reserve to adjust availability and cost of funds.

monument A fixed surveyor's marker for a metes-and-bounds description; can be natural (such as a rock or tree) or artificial (such as an iron stake).

mortgage A security device for real estate. In lien theory states, the mortgagor retains title and gives the mortgagee a lien. In title theory states, the borrower retains possession but gives the lender or trustee title as security.

mortgage banker Mortgage company that originates loans that are then sold in secondary mortgage market.

mortgage broker Broker who arranges a loan between a borrower and a lender.

Mortgage Electronic Registration System (MERS) A private national mortgage database in which MERS may hold a mortgage note.

Mortgage Guaranty Insurance Corporation (MGIC) A private mortgage insurance (PMI) carrier.

mortgage insurance premium (MIP) FHA insurance.

mortgage loan correspondent A firm that arranges the sale of existing loans in the secondary mortgage market.

mortgage loan originator (MLO) Subject to minimum standards of licensing and registration.

mortgage note The note that reflects the promise to pay the mortgage debt. The mortgage is security for the note.

mortgagee One who receives the mortgage; a lender or a seller (under a purchase money mortgage).

mortgagor The owner or the buyer of property who gives the mortgage.

mudsill The lowest board on a house that rests on the foundation. It is often constructed of redwood or treated lumber to resist rot. Also called a sill.

multiple listing A listing, usually an exclusive right-to-sell listing, given out to a group of cooperating brokers who are members of a multiple listing service.

multiple listing service (MLS) An organization of member real estate professionals in which listing agreements are shared to increase the chances of a sale.

muniment of title   Deeds.

mutual consent   The meeting of minds required for a binding contract.

mutual mistake   The mistake of both parties to an agreement. A mutual mistake as to fact allows a mistaken party to void the agreement.

mutual mortgage insurance (MMI)   FHA insurance that protects the lender against buyer default.

mutual savings bank   A bank owned by its depositors and paying dividends, not interest, to the depositors. Located in several northeastern states, such a bank can make real estate loans anywhere in the nation.

naked title   Legal title only, without another right of ownership; for example, a trustee under a deed of trust.

narrative report   An appraisal written in a narrative form; the most comprehensive form of appraisal report.

National Association of REALTORS® (NAR)   A trade organization dedicated to training real estate professionals and ensuring high ethical standards within the field.

National Do Not Call Registry   Federal registry to protect residences from unwanted telephone solicitations.

National Environmental Policy Act (NEPA)   Requires an environmental impact statement (EIS) on federal projects that can significantly affect the environment.

National Flood Insurance Act   Legislation that makes flood insurance available in communities that have developed a flood-protection plan.

natural monument   A surveying point for metes-and-bounds descriptions that is natural, as opposed to manmade; for example, a tree, rock, or river bank.

negative amortization   A loan whose monthly installments are not sufficient to pay the interest, so the principal increases.

negative cash flow   An investment or a business that requires a regular infusion of cash because the cash outlay exceeds the cash receipts.

negative covenant   A promise not to do something; for example, a restrictive covenant that prohibits detached garages.

negative declaration   A statement that a development will not have a significant adverse effect on the environment.

negative easement   An easement right that prohibits an owner from a use.

negative fraud   Fraud resulting from failure to disclose rather than from an affirmative act.

negotiable instrument   A written unconditional promise or order to pay a certain sum in money now or at a definite time in the future.

neighborhood   An area of social conformity.

net lease   A lease under which the tenant pays all operational and maintenance expenses, and gives the lessor a net amount as rent.

net listing   A listing whereby the broker receives as a commission that portion of the sales price that exceeds the listing price. In some states, net listings are illegal.

net operating income (NOI)   Gross annual income less operational costs (does not deduct for debt service or depreciation).

net profit   The profit after all expenses (excludes payment on the principal of loans and taxes on the profit).

net worth   The difference between total assets and total liabilities.

nominal damages   A token amount awarded by a court when no actual damages result from a wrongful act.

nominal   (1) The rate stated in the instrument. (2) A minimum quantity.

nonconforming loan   A loan that fails to meet the purchase requirements of Fannie Mae or Freddie Mac; usually held by the lender as a portfolio loan.

nonconforming use   A use existing before zoning that does not conform with the zoning.

noncumulative zoning   Zoning that allows only a specified category of use (not less restrictive uses).

nondisturbance clause   A mortgage condition by which the mortgagee agrees not to terminate the lease (if the lessee is in compliance with lease terms) in the event of mortgage foreclosure.

nonfreehold estate   A leasehold interest.

noninstitutional lender A lender other than a bank, a savings and loan association, or an insurance company; for example, a pension fund or a private individual.

nonjudicial foreclosure Foreclosure under the power-of-sale provision of a mortgage or trust deed.

nonrecourse loan A loan for which the borrower is not personally liable (no deficiency judgment is possible).

note A signed instrument that acknowledges a debt and agrees to pay it either on demand or at a set date in the future. The mortgage or trust deed secures the note in real estate transactions.

notice of completion A notice filed by an owner that starts a statutory period in which mechanics' liens must be filed.

notice of default A notice given under a trust deed that sets the statutory period for the trustor to pay obligations.

notice of nonresponsibility A notice filed by an owner to protect the property from liens for work authorized by another person; for example, a tenant.

notice to quit A statutory notice given by a landlord to a tenant to vacate the premises.

not-to-compete clause A clause in an employment or a sales contract that prohibits competition by former employees or sellers within a reasonable distance and for a reasonable time period. If a court determines that the restrictions are unreasonable, such a clause is not enforceable.

novation The substitution of one agreement for another, or the substitution of parties to the agreement.

nuisance A use of property that interferes with the quiet enjoyment by others of their properties. An abatement action can be taken to stop (abate) the nuisance.

nuncupative will An oral deathbed will for personal property of low value. The witnesses must reduce it to writing. It is not valid in all states.

objective value Market value as opposed to subjective value, which is use value.

obligatory advance Loan advances required by a lender under an agreement as construction progresses.

observed condition method The method of determining the effective age of a property by its condition.

obsolescence Loss in value due to reduced desirability because of built-in design (functional obsolescence) or forces outside the property itself (external obsolescence).

occupancy permit Permit issued by a building inspector when a new structure has been completed in accordance with codes.

offset statement A statement by a lender as to the current status of a loan (balance due). *See* beneficiary statement.

"or more" clause A provision that allows prepayment without penalty.

one-stop shopping A brokerage firm that handles financing and closing functions. *See* controlled business arrangement.

open listing A nonexclusive agency whereby the owner agrees to a fee only if the broker is the first to procure a buyer under the exact terms of the listing or any other terms to which the owner agrees.

open market transaction Federal Reserve action in buying and selling federal securities on the open market.

open mortgage (1) A loan that can be prepaid without penalty. (2) A mortgage in default before the foreclosure sale.

open-end mortgage A mortgage that can be increased in the future up to an agreed-on maximum amount. Also see dragnet clause.

opportunity cost The loss of other opportunities by making an investment; for example, a long-term, low-yield investment could result in illiquidity whereby the investor would have to forgo a later, more attractive investment opportunity.

option arm Adjustable rate loan with borrower's option to make a minimum payment.

option A noncancelable right given by an owner to another to buy or lease a property at an agreed-on price within a stated period. To be valid, consideration must have been given to keep the offer open.

optionee   The party who purchased the option and has the right to exercise it.

optionor   The owner who gives the option.

order paper   A note payable to a named person or order that allows it to be negotiated by endorsement.

orientation   The way a structure is placed on a site.

origination point   Fees charged by mortgage brokers for services.

ostensible agency   An agency that is implied by the actions of the parties.

overimprovement   An improvement that cannot be recaptured by increased income or sale value.

package mortgage   A mortgage that includes personal property as well as real property.

parol evidence rule   The rule that bars verbal (parol) evidence from being used to show that a contract means other than what it says. Parol evidence can be used to clarify ambiguities or to show fraud.

partially amortized loan   An amortized loan that must be paid off with a balloon payment before amortization is complete.

participation loan   A loan agreement under which the lender receives a share of the revenue or profits in addition to the interest. The lender takes an equity share as a limited partner or shareholder as partial consideration for the loan.

partition in kind   The splitting of property into separate parcels to dissolve a joint tenancy or tenancy in common.

partition   A legal action to break a joint ownership.

partnership   An agreement between two or more persons to unite for business purposes and to share profits.

party wall   A common wall on the property line maintained by both owners.

passive loss   A paper loss from depreciation.

pass-through certificate   A certificate sold to investors backed by a pool of Ginnie Mae–insured mortgages. The principal and interest paid by borrowers is passed through to the certificate owners.

patent defect   A defect that is obvious from a visual inspection.

patent   The original conveyance of land from the government.

payback period   The time it will take for the income generated by a property to return the investment (down payment).

Pearson VUE   An independent examination testing service.

penny   A measure for nails shown as the letter *d*. The larger the penny value, the larger the nail.

per stirpes   An inheritance by right of representation. Children share equally in the share their deceased parent would have received. This is different from per capita distribution, where all heirs obtain the same amount.

percentage lease   A lease in which the rent is a percentage of the gross income.

percolation   The ability of soil to absorb water. Percolation tests are required in many areas before a permit is issued for a structure requiring a septic system.

perfect escrow   An escrow in which all signed documents and funds have been deposited with the escrow and the transaction is ready for closing.

performance bond   Bond that guarantees completion of a contract should the contractor default on performance.

periodic tenancy   A rental from period to period that renews itself automatically unless the lessor or lessee gives notice.

personal assistant   A licensed or unlicensed party who works for a real estate salesperson. Generally regarded as employees of the employing salesperson.

personal property   Property that is not classified as real property.

Personal Responsibility and Work Opportunity Reconciliation Act of 1996 (PRWORA)   An act that prohibits public benefits, including professional licensing, to illegal aliens.

physical deterioration   Depreciation caused by age and use.

pitch   The slope of a roof; usually expressed in inches per foot. A 5-12 pitch drops five inches in each horizontal foot. Generally, roofs with steeper pitches have longer lives than more gently sloped roofs.

PITI   Denotes that a payment includes principal, interest, taxes, and insurance.

planned unit development (PUD)   A development with individual lot ownership and shared ownership of common areas such as recreational areas; also called a planned development project.

planning commission   A group of appointed officials responsible for planning and zoning.

plat   A map or plan of a subdivision showing individual lots.

plate   A horizontal board (2" × 4") to which studs are nailed. There is both a top plate and a bottom plate, called a sole plate.

pledge   The depositing of personal property as security for a debt with another while retaining title.

plot plan   The layout of a lot showing placement of the structure in relationship to lot lines.

plottage   The increase in value from the process of assemblage (joining several adjacent parcels to form a larger parcel).

pocket listing   A listing not advertised or made available to other agents.

point   A fee charged by the lender that amounts to advance interest, making up for an interest rate the lender considers too low. Each point paid is 1% of the loan amount.

point of beginning (POB)   The point of beginning in a metes-and-bounds description.

police power   The power of the state to adopt and enforce laws to promote order, safety, health, morals, and general welfare. No compensation is given for financial losses resulting from the exercise of police power. It cannot be delegated to a nongovernmental body. Examples include zoning, health code, and building code enforcement.

ponding   Floodwater accumulation in depressions.

portfolio income   The passive income received from investments rather than from a salary or business.

portfolio loan   A loan held by the lender as an investment rather than one made for resale on the secondary mortgage market.

power of attorney   A written agency agreement given by a principals to an attorney-in-fact to act on their behalf.

predatory lending   Abusive lending practices to strip an owner of home equity.

preliminary title report   A report indicating the present condition of the title and indicating the conditions upon which title insurance will be issued.

prepayment penalty   A penalty for prepaying a loan before the payment schedule of the note.

prescription   Obtaining an easement by open, hostile, and continuous use for a statutory period of time.

price-fixing   Illegal practice of conspiring to set fixed prices for goods or services.

primary financing   First mortgages and trust deeds.

primary mortgage market   Characterizes the actual granting of loans from the lender to the borrower.

principal   (1) One who engages an agent to act on his behalf. (2) A party to a contract. (3) A sum of money.

principle of balance   The highest value is created and maintained by a proper mix of land use resulting in the highest and best use for a site.

principle of change   Real estate values do not remain constant.

principle of competition   When extraordinary profits are being made, competition will enter the area and profits will drop.

principle of contribution   Improvements should not be made to a property unless the value of the property or rent is increased enough to justify the improvements.

principle of dependency   The value of a parcel changes based on changes in the use of surrounding parcels.

principle of integration and disintegration   Property goes through three phases of development: integration, equilibrium, and disintegration (growth, stability, and decline).

principle of substitution   A person will not pay more for a property than the price of a property of equal utility and desirability.

prior appropriation   A theory used in some western states that the first user of water has priority rights over later users of water from the same source.

private mortgage insurance (PMI)   Insures conventional loans.

privity   The relationship of parties to a contract.

pro forma   An estimated operating statement based on anticipated returns and expenses. It is used where no actual data are available.

probate   The legal proceedings to pay debts and distribute assets of a deceased.

procuring cause   The cause originating a chain of events that, without a break in continuity, resulted in the object of an agent's employment (sale or lease).

profit a prendre   The right to take crops, soil, or profit from the land of another.

profit and loss statement   A financial operating statement showing profit or loss for a designated period.

progression   The increase in value of a less expensive home resulting from more expensive homes being built around it.

property management   Real estate activity focused on leasing and maintenance of property.

proprietary lease   A lease by a cooperative to a shareholder providing a right to occupy a unit.

proration   To apportion based on actual time to the date of closing, as with taxes, insurance, and rents.

Protecting Tenants at Foreclosure Act   Provides for leases surviving foreclosures, as well as a notice period.

puffing   A statement of opinion given in a sale; not a warranty.

punitive damages   Exemplary damages beyond actual damages awarded for a wrongful, willful act for the purpose of punishing the wrongdoer.

pur autre vie   A life estate for the life of a person other than the life tenant.

purchase sale-back   The investor buys property and sells or leases it to the original owner. Normally, a leaseback is used by an owner to free capital for operational purposes. A purchase sale-back is sometimes used in place of a mortgage to provide greater security for the lender. Also called a sale-leaseback.

purchase money mortgage (PMM)   (1) A mortgage given by the buyer to the seller to finance the purchase. The seller is financing the buyer. Actual cash does not change hands. (2) A loan given to a buyer to finance a property purchase.

pyramiding   Refinancing or selling property that has increased in value to buy additional or larger property.

qualified endorsement   An endorsement of a negotiable instrument "without recourse." The endorser is not liable if the maker does not honor the instrument.

quantity survey   A detailed method to determine replacement cost by pricing out all the elements of a structure in the same manner as a builder would estimate costs.

quiet enjoyment   The right of an owner or a tenant to use the property without interference.

quiet title   A court action to determine ownership rights.

quitclaim deed   A deed conveying whatever interest the grantor may have without making any claims as to ownership.

R factor   The resistance factor used to measure insulation.

radon   A colorless and odorless naturally occurring gas resulting from decomposition of radioactive minerals.

rafter   A diagonal roof beam running from the eaves to the ridge of the roof.

range   A vertical row of townships, measured east and west from the meridian.

ratification   The approval of an act of the agent by the principal when the agent exceeded her authority. By taking the benefits of the act, the principal also accepts its obligations.

real estate board   An organization of brokers and associates (salespeople).

real estate owned (REO)   Property that is lender owned as the result of a foreclosure.

real estate investment trust (REIT)   An unincorporated group of 100 or more investors who have limited liability. Under federal law, REITs are taxed on retained earnings only.

Real Estate Settlement Procedures Act (RESPA)   A federal disclosure act requiring that a borrower be given an estimate of settlement costs and an information booklet. The Consumer Financial Protection Bureau administers RESPA.

real property   Land and all that goes with the land (appurtenances).

Realtist   A real estate broker who is a member of the National Association of Real Estate Brokers.

REALTOR®   A member of the National Association of REALTORS®.

recapture clause   A provision in a percentage lease that gives the lessor the right to terminate the lease if a specified volume of sales is not reached.

reconciliation   The process whereby an appraiser assigns various weights to value determined by different appraisal methods (correlation).

reconveyance deed   The deed from the trustee returning title to the trustor when the trustor has satisfied the debt to the beneficiary.

recordation   The act of recording with the county recorder so as to give constructive notice to all of the instruments recorded.

recovery fund   A fund maintained by many state real estate departments to repay persons who suffer losses because of wrongful acts of licensees. Recovery is up to a statutory limit and usually requires an uncollected judgment against the licensee.

red flag   Anything that should alert an agent as to a property problem.

redemption right   The right of the mortgagor to redeem the property after a foreclosure sale. Before a sale, it generally is a reinstatement right.

redlining   Refusing to make loans within designated areas; violates the Civil Rights Act of 1968.

reformation   A court action to rectify a mistake in a deed or contract so it reads as it was intended to read.

regression   A loss in value because a home was placed in an area of less expensive homes.

Regulation Z   The portion of the Consumer Protection Act of 1968 called the Truth in Lending Act (TILA).

rehabilitation   Repair without changing.

release clause   A provision in a blanket encumbrance allowing separate releases from the encumbrance by paying a stated sum of money.

remainder depreciation   The depreciation that an owner has left to take.

remainder interest   An interest that a third person has in property after the death of a life tenant.

renegotiable-rate mortgage (RRM)   A short-term mortgage where the lender will rewrite the loan, when due, at the current interest rate (rollover mortgage).

renewal of lease   An extension of a lease that continues the old lease.

replacement cost   The cost of replacing a structure of the same desirability and utility values using modern methods and materials.

reproduction cost   The cost to reproduce a structure exactly with the same design and materials.

rescission of contract   Setting aside the contract and placing the parties back in the conditions they were in before the contract (as opposed to a waiver, which leaves them as they are).

reservation   The retention of a right, such as an easement, when property is conveyed. An exception retains part of the property.

reserve for replacement   A reserve fund established to replace an asset.

respondeat superior   The doctrine that a master is liable for the acts of his servants. It applies to employees, as well as agents.

restoration   Returning to an original condition.

restricted license   A probationary license granted by some states after a license has been revoked, suspended, or denied.

restrictive covenant   A private beneficial restriction whereby an owner is limited as to the use of her property; for example, minimum size, setback, and height limitations. Also called covenants, conditions, and restrictions (CC&Rs).

restrictive endorsement   An endorsement on a negotiable instrument that restricts any further endorsement; "for deposit only."

restrictive use appraisal   Report limited to specific valuation purposes.

retaliatory eviction   Eviction resulting from a tenant's good-faith complaint. May violate the Uniform Residential Landlord and Tenant Act, Fair Housing Act, and state law.

reverse annuity mortgage (RAM)   A mortgage in which the mortgagee makes monthly payments to the mortgagor. The loan is paid back when the property is sold or the mortgagor dies.

reverse mortgage   A loan where the borrower receives annuity-like payments from the lender but the loan is not repaid until the property is sold or the borrower(s) dies.

reversionary interest   An interest whereby a property goes back to the original grantor on the occurrence of an event such as the death of a life tenant.

rezoning   Change of zoning, as opposed to a variance, which is an exception to zoning.

ridge board   The highest board in a house, located horizontally between the tops of the opposing rafters.

right of correlative user   The right of a landowner to the reasonable use of underground percolating water (the water table).

right of first refusal   A right sometimes given to a tenant to meet the price and terms at which the owner will sell or lease the property to another party. The owner must offer it to the holder of the right before a sale or lease can be made to another. In this case, the owner is not required to sell or lease, as he is with an option.

right-of-way   The right to pass over another's land, as in an easement.

riparian rights   Rights of a landowner to reasonable use of the flowing water located on, under, or adjacent to her property.

rod   A surveyor's measure equal to 16.5 feet.

rule against perpetuities   Requires that a private trust for heirs be restricted to a statutory life limit. The deceased or grantor is limited as to how long he can continue to exercise control over property after death.

S corporation   A small, closely held corporation that has elected to be taxed as a partnership.

safety clause   A listing provision that grants the broker a commission for a sale made within a specified period of time after a listing expires, if the broker submits the name of the buyer to the owner within a stated period of time as a party with whom the broker had negotiated before expiration of the listing.

sale-leaseback   A sale in which the grantor becomes the tenant of the grantee.

sans   French for *without*. Used to exclude property from a grant.

satisfaction of mortgage   Given by the mortgagee to the mortgagor when the mortgage has been satisfied. Recording the satisfaction removes the lien.

scheduled gross income   Gross income based on 100% occupancy and scheduled rents.

seal   An impression or a stamp to authenticate the signature on a document, which is required in some states on formal documents. Generally, "(seal)" or the letters "L.S." (*locus sigilli*, Latin for *place of the seal*) are sufficient.

seasoned loan   A loan with a payment history. Such a loan is desirable on the secondary mortgage market.

secondary financing   Second mortgages or trust deeds.

secondary mortgage market   Describes the buying and selling of existing mortgages.

secret profit   An undisclosed profit of the agent, regardless of the amount.

Section 8   A federal rent subsidy program for low-income families.

section   A parcel of land one mile square containing 640 acres, formed by government survey.

Secure and Fair Enforcement for Mortgage Licensing Act (SAFE Act)   Sets requirements for state licensing of mortgage loan originators.

security agreement   A security interest that a creditor retains in personal property of a debtor (under the Uniform Commercial Code).

security   An investment where the investor invests money but has no control or management over the investment.

seisin   Possession by one who claims rightful ownership.

sellers' market   A market condition characterized by more buyers than sellers, so sellers have a more commanding position.

send-out slip   An agreement that if a broker discloses a property to a prospective buyer, the buyer will negotiate for that property only through that broker.

separate property   Property owned individually by a spouse in which the other spouse has no interest.

Service Members Civil Relief Act (SCRA)   Provides protection against eviction and foreclosure as well as excessive rates of interest.

servicing a loan   The business of loan collection, maintaining impound accounts and recordkeeping.

servient tenement   An estate that is used by another under an easement.

setback   The building line distance from the lot line.

severalty ownership   Ownership by one person or entity alone.

severance   Removing something from the land such as cutting down a tree or demolishing a structure. The real property becomes personal property.

shared appreciation mortgage (SAM)   A mortgage under which the mortgagee shares in the appreciated value of the property.

sheathing   A covering over studs and rafters, which may be plywood, board, or composition board, over which the siding or roofing is placed.

sheet flooding   Flooding down an incline but not in a watercourse.

sheriff's deed   A deed given by the sheriff when property is sold for execution of a judgment or sheriff's foreclosure sale.

Sherman Antitrust Act   Federal law that makes price-fixing, market allocation agreements, and other actions to reduce competition illegal.

short rate refund   A less-than-prorated refund received by an insured who cancels an insurance policy.

short sale   A sale where the lender agrees to accept sales proceeds for the debt because sale price is less than the amount owed. When mortgage exceeds value, it is called an upside-down-sale.

situs   The preference of buyers for particular areas.

soil pipe   The sewage pipe carrying waste from a building to the sewer or septic system.

solar easement   Easement of light.

special agent   An agency in which the agent is authorized to perform only designated acts (specific agency).

special assessment   A charge against a property for a specific improvement, such as a street or sewer; usually assessed based on benefits received.

special warranty deed   A deed in which the seller warrants title only as to defects arising during the grantor's ownership.

specific lien   A lien against a particular property only, as opposed to a general lien, which applies to all property of the debtor.

specific performance   The legal remedy of requiring a party to perform as agreed; ordinarily granted when money damages are inadequate.

spite fence   A fence that exceeds statutory height; considered a nuisance.

spot survey   A survey that shows the location and outline of improvements, easements, and encroachments.

spot zoning   Small areas of zoning use that do not fit with the general use of the area (frequently resulting from political influence).

square footage   The measurement arrived at by taking exterior dimensions, excluding the garage.

standard parallels   East-west survey lines that run north and south of the base line. They are 24 miles apart.

stare decisis   The legal principle stating that previous decisions (precedent) should be considered by the courts.

Starker exchange   A delayed exchange where the exchange property must be designated within 45 days of closing on the first property, and the exchange must be completed within 180 days of the closing on the first property.

statute of frauds   Legislation requiring that certain contracts, including those dealing with real estate, be in writing to be enforceable.

statute of limitations   Sets forth the time limit within which legal action must be taken or rights will lapse.

statutory dedication   Dedication that results from the recording of a subdivision map that indicates land dedicated to public use.

steering   The illegal practice of directing buyers to certain areas, based on race or national origin.

step lease   A lease with graduated increases.

stigmatized property   Nonphysical factors that affect desirability of a property.

stock cooperative project   A cooperative in which each owner owns stock in the project and has the right to occupy a unit.

straight note   A note on which interest only is paid, with the entire principal payable on the due date (a term loan).

straight-line depreciation   A method of depreciation whereby an equal amount is deducted each year over the life of the asset.

straw man   A substitute used to conceal the identity of an actual purchaser.

strict foreclosure   Foreclosure by peaceful entry of the mortgagor without a sale (allowable in several states).

studs   Vertical 2-by-4-inch boards in a wall; usually 16 inches on center (from the center of one to the center of the next stud).

subagent   A person whose agency status was conferred by an agent, not the principal.

subdivision   Land division in accordance with state subdivision laws.

subjacent support   Support of the surface by the underlying ground.

"subject to" loan   An agreement that allows the buying of real estate without agreeing to pay an encumbrance. Buyer is not personally liable on the loan, so a deficiency judgment is not possible. Buyer must make payments, however, or lienholder will foreclose.

subjective value   The use value to the owner.

sublease   A lease given by the original lessee, who becomes a sublessor. The sublessee is the tenant of the sublessor, not of the original lessor. Also called a sandwich lease.

subordinate   An agreement that a loan will be secondary to another encumbrance.

subprime lender   Lender that will make loans deemed too risky by most conventional lenders. They charge higher interest and/or origination fees.

subrogation   The substitution of one party for another as to her interests.

substantial performance   An unintentional contract breach that is not substantial. Contract remains enforceable, but price is reduced based on reduction in value.

Summary Appraisal Report   Report that summarizes the market conditions and analysis performed.

supplemental tax bill   An additional tax bill given when property is reassessed on sale to cover the increased tax for the increased assessment.

supply and demand   The greater the supply, the lower the value; the less the supply, the higher the value. The greater the demand, the greater the value; the less the demand, the less the value.

surface water   Water not in a defined channel.

surrender   The mutual agreement of the parties to end a lease. All further obligations of the parties are terminated.

survey   A location or verification of property lines by a surveyor.

survivorship   On the death of a joint tenant, the tenant's interest ceases to exist, and all interests remain undivided with the survivors.

sweat equity   Equity earned through an owner's construction or improvements.

syndicate   Two or more persons who have joined together for investment purposes. A descriptive term for multiple ownership. Syndicates may be general partnerships, limited partnerships, corporations, or REITs, although most syndicates are limited partnerships.

tacking on   Adding a previous owner's use to satisfy the statutory period of use for an easement by prescription or a title by adverse possession.

take-out loan   Permanent financing that replaces (takes out) a construction loan.

tandem program A program under which Fannie Mae buys below-market-interest mortgages at par value and resells them to encourage low-interest housing loans. Ginnie Mae makes up the loss between market value and par value.

tax base An assessed value of all taxable property within a tax region (needed revenue ÷ tax base = tax rate).

tax collector Collects property tax and conducts tax sales.

tax deed The deed given at a tax sale.

tax shelter A way of excluding income from taxes by such means as depreciation, which is a paper expense and can offset other income.

tax-deferred exchange (1031 exchange) An exchange of like-for-like property held for income or investment. Only boot received is taxed.

team concept Team within a brokerage office where a salesperson or associate broker form teams and share income.

tenancy at sufferance A situation arising when a tenant holds over (continues occupancy) after expiration of a lease. Tenant is subject to an ejectment or an unlawful detainer action.

tenancy at will A tenancy for an indeterminate period.

tenancy by the entirety A form of joint tenancy for husbands and wives. Neither spouse can separately convey to break the tenancy.

tenancy in common Ownership by two or more persons, each of whom has an undivided interest without the right of survivorship.

tenancy A mode of holding ownership or interest in property.

tender An unconditional offer to perform (legal tender is money).

tenement Right that transfers with the real property.

testate To die with a will.

testator A person who has a will.

tie-in agreement A requirement that a buyer of goods or services agree to purchase other goods or services as a condition of the original agreement; generally illegal.

tier A horizontal row of townships, measured north or south from the base line.

"time is of the essence" A statement that makes prompt performance mandatory.

time-share An interval ownership plan used for vacation property.

Title I loan FHA home improvement loan.

Title II loan FHA home purchase loan for one to four residential units.

title insurance An insurance policy that agrees to indemnify the owner for defects in title caused by specified risks.

title theory The theory that a mortgage is a transfer of title to secure a loan and not just a lien (used in a minority of states).

title Ownership. Title is passed by deed.

topographical line Line on a map indicating the contour of the land.

topography The surface elevations of a property.

Torrens title A system of registering ownership in which the court keeps the record of title and issues certificates of title.

town house Row housing having common walls with adjoining housing.

township An area established by U.S. government survey that is six miles square and contains 36 sections.

toxic mold Mold, usually black mold, that negatively effects health.

trade fixture Personal property installed by a tenant to carry on a trade or a business; remains personal property and can be removed by the tenant any time before the lease expiration.

trading on equity Borrowing money on equity in property in order to invest it at a higher rate of return.

transfer-on-death deed Revocable deed that allows real estate to go to heirs without probate.

trespass A wrongful intrusion on the land of another.

triple net lease A net lease where the tenant pays taxes and insurance in addition to all maintenance and operational expenses.

trustee The third party who holds the trust deed.

trustor The debtor who gives title to the trustee as security for the loan.

Truth in Lending Act (TILA) Part of the Consumer Credit Protection Act; also called Regulation Z. It is a disclosure act requiring the lender to show the interest as an annual percentage rate (APR).

turnkey project Completed project from building permit to occupancy permit.

turnover The number of times an inventory is sold in one year.

ultra vires An act outside the authority of the person acting. That person is responsible personally for his actions.

unconscionable contract A contract that is so unfair or harsh that the courts will refuse to enforce it.

underimprovement An improvement that, because of a deficiency in size or cost, fails to achieve the highest and best use for the property.

undivided interest An unspecified interest in the whole rather than a separate interest in a particular portion of a property.

undue influence Taking advantage of another because of a unique position of trust, such as a doctor-patient or an attorney-client relationship.

unearned increment An increase in value that is not due to any effort of the owner.

Uniform Commercial Code A group of standardized commercial laws adopted in whole or in part by most states. They cover negotiable instruments, as well as liens on personal property (financing statements).

Uniform Electronic Transactions Act Gives legal recognition to electronic signatures.

Uniform Residential Appraisal Report (URAR) A form used for HUD, VA, Fannie Mae, Freddie Mac, and Farmers Home Administration (FmHA) loans.

Uniform Residential Landlord and Tenant Act An act adopted in whole or in part by a number of states and designed to provide uniformity as to rights and obligations of residential tenants and landlords.

Uniform Residential Loan Application A standardized Fannie Mae and Freddie Mac form adopted for most residential loans.

Uniform Standards of Professional Appraisal Practice (USPAP) Standards developed by the Appraisal Foundation with which appraisers for federally related transactions must comply.

Uniform Vendor and Purchaser Risk Act (UVPRA) Sets the risk of loss on property damaged or destroyed before completion of transfer.

unilateral contract A promise in exchange for an act; accepted by the offeree's performance.

unit-in-place method An appraisal method whereby cost is priced per unit, such as price per square foot.

universal agent An agent appointed to perform all acts that the principal can delegate lawfully to another.

unlawful detainer A legal eviction procedure.

upset price The minimum bid at an auction.

upside down loan A loan that exceeds the fair market value of the security property.

upzoning Rezoning to a more intensive use.

usury An unlawful rate of interest.

valid escrow Escrow in which an agreement has been reached and there has been conditional delivery of transfer agreements (deeds) to escrow. Delivery is conditioned upon escrow receiving all required funds and/or liens.

valley An internal angle in a roof. Metalwork often is used in a valley to prevent leaks.

variance An exception to zoning.

vendee The buyer.

vendor The seller.

verification A sworn statement before an officer of the court as to the correctness of the contents of an instrument.

vested remainder A remainder interest that cannot be defeated, such as a remainder interest to a life estate. The remainder holder or heirs are bound to get the property.

vested A present or sure interest that cannot be revoked.

vicarious liability Liability for acts of another based on the relationship of the parties such as liability of a broker for acts of a salesperson while acting for the broker.

void Having no legal effect.

voidable   Capable of being voided by one party only; valid until voided.

voluntary lien   A lien, such as a mortgage, placed by an owner.

wainscoting   The treatment of the lower portion of a wall in a different manner than the rest of the wall; half paneling.

waive   To give up or relinquish a right.

waiver   Accepting something less than contracted for. A waiver leaves the parties as they are. Rescission places them back as they were.

walk-through   Buyer's final inspection of property before closing of a sale.

warehousing   The practice of mortgage companies of accumulating a stock of mortgages and borrowing on them until they can be sold.

warranty deed   A deed under which the grantor warrants the marketability of the title. *See* general warranty deed, special warranty deed.

waste   Destruction or damage to a property (usually by a tenant).

wetlands   Marsh or swampland where the water table is close to or at the surface. They are protected from development by federal and state conservation regulations.

wild document   A recorded deed or lien on a property outside the chain of title (placed by one not having a recorded interest in the property).

will   Testamentary statement.

workers' compensation insurance   Provides wage replacement and medical benefits to employees injured in the course of employment.

wraparound loan   A loan written for the amount of both junior and senior liens. The borrower makes the entire payment to the lienholder, who then makes the payment on the senior encumbrance. Also called an all-inclusive mortgage.

zero interest loan   A loan in which the seller buys down the interest rate to zero; usually a short-term loan.

zero lot line   A building can be erected to the edge of the property.

zoning   City or county regulation on land use; considered to be an exercise of police power.

INDEX

Notes

Notes

Notes

Notes

Notes

Notes

Notes